James Hannay

The History of Acadia

From its First Discovery to its Surrender to England by the Treaty of Paris

James Hannay

The History of Acadia

From its First Discovery to its Surrender to England by the Treaty of Paris

ISBN/EAN: 9783337326081

Printed in Europe, USA, Canada, Australia, Japan

Cover: Foto ©ninafisch / pixelio.de

More available books at **www.hansebooks.com**

THE HISTORY OF ACADIA,

FROM

ITS FIRST DISCOVERY

TO

ITS SURRENDER TO ENGLAND

BY THE

TREATY OF PARIS.

BY

JAMES HANNAY.

ST. JOHN, N. B.:
PRINTED BY J. & A. McMILLAN.
1879.

Entered according to Act of Parliament of Canada, in the year 1879, by
JAMES HANNAY,
In the Office of the Minister of Agriculture.

PREFACE.

THIS BOOK is the result of a resolve formed some fifteen years ago to write a History of Acadia during the period of its occupation by the French, and up to the time when it was finally surrendered to England by the Treaty of Paris. No doubt I entered upon the undertaking with but a slight conception of the labor it would involve; but that, perhaps, was a fortunate circumstance, for otherwise I might have been deterred by the magnitude of the task. Owing to the lack of well equipped libraries in New Brunswick, I had to collect, at great labor and much expense, all the books and publications bearing on the early history of New England and Acadia; and having collected them, I had the satisfaction of discovering that very few of them were of the slightest value as works of authority. The only use of most of them is to put the inquirer on his guard and to stimulate him to more exhaustive researches into the annals of the period of which he proposes to write.

After years spent in collecting books, in preliminary inquiries, in making myself familiar with minute matters of detail, which, perhaps, belong rather to the antiquarian than the historian, and after having to lay aside my work many times, often for months together, in consequence of the demands of a most exacting and laborious profession, this history was to have been published in the Summer of 1877. I was at Oak Point, on the St. John River, whither I had gone to obtain quiet and complete the last chapters of this volume, when one pleasant morning in June a little boy came running across the fields with the tidings that the city of St. John had been burnt down the previous day. Before night I reached the city, and discovered the worst, that my book, then half printed, my library, and the whole of the manuscript in the printing office had been destroyed in the great conflagration, which carried ruin to so many homes. With the exception of about one hundred and eighty pages, of which I had a printed copy, the whole work of writing the history of Acadia had to be done over again. This has been accomplished, and now the result is before the reader.

In this volume I have not adopted the plan which is usual in historical works of original research, of placing the names of the authorities in notes on each page. In cases where it seemed necessary to do so, I have rather chosen to name the auth rity in the text, as the more simple and convenient method. For the discoveries of Champlain and the settlement at Port Royal, the authorities I have mainly relied on are, Champlain's work, Lescarbot, and the first volume of the Jesuit Relations. For the subsequent events, up to the capture of Port Royal by the English in 1654, the work of Denys, Governor Winthrop's Diary, and a vast number of public documents in the volume of the E. and F. Commissioners, Hazard's and Hutchinson's collections and similar works have been consulted. After the surrender of Acadia to France in 1670, the memoirs and despatches obtained by the several Provincial Governments from the archives of Paris, furnish abundance of historical material down to the taking of Port Royal in 1710. After that period, the public documents of Nova Scotia, some of which have been reprinted by the Government of that Province, serve as the basis of my story.

My aim has been to trace every statement to its original source, and to accept no fact from a printed book at second hand where it was possible to avoid doing so. Champlain, Lescarbot, Denys, Winthrop, and one or two other books, I consider nearly of equal authority with documentary evidence, because these authors relate facts which happened in their own time, and which mainly came under their own personal observation. Winthrop, especially, is of great value, and without his aid it would have been impossible to give an accurate statement of the singular story of La Tour.

The first and principal object I have kept in view has been to tell the simple truth, and for the sake of this I have been willing to sacrifice mere picturesque effect and all attempts at fine writing. Indeed, the necessarily annalistic character of much of the narrative would prove an effectual barrier against anything more ambitious, and it would be ridiculous to clothe the petty struggles of Acadian history in grandiloquent language. Up to the capture of Port Royal in 1710, I have been very full in my treatment of events in Acadia, but from that date to the end of the period of which the volume treats, I have disregarded everything relative to the mere English Colony of Nova Scotia, which did not properly fall within the scope of my narrative. I have given a good deal of space to the question of the expulsion of the Acadians, and I think that very few people, who follow the story to the end, will be prepared to say that it was not a necessary measure of self-preservation on the part of the English authorities in Nova Scotia.

When I had made some progress in my researches, the manuscripts of the late Professor Robb, of the University of New Brunswick, who had devoted a good deal of attention to Acadian history, were placed in my hands. Dr. Robb had made copious extracts from the manuscripts in the library of Quebec, and I derived much assistance from the result of his labors. I am indebted to Mr. E. Jack of Fredericton for much valuable aid, and to Mr. I. Allen Jack of St. John for manuscripts and maps. Mr. Thomas B. Aikens of Halifax is also entitled to my thanks for assistance courteously and promptly rendered on one occasion. But my thanks are especially due to Miss E. Wagstaff of St. John, whose aid in making translations of difficult French manuscripts has been invaluable. This lady during the great St. John fire let her own property burn while she saved two of the precious volumes of manuscripts copied from the archives of Paris.

I cannot close this Preface without paying my tribute of respect to the labors of the late Beamish Murdoch, my predecessor in this field, whose history of Nova Scotia is a wonderful monument of industry and research, which will serve as a guide to all future historians to the sources of the history of Acadia. Mr. Murdoch only essayed "the task of collecting and reducing into annals, facts of interest" with reference to the history of his native Province; had he done more, this book would never have been written. But having paused at that point, I felt that the field was free for me to attempt to weave into a consistent narrative the facts which he had treated in a more fragmentary way. It will be for the reader to say with what measure of success this has been accomplished.

St. John, N. B., March, 1879.

HISTORY OF ACADIA.

CHAPTER I.

EARLY VOYAGES TO THE NORTHERN PARTS OF AMERICA.

THE 4th of March, 1493, was a day of glad tidings for Europe and for mankind. Yet it was not the witness of any great triumph on the field of arms; nor the birth day of any man of illustrious name; nor the date of any royal pageant. But on that day a little bark, leaky, frail, and shattered by the tempest, sought shelter in the port of Lisbon; no anxious merchant awaited her arrival; no salute thundered her a welcome, but she brought to the shores of Europe "the richest freight that ever lay upon the bosom of the deep—the tidings of a new world." For ages before, commerce had languished within the narrow compass of the Mediterranean Sea, and the enterprise of man had been restrained by the stormy Atlantic, now the highway of nations, but which was believed by the men of those days to be a limitless ocean. It took a succession of the boldest Portuguese navigators upwards of seventy years to reach that stormy Cape which marks the southern limit of the continent of Africa, and no man but Columbus had dreamed of passing over that vast waste of water which rolled in untamed majesty to the west.

The discovery of America dispelled in a moment the superstitious fears which had enslaved the minds of men for so many centuries, and swept away, so far as geography was concerned, the much vaunted wisdom of antiquity.

Here was a field for the enterprise of man such as had never before been opened up, and which modern discovery has made it impossible to parallel in these days. Europe was in a great ferment over the event, which disclosed new visions of wealth and power to the enterprising and bold. Every needy adventurer saw in it a means of bettering his fortune, and every monarch recognized in it an easy mode of extending his dominions. The golden lure stimulated national as well as individual cupidity, and thousands were ready to brave the dangers of that same stormy Atlantic which they had considered Columbus a madman for attempting to pass. The thirst for gold was as keen in the fifteenth century as it is to-day. Amongst those who turned their eyes towards the new continent was Henry VII. of England, a monarch who combined in a surprising degree, caution, with a spirit of enterprise, and avarice with ambition. He had only been prevented by a narrow chance from becoming the patron of Columbus in his great discovery, and had this prudent English King been the first to obtain possession of the rich tropical portions of the western continent, the history of the British Colonies of America, and probably of the mother country also, would have been different. More colonial gold might have flowed into the coffers of England, but a colony planted beneath the equator would have had little in common, either in mental or physical characteristics, with that hardy race of men which seized with iron hand the rugged shores of New England.

At the close of the fifteenth century the position of England as a maritime power was very different from that which she occupied a hundred years later. Her war ships were few; the first of that long line of illustrious admirals, who have borne her flag in triumph on every sea, had not then been born; and he would have been a bold man who would then have ventured to predict that England would become the first maritime nation in the world, without a rival in commercial enterprise or naval power, unless she found one among the vigorous colonies she planted with her own hand. In consequence of the lack of experienced navigators of English birth, Henry VII. was obliged to accept the services of foreigners to carry out his plans of discovery.

In 1495 there was residing in Bristol a native of Venice named John Cabot, who in his youth had been a pilot, but who subsequently had embarked in mercantile pursuits. No part of the world was at that period more famous for the skill of its navigators than the Italian Peninsula, and Venice, from its favorable situation in the Mediterranean, and its large commerce, was, above all others, the place from which a bold and skilful mariner might be expected to come. Cabot had caught the enthusiasm which the discovery of America had wrought upon the minds of men, and embraced the idea that by sailing to the north-west a passage to India might be found. He found in the English monarch a willing and eager patron, and on the 5th March, 1495, received from the King a royal commission granting to him and his sons Sebastian, Louis and Santius, full authority to sail to all countries and seas of the east, west and north, under the flag of England, for the discovery of the "isles, regions and provinces of the heathen and infidels," with power to set up the banner of England in the newly discovered countries, and to subdue and possess them as lieutenants of the King. Cabot and his sons were to enjoy the privileges of the exclusive trade, but one-fifth of the profit was to go to the King.

In the Spring of 1497 Cabot set sail in a ship named the Matthew, provided by the King, and essayed for the first time the passage of the North Atlantic. He was accompanied by his son Sebastian, and in company with their ship, sailed three or four small vessels fitted out by the merchants of Bristol, and laden with goods for the purpose of trading with the natives. On the 24th of June they discovered the main land of America, probably the coast of Labrador in the vicinity of the Straits of Belleisle, and on the same day they saw an island lying opposite to the mainland. To the land first discovered Cabot gave the name of Prima Vista, while the island received the name of St. John, probably from the circumstance of the day of its discovery being St. John's day. There are good grounds for believing that this island of Cabot's discovery was Newfoundland, although, unfortunately, the meagre record of the voyage which has survived, is insufficient to determine the matter with absolute certainty. The inhabitants of this new land were clad in the skins of wild animals, and armed with bows and arrows, spears, darts, slings and wooden clubs. The country was sterile and uncultivated, producing no fruit. White bears, and stags of an unusual height and size, were numerous. The waters around it abounded in fish, especially a kind called by the natives baccalaos, which, during the centuries which have passed since then, has been the means of bringing vast fleets from Europe to gather the rich harvest of this now famous sea.* Salmon were also found in great plenty in the rivers of the new land, and seals were abundant along its shores. It had, likewise, so the chronicle informs us, hawks which were black like ravens, and partridges and eagles with dark plumage.

Cabot, after skirting along the coast for some distance, took two of the natives and returned to England, which he

* This fish has since then received the less musical name of the cod.

reached in August. Thus was the continent of America discovered under the auspices of the crown of England, more than a year before Columbus reached the coast of South America.*

In the following year the King granted a new patent to the Cabots, and gave them authority to engage in another voyage of discovery to the coast of North America. John Cabot, who had been knighted for the discoveries made by him on the former voyage, was unable to accompany this second expedition, and the command of it was given to his son Sebastian. Two ships were provided and fitted out for the voyage, and on board of them embarked three hundred sailors, traders, and adventurers. Early in the summer of 1498 they set sail. The discovery of a north-west passage to India was one of the main objects of this, as it had been of the former voyage, and, accordingly, Cabot, after reaching the coast of Newfoundland, turned the bows of his ships towards the north-west. He did not dream then that the solution of the curious geographical problem which he was the first to attempt, would not be attained until more than three centuries and a half had passed, and hundreds of human lives and an untold amount of treasure had been sacrificed in the endeavour, or he would scarcely have ventured with his frail ships to brave the dangers of that unknown northern sea. But men, happy in their ignorance of the future, press forward in search of an unattainable goal, and so Cabot, undismayed and without misgiving or doubt, swept on with free sail towards the ice-locked ocean of the North.

Cabot as he sailed northward found the shores free from ice, for it was then the month of July, but he was alarmed

---

*This discovery of Cabot was made the foundation of the English claims to North America.

at the appearance of numerous icebergs seaward, and before many days the field ice became so abundant that he found it impossible to proceed, and was reluctantly obliged to return south. He followed the coast of America, looking for a passage to India, until he reached the coast of Florida; then he gave up the attempt in despair and returned to England. Cabot subsequently received high honors from the English King, and, during the reign of Edward VI., was made grand pilot of England, and granted a large pension.

No nation during the fifteenth century exceeded the Portuguese in maritime enterprise. Beginning in 1412, they, with equal perseverance and success, pushed forward the work of exploring the western coast of Africa, which before that time had only been known to Europeans as far south as Cape Non. Six years later they succeeded in reaching Cape Bojador. In 1420 they discovered Madeira. In 1433 Cape Bojador, which had been so long the limit of their navigation, was doubled, and in 1449 the Cape de Verd Islands were discovered. In 1471 they ventured to cross the equinoctial line, which they—following the absurd teachings of the ancients—had believed to be impassable. Finally, Bartholomew Diaz, in 1486, attained that lofty promontory which he called the Cape of Storms, but which his King re-named the Cape of Good Hope. Thus had the Portuguese, in the course of three quarters of a century, explored the whole west coast of Africa to its southern limit, and showed the way by which India might be reached. It is, therefore not surprising that a people so enterprising and sagacious should have looked with interest, not unmixed with jealousy, on the discoveries which the English and Spaniards were making in the new world. Of the Portuguese adventurers who were thus animated by a desire to make discoveries in America, there was none more ardent and resolute than Gaspar de Cortereal. He resolved to pursue the track of Cabot to the north and gain imperishable renown by the discovery of that passage to India which Cabot had been unable to find. In 1500 he set sail from Lisbon with two ships and reached the coast of Labrador, which he named Terra Verde. He entered the Gulf of St. Lawrence, and it is by no means improbable that he landed on some portion of Acadia. He followed the coast to the north for several hundred miles until, like Cabot, he was compelled by the ice to return. But the most notable circumstance in connection with the voyage of Cortereal was the fact of his capturing fifty-seven of the natives, and taking them to Europe, where they were sold as slaves. The country from which those unfortunates were taken, is described as abounding in immense pines, fit for masts, which shows that it could not have been very far to the north. It was thickly peopled, and the natives were attired in the skins of wild animals; they lived in huts, and used knives, hatchets, and arrow-heads made of stone. They were described as a well-made and robust race, well fitted for labor. This description might very well apply to the Indians of Acadia.

Encouraged by the success of his first venture in human blood, Cortereal set out in 1501 on another voyage for timber and slaves. But the fetters which he had forged for his fellow men were destined never to confine the free-born natives of America. That shore which he had polluted for the first time with the touch of slavery, he was fated never more to behold. Many months passed without any tidings of the lost adventurer, and his brother, Michael de Cortereal, fitted out two ships and went in search of him. But the same avenging spirit which had overwhelmed the one, now pursued the other. He also passed away over the trackless ocean, and no friendly gale ever brought back to Europe an intimation of the fate of either.

In 1504 the Basque and Breton fishermen first cast their lines on the Banks of Newfoundland, and to the latter the island of Cape Breton owes its name. Then commenced the gathering of that bountiful ocean harvest which has since rewarded the toil of so many generations of fishermen. Never was so rich a mine of wealth opened by the most fortunate adventurer of the south as those ocean plains, and, although untold millions have been taken from the apparently inexhaustible store, the deep still yields as rich a return for the labor of man as in the days of those ancient toilers of the sea.

The accounts which the fishermen brought back to Europe of the coasts which they had visited in the pursuit of their calling were not so favorable as to tempt many colonists to the new world. The pursuit of gold was then the object which mainly engrossed the minds of the adventurers of France and Spain, and, beyond the pursuit of the fisheries which were early recognized as a source of wealth, nothing was done to profit by the discoveries which had been made.

In 1524 a native of Florence, named John Verazzano, was sent by Francis I. of France on a voyage of discovery. That monarch had viewed with some degree of jealousy the progress which Spain and Portugal had made in the exploration and settlement of America, the more especially as Pope Alexander VI. had issued a bull bestowing the new world on the Kings of those two countries. The King of France was but little disposed, either to bow submissively to the decrees of Rome, or to acknowledge the right of Spain and Portugal to the whole of America. Charles V.

of Spain remonstrated with Francis against his founding any colonies in America, an act which he considered an invasion of his rights, but the French King sarcastically replied that he would like to see the clause in father Adam's will which bequeathed to his royal brother alone, so vast a heritage. Verazzano set sail from a rocky island near Madeira on the 17th of January, in a ship named the Dolphin, with a crew of fifty men, and provisions for eight months. After a tempestuous passage to the west he came in sight of a country, up to that time unknown, which was thickly inhabited by a race of friendly savages, who beheld the white strangers with astonishment and delight. The difficulty of landing on account of the surf made trading impossible, but a bold young sailor who swam ashore was treated by those simple-minded natives with much kindness. This land, according to Verazzano's reckoning, was in thirty-four north latitude, and was doubtless part of North Carolina. Verazzano followed the coast to the northward, landing at many places to barter with the natives, whom he found more savage and less friendly the further north he went. He sailed as far as fifty degrees of north latitude, having explored seven hundred leagues of the coast of America. An enterprise of such magnitude entitles Verazzano to a high place among the navigators of the sixteenth century, and the record of his voyage, which has been preserved, shows him to have been a man of much judgment and ability.

To the whole of the newly explored region he gave the name of New France, and, after his return to Europe, he propounded a scheme for the further exploration and colonization of the new land, which received the countenance of the King. But this plan was never carried to success, and the subsequent fate of the navigator is at this day a matter of doubt. It is related on the authority of Ramusio, that he made a subsequent voyage in which he was killed and devoured by the natives, but other authorities go to show that he was alive after the alleged date of this catastrophe. Whatever his subsequent adventures or fate may have been, he added nothing more to the world's knowledge in regard to America.

In 1527 Master Thomas Thorne, a learned and wealthy resident of Bristol, addressed a letter to King Henry VIII., in which he argued that the discovery of the northern parts of America might be carried even as far as the North Pole, and urged the King to assist in the undertaking. Henry VIII., stimulated no doubt by the example of some of the other European nations, accordingly fitted out two ships, one of them bearing the pious name of Dominus Vobiscum, and in May of the same year they set sail. A Canon of St. Paul's, a man of much wealth, and imbued with an ardent desire for scientific discovery, accompanied the expedition. But the voyage was not prosperous, and the adventurers do not appear to have reached farther north than the Straits of Belleisle, through which they passed; but they had scarcely entered the Gulf of St. Lawrence when one of their ships was cast away. The other then followed the coast south as far as Cape Breton and Arambec—which was the name then given by the English to Acadia—returning to England in October of the same year.

Francis I. still continued to cherish the desire to make further discoveries in the new world, and in 1534 two small vessels of sixty tons burthen were fitted out for a voyage to America by his directions. Each vessel carried a complement of sixty-one men, and the expedition was placed under the command of Jaques Cartier, a very bold and skilful pilot of St. Malo. He departed from that port on the 20th

April, 1534, and holding a due west course, on the 10th May came in sight of Cape Bonavista in Newfoundland. He found this Cape so much beset with ice that he was unable to enter the Bay of Bonavista, and was constrained to take refuge in St. Catharine's Haven, five leagues to the south-east. There he remained ten days. From thence, sailing to the northward, he skirted the eastern coast of the island, and passing through the Straits of Belleisle, entered the Gulf of St. Lawrence, and followed the coast as far south as Cape St. George. He admired the fisheries and harbors of Newfoundland, but speaks very unfavorably of the soil.* He found the inhabitants to be men of good stature, but wild and unruly. Both sexes were clothed with the skins of wild animals. They painted their faces a roan color, and decorated their hair with feathers. They had canoes of birch bark in which they fished and captured seals. He understood from them that they did not reside permanently on the island, but came from hotter countries on the main land to catch seals.

Leaving Newfoundland, Cartier sailed to the south-west and visited the Magdalene Islands; from thence proceeding west, on the 30th June, he came in sight of the coast of Acadia. The land first seen by Cartier appears to have been Cape Escuminac at the southern entrance of Miramichi Bay.† The next day he landed and found the country to be fertile and well wooded. He there saw a large number of the inhabitants crossing a river in their canoes. Cartier entered this river, and speaks of it as "a very goodly river

* He says, "If the soil were as good as the harbors are it were a great commodity, but it is not to be called New Land but rather stones and wild crags and a place fit for wild beasts, for in all the North Island I did not see a cart load of good earth. Yet went I on shore in many places. * * To be short I believe that this was the land that God alloted to Cain."—Hakluyt, Vol. 3, p. 268.

† Named by the French, Cape Orleans; it appears to have been known to the French fishermen by that name before Cartier's visit.

but very shallow." It is now difficult to determine which of the many rivers of that portion of the coast of New Brunswick is the one thus described. Cartier was charmed with the beauty and fertility of the country, and speaks of it in glowing terms.* The forest trees were principally pines, cedars, white elms, ash, willows and yew trees, and many other kinds with which the navigator was unacquainted. Where there were no trees the ground was covered with gooseberries, strawberries, blackberries, wild peas and a species of wild corn which resembled rye. The climate was as warm as that of Spain, and the birds were very numerous. The land was level, and the natives manifested a friendly disposition. Such is, in substance, the account which is given of this part of New Brunswick by its first recorded discoverer, who, fresh from the rugged coast and severe climate of Newfoundland, was the better able to appreciate its beauties.

From Miramichi Bay, Cartier sailed towards the north, and, rounding Point Miscou, entered a fine bay to which, in consequence of the excessive warmth of the climate, he gave the name of Bay Chaleur or Bay of Heat. Crossing to the northern shore of this Bay he entered an open haven now known as Port Daniel, and from this point explored the whole of the Bay, going within it a distance of twenty-five leagues, which must have brought him very near the mouth of the Restigouche River. Singularly enough, the

---

* "Nevertheless we went that day ashore in four places to see the goodly and sweet smelling trees that were there. We found them to be cedars, ewe trees, pines, white elms, ashes, willows, with many other sorts of trees to us unknown, but without any fruit. The grounds where no wood is are very fair and all full of peason, white and red gooseberries, strawberries, blackberries and wild corn even like unto rye, which seemeth to have been sown and ploughed. The country is of better temperature than any other that can be seen, and very hot. There are many thrushes, stock doves and other birds; to be short, there wanteth nothing but good harbors."—Hackluyt, 3 Vol., p. 255.

same evil fortune which caused him to miss the discovery of the Miramichi River, now attended him, and he turned back without entering the Restigouche. In the course of his exploration of the Bay Chaleur, Cartier had frequent and friendly intercourse with the Indians. He visited Bathurst harbor, and there found three hundred Indians, who received him with many demonstrations of joy, and regaled him with the flesh of seals. They were disposed to engage in traffic with the white strangers to the extent of their limited means, and so brisk was the demand for hatchets, knives and beads, that most of them sold the very skins with which they were clothed and went away naked. These Indians were of the Souriquois or Micmac tribe.* From their pacific disposition and friendly conduct, Cartier formed the impression that they might easily be converted to the Christian religion. Their habits, he says, were migratory, and they lived principally by fishing. Cartier speaks of the great abundance of salmon in the rivers on that coast, a quality for which they are still celebrated.

Leaving behind the beautiful and fertile country on the southern shore of the Bay Chaleur and its friendly and hospitable inhabitants, Cartier sailed north-east and entered the harbor of Gaspè. The inhabitants were of an entirely distinct tribe from those of Bay Chaleur, speaking a different language, eating their food almost raw, and having no other dwellings but their canoes. On a point of land which lies at the entrance of this harbor, the French erected a cross thirty feet high, and hung upon it a shield with the

---

* This was established in a very singular manner. When Champlain had settled his colony at Port Royal in 1605, he was visited by the Micmac Indians, headed by their chief Membertou, who was nearly one hundred years of age. This aged warrior remembered Cartier's visit to the Bay Chaleur, and was at that time a married man with a family. Membertou became a Christian, and was baptized at Port Royal in 1610. He died in the following year.

arms of France. This typical act of taking possession of the country was ingeniously performed so as to appear to the natives a religious ceremony. After the cross was erected the old Chief seems to have had his suspicions aroused that something more than worship was intended, and he visited the ships to remonstrate with Cartier. He was however assured that the cross was merely for a landmark to guide the white visitors to the entrance of the harbor on their next voyage. On the 25th July Cartier departed from Gaspè, taking with him two sons of the Chief whom he had seized by stratagem. They were, in some measure, reconciled to their lot by liberal presents of savage finery and promises of being brought back to their own country in the following year.

Cartier sailed north as far as the north shore of the St. Lawrence, but, although he was actually within the estuary of that river, he does not appear to have suspected its existence. He was on the verge of a great discovery; the noblest river in America was open before him, but he was unaware of its presence. The weather suddenly grew stormy and tempestuous; autumn was approaching. Strong easterly winds began to prevail, and he feared that if he remained longer they would be obliged to pass the winter in that unknown region. These considerations induced him to resolve on an immediate return to Europe, and, shaping his course once more towards the east, the little fleet reached St. Malo in safety on the 5th September.

The favorable account which Cartier gave of his discoveries, made the French King eager to found a colony in the new world, and another expedition was accordingly undertaken under the command of the same great navigator. Three ships were fitted out, the largest of one hundred and twenty tons, and the others of sixty and forty tons respectively. Many gentlemen of means had been induced to engage in the adventure. The voyage was inaugurated as became so important an undertaking, and before embarking, the crews with their commanders repaired to the cathedral of St. Malo and received the blessing of the Bishop. On the 19th May, 1535, the expedition set sail from St. Malo. Shortly after their departure a gale sprang up which speedily increased to a tempest, and the ships were in danger of being lost. Cartier's vessel became separated from the other two, but on the 26th July, met them again at the appointed rendezvous in Newfoundland. It was August before they entered the Gulf of St. Lawrence.

Keeping more to the north than he had done on his former voyage, Cartier discovered a large island to which he gave the name of Assumption, but it is known as Anticosti at the present day.* Cartier had on board of his vessel the two Indians taken on his former voyage, and they informed him that they were near the kingdom of Saguenay, and that beyond it was Canada.† Passing up the river St. Lawrence, the adventurers entered the deep and gloomy Saguenay, where they met four canoe loads of natives, who were timid at first, but came to them when spoken to by Cartier's Indians, who understood their language. The lateness of the season prevented them from exploring the Saguenay, and they continued their voyage up the St. Lawrence. On the 6th September they reached an island which abounded in hazel trees, which in consequence received from Cartier the name Isle au Coudres, which it still bears. On the 7th they came to a large and fertile island of great beauty, which abounded in vines. This Cartier named Isle de Bacchus:

* Anticosti is an evident corruption of Natiscotec, the name which the Indians gave it.
† The name Canada, which has since been applied to the whole of this region, is an Indian word, and signifies a collection of huts, a town.

it is now called Orleans. There they cast anchor and went ashore, taking the two Indians with them. By their aid, they were at once put on a friendly footing with the natives, and the feeling of distrust with which the savages had regarded the white visitors was entirely extinguished.

On the following day Donnacona, King of the country, came to visit them accompanied by twelve canoes filled with warriors. An interchange of civilities took place, and the Indian King testified by signs his delight at the arrival of the white strangers. Cartier now advanced up the river to find a secure haven for his vessels, and he found a place in every respect suitable, at the mouth of a small river now known as the St. Charles. Close by, on a high bluff overlooking the St. Lawrence, stood the Indian town of Stadacona, and beneath the black and frowning precipice the great stream, cramped and confined within a narrow channel, swept swiftly onwards to the sea. To this passage the Indians had given the name of Quebec, which in their language signifies a strait,—a name destined to become great and glorious in our country's story.

It needs not the gilding of romance to invest Quebec with the dignity which belongs to it as the scene of illustrious deeds and the birth-place of Canadian history. The rock upon which it stands will not be more enduring than the fame of the achievements which it has witnessed, or the renown of the soldiers who contended for it in wager of battle. The ancient Indian town of Stadacona, which stood upon its site, has long since perished; the warlike race who made it their home have been driven forth, and are now a feeble and despised tribe; the great forest which extended on every side like a boundless ocean, has been cut down by the patient industry of man; all is changed save the beetling cliff which overshadows it; for the frowning battlements of a walled and fortified city have usurped the place of the fragile homes of the Algonquin race.

This city was for a century and a half the capital of the great French empire in America, the heart whose pulsations were felt from the coast of Labrador to the mouth of the Mississippi. Its name has been in times past ominous of disaster and bloodshed to the English race, and it has also yielded our country triumphs which illuminated every city in Britain, and filled the hearts of its people with joy and pride. From it the bloody edicts went forth which gave over the border settlements of New England to the hands of the merciless savage, and which covered her villages with mourning. Over the sea from this barren rock echoed the tidings of that famous victory which gave the vast territory of Canada to the English crown, and in which Wolfe by a soldier's death, immortalized his name. Nor should it be forgotten, that during the war of the Revolution, in a dark hour for England, the strong battlements of Quebec resisted the tide of invasion and preserved England's greatest colony.

The unsuspecting savages, unconscious of the ruin which the white man's presence would bring upon their race, treated the French with kindness and hospitality. Their King, Donnacona, brought them many presents, a good understanding was speedily established, and a league of friendship entered into. But when Cartier proposed to proceed further up the river, the Indians attempted to dissuade him. The navigation, they told him, was dangerous, the country was barren, and the native tribes warlike and hostile. When such remonstrances failed, Donnacona attempted to terrify the French, and deter them from going up, by dressing three Indians to represent evil spirits who declared that they had been sent by their god Cudruaigny,

to say that the country up the river was full of ice and
snow, and that whoever went there would die. Cartier
of course laughed at this attempt to influence him, and
told the Indians that Cudruaigny was a fool. Finding all
his efforts unavailing, Donnacona ordered the Indian
interpreters not to accompany Cartier, and they were
obliged to obey the command of their King. Nevertheless,
on the 19th September, Cartier started up the river with
his pinnace and two boats with a large company of men.
The farther they advanced inland the more the country
improved; the forest trees became larger, grape vines were
seen hanging with thick clusters of fruit, and the meadows
grew broader and more fertile. The natives were everywhere friendly, bringing them fish and such articles as they
had to sell, but they warned them of the dangers of the
navigation farther up. At length, after various adventures, Cartier arrived at the Indian town of Hochelaga,
the home of the Huron tribe, a race less warlike and more
inclined to agriculture than most savages.* Their town
was large, situated in the midst of corn fields, and surrounded by a triple row of palisades thirty feet high. Like
the Indians of Stadacona, the people of Hochelaga were
governed by a King or Agouhanna, who, instead of being
a great warrior, was a feeble and palsied old man. Cartier
visited Hochelaga and was very kindly received, and, as
those simple minded savages believed him to be a superior
being, all their sick and feeble were brought to him to be
healed by the touch of his hand. When he departed they
grieved as at the loss of an old and tried friend, and many
of them followed him along the bank after he had em-

*That these Indians of Hochelaga belonged to the Huron-Iroquois family of
tribes is proved by a variety of circumstances, among which may be named the
affinities of their language, the character of their towns and defensive works, and
of the remains of pipes and pottery dug up at Montreal in 1860.

barked, until, borne rapidly away by a favorable wind and the swift current, he was lost to their sight.

Above the town of Hochelaga rose a mountain from whose summit can be seen a vast extent of level country from which the last vestige of the forest has long since disappeared. The territory beneath is rich in all the material wealth of fine farms, noble orchards and splendid residences. It is rich, too, in historical associations, for it is the great campaign ground of Canada, and its glory is kept fresh in the memory of the French Canadian by the echoes of Chateaugay. Beneath the mountain, on the site of the ancient Hochelaga, lies a great city, where a hundred and fifty thousand people of European origin have their homes, the centre of a vast commerce and of a great railway system, and widely renowned for its beauty, enterprise and wealth. To the mountain Cartier gave the name of Mount Royal, which it still retains, and thus the city beneath it, and the island upon which it stands received the name of Montreal.

Cartier hastened to Quebec, where he had decided to spend the winter. But when winter came, the French were found unprepared for its rigors. The almost tropical summer gave them no intimation of that season of Siberian cold which was to follow it. Their ships were hemmed in by thick ice and covered with drifting snow, and an unknown sickness, probably the scurvy, broke out among the men. By the middle of March, of one hundred and ten men who composed the crews, twenty five had died, and all the others, with three or four exceptions, were affected by the disease. The living were too feeble to bury the dead, and the only resource was to cover them with snow. While in this pitiable condition the ingenuity of Cartier was taxed to the utmost to disguise their real condition from the Indians, whose friendship he had good reason to doubt. Fortunately for him, the savages were affected by the same malady, and, by pretending that one of his servants who had been with them had taken the disease, he managed to discover the remedy they used, which was to drink the liquor in which the bark and leaves of a certain tree had been boiled. In a few days they used up an entire tree in this way, and in a week every man was cured. Indeed so marvellous were the effects of its use that the old chronicle of the voyage declares, "If all the physicians of Mountpelier had been there with all the drugs of Alexandria, they could not have done so much in one year as that tree did in six days." This wonderful tree is believed to have been the white pine.

When Spring returned, Cartier prepared to depart for France, and he signalised his leave-taking by an act that was alike treacherous and cruel. He invited the King, Donnacona, and four of his principal chiefs to a great feast, and in the midst of the festivities, violated the laws of hospitality by seizing and imprisoning them on board his vessels. He departed amidst the lamentations of the Indians, although he caused Donnacona to tell them that he was going to Europe of his own free will and would return to them in a year. But the promise was never fulfilled, for the Indian King died in the land of his captivity. Cartier reached France on the 8th July, 1536, bearing the tidings of his great discovery, which was thenceforward to be known to the world by the name of CANADA.

In the spring of 1536, while he was still at Quebec, a number of London merchants sent out two vessels on a trading voyage to the coast of America, under the command of one Master Hore. They spent some time in the Gulf of St. Lawrence, and afterwards anchored in a harbor on the western coast of Newfoundland. They found the natives so shy that they were unable to communicate with them, and, falling short of provisions, were driven to the necessity of eating such herbs and roots as they could find, although, close to the finest fishery in the world, it is difficult to understand why they should have suffered from hunger. At last, when every other resource was exhausted, they were reduced to the extremity of casting lots to determine who should perish for the sustenance of the remainder. They were finally relieved from their dreadful position by the arrival of a French vessel, which they immediately seized, and which was found to be well stored with provisions. The two countries were then at peace, and the Frenchmen complained of the outrage to Henry VIII. The King, on finding the great straits to which his subjects had been reduced, forgave the offence, and generously recompensed the Frenchmen out of his own private purse.

The failure of Cartier to discover gold in the new world, added to the dreadful severity of the winter and the privations his men had suffered, for a time put an end to any further expeditions to Canada, although the arrival of the Indian King at the French Court produced a profound sensation. But no human enterprise was ever suffered to languish for want of men bold enough to undertake it, and accordingly in 1541, Cartier, in connexion with Francis de la Roche, lord of Roberval, prepared another expedition for the exploration of Canada. King Francis, who had provided most of the funds for the enterprise, conferred the chief command on Roberval, making him his lieutenant general and viceroy in Canada. Cartier was appointed captain general of the fleet.

Roberval's intention was to found a colony in Canada, and his preparations were made on so extensive a scale that they were still incomplete in the Spring of 1541, when Cartier was ready to depart. The latter accordingly set sail on the 23rd May, without his chief, with five vessels and a large company of gentlemen, soldiers and mariners. He also took with him cattle, goats and hogs for the new colony. After a tempestuous passage they reached Newfoundland, where they awaited the arrival of Roberval, but, after a long delay, despairing of his coming, they sailed for Canada, arriving at Quebec on the 23rd August. The ships were immediately surrounded by an eager multitude of Indians enquiring for their King. Cartier was obliged to tell them that Donnacona was dead. Those savage stoics heard the tidings with apparent indifference, but from that moment they regarded the French as their enemies. Cartier felt that he had not deserved their friendship, and he did not dare to trust it. He selected a spot higher up the river where he laid up three of his vessels under the protection of two small forts which he erected. The remaining two he sent to France to inform the King of his position, and that Roberval had not arrived. He spent the winter without any serious encounter with the Indians, but he was well aware that they only awaited a favorable opportunity to attack him. He had to be continually on the alert, and in the Spring he became so much disheartened by the difficulties which surrounded him and the continued absence of Roberval, that he resolved to return to France.

When he arrived at St. John's, Newfoundland, on his return voyage, he found Roberval there with three ships on his way to the new colony. He informed Roberval that he had left Canada because with his small force he was unable to withstand the savages, who went about daily to annoy him. Roberval commanded Cartier to return with him to Canada, but his ambition as a discoverer was satisfied, and he was unwilling to endure the dangers and privations of another winter in the midst of hostile savages. To avoid an open rupture with his commander, he weighed anchor silently in the night and departed for France. Roberval proceeded to Canada, took possession of the forts built by Cartier, and there spent the winter. Their provisions, however, fell short, and each man was put on a very meagre allowance. The scurvy broke out, and, not having the remedy that Cartier had used, fifty of the colony died before Spring. Roberval's colonists must either have been a very bad lot or he an extremely severe ruler, for during the winter one man was hanged for theft,* several put in irons and many whipped, both men and women, "by which means," as the old chronicle informs us, "they lived in quiet." Roberval's colony was a failure, and next summer he returned to France with what remained of it. In 1549 he organized another expedition, but the hopes that were founded on it were doomed to be blasted. He set sail for Canada accompanied by his brother Achille and a band of brave adventurers, but never reached the shores of the New World. Their fate is still one of the secrets of the sea. Canada had reason to regret the event, for the loss of that expedition retarded its colonization for more than fifty years.

For many years after the loss of Roberval's expedition, Canada was almost entirely forgotten by the French. Religious wars and civil dissensions occupied the whole attention of the nation, and a court that was busily engaged in slaughtering its subjects at home, could not be expected

---

*This was the first civil execution in Canada. The name of the offender was Michael Gaillon. One of those kept in irons during the winter was John of Nantes. His offence is not stated.

to take much interest in any scheme for increasing their numbers abroad. A Huguenot colony, which was founded in Florida in 1564, under the auspices of Admiral Coligny, was, after it had been a single year in existence, utterly destroyed by the Spaniards. All the colonists were barbarously murdered, and Ribault, the governor, is said to have been actually flayed, by order of Menendez, the Spanish leader. The corpses of the murdered colonists were hung on trees on which were placed the inscription: "These wretches have not been thus treated because they were Frenchmen, but because they were heretics and enemies of God." There is good reason to believe that the French Court connived at the destruction of this colony. This was worthy of the perpetrators of the massacre of St. Bartholomew. The unchristianized and uncivilized savages of America would have been more humane.

England was the next power to engage in the work of colonizing the northern regions of America, and, although late in the field, was destined to eclipse all competitors in the end. Her first venture, however, was far from being encouraging.

In 1583, Sir Humphrey Gilbert, an elder brother of Sir Walter Raleigh, set sail for the new world with a fleet of five vessels, for the purpose of founding a colony. No expedition of that day had left the shores of Europe better prepared for the purposes of discovery and colonization. Of the two hundred and sixty men who composed it, many were mechanics, such as shipwrights, masons, carpenters, blacksmiths, workers in metal and refiners. A large stock of provisions and articles of traffic was also taken, and, indeed, nothing that the skill and ingenuity of that age could devise appears to have been omitted. But Gilbert was unlucky from the very inception of his voyage. He had only been two days at sea when the Raleigh, the largest vessel in the fleet, turned back in consequence of a contagious sickness having broken out among her crew.* After a foggy and disagreeable passage, the fleet entered the harbor of St. John's, Newfoundland, where were found thirty-six vessels of different nationalities. Gilbert, by virtue of his commission, took possession of the Island in the name of Queen Elizabeth, and enacted and proclaimed laws for the government of the inhabitants and traders.† Some time was spent there in searching for silver mines, and a quantity of ore was obtained which was believed to be precious. What its real value was can never be known for it was on board the Delight, which was lost with most of her crew on the rocks of Cape Breton. This event and the wishes of his officers induced Gilbert to return to England. He shifted his flag to the Squirrel, the smallest of his fleet, in fact a mere boat of ten tons burthen. When about mid-Atlantic on their way back, a terrific gale arose which placed the vessels in imminent danger. The Squirrel during the day labored terribly and was nearly overwhelmed. Gilbert sat calmly in the stern with a book in his hand, and when the Golden Hind approached within hearing, called out to those on board of her: "We are as near Heaven by sea as by land." At midnight the lights of the Squirrel suddenly disappeared; the mighty ocean had swallowed up both her and

---

* This vessel was fitted out by Sir Walter Raleigh.

† "For a beginning he proposed and delivered three laws to be in force immediately. That is to say, the first for religion which in public exercise should be according to the Church of England. The second for maintenance of her majesty's right and possession of those territories against which, if anything were attempted prejudicial, the party offending should be adjudged and executed as in case of high treason. The third, that if any person should utter words sounding to the dishonor of her majesty, he should lose his ears and have his ship and goods confiscated."
—Hackluyt's Voyages, 3 Vol., p. 193.

her gallant commander. The Golden Hind, the last of this fleet which had left England under such promising auspices a few months before, arrived home late in September. The death of Sir Humphrey Gilbert was a sad loss to the new world as well as to the old, for in his ocean grave was buried the hope of Acadia being made a British colony. How different might its history have been had that navigator's designs been carried into effect!

At length, after many years of gloom and misery, France obtained a respite from her religious wars, and Henry IV. was firmly seated on the throne. Then the spirit of adventure began to revive, and the attention of the more enterprising was directed to the new world as a place where they might have scope for their ambition. The office of lieutenant general and viceroy of Canada, which, since the death of Roberval, had been an empty title, was in 1598 bestowed by Henry IV. on the Marquis de la Roche, together with a commission which gave him very extensive powers in the regions he proposed to colonize. In that year he sailed for America, taking with him forty-eight convicts from the French prisons. He left these unfortunate beings on Sable Island, a barren and desolate desert of sand which lies a hundred miles from the coast of Nova Scotia. He then proceeded towards the main land with the avowed object of seeking a suitable place for his colony. He visited the coast of Acadia and was returning to Sable Island when his ship was caught in a tempest and driven back to the coast of France. The wretched convicts were left to their fate. It was five years before Henry IV. heard what had become of them, and then, with that spirit of humanity which ever distinguished him, he immediately sent Chedotel, who had been de la Roche's pilot, with a vessel to ascertain their fate. He found that twelve of them had survived the terrible hardships of their condition. They had subsisted chiefly on cattle which were running wild on the island, probably the produce of animals which had escaped from wrecked vessels.* They were clothed in seal skins, and their shelter was a rude hut made out of the planks of a wreck. It is a striking illustration of the acquisitive nature of man, that these unfortunates in their forlorn condition had collected a large quantity of valuable furs. They presented themselves before the King on their return, by his desire, attired in their singular dress just as they had been found. He commiserated their condition so much that he immediately granted them their liberty and gave each of them fifty crowns. Their sufferings had indeed been terrible enough to expiate almost any crime. Their faces, in consequence of the hardships they had endured, had assumed a savage and ferocious expression, so that they appeared more like wild animals than civilized men. De la Roche, whose cruelty or neglect had been the cause of their misfortunes, died miserably of a broken heart, harassed by lawsuits and ruined in fortune.

While costly expeditions under the patronage of wealthy monarchs were contributing to the sum of human knowledge by trans-atlantic discoveries, a set of humbler adventurers were not less busily engaged in making America known to the people of Europe. The fisheries of Newfoundland and Acadia attracted to their shores large numbers of adventurous men, who were equally ready to fish or to trade with the Indians as occasion offered. In this way the whole coast of the Gulf of St. Lawrence became well known long before Canada or Acadia contained a single white settler, and the Atlantic coast of Acadia was equally familiar to those

* The Baron de Lery is believed to have left some horses and cattle on Sable Island in 1518.

traders and fishermen. There is no positive proof that they ever entered the Bay of Fundy during the sixteenth century, but the probabilities are strongly in favor of their having done so. Thus slowly but steadily the dim outline of the new world displayed its form to the people of Europe, and the spirit of adventure, no longer confined to the great and wealthy, grew in the breasts of the people. Already a new era of colonization and progress was beginning to dawn. Who could have ventured to predict the glory of its meridian splendor?

CHAPTER II.

THE ABORIGINES OF ACADIA.

THE exploration of America established the fact that it was everywhere inhabited, from the shores of the Arctic Ocean to its extreme southern limit. Even the islands which surrounded it were in most cases found to be peopled, and there was no large extent of territory on the continent without its quota of natives. It then became an interesting question for philosophers to determine from what part of the old world America was peopled, and by what means the ancestors of its inhabitants reached the new continent. Surrounded on both sides by vast oceans, it seemed incredible that savages who had no vessels larger than a canoe could come to America by sea, and although ingenuity has exhausted itself in conjectures, and modern research thrown all its available light upon the subject, the question of how America was peopled has not yet been satisfactorily determined.

It is not to be denied that in modern times this question has assumed a very different aspect from that which it presented a century ago, when Robertson wrote his history of America. He assumed—and he has been followed in this respect by many subsequent writers—that the inhabitants of the new world were all of one race, and in the partially civilized communities of Mexico and Peru, he recognized only races of people who had improved to some extent on the customs of the rude Tartar ancestors, from whom he conceived them to have sprung. Finding it difficult to make this hypothesis agree with the undoubted progress they had made in the arts, he cavalierly treated the Spanish accounts of their skill as the exaggerations of a people who desired to augment, as much as possible, the importance of the nations they had subdued. While he did scant justice to the civilization of Mexico and Peru, he ignored altogether the existence of any remains of civilization beyond their limits. It would, of course, be unjust to charge this distinguished historian with any desire to suppress the truth, but it would be equally absurd, at the present day, to adopt him as a guide. Since his day the substantial correctness of the Spanish accounts of the civilization of Mexico and Peru has been fully vindicated. The remains of their temples, pyramids and palaces still bear silent testimony to their former grandeur; and in other portions of America have been brought to light the remains of cities whose inhabitants, although they have utterly perished and left no record, must have had some pretensions to cultivation and refinement.

The archæological remains of America are of so extensive a character as to strike any one who pursues the subject for the first time with astonishment. They are naturally divided into two classes, those that appear to have originated among cultivated races, and those that have manifestly belonged to uncivilized peoples. Of the former class Acadia is entirely destitute, and the same remark is true in regard to the whole Atlantic seaboard of the United States, as far south as Florida. But such remains abound from the State of New York along the western slope of the Alleghanies, through Georgia to the southern portion of Florida. They are very numerous in Kentucky, Illinois and Ohio, and are to be found in great numbers along the margins of all the western rivers, on the head waters and branches of the Mississippi and Missouri, and down to the

HISTORY OF ACADIA. 31

Gulf of Mexico. They are abundant in Mexico, but are found in the greatest numbers and in the highest state of perfection in Central America. A large proportion of the remains of partially civilized races throughout the United States consists of the ruins of fortresses and fortified towns, and tumuli or pyramids of earth. In Onondaga county, New York, was the ruin of a fortified town which covered more than five hundred acres of ground, and there are said to be at least a hundred ruined fortifications of various sizes in that State. In many other States they are still more numerous. In short, throughout the whole extent of country from the Alleghanies to the Rocky Mountains, are found the ruins of a perpetual succession of intrenched camps, and fortresses of earth and stone, constructed on the most gigantic scale, with redoubts, breastworks, ramparts and mounds of observation. Still more stupendous are the tumuli and pyramids which abound throughout the same territory, and which may be numbered by hundreds. One of the largest of these in Illinois, is seven hundred feet in length, five hundred feet wide at the base, and ninety feet in height, and its solid contents may be roughly estimated at twenty million cubic feet. Some of the smaller class of mounds appear to have been used for the purposes of sepulture. One near Circleville, Ohio, was found to contain an immense number of human skeletons of every size and age, all laid horizontally with their heads towards the centre of the mound. In a mound near the town of Chillicothe in the same State was found a single human skeleton covered with a mat, and decorated with a stone ornament, a string of bone beads, and a piece of copper made in the shape of a cross. Still more remarkable was the discovery made in one of the sepulchral mounds in Marietta. There the skeleton of a warrior was found with the remains of a buckler of copper, overlaid with a thick silver plate, lying across his breast. By his side were several broken pieces of copper tubing filled with iron rust, the remains, it was thought, of his sword and its scabbard. A piece of iron ore was also found with them.* This discovery seems to prove that the use of iron was known to the natives of America at a very remote period, and that this knowledge was subsequently lost, for at the time of the conquest of Mexico and Peru by the Spaniards, no iron utensils were in use. Implements of copper are very frequently found in these mounds, and specimens of pottery, some of them displaying excellent workmanship and a knowledge of chemistry, are abundant. In some of the mounds bracelets and rings of brass, ornaments of silver and specimens of sculpture have been brought to light. Some of these pieces of pottery have been compared in beauty and workmanship to the choicest antique vases of Europe; others are remarkable for their enormous size. An earthen vessel was discovered in a mound at Lancaster, Ohio, which was eighteen feet long and six feet in width.

Such discoveries incontestibly prove the former existence in those regions of a people who were acquainted with many of the arts of civilization, and the ancient character of the ruins is attested by the fact that in many instances a heavy growth of forest trees had arisen above them. But grand and imposing as are those ruined fortresses and pyramids, they are far surpassed by the ancient cities of Central America. Messrs. Stephens and Catherwood, in their wanderings through Central America, Chiapas and Yucatan, discovered the ruins of no less than fifty-four cities, and there were others of which they heard, but which they had

---

* An interesting account of this discovery will be found in Vol. I. of the collections of the American Antiquarian Society.

not time to visit. They brought back with them drawings of the principal objects of interest among the ruins, and, in many instances, plans of the cities themselves. One of the most remarkable and probably the most ancient of those cities is Copan, in the State of Honduras. It is situated on a river of the same name, and extends along its banks for upwards of two miles. The principal structure is what has been termed the temple, an oblong enclosure with a front on the river of six hundred and twenty-four feet, built of cut stone, the wall being from sixty to ninety feet in height. But the most interesting features of the ruins are the statues of Indian deities or kings, which are very numerous. These are executed in bold alto-relievo, on stone columns from eleven to fourteen feet in height, and covered on the back with fantastic hieroglyphics. In front of several of these idols were altars, probably intended for the purposes of sacrifice. One of these, made out of a solid block six feet square and four feet high, was ornamented on its side in a remarkable manner in bas-relief, with sixteen figures of men wearing turbans, and sitting cross legged, in Oriental style, while the top of the altar was covered with hieroglyphics. Of the workmanship of these monuments of Copan, Mr. Stephens, himself an Oriental traveller and entitled to speak with authority, declares that it is equal to the finest Egyptian sculpture, and that it would be impossible with the best instruments of modern times to cut stones more perfectly. Yet of the people who executed those great works or of their history we have no record, and tradition has preserved nothing which can aid us in discovering the origin or fate of the inhabitants of this deserted city.

The ruins of Palenque are of a still more remarkable character, and consist of temples and palaces, elevated on pyramids of earth faced with stone. The principal building is two hundred and twenty-eight feet long and one hundred and eighty feet wide. The outside walls, which are about twenty-five feet in height and surmounted by a broad projecting cornice of stone, were, at the time of Mr. Stephens' visit, still in an excellent state of preservation, and many of the interior partition walls were entire. This building was of stone, with a mortar of lime and sand, the front covered with stucco and painted. Its walls are ornamented with sculptures in bas-relief, representing human figures, warriors exacting submission from suppliant enemies, and priests offering sacrifices. One of these sculptures represents a cross, and beside it are two men, who are probably priests, who appear to be engaged in some religious ceremony. All the sculptures are distinguished by a profusion of ornaments, especially in the head dresses of the figures represented. They are all well and firmly drawn, but the profiles of the faces are remarkable for the smallness of the facial angle and the prominence of the nose. Hieroglyphics, similar in character to those found at Copan, co er the walls of the palaces and temples. Everywhere the ruins give evidence of the artistic taste and skill of their form inhabitants.

At Uxmal, in Yucatan, are the ruins of a city which differs entirely in many respects from Copan and Palenque. Although neither history nor tradition has preserved any record respecting its existence, its buildings are in a much better state of preservation than any of the other ruined cities of Central America. One enormous building, which was probably a palace, has a front three hundred and twenty feet in length, and, when visited by Stephens thirty-eight years ago, stood with its walls erect, almost as perfect as when deserted by its inhabitants. It stood on three ranges

of terraces, the summit of the upper range being elevated thirty-five feet above the ground and the lower range being six hundred feet in length at the base. Stephens says of it: "If it stood at this day on its grand artificial terrace in Hyde Park or the Gardens of the Tuilleries, it would form a new order, I do not say equalling, but not unworthy to stand side by side with the remains of Egyptian, Grecian and Roman Art." In another place he says: "The roof was tight, the apartments were dry, and, to speak understandingly, a few thousand dollars expended in repairs would have restored it and made it fit for the re-occupation of its royal owners." In one of the apartments the walls were coated with very fine plaster of Paris; the walls of the other apartments were of smooth polished stone. There were several other buildings at Uxmal in a very perfect condition, one of them still larger than the building above described, and all of them distinguished by one remarkable feature. They were built of plain cut stone to the tops of the doors, above them there was a rich cornice and moulding, and from this to the top of the building the whole wall was covered with rich and elaborately sculptured ornaments, differing entirely in character from those of any of the other ruined cities that have been explored in modern times. Stephens says: "The designs were strange and incomprehensible, very elaborate, sometimes grotesque, but often simple, tasteful and beautiful. Among the intelligible subjects are squares and diamonds, with busts of human beings, heads of leopards, and compositions of leaves and flowers, and the ornament known everywhere as 'greques.' The ornaments which succeed each other are all different; the whole form an extraordinary mass of richness and complexity, and the effect is both grand and curious."
* * * "The reader will be able to conceive the

immense time, skill and labor required for carving such a surface of stone, and the wealth, power and cultivation of the people who could command such skill and labor for the mere decoration of their edifices. Probably all these ornaments have a symbolical meaning; each stone is part of an allegory or fable hidden from us; inscrutable under the light of the feeble torch we may burn before it, but which, if ever revealed, will show that the history of the world yet remains to be written." One singular circumstance in connection with this deserted city is the fact that no water is to be found near it, so that water must have been brought into it by artificial means.

While the former existence of highly civilized communities in America is thus attested, we have the additional evidence which is furnished by the statements of contemporaneous Spanish writers as to the condition of Mexico and Peru at the time of the conquest. Here were two empires containing large and populous cities, with buildings of lime and stone, painted and sculptured ornaments, idols, courts, strong walls, palaces and lofty temples. At Cholula are still to be seen the ruins of the largest pyramid in Mexico. It covers upwards of twenty-six acres of ground, or double that of the largest Egyptian pyramid, and it is one hundred and seventy-seven feet in height. It was constructed of alternate layers of clay and unburnt brick, divided into four separate stages or stories, and ranged exactly in the direction of the cardinal points. At the time of the Spanish conquest this pyramid was surmounted by a stately temple, and it was only one of many, for every city or populous village had its temple. Bernal Diaz, himself one of the conquerors of Mexico, speaks with enthusiasm of its scenery. Approaching the city, he says: "We could compare it to nothing but the enchanted scenes we had read of in Amadis de Gaul, from the great towers and temples and other edifices of lime and stone which seemed to rise up out of the water." And again he says: "At the great square we were astonished at the crowds of people and the regularity which prevailed, and the vast quantities of merchandize." He adds that the ascent to the great temple was by one hundred and fourteen steps, and that from its summit could be seen the temples of the adjacent cities, built in the form of towers and fortresses, all white-washed and wonderfully brilliant. The noise and bustle of the market-place could be heard almost a league off, and "those who had been at Rome and Constantinople said that for convenience, regularity and population, they had never seen the like." In addition to the knowledge of agriculture, which the Mexicans possessed, they had the art of working in metal, and their implements of bronze supplied, in a large measure, the want of iron. They had also a considerable knowledge of astronomy, and had a solar year more accurately calculated than that of the Greeks and Romans. It is unnecessary to describe the institutions of the Peruvians or their progress in the arts. They were in some respects a more advanced people than the Mexicans, and the ruins of their cities, temples and highways are wonderful monuments of the power and wealth of the Incas.

The second class of ancient remains, such as are manifestly the production of uncivilized races, has a very wide distribution over the whole continent. Such remains consist generally of axes, hatchets, pipes and arrow and spear heads of stone, exhibiting much mechanical skill, but little or no knowledge of art. They are uniform in their character throughout the whole of America, and resemble the implements belonging to what has been termed the stone age, found in many parts of Europe. Some of them are found on the surface of the ground, and some beneath it; but those that belong to a remote age do not appear to be either better or worse in point of workmanship than those of more modern date. They are just such implements as were found in the hands of the savages of Acadia when they were first visited by Europeans. All along the Atlantic coast of America from Nova Scotia to Florida are shell heaps which mark the camping grounds of the Indians from time immemorial. Some of these shell heaps are upwards of three feet in thickness, cover more than an acre, and many of them are of very great antiquity, for when seen by the first settlers more than two centuries ago they were covered with a heavy growth of forest trees. Most of the shell heaps that have been examined yield implements of bone, such as arrow and spear heads and a variety of other articles of the same material of which the use can only be conjectured. The bones of fish and of various animals which formed the food of the Indians are also found in them, some of them being the bones of animals which are now extinct in the places where the shell heaps are. An examination of these remains of their savage feasts shows pretty clearly that the Indians were not very nice in their choice of food, and that while they relished moose, bear and beaver, they would eat anything from a dog to a rattlesnake, when hungry. Similar shell heaps exist in various parts of Europe, and those of Denmark which have been carefully examined are similar in their contents to those of America. The resemblance is strong enough to be suggestive of a common origin.

The traditions of the uncivilized aborigines of America throw no considerable light upon their origin, but those of the more polished races are deserving of more attention. The Peruvians trace the origin of their empire to a period four hundred years prior to the Spanish conquest, when, according to their traditions, Manco Capac and his consort appeared among them, and declared themselves to be the children of the Sun, sent by their beneficent parent to instruct them. Under their guidance they became skilled in agriculture and the arts, and from the scattered and barbarous tribes grew a populous and powerful empire: The Aztecs, if their traditions are to be credited, made their journey over from Asia by way of the Aleutian Islands about the eleventh century, and it is well established that they did not reach Mexico until 1324. But they were not the first civilized inhabitants of that country. They founded the Mexican Empire on the ruins of that of the Toltecs, who were by far the most civilized and ingenious people in America of which any record has been preserved. They had been in Mexico for a thousand years prior to the arrival of the Aztecs, and the ruined cities of Central America are believed to have been built by them. Few of the uncivilized Indians have any traditions as to their origin; most of them, the Algonquins among the rest, point to the rising Sun as the direction from which their forefathers came, but the Quiches alone have any definite account of their route. According to their traditions their ancestors came from the East, making a perilous journey through fields of ice and in protracted darkness. Some have inferred from this that they must have reached America by some Arctic route.

Great stress has been laid on the fact of the general similarity which all the natives of America have to each other. It is not to be denied that all the tribes of North American Indians have many points of resemblance, but, that they are all entirely alike is not true. The prairie Indians differ greatly from the forest Indians. The

Indians of California and British Columbia have scarcely any resemblance to the eastern nations, and it is not difficult to detect points of difference between tribes which are generally believed to be closely allied in their origin. Be that as it may, and without discussing the question of similarity, which is at the best a very uncertain test of origin, the crania which an examination of the Indian graves brings to light evidently belong to different races. In Peru alone an examination of the crania found proves conclusively that three distinct races dwelt there which have been classified as the Chincas, the Aymaraes, and the Huancas. The crania of the latter offer a very rare and characteristic formation, the head being flattened so that the facial angle is very small. It is possible that to some extent this peculiarity may have been caused by artificial pressure, as is the case with some tribes of Indians on the Pacific coast at the present day; but it has nevertheless been proved that, however this peculiarity may have been exaggerated by art, it was a natural characteristic of the race. Humboldt thought that the origin of such a custom may be traced to the natural inclination of each race to look upon their own personal peculiarities as the standard of beauty. It has been already remarked that in all the sculptured figures of Mexico and Central America the facial angle is very small, for it was natural that a people with this peculiarity, and who regarded it as a standard of beauty, should represent this type of forehead in an exaggerated form in the statues of their divinities and heroes. No more surprise therefore need be expressed at the extravagant forms of profile in the sculptures of Central America, than at those of the Greek statues of their divinities, which were equally untrue to nature, although in the opposite direction.

This digression in regard to the general subject of American Archæology will aid the general reader to understand the bearings of the question of the origin of the Indian races. In most works which profess to speak of the Aborigines, a cursory glance or a passing remark in regard to the antiquarian remains of America, is considered sufficient. It seems to be assumed that every reader has dived deeply into the subject of American Archæology, whereas to many it is entirely new. And the subject is a great one, and well worthy of attentive study. Many works have been written upon it to support particular theories, but as the facts to support the theories propounded have been generally selected after the theories were formed, such works are of little value. It is better to give a general outline of the facts, as has been done here, and let every reader think over the subject for himself. It must be admitted that it affords a tempting field for conjecture.

It seems to be pretty evident that all the American natives can only be said to be of the same race, in the same manner that all men are said to be of the same descent from Adam. It would appear, too, that America has been inhabited from the remotest ages, and that for many centuries before its discovery, civilized communities and savage tribes dwelt side by side. That from time to time immigrants have arrived from Asia by way of Behring's Straits, which are only thirty-six miles in width, or by the Aleutian Islands, which present an almost continuous chain of land from Asia to America. That while an indigenous civilization had grown up in some portions of America, adventurers or castaways from India, or from other portions of Southern Asia, brought to its shores some knowledge of the religion and of the arts of the ancient continent, and that the question—how America was first peopled—can only be solved by a reference to a condition of affairs which has long ceased to exist, and is one of the problems which philosophy has as yet left undetermined in connection with the migrations of pre-historic man.

The Red Indians of America, instead of being, as has been broadly contended, the broken and scattered remains of nations formerly civilized, appear rather to be a race of men who had attained the highest state of advancement which it was possible for a race of hunters to reach with such implements as they possessed. Although savages in their mode of life, they were savages of the highest type, veritable Romans in spirit, eloquent, brave and honorable, with some of the highest qualities and virtues of civilization. Their contact with white men has not improved them in a moral point of view, although it has given them better weapons and more comfortable clothing. Even in the last respect their advance has not been so great as might be supposed. The axe of iron has indeed replaced that of stone; the rifle has supplanted the bow and arrow; but modern ingenuity has not been able to devise a better vessel for the uses to which it is applied than the bark canoe, a more effectual means of ranging the winter woods than the snow shoe, or a more comfortable covering for the feet than that most perfect of all shoes, the Indian moccasin.

The Indians of North America inhabiting the region between the Mississippi, the Atlantic, and the country of the Esquimaux, were divided into eight great families, each speaking a language radically distinct from all the others. Of these, the Algonquins were by far the most numerous; they occupied nearly half of the territory east of the Mississippi, and extended from Labrador to North Carolina. It is to this family that the Indians of Acadia belong. When the French first visited Acadia they found

HISTORY OF ACADIA. 43

it divided between two tribes who differed considerably in language and in their mode of life. The whole of the Peninsula of Nova Scotia, and the Gulf shore of New Brunswick were occupied by the Souriquois, which was the tribe now known as the Micmacs, while the Etchemins occupied the territory from the River St. John to the Kennebec. The latter tribe are now known as Malicites, and they call themselves Wabannakai, or men of the East. There is reason to believe that the Etchemins, or Malicites, did not originally occupy any portion of Acadia, but that they intruded themselves into the territory of the Micmacs about the beginning of the seventeenth century, and gradually spread themselves along the Northern coast of the Bay of Fundy and up the River St. John, pressing the Micmacs back to the gulf and the peninsula of Nova Scotia. The Malicites were a very warlike people, much more so than the Micmacs, and they were generally in league with the Indians of Maine and Canada against the colonists of New England.

Although the Indians, from their peculiar mode of warfare and their contempt for peaceful pursuits, were at all times dangerous enemies, there is reason to believe that their numbers have been greatly exaggerated. By the census of 1871, it appeared that there were in New Brunswick 1403 Indians, 1666 in Nova Scotia, and 323 in Prince Edward Island, or 3392 in all. Of these, 503, most of whom reside on the St. John River, may be set down as Malicites, so that the Micmacs of Acadia number nearly three thousand, which would represent a force of six hundred warriors. It is doubtful if their numbers were ever much greater. In 1607, when Membertou assembled all his Micmac warriors, from Gaspè to Cape Sable, to make war upon Armouchiquois at Saco, their whole number amounted only to four hundred. In 1694, when the Malicites and Canibas, under Matakando, made their grand raid on Oyster River and the other settlements of New Hampshire, the whole number engaged in the expedition was only two hundred and fifty; and two years later, when Fort Nashwaak was besieged by the English, thirty-six warriors was the whole number that the Indian settlement of Aukpaque could spare for the assistance of the garrison. It appears from a memorandum made in 1726 by Captain Gyles, who had resided many years with the Indians, that the number from sixteen years of age and upwards on the River St. John, was one hundred; and at Passamaquoddy, thirty. A letter written in 1753 by Governor Hopson to the Lords of Trade states that there were about three hundred families of Micmacs in the country; but he could not find any person who had been among them who had ever seen two hundred Indians under arms together. From these statements it may be safely inferred that the whole force of the Micmacs and Malicites combined never exceeded seven or eight hundred warriors, and that no material decrease has taken place in their numbers since the first settlement of the country.

Excellent reasons existed to prevent the Indians from ever becoming very numerous. An uncultivated country can only support a limited population. The hunter must draw his sustenance from a very wide range of territory, and the life of hardship and privation to which the Indian is exposed, is fatal to all but the strongest and most hardy. The Indians of Acadia were essentially a race of hunters and warriors. Like most Indian tribes, they despised agriculture, and considered it a pursuit only fit for women and slaves. Some of the northern Indians cultivated the ground to a small extent, and it is certain that the Indians of Acadia did so during the French occupation, but their operations in tillage were on a very limited scale; and to this day our Indians are averse to the steady labor of the field. They had no domestic animals except the dog, and he was useful only in the chase.

During the summer the Micmacs drew a large portion of their subsistence from the sea. Every bay and inlet swarmed with fish, and there they might always reap an unfailing harvest. The Malicites, although living inland, were not without their share of the same kind of food. Fish were abundant in every stream and river, and the salmon was pursued with torch and spear over the shallows by the savage denizens of the St. John. In this way from one to two hundred salmon would be sometimes taken at a time. The Indians also used hooks of bone or shells, and lines and nets made of a coarse kind of hemp. They had weirs, in which they at times captured great quantities of fish; but the torch and spear were their favorite implements of fishing.

Notwithstanding the abundance of fish at certain seasons, the savages were at all times principally dependent on the forest for their food. Game is believed to have been much more abundant in Acadia in former times than it is now, and about the time when de la Tour and Charnisay were fighting with each other for the possession of the country, as many as three thousand moose skins were collected on the St. John River each year. Wild fowl of all kinds gathered in incredible numbers along the shores, on the marsh lands and up the rivers. Charlevoix states that near St. John geese laid their eggs so abundantly that they alone might have sustained the whole population; and the same, according to Lescarbot, was true with regard to the St. Croix. Denys speaks of immense flocks of wild pigeons passing his camp on the Miramichi, every morning and evening for eight days together; and he adds, that it was hardly possible to sleep for the noise made by the salmon going over the shoals, and the immense flocks of geese and ducks. At Bathurst, and all along the northern shore of New Brunswick, their number was such as almost to exceed belief.

The habitations of the Indians were generally huts or wigwams, made of poles and covered with bark; but in some instances they erected dwellings of a more permanent character, and surrounded them with palisades, so as to form a sort of fort. There were several structures of this description on the St. John in early times: one at Aukpaque, another at Medoctec and a third at Madawaska. Denys speaks of a fortified dwelling which the chief of Richibucto had erected on the shore of the Gulf, and in which he describes him as receiving strangers, sitting on the ground, looking like an ape with a pipe in his mouth, and preserving his dignity by being very taciturn and getting drunk only in private.

The Indians cooked their meat by broiling it on live coals, or roasting it on a sort of spit in front of the fire. But soup was their favorite delicacy; they boiled it in a capacious wooden cauldron made out of the butt of a large tree and hollowed out by fire. As such a vessel was not easily made, they frequently regulated their camping ground, in some measure, by the conveniences for establishing such a soup-kettle. The soup was boiled by dropping red hot stones into the cauldron, which, when cooled, were immediately replaced by others hot from the fire, until the meat was cooked. The soup thus made was their great drink, for Denys says "they drank as little water then as now;" and he adds: "Thus they dined without care, or salt or pepper, and quaffing deep draughts of good fat soup, lived long, and multiplied, and were happy."

Yet, although at certain seasons they luxuriated in abundance of food, at times they were subject to the greatest privations and on the verge of starvation. Then, no sort of food came amiss to them; reptiles, dogs, and animals of all sorts, were eagerly sought after and greedily devoured; roots* of various kinds were in great demand, and, sometimes, they were forced to boil even the bones of their former feasts to appease their hunger. Wild grapes, also, it appears, formed a portion of the food of the St. John Indians.† This frequent scarcity of food was in part owing to the uncertainty of the chase, but chiefly to the improvident habits of the Indians, who, when they had abundance of food, gorged themselves with it, and never thought of looking for more until it was all gone. This again was the result of another custom, which required all the food obtained, either by hunting or otherwise, to be equally divided; so that, as the active and indolent shared alike, all incentive to industry was taken away, and no large accumulation of food ever became possible. The St. John Indians were, perhaps, less open to this reflection than most others, and with them there were at times some attempts made to preserve food for future use. They preserved their meat by taking the flesh from the bones and

* Mrs. Rowlandson, who was captured during King Philip's war, says: "Their chief and commonest food was ground nuts. They eat also nuts and acorns, artichokes and lily roots and ground beans. They would pick up old bones and cut them in pieces at the joints, scald them over the fire to make the vermin come out, boil them, and then drink the liquor."

† See narrative of John Gyles' captivity. He was taken by the Indians when the Fort at Pemaquid was captured in 1689, and was a captive on the St. John River nine years—six with the Indians at Medoctec, and three with Louis d'Amours, Sieur de Chauffours at Jemseg. The latter treated him very kindly, and finally gave him his liberty. His narrative, which is the most valuable contribution extant relative to the customs of the Acadian Indians, was published in Drake's Tragedies of the Wilderness, and also with Historical Notes by the author of this History.

drying it in smoke, by which means it was kept sound for months, or even years, without salt. They had a curious way of drying corn when in the milk: they boiled it on the ear in large kettles until it became pretty hard; it was then shelled from the cob with sharp clam shells and dried on bark in the sun. When thoroughly dry the kernels shrivelled to the dimensions of a small pea, and would keep for years. When boiled again they swelled as large as when on the ear, and were said by Gyles to be "incomparably sweeter than any other corn."

An Indian feast, as made by the savages of Acadia two centuries ago, was quite different from anything to be seen at the present day. The ingredients were fish, flesh, or Indian corn and beans boiled together. Sometimes, when pounded corn was plenty, hasty pudding or porridge was made of it. An Indian boiled a sufficient number of kettles full of food, and sent a messenger to each wigwam door, who exclaimed: "Kah menscoorebah," which means "I come to conduct you to a feast." The invited guest then would demand whether he must take a spoon or a knife in his dish, which was a polite way of finding out what the bill of fare was to be. When the guests were met at the wigwam of the host, two or three young men were appointed to deal out the food, which was done with the utmost exactness in proportion to the number of each man's family at home. When the guests were done eating, one of the young men stood without the wigwam door, and called out: "Mensecommock," which means "Come and fetch." This was the signal for the squaws to go to their husbands, and each squaw took the dish, with what her husband had left, which she carried home and ate with her children. Neither married women nor youths under twenty were allowed to be present, but old widow squaws and captive men were allowed to sit by the wigwam door. The Indian men continued in the wigwam, relating their warlike and hunting exploits, or telling comical stories. The seniors gave maxims of prudence and grave counsel to the young men, which were always listened to with a degree of respect and attention not always found in assemblies of white men. Each spoke according to his fancy, but rules of order were observed—there was no coughing down of speakers, as in modern Houses of Parliament—and but one spoke at a time. When every man had told his story, one would rise up and sing a feast song, after which others followed alternately, until the company broke up.

The taciturn and silent character of the Indians has been so much spoken of as to have become almost proverbial, but it seems to be much less a natural quality with them than is generally supposed. They are decidedly fond of speech-making, and equally fond of telling stories of the prowess either of their ancestors or of themselves. The causes of their taciturnity will be easily understood when it it is remembered how limited is the range of subjects on which they are able to converse. Their hunting or warlike exploits, and a few traditions, are almost the only matters on which they can speak. Unlike civilized men, they know nothing of the news of the world, the teachings of history or philosophy, or the politics and business of life. Their education and pursuits entirely unfit them for the discussion of a thousand questions with which civilized men are familiar, and hence they are silent for lack of having anything to say.

But it is as warriors that the Indians have attracted the greatest amount of attention and won the most fame. With the Indians, war was the object that they regarded as most worthy of their efforts, and to be a great warrior was their highest ambition. They taught their children that valor, fortitude and skill in war, were the noblest accomplishments of a man, in which respect they resembled the people of Sparta; but, unlike them, they did not consider that to attain them it was necessary to sacrifice decency, honesty and truth. In these respects the uncivilized and untaught savages were superior to the polished Greeks. Their falsehood never passed into a proverb. They were distinguished for their honesty. They were still more distinguished for their chastity. There is no instance on record of any insult being offered to a female captive by any of the Eastern Indians, however cruelly she might otherwise have been treated. It would be pleasant to learn the name of any civilized people of which the same could be said. When we read the tales of Indian atrocities in war, of the murder of infants and mothers, of stealthy midnight marches and barbarous assassinations, we are struck with horror and indignation at the recital. These are proper and natural feelings which do honor to the sensibilities of mankind. But on turning to the other side of the picture, and reading the bald and often distorted statements which have been recorded of the treatment of Indians by white men, who have themselves been the narrators of their own deeds, our views become greatly modified. In the course of this work, many tales of Indian cruelty and revenge will be told, and others not less harrowing, of atrocities committed by Englishmen and New Englanders on both the French and the Indians. When the Pilgrim Fathers landed at Plymouth, in 1620, they were visited by Massasoit, the great Sachem or King of the tribes in the vicinity, and a treaty of amity was arranged between his people and the Colonists. During the thirty years following, Massasoit ever remained their constant friend. When he died, his son, Alexander, renewed the old treaties of friendship with the New Englanders, and all went on harmoniously until the people of Plymouth, on the pretext that he entertained designs unfriendly to them, caused him to be ignominiously arrested, and threatened with instant death if he did not immediately appear before their council. The insult threw him into a burning fever, and two days afterwards he died, probably from natural causes, but the Indians firmly believed that the white men had poisoned him. King Philip, his brother and successor, with a soul rankling with hatred, resolved to avenge the wrong. The great Indian war of 1675 was the result, and few civilized wars have been undertaken for a better cause. Unfortunately for the Indians, their enemies have been their only historians; the records of their cruelties remain, but the wrongs which provoked them are either untold, or are ignored and forgotten.

The warlike weapons of the Indians before the white men visited them consisted of bows and arrows, the latter tipped with stone or bone, and battle-axes or tomahawks of stone. The scalping knife was made of a sharpened bone, or the edge of a broken silex; the knife now used is a later invention, which the manufacturers of Birmingham or Sheffield were kind enough to supply their red brethren for a consideration, in unlimited numbers, to be used on the scalps of their white brethren in America. The introduction of fire-arms quickly supplanted the bow and arrow, and the tomahawk of later times was made of iron and steel. Before they became demoralized by contact with civilization, the Indians, previous to going to war, were in the habit of informing their enemies of the fact by sending some symbol to put them on their guard. When, in 1622, Canonicus proposed to go to war with the Plymouth colony, he sent his defiance in the shape of a bundle of arrows tied up in the skin of a rattlesnake. Later, it is to be feared, that the sending of a declaration of war was sometimes forgotten. Before starting, they always had a feast of dog's flesh, which they believed made them courageous, and a war-dance, at which the older warriors excited and stimulated the others to engage in the proposed enterprise by dancing in a sort of frenzy to the music of a drum, and by the recital of their former deeds in war. Everything being ready, the expedition started. While in friendly territory they divided into small parties for the convenience of hunting; but when they reached the enemy's frontier they went in close array, and in silence. To conceal their numbers, sometimes they marched in single file, each one in the track of his predecessor. Every device that their ingenious minds could suggest was employed to outwit and surprise the enemy. They enticed them into ambuscades, or waylaid and scalped them while passing in fancied security.* If no straggling parties of the enemy were met with, they sought one of his principal villages, which they attacked under cover of the darkness; a general massacre ensued, and those who were so unfortunate as to be taken alive were carried back with them to die by lingering torments. It sometimes happened that captives were not thus treated, but were adopted into the tribe and made to supply the place of some dead warrior. Their fate was determined by a council, and in any case, whether they were to be tortured to death or adopted as brothers, they were

---

* A remarkable instance of Indian strategy was a trick played by the Catawbas on the Caugnawagas early in the last century. They crept near the hunting camps of the latter, and lay in ambush, and, in order to decoy the Caugnawagas out, sent two or three Catawbas in the night past their camp with buffalo hoofs fixed on their feet. In the morning the Caugnawagas followed the track, fell into the snare, and many were killed.

required to pass through the ordeal. This, with the Iroquois, consisted in the captive running between a double file of the warriors and being beaten by each as he passed. The Acadian Indians had a different system of torture; the captive was held up in the arms of four Indians, and then allowed to drop on his back on the ground, and in this way tortured until the circuit of the large wigwam, some thirty or forty feet long, was completed. Sometimes he was beaten with whips, or shaken head downwards. The squaws always took a great interest in these proceedings, and were more cruel than the men. They seemed to regard the torturing of prisoners as their share in the glory of a victory over the enemy. When a captive was condemned to death, he was mutilated with knives, tortured in every conceivable way, and burnt at the stake; but if adopted by the tribe, no distinction was ever made between him and the rest. He became, to all intents and purposes, one of themselves, and shared equally with them, as well in the pleasures and abundance, as in the misfortunes and privations of the tribe.

When a young Indian considered his acquirements and worldly possessions would admit of it, he generally began to look for a wife. If he possessed a canoe, gun and ammunition, spear, hatchet, a moonodah, or pouch, looking-glass, paint, pipe, tobacco, and dice bowl, he was looked upon as a man of wealth, and very eligible for a husband. A squaw who could make pouches, birch dishes, snowshoes, moccasins, string wampum beads, and boil the kettle, was considered a highly accomplished lady. The courtship was extremely simple and short. The lover, after advising with his relations as to the girl he should choose, went to the wigwam where she was, and if he liked her looks, tossed a chip or stick into her lap, which she would take, and, after looking at it with well-feigned wonder, if she liked her lover's looks, would toss it back to him with a sweet smile. That was the signal that he was accepted. But if she desired to reject him, she threw the chip aside with a frown. The marriage ceremony varied greatly with different tribes, and with most there was no ceremony at all. It is not known that any special marriage ceremony existed among the Indians of Acadia.

The religious views of the Indians of Acadia were of the most vague and indefinite character. Champlain declares that they had no more religion than the beasts they hunted. But it is certain that they believed in a future state of existence, and that they were in the habit of making offerings to departed or unseen spirits. Their system of theology was a structure founded on superstition, for the Indians were the most superstitious of men. They placed implicit faith in the incantation of jugglers; they believed in invisible spirits, some good and some bad, who dwelt in the winds and in the water. But as courage in war and skill in the chase were their standards of virtue, their religious views had little influence on their moral conduct. Their paradise was merely a place of sensual enjoyment, where hunger and fatigue were unknown. There was nothing ennobling or exalted in their system of theology— nothing which appealed to the higher nature of man.*

---

*To illustrate the views which they entertained in regard to objects of devotion, I may mention a circumstance related by Denys. At the time La Tour had his fort at St. John a singular tree, about the thickness of a barrel, was from time to time visible in the Falls: it floated upright, and sometimes was not seen for several days. This was considered a proper object of worship by the Indians. They called it Manitou, and made offerings of beaver skins to it, which they fixed on it by means of arrow heads. Denys states that he has seen it, and that La Tour allowed ten of his men to try to drag it out by means of a rope which they attached to it, but were unable to move it. No doubt the ingenious La Tour had anchored the tree there himself, and history is silent in regard to who gathered the beaver skins from the Manitou.

Their funeral ceremonies were of a touching character. When the head of a family died there was great weeping and sorrowing for three or four days. The faces of the friends were besmeared with soot, which was the common symbol of grief. At the proper time a funeral oration was pronounced, in which the genealogy of the deceased was recited, and the great and good actions of his life, his dinners and feasts, his adventures in war and in the chase recounted. On the third day a feast was held as a recognition of the great satisfaction which the deceased was supposed to feel at rejoining his ancestors. After this the women made a garment, or winding sheet, of birch bark, in which he was wrapped and put away on a sort of scaffold for twelve months to dry. At the end of that time the body was buried in a grave, in which the relatives at the same time threw bows, arrows, snow-shoes, darts, robes, axes, pots, moccasins and skins. Denys states that he has seen furs to the value of a thousand francs thrown in, which no man dared to touch. Once he had a grave on the Gulf shore opened, and he showed the savages that the skins were rotten, and the copper pot all covered with verdigris. They only remarked that the pot was dead too, and that its soul had gone with the soul of 'their friend, who was now using it as before.

Lescarbot gives an account of the funeral obsequies of Pennoniac, a Micmac chief, who was killed by the Armouchiquois in 1607. He was first brought back to St. Croix, where the savages wept over his body and embalmed it. They then took it to Port Royal, where, for eight days, they howled lustily over his remains. Then they went to his hut and burnt it up with its contents, dogs included, to prevent any quarrelling among his relatives as to the property. The body was left in the custody of the parents until Spring, when he was bewailed again, and finally laid in a new grave near Cape Sable, along with many pipes, knives, axes, otter skins and pots.

Before setting forth on any expedition the Indians would hold a pow-wow, at which certain secret ceremonies were performed for the purpose of discovering whether they would meet with success or failure. They had a respect for the devil, which was quite natural, considering the character of some of their actions; and the fear of ghosts, goblins, and evil spirits, was continually before their eyes. Perhaps their solitary wanderings through the forest were a means of instilling into their minds the extreme dread of the supernatural which infected them. They were in the habit of making sacrifices when in difficulty or danger to the spirit or demon which they desired to propitiate. A dog was regarded as the most valuable sacrifice, and if, in crossing a lake, their canoe was in danger of being overwhelmed by the winds and waves a dog was thrown overboard, with its fore paws tied together, to satisfy the hunger of the angry Manitou. They were continually on the watch for omens, and easily deterred from any enterprise by a sign which they regarded as unfavorable. A hunter would turn back from the most promising expedition at the cry of some wild animal which he thought was an omen of failure in the chase. The same superstitions prevail among them to the present day.*

*A good story, in illustration of Indian superstition, is told by Mr. E. Jack, of Fredericton. He was on a surveying journey, and had encamped near Mount Porcupine, in Charlotte County. One of his men, named Smith, had ascended the mountain to look for pine, and on his return told Saugus, an Indian, who was with the party, that he saw an old man on the mountain, twelve feet high, with one eye, who called to him, "Where is Saugus? I want to eat him." Poor Saugus was much terrified at the intelligence. During the night an owl commenced to hoot over the camp, and filled Saugus with such consternation that he woke up Mr. Jack to say that "Smith's old man" was coming. Next morning, Mr. Jack offered Saugus two dollars to go up to the mountain for a knife which Smith had left sticking in a spruce tree, but Saugus was not to be tempted by the bribe to take such a dangerous journey.

The Indians, from their simple mode of life and abundant exercise, were not exposed to many diseases which are known to civilized men. But some of their maladies were extremely fatal. Their uncertain means of subsistence, sometimes exposed to starvation, and at other times indulging in great excesses, undermined their constitutions and sowed the seeds of disease. Consumption, pleurisy, asthma and paralysis, the result of the fatigue and hardships of the chase, also carried off great numbers of them; and at times, epidemics of an unknown and mysterious nature swept them away by thousands. For three or four years previous to the landing of the Pilgrim Fathers, a deadly pestilence raged along the seaboard from Penobscot to Narraganset Bay. Some tribes were nearly destroyed. The Massachusetts were reduced from three thousand to three hundred fighting men; and many districts which had been populous, were left without a single inhabitant. What the disease was which then swept over the land can, of course, never be ascertained. In 1694 another terrible visitation of the same nature swept over Maine and Acadia. At Pentagoet great numbers died of it, and it carried off the Chief of the River Saint John and vast numbers of others. At Medoctec alone, over a hundred persons died, and so great was the terror caused by the plague that the Indians deserted that village entirely and did not settle there again for many years. The symptoms, as described by Gyles, who was an eye witness, were—that a person seemingly in perfect health would commence bleeding at the mouth and nose, turn blue in spots, and die in two or three hours.* Strange to say, the disease was at its worst during the

*The symptoms of the plague which prevails in Egypt are somewhat similar. The most fatal symptom is violent bleeding at the nose, and those thus taken are never known to recover.—*Baker's Albert N' Yanza,* p. 333.

winter. No such plague appears to have visited Acadia since that time; yet, unlike all other races, the Indians rather diminish than increase in numbers. Nor is it difficult to ascertain the cause. All over America, whether the white man is a friend or an enemy, the red man fades before him. Peace is not less fatal than war to the savage: in the latter, he is shot down with an unsparing hand; in the former, he is demoralized and degraded by vicious customs: exposed to temptations he has no power to resist, which enervate his frame and end in misery and death. Every tree which is felled in the forest reduces the area of the hunting grounds which he inherited from his fathers, and on which his existence depends. Every mill which attests the energy and industry of his white brother is an additional omen of his extinction. Every day he sees the girdle of fields and meadows narrowing the circle of his hopes. Driven back, mile by mile, whither shall he at last retire? He is a stranger and an alien in his own land —an outcast, robbed of his birthright by a stronger race. He and his tribe are but a feeble few, and their efforts avail nothing against the ceaseless advance of the pale faced race, who come welded together into a resistless phalanx by the iron hand of civilization.

CHAPTER III.

CHAMPLAIN'S DISCOVERIES, AND THE ISLAND OF
SAINT CROIX.

TOWARDS the close of the sixteenth century France had attained a degree of internal tranquillity which gave the nation some leisure for the pursuit of pacific enterprises. Henry IV. was on the throne, and that large-minded and truly great King was doing his utmost to increase the prosperity of his country by the husbanding of its resources, the improvement of agriculture, and the extension of commerce. Guided by his strong and vigorous hand, the nation rapidly recovered from the effects of its former misfortunes; trade flourished, wealth increased, and luxury followed in their train. It was at this period that those enterprises for the colonization of North America—which had been abandoned under the pressure of civil commotion—began to be renewed. Indeed it was necessary for France to be on the alert, for English adventurers were scouring every sea, and the work of planting English colonies was being carried on with vigor under royal auspices. The time had come for the commencement of the great contest between the rival nations for the rich Empire of the west. Yet it would be extremely absurd to suppose that either the English or French colonizers of America had any conception of the grand destiny of the States whose foundations they helped to lay. Extensive colonial empires were things which had not in Europe at that day been recognized as practicable. It was rather to gather the abundance of the land, than to found empires on its soil, that brought Europeans to America, and those who were prepared to make themselves permanent homes in the new world were chiefly men who expatriated themselves in consequence of civil or religious persecution, or because of loss of fortune.

The first essay of France towards colonizing North America gave little promise of success. In 1599 Pontgravè, a rich merchant of St. Malo, conceived the plan of obtaining possession of a monopoly of the fur trade on the coast, and fitted out a small bark for a voyage up the St. Lawrence. He induced Chauvin,* a captain in the French navy, who had served in the late wars, and had influential friends at Court, to enter into his schemes, and obtained from the King a patent with the same powers which had formerly been granted to De la Roche. Chauvin set sail for America, and reached Tadoussac, where he attempted to establish a trading post. But his men came near dying of hunger during the winter, and but for the savages, who took compassion on their sufferings and supplied them with food, all must have perished. Chauvin abandoned Tadoussac in the Spring, but afterwards made another voyage to that place, in which he was accompanied by Pontgravè and other gentlemen. In 1602, while preparing for a third expedition, he suddenly died.

After the death of Chauvin, Eymard de Chaste, Chevalier of Malta, Commander of Lormetan, Grand Master of the Order of St. Lazarus, and Governor of Dieppe, obtained the same commission which Chauvin had held. To provide for the expense of another expedition, an association was formed consisting of many gentlemen and the principal merchants of Rouen, and others. Pontgravè was chosen to conduct the vessels to Tadoussac, and Samuel

* Chauvin was a native of Normandy, and a Huguenot.

Champlain, a captain of approved intelligence and courage, went with him. They set sail in 1603, and ascended the St. Lawrence as far as the Sault St. Louis. It appears that at this period Hochelaga, which had been the residence of the powerful Hurons in Cartier's time, had fallen into such decay that they did not even visit it. Champlain discovered, however, that Montreal was an island, and drew a chart of the river, which was presented to the king on his return. In the meantime De Chaste had died. His zeal in the cause of colonization, and his powerful influence, made his loss a severe blow to the adventurers; but the mantle which had fallen from his shoulders was destined to grace another equally worthy, and the schemes of colonization, which he had meditated, to be pursued to a successful termination.

Among the persons who had accompanied Chauvin and Pontgravè to Canada, was a gentleman of the bed-chamber of King Henry IV., named De Monts, a much attached follower of the monarch, and one who had done him good service in the wars. He had been struck with the advantages which might be derived from a vigorous prosecution of the fur trade, and still more by the fitness of New France for a Royal Colony. Although Tadoussac had a favorable position as a depôt for the trade, he discerned in Acadia, with its milder climate and more fertile soil, a more suitable place for a colony of farmers, and, with the bold grasp of a man who felt himself equal to the task of establishing the power of his country in America, he resolved to combine both schemes in one, and to make the peltry trade and the colony mutually assist and support each other. That he was a person in every way fitted to accomplish the object which he proposed, has been admitted by the united voice of contemporary writers. He was distinguished for his great talents and wide experience. To the accomplishments of a soldier, he added the tact of a statesman. He was ever zealous for the glory of his country, and upright in his views. He was also, what was equally necessary for the founder of a colony, incorruptibly honest and firm in his resolves. That he was a Protestant perhaps detracted something from his influence as the founder of a Catholic colony; but that fact has been so far useful to his reputation by making his just dealing and integrity under trying circumstances the more conspicuous. That he did not succeed in all his undertakings, must be attributed partly to the fact that he was often badly served, partly to inexperience, the result of want of knowledge of the country, and partly to fortune. Nothing can rob him of the honor of being the founder of the first permanent settlement in the Canadian Dominion, and his name will go down to posterity with that distinction attached to it as long as its people take an interest in their country's early history. He obtained from the King, on the 8th November, 1603, a patent constituting him Lieutenant General of the Territory of Acadia, between the 40th and 46th degrees of latitude, with power to take and divide the land, to create offices of war, justice and policy; to prescribe laws and ordinances; to make war and peace; to build forts and towns, and establish garrisons. He was also directed to convert the savages to the Christian religion; and in fine, to use the words of the commission, "to do generally whatsoever may make for the conquest, peopling, inhabiting and preservation of the said land of Acadie." The association formed by his predecessor, De Chaste, being still in existence, De Monts induced many wealthy merchants of Rochelle and other places to join it, and on December 8th, 1603, obtained from the King letters patent granting to him and his associates the exclusive right to trade with the savages in furs and other articles between Cape de Raze* and the 40th degree of latitude, for ten years. Four ships were then made ready for a voyage to his new government, and many gentlemen, induced by curiosity to see the new world, or moved by a desire to make it their home, came forward and volunteered to accompany him. The most distinguished of these was a gentleman of Picardie, named Jean de Biencourt, Baron de Poutrincourt, who wished to remove with his family to Acadia. He was highly esteemed by the King as a brave soldier, and proved a most valuable addition to the colony.

Champlain was the person chosen to conduct the vessels to Acadia, and he gladly consented to perform the service. This illustrious man, who has left his name for ever inseparably connected with the history of Canada, had even then earned a good title to be called an experienced voyager. He was remarkable, not only for his good sense, strong penetration and upright views, but for his activity, daring, firmness, enterprise, and valor. He had a natural gaiety of spirit, which made him at all times a cheerful companion, and no one understood better than he how to make the irksome tediousness of a long residence on shipboard endurable for those under his command. His zeal for the interest of his country was ardent and disinterested; his heart was tender and compassionate, and he was thoroughly unselfish. He was a faithful historian, intelligent and observant as an explorer, and an experienced seaman. But,

*.Cape de Raze, no doubt, means Cape Race. It is so marked on the old maps. This grant seems never to have been seen by Charlevoix, for he describes it as extending from the 40th to the 54th degree. The words are, "Depuis le Cap de Raze jusqu'au quarantieme degre comprevant toute la cote de l'Acadie, terre et Cap Breton, baie de Saint [illegible], de Chaleur, isles percees Gaspay, Chichedec, Mesamichi, Lesquemin, Tadoussac et la riviere de Canada, tant d'un cote que d'autre et toutes les bales et rivieres qui entrant au dedans desdites costes."

perhaps, the strongest and noblest feature of his character was his untiring zeal for the propagation of the Christian religion among the savages. To accomplish this end, he was ready to encounter difficulties, dangers, and death. No Jesuit father was ever imbued with a more resolute missionary spirit. It was a common saying of his, "that the salvation of one soul was of more value than the conquest of an empire," and "that kings ought not to think of extending their authority over idolatrous nations, except for the purpose of subjecting them to Jesus Christ." For thirty years, often with slender resources, but always with untiring energy, he toiled to extend the possessions of his country in America, and to convert the savages; and it has been truly said that "when he died, Canada lost her best friend." Of the four vessels which De Monts and his associates had provided, one was ordered to Tadoussac, to prosecute the fur trade. Another, under Pontgravè, whose zeal in voyages to the new world nothing could tame, was sent to Canso, to scour the straits between Cape Breton and the island of St. John, for the purpose of driving those away who might venture to interfere with the fur trade. The other two vessels, under the immediate command of De Monts himself, formed the main expedition, and were for the purpose of conveying the colony which was destined to carry the arts of civilization to the shores of Acadia. The colonists numbered about one hundred and twenty persons, consisting of artizans, agriculturists, priests, Huguenot ministers, and gentlemen. They were of both religions—Catholic as well as Protestant—but the former were the more numerous. Champlain believed that in this mixture of religions there would be a source of difficulties for the colony, but none of a serious nature arose from this cause. Everything that the ingenuity of that

HISTORY OF ACADIA. 65

day could suggest was done to ensure success. Tools of all kinds were provided in abundance, building materials were also taken, and arms and ammunition were supplied in sufficient quantities for any possible contingency. The only thing wanting was knowledge of the difficulties from climate and other causes, against which they would require to provide, but that knowledge was only to be gained in the rude school of experience.

De Monts set sail from Havre de Grace on the 7th March, 1604, leaving his consort, commanded by Captain Morrel, which contained most of the implements and provisions for the winter, to follow him. The vessels were to meet at Canso, but De Monts made a bad land-fall, was driven too far to the south, and in a month from the day of his departure, found himself off Cape la Have. In the first harbor he entered he found a vessel engaged in trading in violation of his monopoly. This vessel he seized and confiscated, but he perpetuated the name of his victim by calling the harbor where the seizure was made Port Rossignol, after the master of the vessel. Passing to the westward he entered a harbor which he named Port Mouton, to preserve the memory of another victim, an unfortunate sheep which fell from the vessel and was drowned. By this time they had grown weary of life on board a ship, and De Monts landed his company and sent exploring parties east and west, to see if a suitable place for a settlement could be found. In the meantime he had become anxious at the delay in the arrival of his consort, which had not yet appeared. Finally she was discovered near Canso, and her stores brought from her by the aid ot the Indians, with whom he was on excellent terms, and whose families he in the interval fed. Morrel then,

E

having received his instructions, proceeded with his vessel to Tadoussac.

The exploring parties sent out by De Monts having found no suitable place for the colony, they again embarked and sailed to the south-west. Following the coast as closely as they could with safety, they passed on, and, rounding Cape Sable, entered the Bay of Fundy. This De Monts named le grand Baie Françoise, a name which it retained until the English got possession of the country. They next entered St. Mary's Bay, to which De Monts gave the name it still bears, and finding the country pleasant, anchored and sent out exploring parties. There was on board the ship a priest from Paris, named Aubrey, a man of good family, who being an active, intelligent person, and a naturalist of some ability, was in the habit of landing with the exploring parties to examine the productions of the country. While at St. Mary's Bay, he went out as usual with one of the parties, but his companions were dismayed on their return to the vessel to discover that he was still absent. Guns were fired from the vessel to guide him in case he had lost his way, but night came and passed without any sign of his return. For four days the woods were searched in all directions without finding any traces of the wanderer, until hope died, and it was the opinion of all that he was no longer living. Then indeed a horrible suspicion of foul play disturbed, for the first and last time, the harmony of the two religious parties which composed the colony. One of those who had been with him was a Protestant. He and the lost Aubrey had been heard to dispute on religious matters, high words had passed between them, and zealous friends of the missing man searched their memories to recall some word or look of his rival in the controversy, which could be strained into evidence of revenge and assassination. To the honor of that company, be it said, that though cruelly suspected, no violence was done him, but it was with bitter hearts they sailed out of the Bay of St. Mary.

But this gloom was soon dispelled. Scarce a score of miles from the scene of their mournful adventure, they entered a narrow channel, between two lofty hills, and found themselves sailing in a spacious basin some leagues in extent. All around them were vast woods, covering elevations which gradually grew to be mountains as they receded from the sea. Little rivers added their contribution of waters to the great basin, and the wide meadows beyond seemed like a sea bearing a forest on its breast. This noble harbor filled Champlain with admiration, and struck by its spaciousness and security, he gave it the name of Port Royal. He found that a large river flowed into the basin from the eastward, and was divided at its entrance by an island, within which a vessel might anchor in deep water. Champlain ascended it as far as his boats could go, which was fourteen or fifteen leagues, and he gave it the name of River de l'Esquille,* from a fish of

*Champlain describes the river thus:—'I named it Port Royal, to which descends three streams, one sufficiently large, drawing from the east, called the river of the Esquille, which is a little fish the length of a span, which they catch in quantities, also plenty of herring, and many other sorts of fish, which are abundant in their season. This river is almost a quarter of a league wide at its entrance, wherein there is an island which is about half a league in circuit, filled with wood like the rest of the land, as pines, firs, vines, birches, aspens, and some oaks, which are, with the other trees, in small numbers. There are two entrances to the said river, one to the north and the other to the south of the island. That to the north is the best, where vessels may lie at anchor sheltered by the island in 5, 6, 7, 8 and 9 fathoms of water, but must take care of some shoals which are joined to the island and the main land, very dangerous if you do not observe the channel. I went 14 or 15 leagues to where the tide flows and could not go further into the interior on account of the navigation. In this place it is 60 paces in width, and has a fathom and a half of water. * * Within the harbor is another island, distant from the first about two leagues, where there is another small river which goes some distance inland, which I named the river St. Anthony. Its entrance is distant from the head of St. Mary's Bay about four leagues by traversing through the woods."—*Champlain, Vol. I, pp.* 70, 71, 72.

that name, with which it abounded. To another river, lower down the basin, he gave the name of St. Anthony. When they landed they found that the fertility of the soil and the variety of its natural productions did not deceive their expectations. The woods were composed of oaks, ash, birches, pines and firs; the basin swarmed with fish, and the meadows were luxuriant with grass. They visited a point of land near the junction of the main river which flowed into the basin and a smaller tributary which entered it from the south, a place long destined to be memorable as the seat of French power in Acadia.* Poutrincourt was so charmed with the beauty of Port Royal and its surroundings that he resolved to make it his home, and requested a grant of it from De Monts, which he received, coupled with the condition that during the ensuing ten years he should bring out to it from France a sufficient number of other families to inhabit and cultivate the place. In 1607 this grant was confirmed by the King.

Leaving behind them the beautiful basin of Port Royal, they again set sail in quest of further discoveries and followed the coast towards the east. Champlain's simple and truthful narrative of the voyage makes it possible to follow his track almost with the accuracy of an actual observer of his movements. They came in sight of Cape Chignecto, which Champlain named the Cape of two Bays, because it was the western extremity of the land which divides Chignecto Bay from the Basin of Mines. They observed the lofty island which lies off from the Cape, and to this, in consequence of its elevation, the name of Isle Haut was given. They landed on its solitary shore, seldom even at the present day profaned by the presence of man, and climbed to its summit. There they found a spring of

* This was afterwards the site of the town of Port Royal.

delightful water, and in another place indications of copper. From this island they went to Advocate Harbor, a natural haven, but dry at low water, and one which seems to have struck Champlain's fancy much, for he has left sailing directions for entering it. At the cliff beyond it, which is now named Cape d'Or, they found another copper mine, which has been often explored since but never worked with success. They then sailed eastward as far as Partridge Island, Parrsboro, observed the remarkable rise and fall of the tides, and discovered the river by which the Indians reached the Basin of Mines from Tracadie, Miramichi, and other parts of the Gulf of St. Lawrence.* At Partridge Island Champdore discovered some rude amethysts; one large cluster was divided between De Monts and Poutrincourt, who afterwards set the stones in gold and gave them to the King and Queen. Champlain, notwithstanding the richness of the land in minerals, was discouraged by the forbidding aspect of its rock-bound shore, and he has recorded in his book his unfavorable opinion of its soil.

The voyagers then crossed the Bay of Chignecto, and arrived at Quaco, where they landed and found indications of iron, and passing to the westward reached a fine bay which contained three islands and a rock, two bearing a league to the west, and the other at the mouth of a river, the largest and deepest they had yet seen. This Champlain named the River St. John, because they arrived there on the day of St. John the Baptist. By the Indians it was called the Ouygoudy.† It has been generally stated by those who have written on the subject, and accepted as true, that Champlain on this occasion ascended and explored

* This stream is now called Partridge Island River; from it, by a short portage, the Indians passed to the river Hebert, which flows into Cumberland Bay.

† Wigoudi would probably better express the Indian pronunciation of the name of this river. It means a highway.

the St. John River, but it is quite clear that he did not. No such statement is to be found in his book, and such an important expedition would not have been passed over in silence. Lescarbot states, and his authority cannot be impeached, that the expedition for the exploration of the St. John was undertaken in 1608, or four years later. Champlain gives a minute account of the Falls at the mouth of the St. John and of the mode of passing them, and also some account of the river above, but the latter was doubtless furnished to him by Champdore, who visited the river in 1608. He states that the Falls being passed, the river enlarged to a league in certain places, and that there were three islands, near which there were a great quantity of meadows and handsome woods, such as oaks, beeches, butternuts, and vines of the wild grape. The inhabitants of the country, he says, went by the river to Tadoussac on the great river St. Lawrence, and had to pass over but little land to reach that place. Shallops could only ascend fifteen leagues on account of the rapids, which could only be navigated by the canoes of the savages. Such an account, though correct enough in some particulars as regards the width of the river, the islands near Oak Point, which are those which are evidently meant, and the wild grapes which they produce is manifestly not the result of Champlain's personal observation. He was too accurate and painstaking to have erred so grossly as to think that the stream was only navigable for fifteen leagues by shallops, in consequence of the rapids. Some less conscientious lieutenant must be credited with the misstatement.

If it were possible to bring together but for a moment the past and the present, and to place the scene as it was viewed by Champlain, and as it is to-day, side by side, we should be able to realize more clearly than any pen can describe how vastly the face of nature may be changed by the industry of man. Could Champlain, as he gazed on the cedar-clad rocks which surrounded the harbor of St. John, have looked into the future with the eye of prophecy, it would have taken nothing less than a Divine revelation to induce him to believe that his vision would ever come to pass. He would have seen himself surrounded by unheard of scenes and unknown inventions. Here and there a glimpse of the primeval rock might for a moment strengthen his faith that the busy city before him stood on the banks of his own St. John, but the snorting locomotive, the splashing steamboat and the clashing sound of strange machinery would have sadly tried his belief. And if, indeed, he trusted his vision, and saw with complacent eyes the flourishing community which had grown on the place of his discovery, his mind would be embittered by the reflection that his own countrymen had lost the fair heritage to which he had pointed the way, and had been supplanted by an alien race, speaking a strange tongue, who valued little the memory of the man who had been the first to tread their shores.

Leaving the River St. John, Champlain sailed to the west, and came in sight of four islands, now called the Wolves, but which he named Isles aux Margos, from the great number of birds which he found on them. The young birds, he says, were as good to eat as pigeons. He saw an island six leagues in extent, which was called by the savages Manthane. He presently found himself sailing among islands, of which the number was so great that he could not count them, many of them very beautiful, and abounding in good harbors. They were all in a *cul de sac*, which he judged to be fifteen leagues in circuit. The bays and passages between the islands abounded with fish, and the voyagers caught great numbers of them. But the season was advancing, and De Monts was anxious to find some place where he might settle his colony, now grown weary of the ship, and eager for a more active life. In this beautiful archipelago he saw that, whatever might be their success in agricultural operations, the abundance of fish would always make their means of subsistence sure, and as this was a central point from which he could hold intercourse with the Indians, he sought for a proper place on which to erect a fort and dwelling. He finally fixed upon an island in the St. Croix River, a few miles above St. Andrews, as his head-quarters, and there commenced preparations for making it a permanent settlement. Looking at his selection now by the light of common experience his choice of a locality seems to have been a most unwise one; but his error may well be excused, considering his want of knowledge of the country and climate. To this island, which is now known on the maps as Doucett's Island, he gave the name of St. Croix. Its position has been the subject of much controversy, but that has only been so because national boundaries depended on the determination of its locality. The description given of it by Champlain and Lescarbot are so full and exact that any stranger taking them in his hand could easily identify it—for it had peculiarities in shape and surroundings which could scarcely be found in any other island on the coast of America, quite independently of its latitude, which is accurately stated by Champlain.

De Monts lost no time in commencing the erection of suitable buildings for his colony, and in the mean time an event occurred which caused universal rejoicing. Champdore was ordered to convey Master Simon, a miner, who had been brought with the expedition, to examine more carefully the ores at St. Mary's Bay. While engaged in their researches at that place their attention was attracted by the signal of a handkerchief attached to a stick on the shore, and immediately landing, they were overjoyed to find the missing Aubrey, weak, indeed, and perishing of hunger, but still able to speak. For seventeen days he had subsisted on berries and roots, and was sadly emaciated. It appeared that he had strayed from his companions while in search of his sword, which he had left by a brook where he stopped to drink. Having found it, he was unable to retrace his steps, and had wandered he knew not whither. De Monts and the whole colony were greatly delighted at his safe return, which relieved the little community from the misery of unjust suspicions.

St. Croix Island is oblong in shape, and lies from north to south. It contains probably ten acres of land.* At its southern extremity, lying towards the sea, was a little hill, or islet, severed from the other, where De Monts placed his cannon. At the northern end of the island he built a fort, so as to command the river up and down. Outside of the fort was a large building which served as a barracks, and around it several smaller structures. Within the fort was the residence of De Monts, fitted up, as Lescarbot tells us, with "fair carpentry work," while close by were the residences of Champlain, Champdore and d'Orville. There was also a covered gallery for exercise in bad weather. A storehouse, covered with shingles, a large brick oven, and a chapel, completed the structures of the colony on the

* St. Croix Island, according to the plan made in 1797 by Thomas Wright, Surveyor-General of the Island of St. John, is sixteen chains in length and seven in extreme width.

island.* On the western shore of the St. Croix a watermill was commenced for grinding corn, while some of the settlers erected buildings close to the brook on the eastern bank of the river, where the colonists obtained water, and laid out land for a garden.

While the colonists were engaged in their various works, Poutrincourt took his departure for France. He had seen the country, and was satisfied with its excellence; he had chosen Port Royal as the place where he should reside, and it only remained for him to return for the purpose of removing his family to their new home. He took with him the best wishes of his friends, who hoped for his speedy return, and he was the bearer to the King of the glad tidings that France had at last founded a colony in the new world.

During the course of their explorations the adventurers had found the savages everywhere friendly. They had received the French, not with the distant and cold civility of suspicious strangers, but with the cordiality of old friends. They were eager to trade with them, and had rendered them valuable services on more than one occasion. Thus commenced that friendship and amity between the French and the Indians of Acadia which was never broken or disturbed, which alone enabled the former to maintain a long contest against the powerful colonies of England with some show of equality, and which made the Indians faithful to their memory long after the last vestiges of French power had been swept away.

Scarcely had the colonists concluded their labors when

* In 1797 the stone foundations of these buildings were brought to light by Robert Pagan and others. Five distinct piles of ruins were discovered at the north end of the island, and from the manner in which the work had been done, it was quite evident that a permanent settlement had been intended. The evidence of this discovery was placed before the Commissioners appointed to determine the locality of St. Croix island, and, no doubt, materially influenced their decision.

the winter came upon them with awful and unexpected severity. They were struck with terror and surprise at the fury of the snow storms and the severity of the frost. The river became a black and chilly tide, covered with masses of floating ice, and the land around them a dreary and frost-bound desert. It soon was painfully apparent that their residence had been unwisely chosen. The island was without water, and the wood upon it had been exhausted by the erection of the buildings and fort. Both these articles of prime necessity had to be brought from the main land, and this was a service arduous and difficult to men who had been accustomed to the milder temperature of France. To add to their troubles a number of Indians encamped at the foot of the island. Their entire friendliness was not then so well understood as it afterwards became, and the French were harassed and wearied by continual watching to guard against attack. In the midst of this suffering and anxiety there came upon them a frightful visitation. A strange and unknown disease broke out among them, which proved alarmingly fatal. No medicine seemed to relieve it, and the natives knew of no remedy against its ravages. Out of the small colony of seventy-nine, thirty-five died, and many of the survivors were only saved by the timely arrival of warmer weather. Those who were not attacked were scarcely able to provide for the wants of the sick and to bury the dead.* Many

*Champlain describes this disease as follows:—"During the winter a certain disease broke out among many of our people, called the disease of the country, otherwise the scurvy, as I have since heard learned men say. It originated in the mouth of those who have a large amount of flabby and superfluous flesh, (causing a bad putrefaction,) which increases to such an extent, that they can scarcely take any thing, unless it is almost entirely liquid. The teeth become quite loose, and they can be extracted by the fingers without causing any pain. The superfluity of this flesh requires to be cut away, and this causes a violent bleeding from the mouth. They are afterwards seized with a great pain in the legs and arms, which swell up and become very hard, all marked as if bitten by fleas, and they are unable to walk from the contraction of the nerves, so that they have no strength left, and

a longing eye was cast over the pitiless sea which severed them from their own fair land, which so many of them were fated never to behold again.

The return of Spring brought with it brighter skies and better hopes, but De Monts determined to remove his colony from St. Croix Island. As soon as the state of the seas would permit, he fitted out and armed his pinnaçe, and, accompanied by Champlain, sailed along the coast towards the south-west, with a view to the discovery of a more favorable situation and a more genial climate. They made a careful examination of the whole coast as far as Cape Cod, entered the bay of Penobscot, and at the Kennebec erected a cross. Some of the places which they visited appeared inviting, and suitable for settlement, but the savages were numerous, unfriendly and thievish, and their company being small, it was considered unsafe to settle among them. For these reasons they returned to St. Croix with the intention of removing the colony to Port Royal.

In the meantime Pontgravè, who was quite indefatigable in his Acadian schemes, had arrived with an accession of forty men and fresh supplies from France, a most welcome addition to their diminished numbers and resources. Everything portable was removed from St. Croix Island, but the buildings were left standing. The embarkation of the colonists and stores was speedily accomplished under the direction of Pontgravè, and with mingled feelings of pleasure and regret they bade farewell to that solitary island

suffer the most intolerable pain. They have also pains in the loins, the stomach and intestines, a very bad cough, and shortness of breath; in short, they are in such a state that the greater part of those seized with the complaint can neither raise nor move themselves, and if they attempt to stand erect they fall down senseless, so that of seventy-nine of us, thirty-five died, and more than twenty barely escaped death. The greater part of those unaffected with the complaint, complained of slight pains and shortness of breath. We could find no remedy to cure those attacked by the complaint, and we could not discover any cause for the disease."

which had been the scene of so much misery and suffering, but which was still, in a measure, endeared to them because it was their first home in the new world, and the last resting place of so many loved companions and friends. Before they departed, some of the colonists sowed portions of it with rye, and when visited in the autumn, two years later, a heavy crop of grain was found on the island, which the colonists reaped and carried away. Thus suddenly ended the occupation of an island which since that time has never been inhabited by any permanent resident, except the keeper of the light-house, whose beacon warns the voyager on the St. Croix to avoid its rocky shores.

CHAPTER IV.

THE COLONY AT PORT ROYAL.

THE place chosen for the residence of the colony at Port Royal was opposite Goat Island, on the north bank of the river of Port Royal,* distant about six miles from the present town of Annapolis. It was a position easily fortified, favorable for traffic with the savages, and beautiful by nature. The land around it, although somewhat stony, was strong and fertile, and the marsh lands, some distance away, were of inexhaustible richness. The climate, too, was milder than that of the greater portion of the peninsula, and well adapted to the cultivation of fruit. Timber of the best quality was abundant, and extensive fisheries were close by. Nothing, it would seem, was wanting that nature could bestow to make Port Royal a flourishing colony. The work of erecting buildings was rapidly advanced, dwellings and storehouses were built, and a small palisaded fort constructed. When this work was being carried on, De Monts sailed for France to provide for the provisioning of the colony, until crops could be raised, and to attend to his trading interests. He left Pontgravè as his lieutenant to govern the colony in his absence, and with him Champlain and Champdore, to assist in the general conduct of affairs, and take charge of any exploring expeditions that might be required. Pontgravè was an energetic and active man, zealous in the work of colonization, and equally zealous in the prosecution of trade. While he

* Now Annapolis River. It was named by the French the Dauphin, but popularly known and marked on their maps as the River of Port Royal.

pushed forward the preparations necessary for the comfortable wintering of the colony, he did not neglect the commercial pursuits, without which the colony could not then subsist. The savages, among whom he was, were of the Souriquois or Micmac tribe, and well disposed towards the whites. For the purpose of deepening this attachment, and at the same time carrying on a profitable business, he commenced an active trade with them for the skins of moose, otter and beaver. After the winter had set in, this barter became very brisk, and the good disposition of the natives was to the advantage of the French in another way, for they brought them abundance of fresh meat, and enabled them to live through the cold season in comparative comfort. They were quite free from any serious epidemic, such as had proved so fatal at St. Croix, and only six died during the winter. Their supplies of breadstuffs were abundant, but the labor of grinding their grain by hand proved most irksome, and Lescarbot gravely states that he believed this had contributed to kill those who died. The Indians, although so liberal with their venison, refused to assist in this severe work, which was not surprising, considering how averse the savages were to labor of any description. A more probable cause of the mortality was the fact that they had neglected to drain their dwellings, which were consequently damp and uncomfortable.

In the Spring of 1606 Pontgravè made an attempt to find a warmer climate and a better place for his colony in a more southern latitude. He fitted out the barque which had been left with him, and set sail for Cape Cod; but his venture proved disastrous. Twice he was driven back to Port Royal by the violence of the tempest, and on the third essay was so unfortunate as to have his vessel injured on the rocks at the mouth of the port. This deterred him from any further attempt, which, indeed, could only have been attended with greater disasters; such was the weakness of his vessel, and so great were the dangers of that tempestuous sea. Pontgravè then built another barque, or shallop, so that he would not be quite without means of transport in case of accident, or shortness of provisions. The result proved that he had been guided by a wise forethought. The Spring advanced, and provisions began to grow scarce, but there was no sign of De Monts' arrival. Summer was ushered in, but still the expected supplies did not come, and Pontgravè, now really alarmed for the safety of De Monts, and apprehensive that the colony would soon be without food, determined to embark his people, and run along the coast as far as Canso, in the hope that he might fall in with some fishing vessel, by which their wants might be relieved, and in which they might obtain a passage to France. Having finally given up all hope of the arrival of the expected succor, Pontgravè set sail on the 25th July from Port Royal, leaving two men behind, who had volunteered to remain and take charge of the stores.

In the meantime De Monts had been hastening to the relief of his colony. On his arrival in France his accounts of Acadia had been coldly received. The expense of the venture had been heavy and the returns small. Many of the merchants who belonged to the company were dissatisfied, and it appeared equally difficult to fit out ships for the relief of the colony or to get men to embark in them. In this juncture Poutrincourt nobly came to his aid. His presence in France at that time was of vital importance to his own interests in consequence of some lawsuits in which he was engaged; but notwithstanding this position of affairs he agreed to return to Acadia and assist De Monts in placing the colony on a permanent footing. Poutrincourt was now more resolute than ever to establish himself there with his family. He also persuaded Lescarbot, an advocate who resided in Paris, to accompany them. After many vexatious delays a vessel of one hundred and fifty tons, named the Jonas, was fitted out at Rochelle, and set sail for Acadia on the 11th May 1606. The voyage was long and tedious from adverse winds, and rendered still more so by visits which were made to various parts of the coast from Canso to Cape Sable. They passed Cape Sable on the 25th July, and reached Port Royal on the 27th with the flood tide, saluting the fort as they entered the basin. They were much surprised to discover that Pontgravè had departed, and that only two men had been left. It seems that they had sailed outside of Brier Island in coming up the bay, while Pontgravè had gone through the Petite passage between Long Island and the main, in consequence of which they had missed each other. Pontgravè, however, fell in with a shallop which had been left on the coast by De Monts, and was informed that the Jonas had arrived. With all haste he retraced his course and reached Port Royal on the 31st July, to the great delight of De Monts and his companions. The occasion was celebrated by a festival. Poutrincourt opened a hogshead of wine, and the night was spent in bacchanalian revelry.

Poutrincourt lost no time in commencing the cultivation of his territory. Although the season was well advanced, he sowed a variety of vegetables and grain, and soon had the satisfaction of seeing them start from the virgin soil. He would have been content to settle down and make Port Royal his permanent residence, but De Monts, who was about to return to France, besought him to make one effort more to find a place for the colony farther south. To do this it became necessary for him to give up the superin-

F

tendence of his agricultural operations, and the rest of the summer was employed in a fruitless search. He left Port Royal on the 28th August, accompanied by Champdore, and on the same day the Jonas also put to sea with De Monts and Pontgravè, who were returning to France. Lescarbot, who was a valuable addition to the colony, was left in charge of the establishment at Port Royal, and directed to keep the colonists in order.

Poutrincourt's voyage south began in the midst of difficulty and ended in disaster. The elements were unpropitious, and the barque in which he sailed was small and leaky. They were twice forced back by stress of weather before they reached St. Croix Island. There they found the grain ripening, and gathered some of it, which they sent back to Port Royal. They then proceeded south as far as Cape Cod, where, from its more southern latitude, they hoped to find a situation where the cold would be less extreme than at Port Royal; but their barque became entangled among the shoals, the rudder was broken, and they were obliged to come to anchor three leagues from the land. It took them fifteen days to make the necessary repairs. While some of Poutrincourt's men were ashore they got into collision with the savages, in consequence of some thefts of the latter which they resented. To prevent further difficulty he ordered his men to go on board the vessel, as from the hostile appearance of the savages, it was evident that bloodshed could not otherwise be prevented. Five of them who neglected to obey this wise order were surprised, two of them killed on the spot and the others wounded, two of them mortally. Poutrincourt immediately went ashore with ten men and buried their dead comrades, over whom they erected a cross, the savages in the meanwhile yelling in triumph at a safe distance. When they returned to their vessel the brutal natives dug up the bodies and tore down the cross, insulting the French by shouts and gestures of defiance. The latter were then unable to return to the shore in consequence of it being low water, but when the tide served they replaced the cross and bodies. After an unsuccessful attempt to pass beyond the Cape, Poutrincourt was forced back to the same harbor where his men had been killed, and while there, some of the natives, who came down on pretence of trading, were captured and put to death. Another attempt was made to sail farther south, but they were again driven back, and— the condition of his wounded men being extremely precarious—Poutrincourt bore up for Port Royal, which he reached on the 14th November.

He was received with great joy by the colonists, who had despaired of his safety. Lescarbot celebrated his return by a sort of triumph, crowning the gates of the fort with laurel, over which was placed the arms of France. Below were placed the arms of De Monts and of Poutrincourt, also wreathed with laurel, and a song was composed by Lescarbot in honor of the occasion. That indefatigable and light-hearted Frenchman had not been idle during Poutrincourt's absence. With the assistance of Louis Hebert, the apothecary, who had much experience in such matters, he had superintended the preparation of ground for gardens and fields. He also had a ditch dug round the fort, which drained it completely and made it dry and comfortable. He had the buildings more perfectly fitted up by the carpenters; had roads cut through the woods to various points, and charcoal burnt for the forge, which was kept in active operation for the preparation of tools for the workmen and laborers. And he had accomplished all this without any great strain on the strength of the men, for he only required them to work three hours a day. The rest of the time they spent as they pleased—in hunting, fishing, ranging the forest, or in rest.

The next winter was passed in comfort and cheerfulness. This was owing to the care which had been taken to make the fort and dwellings dry, and also to an admirable arrangement which had been established at the table of Poutrincourt by Champlain. He organized the guests, fifteen in number, into a society which he called the *ordre de bon temps*. Each guest in his turn became steward and caterer for the day, during which he wore the collar " of the order and a napkin, and carried a staff." At dinner he marshalled the way to the table at the head of the procession of guests. After supper he resigned the insignia of office to his successor, with the ceremony of drinking to him in a cup of wine. It became a point of honor with each guest, as his day of service came, to have the table well supplied with game, either by his own exertions, or by purchasing from the Indians, and in consequence they fared sumptuously during the whole winter, so that Lescarbot was enabled to reply with truth to some Parisian epicures, who made sport of their coarse fare, that they lived as luxuriously as they could have done in the street Aux Ours in Paris, and at a much less cost. It is painful, however, to be obliged to record that, although bread and game were abundant, the wine of those festive Frenchmen fell short, so that before Spring they were reduced from three quarts a man daily to the inconsiderable allowance of a pint. The winter was mild and fair, and only four died, who are described as having been sluggish and fretful. These men died in February and March, and in January it seems that the whole company went two leagues to see their cornfield, and dined cheerfully in the sunshine. People accustomed to the climate may be pardoned for supposing that a few experiments of that description might have a tendency to thin the ranks of the colonists, many of whom might not be the most rugged of men.

The Micmacs were their constant visitors throughout the winter, making them presents of venison, and selling the remainder at a fair price. Membertou, their great Sachem—who was chief of the whole tribe from Gaspè to Cape Sable—and many of their lesser dignitaries were the frequent guests of Poutrincourt. Membertou had been a noted warrior, and was a great friend of the white men. He was very aged, and remembered Cartier's visit to the Bay Chaleur in 1534.

In the Spring, Poutrincourt, with his accustomed energy, renewed the work of improvement. He had a water-mill erected for the purpose of grinding grain, which they had previously done with great toil by hand labor. The fisheries were also prosecuted vigorously, two small vessels for coasting voyages built, and all the available land prepared for cultivation. Everything promised fair for a busy and prosperous season, when their labors were brought to a sudden termination by an untoward event.

One morning, in May, a vessel was observed by the Indians making her way up the Basin. Poutrincourt was immediately informed of the circumstance, and set out in a shallop with Champdore to meet her. She proved to be a small barque from the Jonas, which then lay at Canso, and brought the evil tidings that the company of merchants was broken up, and that no more supplies would be furnished to the colony. This, then, was the inglorious termination of all Poutrincourt's hopes and labors. Just as the community was being put in a position to become self-sustaining, the message came which sealed its fate. As the vessel brought no sufficient supplies, nothing remained but to leave Port Royal, where so much money and toil had been fruitlessly expended.

The cause of so sudden a change in the conduct of the company of merchants was the revocation by the King of the exclusive monopoly of the fur trade, which had been granted to De Monts and his associates for ten years. The grant of this monopoly had provoked great jealousy in France among merchants and traders, who were debarred from this lucrative trade, and their jealousy was not lessened by the knowledge that the Dutch, who cared nothing for De Monts' patent, were prosecuting the trade which Frenchmen were unable to pursue, without violating the laws. It was also urged by the enemies of this monopoly that De Monts, during the three years he had held the patent, had made no converts among the natives. These seem to have been the reasons which influenced the King, and the patent being revoked, the dissolution of the company followed. Accordingly the Jonas was sent out to bring back the colony, and, to defray the expenses of the voyage, was ordered to fish and trade at Canso, while the people were brought round from Port Royal in the smaller vessel.

Pourtrincourt, however, had resolved that he would return to Acadia, even if he brought with him none but the members of his own family. To enable him to take home with him to France visible tokens of the excellence of the products of the country, it was necessary for him to stay until his corn was ripe, and to accomplish this without sacrificing the interests of the merchants, at whose charge the vessel had been sent, he employed Chevalier, the commander of the barque, to trade with the Indians for beaver at St. John and St. Croix, and went to Mines himself with the same object. By this means the departure of the colonists was delayed until the end of July.

Some time prior to this a war had broken out between the Indians of Acadia and the tribes west of the Penobscot. The whole available force of the Micmacs was called into the field, and Port Royal was the place of rendezvous.* Early in June the Chief, Membertou, took his departure for Saco, with four hundred warriors, to attack the Armouchoquois, who dwelt there. This savage pageant was a novel and interesting sight to the French, as the great flotilla of canoes swept past the fort and settlement towards the west. Before Poutrincourt departed; Membertou and his warriors returned from their campaign, which had been attended with success, but for several years the warfare between the tribes east and west of the Penobscot continued. It was characterized by revenge, violence and extermination; the great Bashaba, or Prince of the western tribes, was slain, and his nation totally defeated. His death was followed by a civil war amongst his now divided tribes; a fearful pestilence succeeded and swept over the whole coast from Penobscot to Cape Cod. Some tribes were totally exterminated, and others reduced to one-tenth of their former strength in warriors. Such was the tragic termination of this great savage war. On the 30th July most of the colonists left Port Royal in the small barque. Their destination was Canso, where the Jonas was awaiting them to take them to France. On the 11th August, Poutrincourt, finding that his grain was ripe, gathered a quantity of it to take to France as a proof of the excellence of the soil and climate. He also took with him a number of other natural productions of the country.

* The cause of the war was the killing of Pennoniac, a Micmac Chief, by the Armouchoquois who dwelt at Chouacoit or Saco.

He gave Membertou and his people ten hogsheads of meal and all the grain that was left standing. He enjoined them to sow more in the Spring, and, if any of his countrymen came there from France, to give them their friendship and assistance. They were deeply grieved at Poutrincourt's departure, and promised faithfully to carry out his wishes. A system of mutual forbearance and assistance had endeared those polished Frenchmen to the savages of Acadia, and their departure seemed like the loss of old and tried friends. It is an honorable feature in the character of the first colonists of Acadia that they could awaken such sentiments in the breasts of those barbarous warriors.

Poutrincourt and his company reached France in the Jonas in the latter part of September, and he immediately waited on the King, to whom he presented wheat, barley and oats, grown in Acadia, and other specimens of its productions—animal, vegetable and mineral. Among the former were five living wild geese, which had been hatched from eggs found near Port Royal. King Henry was much pleased with those specimens of the natural products of the colony, and encouraged Poutrincourt to continue his efforts in that direction. He ratified the grant of Port Royal, which had been made to him by De Monts. He desired him to procure the services of the Jesuits in the conversion of the Indians of Acadia, and offered to give two thousand livres towards their support. All these inducements coincided with Poutrincourt's resolution to continue the colony, and encouraged him to follow out his plans for that purpose, but time was required to complete them, and for two years Port Royal remained without white inhabitants. All the buildings had, however, been left untouched, and only awaited new occupants. The grain fields also were kept in order by the savages, and

Champdore, who was on the coast in 1608, and visited Port Royal, found the grain growing finely, and was received by Membertou and his people with every demonstration of welcome. Everything was favorable for a new essay in colonization, which could not fail to be successful, considering the experience of its chief promoter, and that so much had already been accomplished in the way of conciliating the savages and erecting habitations for the people.

CHAPTER V.

POUTRINCOURT'S COLONY.

POUTRINCOURT was detained in France much longer than he had intended, owing to his relying on the assistance of others, who promised to join with him in the settlement of Acadia, but who finally withdrew from the engagements into which they had entered. He at last concluded an arrangement with a merchant named Robin, who was to supply the settlement for five years and provide funds for bartering with the Indians for certain specified profits; and on the 26th February, 1610, he set sail for Port Royal, which he did not reach until June. Poutrincourt, who was a devout Catholic, had entered willingly into the schemes proposed to him for the maintenance of Jesuit missionaries in Acadia, and had brought with him to the colony a priest named Jossé Flesche, who, however, was not a member of that order. This father prosecuted the work of converting the savages with such good results that on the 24th of June of the same year twenty-five of them were baptized at Port Royal, one of whom was Membertou, their great Sachem. This aged chief was so zealous for his new faith, that he offered to make war on all who should refuse to become Christians. This mode of compelling conformity of faith was thought rather to savor of the system pursued by Mahomet, and was declined. Poutrincourt, who was skilful in music, composed tunes for the hymns and chants used by the Indian converts in the ceremonial of the church, and, under his instructions and that of the priest, they soon became devout worshippers.

Early in July he had sent his son, Biencourt, who was a youth of nineteen, to France, to carry the news of the conversion of the natives, and obtain supplies for the winter. He was expected to return within four months, as the colony was greatly in need of provisions. Poutrincoúrt had with him twenty-three persons for whom he had to provide, and when winter set in, without any appearance of the expected succor, he began to be seriously alarmed. By prudent management, and by the aid of diligent hunting and fishing, they contrived to subsist through the winter without losing any of their number, and it was well that their experience of Acadian life in winter enabled them to depend on their own exertions for sustenance, for had they relied on Biencourt for supplies, they must all have perished.

Biencourt's detention was caused neither by want of zeal nor of industry on his part. He reached Dieppe on the 21st August, 1610, but found on his arrival that many startling changes had taken place in the position of affairs in France. Henry IV. had been assassinated three months before, leaving behind him a son and successor, Louis XIII., only nine years of age. The power which Henry had so wisely and firmly wielded for the good of his country had passed into the hands of the queen mother, Mary de Medicis, a woman of strong passions and narrow understanding, who was wholly controlled by Italian favorites. Shortly after his arrival Biencourt presented himself at court, and informed the Queen of the conversions that had taken place in Acadia. The news was gladly received, and she desired him to take two Jesuit missionaries with him on his return. Two members of that order—Fathers Pierre Biard and Enemond Masse—were appointed to accompany him, and the Queen and ladies of the court provided liberally for the voyage. The young King gave the missionaries five hundred crowns, and every requisite in the shape of clothing and supplies was provided for their comfort. Biencourt's vessel was to have sailed from Dieppe in the latter part of October, but, on proceeding there to embark, the missionaries were met by a new and unexpected difficulty. Two Huguenot traders, who were engaged in the adventure with Biencourt and Robin, refused to allow any Jesuits to go in the vessel, although they professed their willingness to allow any other priests to go. Biencourt and Robin were obliged to submit, but this illiberal conduct did not succeed in its object. Madame de Guercheville, a lady of the court, quickly succeeded in collecting among her friends sufficient funds to buy out the interest of the obstinate traders, which did not exceed four thousand livres, and the missionaries were allowed to embark. It was also arranged that the sum thus collected should belong to the Jesuit mission, and that they should receive the benefit of it.

The vessel in which Biencourt and his company of thirty-six persons were embarked was a small craft of about sixty tons burthen. It speaks well for his boldness and skill that, with this little barque, he should have essayed a winter voyage to Acadia; but he had a strong motive to urge him forward, for he knew well the straits to which his father and the colonists would be reduced by his delay, and he set sail from Dieppe on the 26th January, 1611. They met with very rough weather, and were forced to take shelter in an English port, and their voyage altogether lasted about four months. On their way out they fell in with Champlain, who was bound for Quebec, and at one time were in considerable danger from icebergs. They finally reached Port Royal on the 22nd May, but with their stores sadly diminished in consequence of the extreme length of the passage.

Poutrincourt, who had been greatly alarmed for their safety, was proportionally pleased at their arrival, but, as their provisions were nearly exhausted, and the number to be provided for greatly increased, it became necessary for him to look for further supplies. With this view he went to a harbor named La Pierre Blanche, (the white stone),* which lay twenty-two leagues due west from Port Royal, and which he knew was frequented by fishermen and traders. Here he found no less than four French vessels, one of which belonged to De Monts and another to Pontgravè. Poutrincourt expressed his intention of going to France, and made them recognize his son, Biencourt, as vice-admiral in his absence. He also requested them to furnish him with supplies, promising to repay them on his return to France. The necessary supplies were obtained on these terms, and they returned to Port Royal.

It then became necessary for Poutrincourt to make another voyage to France for the purpose of arranging for the regular furnishing of supplies until the colony became self-sustaining. He accordingly left Port Royal in July, leaving Biencourt in command of the colony, which then consisted of twenty-two persons, including the two Jesuit missionaries. These two fathers, with the zeal which has ever distinguished their order, engaged vigorously in the study of the native languages, and the manners and customs of the aborigines. To forward this as much as possible, father Masse took up his abode in the Micmac village, which then existed at the mouth of the St. John, where

* This must have been at Grand Manan, which is about twenty-two leagues due west from Port Royal, and where there is an island which is still called Whitehead Island.

Louis Membertou, the son of the old chief, resided, while father Biard devoted himself more particularly to the Indians about Port Royal. He also frequently accompanied Biencourt in the numerous trips which he made to various parts of the Bay of Fundy. While they were absent on one of these occasions, on a visit to St. Croix Island, Membertou was brought from St. Mary's Bay to Port Royal in a dying condition. It soon became apparent that he could live but a little time, and an unseemly dispute arose as to where he should be buried. Biencourt wished him to be buried with his own people, agreeably to a promise which he had made to the dying Chief, who desired to be laid with his forefathers. The Jesuits, on the other hand, contended that he should be buried in consecrated ground, as a proof of the reality of his conversion. Biencourt curtly told them that they might consecrate the Indian burial place, but that he should see Membertou's wishes carried out. The old Chief finally consented to be buried with the Christians, and he was accordingly interred in the burial ground at Port Royal. This, unfortunately, was only the first of a series of disputes between the Jesuits and the young governor, all of which were not so satisfactorily adjusted.

In the meantime the colonists were becoming straitened for provisions, and, as a precaution against absolute want, were put upon short allowance when the first fall of snow came, which was on the 16th November. As the year closed their prospects looked gloomy enough; but relief speedily came, for on the 23rd January, 1612, a vessel arrived with supplies. This vessel had been sent in pursuance of an arrangement which Poutrincourt and Robin had made with Madame de Guercheville, who had already exerted herself so strenuously to promote the mission of the Jesuits. She advanced a thousand crowns for supplies, but Poutrincourt soon discovered that he had called in an ally who would fain become his master. This ambitious lady had indeed formed the design of establishing in Acadia a sort of spiritual despotism, of which the members of the Order of Jesus should be the rulers and she the patroness. To carry out this plan, it might be necessary to dispossess Poutrincourt, or, at all events, to obtain possession of the rest of Acadia. She had abundance of influence at court, and the Queen and her adviser, Concini, held views similar to her own. She quickly proceeded to put her plans into operation. Finding that the whole of Acadia, except Port Royal, belonged to De Monts, she obtained from him a release of his rights, and immediately obtained a grant of it from the King for herself. She did not doubt that Poutrincourt's necessities, and the burthen of the charge which the Jesuit mission inflicted on the trade of the colony, would speedily compel him to abandon Port Royal to her also. He did not purpose at that time to return to Port Royal, but put the vessel which he sent with supplies in charge of one Simon Imbert, who had been a long time his servant, and in whom he had entire confidence. Madame de Guercheville, with equal forethought, sent out another Jesuit, named Gilbert Du Thet, who went in the vessel, ostensibly as a passenger, but in reality as a spy upon Imbert, and to look after her interests.

The result of such arrangements might easily have been foreseen. Scarcely had they landed at Port Royal when a bitter dispute arose between Du Thet and Imbert. The former accused the latter of misappropriating a part of the cargo, and Imbert retorted by accusing the Jesuits of a plot to expel Biencourt and his people from the country and obtain Port Royal for themselves. These recriminations caused the differences which had formerly existed between Biencourt and the Jesuits to be renewed with fresh animosity and vigor.

Fathers Biard and Masse had, on their first arrival, refused to administer baptism to the savages without fully instructing them in the doctrines of the Christian religion, and had sent Flesche, the priest, by whom Membertou had been baptized, back to France. This produced remonstrances from Biencourt, who was a hot-headed and determined young man, but little impressed, it is to be feared, with the sacred character of the ordinances which he called upon them to exercise. The dispute had been so warm that the Jesuits had actually obtained a chart of the coast and proposed to leave Port Royal by stealth; but Biencourt discovered the plan, and pointed out to them that they could not leave without the command of the head of their Order, and that it would be highly contrary to the Order of Jesus for them to forsake their posts without any authority to do so, leaving the little colony to which they had been sent without the exercises of religion. These arguments prevailed for the time, but fresh disputes arose. Biencourt resented their attempts to interfere with his authority, and so scandalous did the differences become that they threatened to excommunicate Biencourt, and, Lescarbot says, actually carried their threats into execution. The governor, on his part, coolly informed them that, however high their spiritual authority might be, he was their governor on earth, and that he would have obedience from all under him, priests included, even if it required the lash to compel it.

These threats had not been forgotten when the mutual accusations of Du Thet and Imbert opened the old wounds. The Jesuits accused Biencourt of carrying on the colony as a mere trading speculation for his own profit, and neglecting the interests of religion, which he only used as a cover for his schemes of gain. He retorted in terms equally bitter, that the missionaries, instead of attending to their legitimate functions, were seeking to subvert his government and ruin his colony. In consequence of this last contest, the public exercises of religion were entirely suspended for three months. Biard and Masse, who appear to have been entirely innocent of any participation in Madame de Guercheville's schemes, and only sincerely desirous of converting the savages, felt that there was some show of truth in the statements made by Imbert, as it was evident Du Thet had not come out as a missionary, and that his presence, under the circumstances, was a bitter injustice to them and their mission. At length on the 25th June, 1612, a reconciliation took place between them and Biencourt, father Biard administered mass, and then begged of Biencourt that he would send Du Thet back to France, which he did, and the colony was once more tranquil.

In August, Biencourt, accompanied by father Biard, went up the Basin of Mines in a shallop to trade with the Indians, and afterwards up Chignecto Bay, where for the first time they beheld that immense tract of marsh which now forms so large a portion of the wealth of two great counties. They gazed with surprise and admiration on the almost boundless expanse of virgin soil, but no thought seems to have entered their minds of utilizing its fertility. The Indians there, they found to be less migratory in their habits than most others. Game was abundant, and the natives seemed quiet and contented. On their return, the wind continued for a long time contrary, and they were in danger of perishing for want of food. In their extremity, father Biard made a vow that if God would grant them a fair wind, he would make the poor savages who accompanied them Christians. But they frustrated that good design by deserting the shallop in search of something to eat.

Gilbert Du Thet returned to France with the report that there was little hope of the conversion of the savages at Port Royal, and informed Madame de Guercheville that the character of Biencourt afforded no prospect of the influence of the Jesuits becoming predominant in the colony. She therefore resolved to remove them from Port Royal and establish a colony of her own. Poutrincourt had, by this time, begun to be aware of the character of his new ally, and serious misunderstandings had, in consequence, arisen between them. The prospect of getting rid of the Jesuits was, therefore, a very agreeable one to him, for although he was a most zealous Roman Catholic, and anxious for the conversion of the savages, he had, like many worthy men of his church, acquired a strong dislike to the members of the Order of Jesus. It was pretended by those who favored the Jesuits—and the statement has been repeated by their partizans—that Poutrincourt's object in establishing the colony at Port Royal was solely to trade with the savages, and that his avowed desire to convert them was only a pretence and a cloak to cover his real design. But it cannot be said that he ever displayed any want of zeal for the propagation of the Christian faith. It was by the missionary whom he brought to Acadia that the first of its savages were converted. The Jesuits, whatever may have been their religious zeal, were the first to cause dissensions in the colony, and they appeared more disposed to seize the reins of government than to engage in the more humble work of converting the natives to the Christian faith.

Madame de Guercheville fitted out a vessel of a hundred tons burthen at Honfleur, and gave the command of the expedition to M. de La Saussaye, who was to be governor of the colony. This vessel was appointed to take out twenty-seven persons and provisions for one year. Amongst others, there went in the vessel two Jesuits, Father Quantin and brother Gilbert Du Thet, of whom mention has already been made. They were to return to France after the colony was properly established, if fathers Biard and Masse were then alive and able to undertake their missionary duties. The whole company, including sailors, numbered forty-eight persons. The vessel was better provided with stores and implements than any that had gone to Acadia before that time. She carried, also, horses for the cultivation of the fields, and goats to provide the colony with milk. The Queen contributed four tents from the royal stores, and some munitions of war. She also wrote a letter, commanding that fathers Biard and Masse be allowed to leave Port Royal. The ship set sail on the 12th March, 1613, and on the 16th May reached Cape La Have, where they held high mass and erected a cross, on which was placed the arms of the Marchioness de Guercheville, as a symbol that they took possession of the country for her. When they arrived at Port Royal, they only found five persons—fathers Biard and Masse, their servant, the apothecary Hébert, and another. All the rest were absent, either hunting or trading. They shewed the Queen's letter to Hébert, who represented Biencourt in his absence, and taking the two Jesuits, with their servant and luggage aboard, again set sail. It was their intention to establish the colony at Pentagoet, which father Biard had visited the year previous, but when off Grand Manan a thick fog came on, which lasted for two days, and when it became clear, they put into a harbor on the eastern side of Mount Desert Island, in Maine. The harbor was deep, secure and commodious, and they judged this would be a favorable site for the colony, and named the place St. Sauveur. All the company were speedily engaged in clearing ground and erecting buildings. La Saussaye was advised by the principal colonists to erect a sufficient fortification before commencing to cultivate the soil, but he disregarded this advice, and nothing was completed in the way of defence, except the raising of a small palisaded structure, when a storm burst upon the colony, which was little expected by its founders.

In 1607 a company of London merchants had founded a colony on the James River, in Virginia, where, after suffering greatly from the insalubrity of the climate and want of provisions, they had attained a considerable degree of property. In 1613 they sent a fleet of eleven vessels to fish on the coast of Acadia, convoyed by an armed vessel under the command of Captain Samuel Argal, who had been connected with the colony since 1609. Argal was one of those adventurers formed in the school of Drake, who made a trade of piracy, but confined themselves to the robbery of those who were so unfortunate as not to be their own countrymen. He was a man of good abilities and great resolution, but he was also rapacious, passionate, arbitrary, and cruel, a fit instrument in every way to accomplish the designs of the people of a greedy colony, who, having just barely escaped destruction themselves, were bent upon destroying every one else.

When Argal arrived at Mount Desert, he was told by the Indians that the French were there in the harbor with a vessel. Learning that they were not very numerous, he at once resolved to attack them. All the French were ashore when Argal approached, except ten men, most of whom were unacquainted with the working of a ship. Argal attacked the French with musketry, and at the second discharge Gilbert Du Thet fell back, mortally wounded; four others were severely injured, and two young men, named Lemoine and Neveau, jumped overboard and were drowned. Having taken possession of the vessel, Argal went ashore and informed La Saussaye that the place where they were was English territory, and included in the charter of Virginia, and that they must remove; but, if they could prove to him that they were there under a commission from the crown of France, he would treat them tenderly. He then asked La Saussaye to show him his commission; but, as Argal, with unparalelled indecency, had abstracted it from his chest while the vessel was being plundered by his men, the unhappy governor was of course unable to produce it. Argal then assumed a very lofty tone, accused him of being a freebooter and a pirate—which was precisely what he was himself—and told the French it was only by his clemency they were allowed to escape with their lives. By the intercession of Biard and Masse, he affected to be disposed to deal more leniently with them. It was finally arranged that fifteen of the French, including Flory, the captain of the vessel, Lamotte le Vilin, La Saussaye's lieutenant, fathers Biard and Quantin, and a number of mechanics, should go with Argal to Virginia, where they were to be allowed the free exercise of their religion, with liberty to go to France at the expiration of a year. The remainder were to take a shallop and proceed in search of some French fishing vessel, in which to return to France. They accordingly started, and were fortunate enough to fall in with two vessels on the coast, one of which belonged to Pontgravè, and reached France after some hardship and suffering.

When Argal arrived in Virginia, he found that his perfidious theft of the French governor's commission was likely to cause his prisoners to be treated as pirates. They were put into prison and in a fair way of being executed, in spite of Argal's remonstrances, until struck with shame and remorse, he produced the commission which he had so dishonestly filched from them, and the prisoners were set free. But the production of this document, while it saved the lives of one set of Frenchmen, brought ruin upon all the others who remained in Acadia. The Virginia colonists, although utterly unable to people a hundredth part of the State which now bears that name, were too jealous-minded to allow any foreigners to live peaceably within eight hundred miles of them, and resolved to send Argal to destroy all the French settlements in Acadia, and erase all traces of their power. He was furnished with three armed vessels, and was accompanied by the two Jesuit fathers, Biard and Quantin. Argal first visited St. Sauveur, where he destroyed the cross which the Jesuits had erected and set up another in its place with the name of the King of Great Britain inscribed upon it. He then burnt down all the buildings which the French had built there, and sailed for St. Croix Island, where he found a quantity of salt which had been stored there by the fishermen. He burnt down all the buildings at St. Croix, and destroyed the fort. He then crossed to Port Royal, piloted, it is said, by an Indian, but it was shrewdly suspected and generally believed in France, that father Biard was the person who did this favor to the English. At Port Royal he found no person in the fort, all the inhabitants being at work in the fields five miles away. The first intimation they had of the presence of strangers was the smoke of their burning dwellings, which, together with the fort, in which a great quantity of goods was stored, he completely destroyed. He even effaced with a pick the arms of France and the names of De Monts and other Acadian pioneers, which were engraved on a large stone which stood within the fort. He is said to have spared the mills and barns up the river, but that could only have been because he did not know that they were there. No one acquainted with Argal's character could accuse him of such absurd clemency towards a Frenchman.

Biencourt made his appearance at this juncture, and requested a conference with Argal. They met in a meadow with a few of their followers. Biard endeavored to persuade the French to abandon the country and seek shelter with the invaders, but his advice was received so badly that he was denounced as a traitor, and was in danger of violence from his countrymen. Biencourt proposed a division of the trade of the country, but Argal refused to accede to this, stating that he had been ordered to dispossess him, and that if found there again he would be treated as an enemy. It is related that while they were engaged in this discussion a Micmac savage came up, and in broken language and with suitable gestures, endeavored to mediate a peace, wondering that persons who seemed to be of one race should make war upon each other. If this ever took place, which is very improbable, it would only serve to show that the Indians were as great hypocrites as civilized men, who profess the greatest regard for peace, while cutting each others throats, and invoke the aid of heaven to assist them in their efforts to shed human blood.

When Argal departed from Port Royal, he left that settlement—on which more than a hundred thousand crowns had been expended—in ashes, and more dreary and desolate than an uninhabited desert could have been, because its soil was branded with the marks of ungenerous hatred, unprovoked enmity, and wanton destruction. The continent was not wide enough, it would seem, for two small colonies to subsist harmoniously upon it, even if their settlements were close upon a thousand miles apart. The only excuse offered for this piratical outrage of Argal—which was committed during a period of profound peace—was the claim which was made by England to the whole continent of North America, founded on the discoveries of the Cabots more than a century before. That claim might, perhaps, have been of some value if followed by immediate occupancy, as was the case with the Spaniards in the South, but that not having been done, and the French colony being the oldest, it was entitled to, at least, as much consideration as that of Virginia. Singularly enough, this act produced no remonstrance from France. As has been well said by one of her sons: "The Queen Regent's court was a focus of intrigues which eventuated in a civil war, and put the independence of the kingdom in peril." There was no room for patriotism in the hearts of the people who governed France in those days.

Poutrincourt, who attributed all his misfortunes to the Jesuits, took no further part in the affairs of Acadia, but entered into the service of the King, where he distinguished himself, and was killed in the year 1615, at the siege of Méry-sur-Seine, which he had undertaken to capture for the King. Biencourt, however, refused to abandon the country, but, with a few chosen and faithful companions, maintained himself in it during the remainder of his life. One of the friends who shared his exile and enjoyed his confidence was Charles de La Tour, a name afterwards memorable in the annals of Acadia. Sometimes they resided with the savages, at other times they dwelt near Port Royal, but of their adventurous life little is known. The trials and sufferings of those who reside in the wilderness seldom see the light, unless at the instance of the adventurers themselves. But Biencourt left no record behind him, and La Tour, who might have told the story, was a man of the sword rather than of the pen.

CHAPTER VI.

SIR WILLIAM ALEXANDER AND THE LATOURS.

WHILE the French were struggling to maintain their Colony in Acadia, in the midst of many adverse influences, the English had begun to turn their attention to colonizing the coast of New England. In 1605, Captain Weymouth, a navigator of considerable experience, was despatched by the Earl of Southampton, Lord Arundel of Wardour, and several other English gentlemen, ostensibly to discover a north-west passage, but really to explore a portion of the coast of North America, with the view to the settlement of a colony.

Weymouth, instead of keeping well to the north, came in sight of the coast of America, as far south as Cape Cod, and from there sailed towards the north until he reached the mouth of the Kennebec, and entered the Sagadahock, a river which is now known as the Androscoggin. While on the coast he seized five of the natives and returned with them to England. The favorable description he gave of the country induced several gentlemen—among whom were the Lord Chief Justice Popham and Sir Fernando Gorges—to form a Company for the purpose of colonizing it. The Crown, on being petitioned, granted a charter for two Colonies, then called the London Company and the Plymouth Company, but better known at the present day as the South and North Virginia Company. Both Companies were immediately organized. The establishment of the former colony has already been mentioned; the latter, in which Gorges and Popham were more immediately interested, had for its boundaries the 38th and 45th parallels of latitude. In August, 1606, a ship commanded by Captain Henry Chalounge, was fitted out to go to Sagadahock with a number of colonists. Two of the natives Weymouth had captured were on board to pilot the vessel into the river. Chalounge neglected his orders, kept too far to the south, and was captured by a Spanish fleet. A few days after he had sailed, Popham fitted out another vessel, commanded by Captain Pring, and sent by her a few more colonists and additional supplies, with two of the natives as pilots. Pring reached Sagadahock in safety, but found no colony there. After waiting some time for Chalounge's arrival, he concluded that some disaster had happened to him, and returned to England, where he found the Company and the public greatly discouraged at the termination of the enterprise. Pring's favorable account of the country induced the Company to fit out two other vessels in the following year. They arrived at Sagadahock on the 15th of August, 1607, with over one hundred colonists. They first landed on an Island, some eight or ten acres in extent, now called Stage Island, and erected some buildings; but, finding the place unsuitable, they removed to the mainland—to a place now called Hunnewell's Point —where they erected dwellings and a small fort, and continued nearly a year. The winter was very severe, and the colonists were much discouraged at the prospect before them. If tradition is to be credited, they were a sorry lot, and conducted themselves in a very unbecoming manner towards the friendly natives. It is related that—unable to endure their insolence any longer—the savages killed one of them and drove the rest out of their fort. They then opened one of the casks of powder, and, being unacquainted with its properties, it blew up, destroying nearly everything in the fort and killing many of them. Thinking that this was an evidence of the anger of the Great Spirit for quarrelling with the whites, they very humbly begged forgiveness, and friendship was restored. When the winter was over the colonists embarked on board their vessels and sailed for England, taking with them the most unfavorable account of the country—its climate, resources and salubrity. They represented it as intolerably cold and sterile, and not inhabitable by the English nation. This unfavorable account of the country, together with the death of Chief Justice Popham, greatly discouraged all those who had interested themselves in the undertaking, with the exception of Sir Fernando Gorges, who was not to be daunted by any difficulties whatever. Where others saw nothing but sterility and misery, he looked confidently forward to the establishment of a prosperous colony. Read by the light of our present knowledge, his answer to those who objected to the coldness of the climate, sounds almost like prophecy. He says: "As for the coldness of the clime, I had had too much experience in the world to be frightened with such a blast, as, knowing many great kingdoms and large territories more northerly seated, and by many degrees colder than the clime from whence they came, yet plentifully inhabited, and divers of them stored with no better commodities for trade and commerce than those parts afforded, if like industry, art and labor be used." For several years he employed a vessel on the coast of Maine to trade and make discoveries at his own cost. Richard Vines had charge of this vessel, and he spent one winter with the Indians while the pestilence was raging among them with such destructive effect, that the living could not bury the dead; yet neither he nor any of the white men with him were attacked, though they slept in the same wigwams with many that died. Though Gorges obtained much useful information from his servants whom he thus employed, in regard to the country and its resources, he found that he could at that time obtain neither colonists to settle the territory, nor capitalists to advance money for such an enterprise. New England had to wait a few years longer for the advent of those indefatigable men who were destined to lay the foundations of that great and prosperous community, whose people now look back with reverence on their much honored "Pilgrim Fathers."

For several years after the destruction of Port Royal by Argal, there is a blank in the history of Acadia, and one which it is now impossible to fill. Biencourt still remained in the country, and occasionally resided at Port Royal, and it does not appear that any considerable number of his people returned to France.* A languid possession of Acadia was still maintained, but under such circumstances that little or no improvement in its condition became possible. In 1619, a year of great civil and religious excitement in France, two trading companies were formed for the purpose of developing the resources of Acadia. One company was authorized to carry on the shore fishery, the other to trade with the savages for furs. Both companies appear to have prosecuted their operations with considerable vigor. The fur traders established a post at the River St. John, as the most convenient depôt for traffic with the savages. The fishery establishment was at Miscou, on the Gulf of St. Lawrence. To provide for the religious wants of the employès of the two companies, and of the colonists, who still remained at Port Royal, three Recollet Missionaries were sent to Acadia, where, in addi-

---

* Louis Hébert, who had been the apothecary at Port Royal, appears to have returned to France, for he took his family to Quebec in 1617.

tion to their stipulated duties, they did good service in the conversion of the natives.

On the 9th November, 1620, the Pilgrim Fathers in the Mayflower came in sight of Cape Cod, and, after exploring the coast, concluded to settle their colony at Plymouth Bay. But as it was without the bounds of the charter of the South Virginia Company, from which they had a patent, and symptoms of faction appearing among the servants, they formed an association, by which they agreed to combine for the purpose of mutual protection and the maintenance of order, and submit to such government and governors as should be made and chosen by common consent. This was the first permanent settlement in New England, and through much hardship and suffering, it speedily attained a wealth and importance which none of the French colonies could boast.

In the meantime the work of colonizing Canada had been going on under the direction of De Monts and Champlain. The latter took a number of colonists up the river St. Lawrence in July, 1608, and founded Quebec. The first permanent erection raised was a storehouse, and dwellings for the colonists were soon added. Champlain spent the winter with the colony of which he had the command, and he may be said to have devoted the remainder of his life to the colonization of Canada. But so slow was the growth of Quebec, that, in 1620, when Champlain erected a small fort there, the colony only numbered sixty souls.

After the destruction of Port Royal by Argal, the English continued to assert their right to Acadia by virtue of its discovery by Cabot. The French who continued there were merely regarded as interlopers, whose presence, like that of the Indians, was simply tolerated for the time. The fact of a navigator in the service of England having seen its shores more than a century before, was considered by King James to have established his sovereignty over the country for all time to come. There was at the court of this pedantic monarch a Scottish gentleman, named Sir William Alexander, who claimed to be descended from Somerled, King of the Isles. He was a man of some talents, and like King James himself, was ambitious of being known as an author. He had published a quarto volume of plays and poems, which are now utterly forgotten, and desired to turn his attention to the colonization of America. The King, who delighted in long pedigrees and anti-tobacco tracts, in compliance with his wishes, granted him a piece of territory in America, nearly as large as the kingdoms which he himself governed so badly. This grant was made in September, 1621, and embraced the whole of the Provinces of Nova Scotia and New Brunswick, and the Gaspè Peninsula. The territory granted was to be known by the name of Nova Scotia, and to be held at a quit rent of one penny Scots per year, to be paid on the soil of Nova Scotia on the festival of the nativity of Christ, if demanded. This charter also endowed the grantee with enormous powers for the regulation and government of his territory, the creation of titles and offices, and the maintenance of fortifications and fleets. In pursuance of his charter, Sir William Alexander, in 1622, equipped a vessel for the purpose of taking a colony to his new possession. By the time they reached Newfoundland it was late in the season, and they concluded to winter there. In the following Spring they visited the coast of Acadia and entered Port Joli, where they intended to settle, but some unexpected difficulties arising, they resolved to make discoveries and not to plant a colony; and after remaining some time on the coast, they returned to Scotland in July. At that time the French were in possession of Port Royal, and possibly that circumstance may have influenced the determination of the Scottish colonists. However that may be, it is quite certain that on that occasion no permanent settlement was made by Sir William Alexander's people, and for several years that fortunate grantee did nothing for Acadia beyond sending a vessel annually to explore its shores and trade with the Indians.

In 1625 James I. died, and Alexander obtained from his son, Charles I., a confirmation of his grant of Nova Scotia, and, for the purpose of facilitating the settlement of a colony, and providing funds for its subsistence, an order of baronets of Nova Scotia was created. It was to consist of one hundred and fifty gentlemen, who were willing to contribute to the founding of the colony, each of whom was to receive a tract of land, six miles by three, in Nova Scotia, which Alexander released to them in consideration of their aid in the work of colonization. One hundred and seven of these baronets were created between 1625 and 1635, thirty-four of whom had their estates in what is now New Brunswick, fifteen in Nova Scotia, twenty-four in Cape Breton and thirty-four in Anticosti. Creations to this order of baronetage continued to be made up to the time of the union between England and Scotland, the whole number of creations up to that period being upwards of two hundred and eighty, of which about one hundred and fifty still exist. This was a scheme which undoubtedly gave a fair promise of success, and which, if vigorously carried out, would probably have ended in the founding of a strong colony. But while Alexander was still hesitating and confining his exertions merely to sending a vessel to trade on the coast, suddenly a war broke out between England and France. This war, which was undertaken ostensibly for the relief of the French Huguenots, but which was in reality brought about by the intrigues and ambitious views of Buckingham, commenced early in 1627. During the same year Cardinal Richelieu, then at the height of his power, formed an association for the purpose of colonization, called the Company of New France. It consisted of one hundred gentlemen, many of them persons of much influence. Among the original members of this association were Richelieu himself, De Razilly and Champlain. They were bound by the act by which the Company was created to settle two hundred persons the first year, and at the end of fifteen years to augment the number of colonists to four thousand, every settler to be of French birth and a Catholic. Each settlement was to be supplied by them with three ecclesiastics. King Louis XIII., who took an interest in the undertaking, gave the Company two vessels of war, and the favor with which it was regarded by him, and the wealth and influence of its members, seemed almost to ensure its success. Twelve of its principal members received patents of nobility, the Company was allowed to receive and transmit merchandise of all kinds without paying dues, and free entry was given in France to all articles manufactured or produced in Canada. To these privileges were added the monopoly of the fur trade, of hunting, and of the shore fishery, and the power of governing and ruling the country at will, and of declaring peace and war. Such was the organization which the bold and sagacious Richelieu created for the purpose of engrossing the trade of New France and creating a strong power there to overawe and check the English colonies.

In Europe the war between France and England was conducted in a very languid manner, but more vigor was displayed in America. Indeed, the extreme feebleness of the French colonies exposed them to insult or destruction, and no man saw this more clearly than the person then in command in Acadia, Charles de St. Etienne, afterwards better known as the Sieur de La Tour. This extraordinary man, who is certainly the most notable character in Acadian history, had already experienced vicissitudes such as seldom mark the life of any one individual. His father, Claude St. Etienne Sieur de La Tour, was a French Huguenot, allied to the noble house of Bouillon, who had lost the greater part of his estates in the civil war. He came to Acadia about the year 1609, with his son Charles, who was then only fourteen years of age, to seek in the new world some part of the fortune he had lost in the old. He engaged in trading to some extent until the colony at Port Royal was broken up by Argal. After that unfortunate event, he erected a fort and trading house at the mouth of the Penobscot River, in Maine, of which he was dispossessed by the English of the Plymouth Colony in 1626. His son Charles allied himself with Biencourt, who, driven from his colony, found a temporary home with the Indians. The two soon became inseparable friends. Biencourt made the young Huguenot his lieutenant, and in 1623, when he died, bequeathed to him his rights in Port Royal, and made him his successor in the government of the colony. It could not have fallen into better hands, for he was a man equally bold, enterprising and prudent. He possessed resolution, activity and sagacity of no ordinary kind, and had that art—the most necessary of any for a leader—the art of winning the confidence of those with whom he was associated. About the year 1625 he married a Huguenot lady, but of her family, or how she came to Acadia, nothing is known. She was one of the most remarkable women of the age, and lady de La Tour will be remembered as long as the history of Acadia has any charms for its people.

Shortly after his marriage, Charles de St. Etienne removed from Port Royal, and erected a fort near Cape Sable, at a harbor now known as Port La Tour. This stronghold, which he named Fort St. Louis, seems to have been chosen chiefly on account of its convenience as a depôt for Indian trade. He was residing there in 1627, when the war broke out, and perceived at once that Acadia was in great danger of being lost to France forever. He addressed a memorial to the King, in which he asked to be appointed commandant of Acadia, and stated that if the colony was to be saved to France, ammunition and arms must be provided at once. He had with him, he said, a small band of Frenchmen, in whom he had entire confidence, and the Souriquois, who, to the number of one hundred families, resided near him, were sincerely attached to him, and could be relied on, so that, with their aid, he had no doubt of his ability to defend the colony if arms and ammunition were sent. His father, who then was returning to France, was the bearer of this communication to the King, which was favorably received, and several vessels fitted out under the command of Roquemont and La Tour, with cannon, ammunition and stores for Acadia and Quebec. Scarcely had they reached the shores of Acadia when they were captured by an English squadron, under Sir David Kirk. La Tour was sent to England a prisoner, and Kirk, proceeding to Acadia, took possession of Port Royal, leaving a few men there in charge of the works, with instructions to prepare the place for the reception of a colony in the following year. The whole number of vessels captured by Kirk at this time amounted to eighteen, with one hundred and thirty-five pieces of ordnance and a vast quantity of ammunition, quite sufficient to have put both Port Royal and Quebec in a respectable state of defence. While at

Tadoussac, in July, 1628, Kirk had sent a summons to Quebec to surrender, but Champlain returned a defiant answer, and Kirk not being aware of its wretched condition postponed attacking it until the following year, contenting himself with cutting off its supplies. Had he attacked it then the place must have fallen immediately, for it only contained fifty pounds of powder, and was short of provisions. In 1629 Kirk again made his appearance in the St. Lawrence with a strong squadron, and summoned Quebec to surrender. This time there was no thought of resistance. The place was destitute both of provisions and ammunition, and Champlain had no alternative but to accept the favorable terms offered by Kirk, who took possession of the place on the 29th July, 1629, and carried Champlain to England, leaving his brother, Louis Kirk, in command of Quebec. He was a lenient and popular governor, and most of the French colonists concluded to remain in the country. Early in the same year Lord James Stuart, with three vessels, had taken possession of a fishing craft on the coast, belonging to St. Jean de Luz, which he sent to Port Royal with two of his own, and with the third proceeded to Port aux Baleines* in Cape Breton, where he erected a fort, claiming that the territory belonged to Great Britain. He was, however, not allowed to remain long in peaceable possession of his new acquisition. Captain Daniel, who commanded a French war vessel, heard of the English fort, and immediately attacked and captured it, with its garrison. He utterly destroyed the fort, but erected another at the

---

*Murdoch conjectures this to have been St. Anne's Harbor, but a reference to Charlevoix's map of Isle Royale shows that it was the harbor immediately to the westward of the east point of Cape Breton, and within the island now called Puerto Nuevo Island, which is laid down on the map of Charlevoix "Portenove ou la Baleine." This harbor has now no name on the maps, and it is possible there may be no settlement there. It is about ten miles from Louisburg.

entrance of the Grand Cibou,* which he armed with eight guns and garrisoned with thirty-eight men. He then sailed for Falmouth, where he landed forty-two of his prisoners, and took the remainder—twenty-one in number, including Lord James Stuart—to Dieppe. Thus it appears that the English were the first to recognize the vast importance of Cape Breton as a position which commanded the Gulf of St. Lawrence, but the French improved vastly upon the lesson thus taught them, and it was there that they made their last stand for the preservation of their power in Acadia.

While this conflict was going on in America, all hostilities between England and France had been put an end to in Europe by a treaty made between those powers at Suza, in Piedmont, in April, 1629. It will thus be seen that Quebec had been captured after peace had been concluded, and that some work was still left for the diplomatists to arrange. Port Royal was in the possession of the English, and, with the exception of Fort St. Louis, at Cape Sable, they may be said to have had possession of the entire territory of Acadia. When Charles de St. Etienne found that there was no prospect of help from France, he summoned all the French in Acadia into his fort, and put it in as good a posture of defence as his means would permit. He then calmly awaited any attack that might be made, confident that he had left nothing undone that it was in his power to do, to defend his post.

La Tour, in the meantime, had been conveyed to England as a prisoner of war; but he does not appear to have remained long in that position. He became acquainted with Sir William Alexander, and was presented at court,

---

* This is what is now called Great Brass d'Or, a corruption of Labrador. Fort Dauphin was afterwards built on the site of Daniel's Fort, or in its vicinity.

where he was received with favor. While in London he mingled much with his Protestant brethren who had fled from France, and no doubt his mind became greatly influenced by their strictures on the conduct of the King and Richelieu in breaking faith with the people of Rochelle. Whatever was the cause, he fell away from his allegiance to his native country. He married, while in London, one of the maids of honor to the Queen Henrietta Maria, and from that time he seems to have regarded himself as a subject of Great Britain. An extraordinary degree of favor was shown to him by the King; he was created a baronet of Nova Scotia, his son received the same honor,* and on the 30th April, 1630, La Tour and his son Charles received from Sir William Alexander a grant of a tract of territory in Acadia, from Yarmouth along the coast to Lunenburg, and fifteen leagues inland towards the north, a grant which may be roughly estimated to contain four thousand five hundred square miles. This territory was to be held under the Crown of Scotland, and to be divided into two baronies, which were to be named the barony of St. Etienne and the barony of La Tour. The grantees were also invested with the power of building forts and towns, and with the right of admiralty over the whole coast, which was about one hundred and fifty miles in extent. So munificent a gift required some corresponding return on the part of the grantees, and, accordingly, La Tour undertook to plant a colony of Scotch in Acadia and to obtain

---

*The following is a list of baronets created, and of the places where they held lands, from the creation of de La Tour to his son, inclusive:—

1629—November 30—Sir Claude de St. Etienne Seigneur de La Tour,	. .	Nova Scotia.
1630—March 31—Sir Robert Hannay, of Mochrum, ...	.	New Brunswick.
" April 30—Sir William Forbes, of New Craigeivar, ...	.	New Brunswick.
" " 24—Sir James Stewart, Lord Ochiltree, ...		New Brunswick
" " 24—Sir Peirs Crosbie, -		New Brunswick.
" " 24—Sir Walter Crosbie, of Crosbie Park, Wicklow, . .	.	New Brunswick.
" May 12—Sir Charles de St. Etienne, Seigneur de St. Deniscourt,	. .	Nova Scotia.

possession of his son's fort of St. Louis for the King of Great Britain. Accordingly, in 1630, he set sail with a number of colonists in two vessels well provided, and he appears to have had no doubts as to his ability to carry out what he had promised. When the vessels arrived at Port Latour, he landed and visited his son at fort St. Louis. But Charles de St. Etienne utterly refused to entertain for a moment the proposition made to him by his father to deliver his fort to the English. When the latter endeavored to seduce him from his allegiance by relating the high consideration in which he was held at the English court, and the honors and rewards which he would receive if he would come under English rule, he replied that the King of France had confided the defence of the fort to his keeping, and that he was incapable of betraying the confidence which had been placed in him; that however much he might value any honor or title bestowed upon him by a foreign prince, he would regard still more highly the approval of his own sovereign for having faithfully performed his duty; and that he would not be seduced from his allegiance, even at the solicitation of a parent whom he loved. Overwhelmed with mortification, La Tour retired on board of his ship and addressed a letter to his son, couched in the most tender and affectionate language, and setting forth the advantages which they would both derive from pursuing the course which he desired his son to adopt. Finding this produced no effect, he tried to intimidate his son by menaces; and, finding these disregarded, and utterly driven to desperation, he disembarked his soldiers and a number of armed seamen, and tried to carry the fort by assault. The assailants were driven back with loss, and on the second day made another attack, but with no better success. La Tour was urgent for another assault on the third day, but the commanding officer would not permit any more of his men to be sacrificed, and retired with them to the ships. La Tour was now in a most pitiable position and knew not which way to turn. He had made himself a traitor to his country, and he had broken his promises to the English. To remain with either was only to take a choice of evils, and the earth was not wide enough to enable him to escape from the anger of both. He, however, believed himself safer with the foreigners, whom he had deceived, than with his own countrymen, whom he had betrayed. He therefore went with the Scotch colonists, who retired to join their countrymen at Port Royal. Great as might have been La Tour's grief at this misadventure on his own account, it could not fail to be much increased by the reflection that he had made the lady who had become his wife the innocent sharer of his misfortunes. He told her, in touching language, that he had counted on introducing her in Acadia to a life of happiness and comfort, but that he was now reduced to beggary, and, if she chose, he would release her from her painful position and allow her to return to her family. She replied in the noble language of Ruth, telling him that she had not married him to abandon him at the first breath of misfortune, and that, whatever trials and troubles he had to endure, she would be willing to share with him.

The colony at Port Royal, in which La Tour found refuge, had been established there in 1620 by a son of Sir William Alexander, and consisted chiefly of natives of Scotland. They had erected a fort on the Granville shore, opposite Goat Island, the site of Champlain's fort. Very little is known of the history of the colony, and the little that has been preserved, is chiefly a record of misfortunes. During the first winter, out of seventy colonists, no less than thirty died, and the survivors seem to have had but little heart to withstand the rigors of another winter. The arrival of the vessels in which La Tour had come, with additions to their numbers and supplies, somewhat revived their drooping spirits; but there were dangers menacing the existence of the colony which neither their prudence nor their industry could avert.

The attention of those people in France, who took an interest in the affairs of America, was directed to the capture of Quebec by the English in time of peace, and much indignation was expressed that such an outrage should be permitted. Strong pressure was brought to bear on the King to demand the restitution of this stronghold, and, as Richelieu was favorable to such a demand being made, Louis XIII. was easily induced to accede to their wishes. In the meantime the Company of New France resolved to preserve what possessions still remained to them in America. Accordingly, in 1630, two vessels were fitted at Bordeaux by M. Tufet, a merchant and citizen of that town, and a member of the Company, with supplies, arms, and ammunition for the new fort at Grand Cibou, in Cape Breton, and for Fort St. Louis at Port La Tour. They had a long and stormy passage, and did not reach Cape Sable until late in the season, which was the more annoying, as they had on board a considerable number of workmen and artizans for the purpose of forming a new settlement in Acadia, and three Recollet fathers to perform missionary services. Captain Marot, who had command of this expedition, brought Charles de St. Etienne a letter from M. Tufet, enjoining him to remain steadfast in the King's cause, and expressing the confidence which the Company had in his patriotism and firmness. It also informed him that the vessels contained arms, ammunition,

supplies and men, which were at his service, to build
dwellings and forts wherever he deemed most-convenient.
St. Etienne was naturally much gratified at this illustration
of the favor with which he was regarded in his native
country, but he was much troubled on account of the conduct of his father, who still remained at Port Royal with
the Scotch. After consulting with Captain Marot, it was
agreed that the best plan was to advise his father of the
probability of Port Royal being given up by Great Britain,
and to request him to return to Cape Sable, so that they
might be informed of the numbers and intentions of the
Scotch. La Tour very cheerfully complied with this
invitation, and repaired to Cape Sable, where his son had a
comfortable dwelling erected for the accommodation of his
family and attendants without the walls of the fort. He
brought the intelligence that the Port Royal colonists
intended to make another attack on Fort St. Louis. A
long consultation was then held, in which La Tour, St.
Etienne, Captain Marot and the Recollet fathers took
part, and the question as to what was the best course to be
pursued was discussed in all its bearings. It was finally
concluded to erect a strong fort at the mouth of the St. John
River, where there was a powerful tribe of Indians, which
would serve the double purpose of repelling the intrusions
of the English in that direction, and would give the French
at the same time command of the whole peltry trade of that
vast tract of wilderness, which extended to the River St.
Lawrence. La Tour was to superintend the erection of
this fort, and continue in command until it was completed,
while St. Etienne would still remain at Cape Sable, and
resist any attack which might be made upon him by the
Scotch. Captain Marot was to convey the workmen,

artizans and their supplies to the mouth of the St. John, and the work was to be proceeded with at once.

This plan was equally bold and judicious, and no time was lost in carrying it into effect. The workmen were conveyed to the St. John, and operations commenced with vigor, but as the proposed work was to be constructed on an extensive scale, but little could be done towards its accomplishment that season, and when another season had arrived, the political aspect of affairs appeared to render its immediate construction less necessary. The King of Great Britain seemed little disposed to resist the demand that had been made upon him for the restoration of Quebec and Acadia. The value of these possessions had not then been recognized either in England or France, and Charles I. was not willing to risk further difficulty with his most Christian brother, Louis, for the sake of such worthless acquisitions. Although he professed to regard the territory of Acadia as belonging to the Crown of England, and had granted it to one of his subjects who had partially colonized it, he meanly gave it up to France, when threatened that if he did not do so, four hundred thousand crowns of the portion of Queen Henrietta Maria would be retained. In June, 1631, he authorized his ambassador, Sir Isaac Wake, to conclude a treaty with the French King for the purpose of setting at rest all controversies, and in July informed Sir William Alexander, who, the year previous, had been created Earl of Sterling, that Port Royal was to be restored to the French, and the fort destroyed which the Scotch had erected. On the 29th March, 1632, the treaty of St. Germain-en-Laye was signed, one of its provisions being that Acadia should be restored to France.

In the meantime Charles de St. Etienne's patriotism and courage were recognized in France by the granting of a commission to him, dated 11th February, 1631, by which he was appointed to command as the King's lieutenant-general in Acadia. Great activity was now displayed by the Company of New France, and, while the King invested his loyal subject with dignity and authority, the Company supplied him with ammunition and stores, that his commission might not prove a bootless honor, and sent a well-stocked vessel to Fort St. Louis in April 1631, with a letter confirming, on the part of the Company, the command granted by the King. The fort at Cape Breton was also supplied at the same time, but things had gone badly there, for Gaude, the commander, had basely murdered Martel, his lieutenant, although there were there two missionaries, fathers Vimont and Vieuxpont, whose teachings and example seem to have had no effect in bringing this barbarous commander to respect the proprieties of life.

Thus ended the year 1631, a year which was remarkable as marking the termination of that period of apathy and neglect which had been so prejudicial to the interest of Canada and Acadia, and which had caused their shores to be comparatively deserted, while New England was being filled up with hardy and industrious colonists.

CHAPTER VII.

ISAAC DE RAZILLY'S COLONY.

AGREEABLY to the treaty of peace, France proceeded to resume possession of those portions of her North American dominions which had been seized by England. The Company of New France, then strong in wealth and numbers, and strong also in royal favor, had resolved to colonize Acadia, and to accomplish this, neither money nor labor was to be spared; for the undertaking was not more for the profit of the Company than it was for the honor of the King. Isaac De Razilly was the person selected to effect the restoration of the country to France. This commander, who had served as a captain in the navy at Rochelle, and who added to his titles as commander of the Isle Bouchard and commodore of Brétagne, that of Knight Commander of St. John of Jerusalem, had likewise another claim to notice equally strong. He was a relative of the great Cardinal Richelieu, and stood high in his favor, at a time when to be the Cardinal's favorite was more than to be a favorite of the King himself.

On the 27th March, 1632, De Razilly entered into an agreement with the Company of New France, by the terms of which he was to receive from the Cardinal a vessel called L'esperance en Dieu, free and in sailing order, ready to receive her cargo, armed with her guns, swivels, powder and shot. He was to receive also the sum of ten thousand livres in ready money, in consideration of which he engaged to put the Company of New France in possession of Port Royal, without any further charges. He engaged also to fit out an armed pinnace of at least one hundred tons, and to carry out to Acadia three Capuchin friars, and such a number of men as the Company of New France should judge to be proper. On the 10th of May he received a commission from the King, authorizing him to cause the Scotch and other subjects of Great Britain to withdraw from Quebec, Port Royal and Cape Breton. A few days later he obtained from the Company of New France a grant of the river and bay of St. Croix, twelve leagues in front and twenty in depth, with the adjacent islands, including the Island of St. Croix, on which De Monts spent his first winter in Acadia. De Razilly was furnished also by the Secretary of State with letters patent of the King of Great Britain, under the great seal of Scotland, for the restitution of Port Royal to the French, and an order of King Charles to his subjects in Port Royal for the demolition and abandonment of the place. De Razilly likewise carried with him a letter from Sir William Alexander to Captain Andros Forrester, who was commander of the Scotch colony at Port Royal, requiring him to deliver up that place to the French commander. Thus fully armed, with all necessary authority for carrying out his undertaking, De Razilly set sail for Acadia.

He took with him a number of peasants and artizans to people the new colony, and in his train were two men, whose names are inseparably linked with early Acadian history. One of these, Charles de Menou, seigneur d'Aulnay de Charnisay, became the life-long enemy of Charles de St. Etienne; the other, Nicholas Denys, after a life of adventure in Acadia, became its historian, returned to France, and died at a ripe age in the land of his birth.

As soon as De Razilly arrived at Port Royal, it was surrendered to him by the Scotch commander, the fort having been previously demolished. The Scotch colony was at that time in an extremely feeble state. Nearly half the colonists had died during the first winter, and, although subsequently reinforced, they were much discouraged and in no condition to persevere in the work of settling of Acadia. To most of them, therefore, the order for their return to their native land was most welcome. A few, however, decided to remain and cast their lot with the French who were come to occupy the country. These Scotch families who remained in Acadia became entirely lost amid the French population in the course of a generation, and so the name, and almost the memory, of Sir William Alexander's Scotch colony perished.

De Razilly did not settle his colony at Port Royal. Experience had taught the French that, great as were the advantages of that place, there were other points on the coast more favorably situated for the successful prosecution of the fisheries, and that was one of the main objects of the Company of New France. De Razilly accordingly, after taking formal possession of Port Royal, went to La Have, and there planted his colony. This place had long been known to the French fishermen, and it was admirably situated for carrying on the shore fishery. Its harbor was spacious and easy of access; a considerable river, which flowed into it, supplied a means of communicating with the interior of the peninsula, and the whole shore, to the east and west, abounded in fish. De Razilly's fort was erected at the head of La Have harbor, on its western side, on a little hillock of three or four acres, and was, like all the Acadian forts of that day, merely a palisaded enclosure with bastions at the four corners. Such a stronghold was then considered sufficient for all purposes, for the Indians were friendly, and the New England colonists were too weak to give the French in Acadia any concern. The fort at La Have was, therefore, but a sort of trading house, about which the habitations of the colonists might cluster, and it was entirely overshadowed in importance by the forts of Port Royal and St. John, which afterwards became the scene of so many warlike operations.

De Razilly appears to have been moved by a sincere desire to establish a strong French colony in Acadia; but to accomplish this object was a matter of no small difficulty. The French, like the other Latin peoples, have never been possessed of that migratory spirit which has spread the Anglo-Saxon race over so large a part of the habitable globe, and they have always made indifferent colonists. It was, however, one of the conditions on which the privileges of the Company of New France had been granted, that it should supply Acadia with colonists, and it was necessary to make some effort to fulfil this part of the obligations imposed on the Company. De Razilly, in the first year of his settlement at La Have brought out to Acadia forty families from France, most of whom were cultivators of the soil, and they were settled about the fort on the indifferent and rocky land which surrounds La Have. There is reason to believe that for some years their main pursuit was the shore fishery, which was found more immediately profitable than the cultivation of the soil. La Have, and the coasts about it, abounded in such fish as cod, sturgeon, halibut, salmon, shad, alewives and herrings, and both De Razilly and Nicholas Denys, at that period, engaged in fishing operations on a large scale. Denys established a fishery at Port Rossignol, a harbor to the westward of La Have, and it would seem that De Razilly was interested in his operations. No doubt the new French commander in Acadia had discovered that it was more prudent to employ his colonists in those pursuits which would yield an immediate return for their labor, rather than to engage in the arduous task of developing the agricultural wealth of an unsubdued continent. Whatever may have been De Razilly's views upon the subject, it is at least certain that his colony of Frenchmen never took any strong root at La Have during the years of its existence there.

But weak as was the La Have colony, and uncertain as was its tenure of the soil on which it was placed, it must have looked strong and imposing to the distant colonists of New England, for it filled them with alarm. Governor Winthrop, in his diary, gives expression to the feelings of apprehension and distrust with which the planting of De Razilly's colony was viewed in Boston; and he relates how he called the assistants to Boston, and the ministers and captains, and some other chief men, to advise what was best to be done for the safety of New England. At this meeting it was agreed that a plantation and fort should be forthwith begun at Natascott, that the fort at Boston should be finished, and that a plantation should be begun at Agawam, which was considered the best place in New England for tillage and cattle. Winthrop was apprehensive that if Agawam was left vacant much longer, it might fall into the hands of the French.

No doubt there were some grounds for these apprehensions, for the French in Acadia often exhibited a capacity to annoy and injure quite out of proportion to their actual strength. In June 1632, before De Razilly arrived in Acadia, an event took place which gave some indications of the spirit in which the treaty of St. Germain was likely to be interpreted by the subjects of France. A party of French came in a pinnace to Penobscot, where the New Plymouth colonists had established a trading house, after

I

La Tour had been dispossessed. The French pretended to have just arrived from sea, that they had lost their reckoning, that their vessel was leaky, and that they desired to haul her up and repair her. It happened that the master of the trading house and most of his men had gone to the westward for a supply of goods, leaving only three or four men to protect the fort. The French, seeing the weak state of the garrison, resolved to help themselves to the contents of the trading house, and, having overpowerd the few men in charge, loaded their vessel with their goods, which consisted of three hundred weight of beaver, besides trading stuff, such as coats, rugs, blankets, and biscuit, the whole valued at five hundred pounds sterling. The French did not injure or imprison the Englishmen in charge of the post, but when they had secured their plunder, set them at liberty, telling them to carry to their master the insolent message, that some gentlemen of the Isle of Rhé had been there.

Governor Bradford, who gives a circumstantial narrative of this transaction, does not furnish the name of the French leader who rifled Penobscot, but states that he had with him a false Scot, who acted as interpreter. It is highly probable that Claude La Tour was at the head of the party, and that he took this novel method of carrying out the treaty of St. Germain, and at the same time reimbursing himself for his losses at Penobscot, when it was taken from him by the English. It is clear that the treaty of St. Germain contemplated the restoration of Penobscot to France, but certainly not by the Corsair-like method adopted by the gentlemen from the Isle of Rhé. In their case one act of piracy led to others. While returning with the plunder of Penobscot, the French fell in with the shallop of an Englishman named Dixy Bull, who had been engaged in trading to the eastward, and robbed him of his goods. Bull seems to have been so much discouraged by the ill success of his attempt to make an honest living by trading that he resolved to turn pirate himself. He gathered together fifteen other vagabond Englishmen, who were scattered about the coast east of Boston, and, seizing some boats, made a raid on Pemaquid, where there had been a small English settlement for some years. Bull rifled the fort there, and plundered the settlers, losing one of his men by a musket shot. He was finally chased away by a hastily organized force under Neale and Hilton from Piscataqua. This bold act of robbery excited great indignation at Boston, and a bark was fitted out with twenty men, under the command of Lieutenant Mason, to capture Bull and his gang. After a two months' cruise, however, they returned without having seen anything of him, and he appears to have escaped to England. This man was the first pirate known on the coast of New England.

In the following year Charles La Tour took possession of Machias, where Mr. Allerton of Plymouth and some others had set up a trading wigwam, guarded by five men. La Tour dispossessed them, claiming Machias as French territory. Some resistance being offered, two of the English were killed, and the other three and the goods carried off to La Tour's fort at Cape Sable. Mr. Allerton afterwards sent a pinnace to La Tour to obtain the restoration of the men and the return of the goods which he had taken from Machias. But La Tour made answer that he took them as lawful prize, and that he had done so under the authority of the King of France, who claimed the whole territory from Cape Sable to Cape Cod. He desired Mr. Allerton's men to take notice, and to inform the rest of the English, that if they traded to the east of Pemaquid, he would seize them and their vessels. One of the English was imprudent enough to ask La Tour to show his commission, and he answered with some heat, that his sword was a sufficient commission where he had strength enough to overcome his enemies, and that, when that failed, it would be time enough for him to show his commission. Both men and goods were sent by La Tour to France, where the men were set at liberty, but the goods were adjudged to be lawful prize. La Tour's conduct in this affair shows that he was not merely acting the part of a freebooter, as some of the New England writers pretend, but as the lieutenant of the King, and under a claim to territorial rights, which, however extravagant, was probably quite as good as any of the claims under which America was held at that period.

This claim of the French King was enforced again in the following year (1635). M. De Razilly sent a ship to Penobscot under the command of his lieutenant, Charnisay, who had come to Acadia with him, three years before. The trading house at Penobscot, which had been despoiled of its goods by the French in 1632, was still kept up by the Plymouth people, and was as little capable of defence as it had been on the former occasion. Charnisay took possession of Penobscot without meeting with any serious resistance, and seized all the goods in the trading house, giving bills for them to the men in charge. He gave the men their liberty, but, before they departed, he shewed them the commission which he had from the French commander at La Have to remove all the English from the settlements as far south as the Pemaquid. He bade them tell their people at the English plantations, that he would come the next year with eight ships and displant them all as far south as the fortieth degree of north latitude. At the same time he professed all courtesy for the English and a desire to live on the most friendly terms with them. Charnisay then proceeded to occupy the trading post and to strengthen its defences. The sequel showed that his precautions were by no means superfluous. The Plymouth colonists were highly enraged at the insolence of the French and at the loss of their goods, and resolved to recapture Penobscot. They hired a vessel named the Great Hope from her master, Mr. Girling, who undertook for a payment of two hundred pounds to drive the French out. The Plymouth people also aided him with a bark and about twenty men. When they reached Penobscot they found the French, who were eighteen in number, so strongly intrenched that, after expending most of their powder and shot in cannonading them, they were unable to make any impression on their works. This unexpected repulse rendered a change of policy necessary, and accordingly the Plymouth bark was sent to Boston to obtain assistance, Girling's ship being left to blockade the French in the meantime.

The general court assembled at Boston, and agreed to aid the Plymouth people to drive out the French from Penobscot, which all were satisfied was a measure essential to the comfort and safety of the New England colonies. But when it came to the discussion of details with the Plymouth people, there was found to be a wide difference of opinion as to the terms on which the aid should be granted. Mr. Prence and the redoubtable Captain Miles Standish, who were sent to Boston as commissioners by the Plymouth colony, contended that the removal of the French from Penobscot, was a matter which concerned all the English colonies, and in which they ought all to make common cause. They said that the people of Plymouth should only be made to contribute their proper share of the cost of the removal of the French. The commissioners for the colony of Massachusetts Bay, on the other hand, refused to have anything to do with the expedition to Penobscot, except in aid of the Plymouth colonists and at their cost. So material a difference of opinion made it impossible for the representatives of the two colonies to come to terms, and the result was that the conference fell through, and the French were left in undisturbed possession of the mouth of the Penobscot river for many years. There were mutual jealousies, even at that early day between the people of Plymouth and the people of Massachusetts Bay, which prevented them from uniting in an undertaking which concerned both colonies in an equal degree. If one colony was more interested than the other, it certainly was that one which lay nearest to the French at Penobscot, and was, therefore, most likely to receive annoyance from them. Yet it was Massachusetts which occupied that position, that refused to stir in the matter unless paid by the people of Plymouth. Could the people of New England have looked but a little way into the future, they would not have grudged the cost of an expedition to drive the French to the St. Croix.

At this period, however, there was but little of that bitterness between the people of New England and the French in Acadia which in after years distinguished their contests. Indeed, many acts of kindness on both sides are recorded in the annals of that time, one of which deserves mention, as it brings Charnisay into a more favorable light than he is generally shown in by the old chronicles. A pinnace belonging to Sir Richard Saltonsall, which had been sent out to Connecticut, was, on her return to England, cast away upon the Isle of Sable. The French upon the island treated the shipwrecked company kindly and sent them to

De Razilly at La Have, who used them with great courtesy, giving four of their number a passage to France. The others, who preferred to return to New England, he furnished with a shallop to carry them back to Boston. While sailing carefully round the coast with their frail craft, they were obliged to put into Penobscot, which was just then being blockaded by Girling's ship. Charnisay, at such a time, might have been excused if he had shown some harshness to the countrymen of the people who were just then attacking him. But he displayed no such feeling, merely contenting himself with detaining them until Girling's ship was gone. He then forwarded them on their voyage to Boston, sending by them a letter to the governor of Massachusetts Bay, in which he, in courteous terms, gave expression to his feelings of friendship and esteem.

Sir Richard Saltonsall's men were not the first Englishmen who were so unfortunate as to be cast away on Sable Island. In 1633 Mr. John Rose, a Boston man, lost his vessel, the Mary and Jane, on that inhospitable island desert, but made a pinnace out of the wreck in which he and his crew reached the mainland of Acadia. Rose saw more than eight hundred wild cattle on the island, and great numbers of foxes, some of which were black. The account he gave to the French of this island so tempted their cupidity that they resolved to go thither, and seventeen of them embarked in a small vessel for Sable Island, taking Rose with them as pilot. These Frenchmen built themselves a residence, and proceeded to hunt the wild cattle, foxes and sea-horse, which abounded on the island. Rose returned to New England, but the tidings of his adventures soon spread, and in 1635 two Boston men, named Graves and Hodges, organized a company to go to Sable Island for sea-horse and wild cattle. They went well provided with everything necessary for a residence there, carrying a portable house to dwell in, and other necessary articles. They found sixteen Frenchmen on the island, who had wintered there and built a little fort. They had succeeded in killing a few black foxes, but had slaughtered so many of the cattle that not over one hundred and forty were left. The Englishmen only succeeded in killing a few sea-horse, owing to the distance they had to travel in the sand to their haunts, and they were obliged to come away from the island at the very time when sea-horse were beginning to come ashore in the greatest numbers. They returned to Boston on the 26th August, 1635. Two years later, twenty men went from Boston in a pinnace to kill sea-horse on Sable Island, but after cruising about for six weeks were unable to find it, and returned home. In September 1637, they set out again with more skilful seamen to renew their search, with the intention of wintering there. Nothing was heard from them for nearly two years. In March 1639 a bark was sent to Sable Island to bring them back, but was caught in a tempest and wrecked there, and out of her timbers they made a smaller vessel, in which the men returned to Boston. They reported the island to be very healthful and temperate, not having lost a man in nearly two years, nor had any of them been sick. They had collected a great store of seal oil and skins, and some sea-horse teeth, but the loss of their vessel overthrew their hopes of profit from the venture. After this, the people of Boston sent out several companies of adventurers to Sable Island to hunt wild cattle and sea-horses, one company getting there in 1642 goods to the value of one thousand five hundred pounds. The wild cattle were soon all killed off under the pressure of so many attacks, and expeditions to Sable Island afterwards became unprofitable. The ancestors of the wild horses which are still to be found on Sable Island, we may presume, were left there by some of the English or French adventurers who hunted on it during the first half of the seventeenth century.

The internal history of Acadia for the four years between 1632 and 1636, does not present many points of particular interest. De Razilly's colony of farmers and fishermen at La Have, and Charles La Tour's settlement at Cape Sable, were at first the only inhabited places in Acadia, but within these years the settlement at Port Royal was re-established, and, as has already been stated, in 1635 Penobscot was occupied by Charnisay, acting as De Razilly's lieutenant. This last, however, never was anything more than a fortified trading post with a small garrison.

Several important grants were made by the Company of New France about this time. In 1634 this Company granted to Claude De Razilly, brother of the commander of Acadia, the fort and settlement of Port Royal in Acadia, together with the Isle of Sable and the fort and settlement at La Have. This Claude De Razilly was largely engaged in the fishing business, and the operations which the French were conducting on Sable Island appear to have been for his benefit.

The next grant of importance made in Acadia by the Company was a fitting reward for faithful service and loyalty to the King. Charles de St. Etienne, the sieur de La Tour,[*] who is described in the grant as lieutenant-general for the King on the coast of Acadia in New France, was granted the fort and habitation of La Tour on the River St. John, with the lands adjacent, having a

---

[*] Where La Tour is spoken of hereafter in this history, Charles La Tour is meant, Claude, the father, having taken no active part in the affairs of Acadia after the year 1635.

frontage of five leagues on the river, and extending ten leagues back into the country. The date of this grant was the 15th January, 1635, and during this year La Tour removed part of his establishment from Cape Sable to the River St. John, where a fort had been commenced some years before. This fort was destined in after years to become the scene of some of the most stirring events in Acadian history.

The work of the missionaries, which, during the English occupation had been abandoned, was renewed in 1633. In that year the monks of the Order of St. Francis, from the Province of Aquitane, returned to Acadia, and the missions on the St. John and at Miscou were re-established. Those pious fathers continued to retain the possession of this missionary field, and under their ministrations all the savages of Acadia, in the course of time, became Christians, at least in name. Those humble missionary laborers have had no historian to relate their privations and toils, and, unlike the Jesuits, they did not become their own annalists. It surely was not for an earthly reward that they condemned themselves to spend their days among squalid savages in the deep recesses of the forest, exposed to all the vicissitudes of savage life, discomfort, disease, hunger, and sometimes starvation. The zeal which could carry men so far in the path of duty, without complaining, must surely have been lighted from some more sacred flame than burns on any earthly altar.

In 1636, Isaac De Razilly, in the midst of his plans for the colonization of Acadia, suddenly died, leaving the young colony without its leader and head. His death was a peculiarly severe misfortune, happening when it did, for his work was not finished. Had his life been prolonged, Acadia, instead of becoming for years a field of conflict for rival seigniors, would have settled into a tranquil, prosperous and growing colony. What was wanted in Acadia was a peaceful and industrious population, and neither the glitter of arms nor the splendor of titles could supply its place. The fabric of every nation's prosperity rests on the shoulders of the humble sons of toil, but they had nothing to induce them to come to Acadia, where little else was heard for years but the clashing of swords. The result was that during a period of nearly forty years, while New England was being rapidly peopled, scarcely a family was added to the population of Acadia. The English colonies grew daily in strength, and developed into the vigor of manhood, while Acadia remained always cursed with the weakness of a sickly infancy.

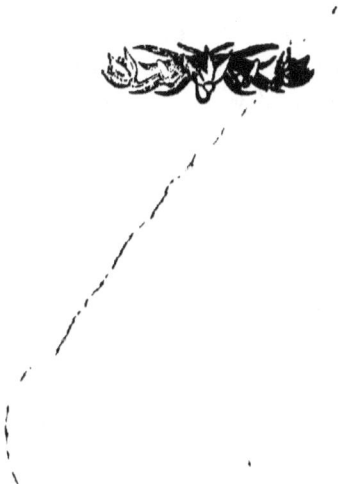

CHAPTER VIII.

CIVIL WAR IN ACADIA.

WHEN Isaac De Razilly died, his property and territorial rights in Acadia came into the possession of his brother Claude, who had been associated with him in fishing enterprises on the coast. Charles La Tour was then settled at the mouth of the river St. John in his new fort, and his father, Claude, was holding for him his old stronghold Fort St. Louis, at Port Latour. The sieur d'Aulnay Charnisay, was in possession of the fort and trading house at Penobscot,* which he was holding as a lieutenant-general for the King, mainly it would seem, for the purpose of resisting the encroachments of the English colonists who were pushing their settlements to the eastward. At that period, as we learn from a letter written in 1636 by Charnisay to the governor of Massachusetts Bay, the French claimed the country as far west as Pemaquid, and substantially the same claim was maintained sixty years later in Villebon's time.

Charnisay was a relative of the deceased commander, De Razilly, and he seems to have been permitted by Claude, his brother and heir, to enter into possession of his estates immediately after Isaac De Razilly's death. The actual deed of transfer of Isaac De Razilly's possessions in Acadia was not given to Charnisay until 1642, but this was but the formal recognition of what was already an accomplished fact, for Charnisay long before that had been treating these

* Called by the French Pentagoet.

possessions as his own. One of his first acts was to take possession of Port Royal and to erect a new fort there, and as soon as this was done, he removed the majority of the La Have colonists to Port Royal, giving them lands on the banks of that beautiful river which flows through the garden of Acadia. He also brought out from France some twenty additional families of colonists, whom he settled at Port Royal, which thenceforth became the principal settlement in Acadia. Charnisay, however, had no desire to see Acadia peopled, and in colonizing Port Royal his motives were purely of a selfish character. Denys charges him with keeping the inhabitants of Port Royal in the condition of slaves, and not allowing them to make any profit from their labor. His great object and aim was to grow wealthy out of the fur trade, and of course, to enable him to maintain the small army of retainers necessary for its prosecution, it was more convenient that he should be able to obtain food for them in Acadia, so that a colony at Port Royal was almost essential to the success of his plans. But beyond that he did not go, and there is too much reason to fear that what his contemporaries said of Charnisay was true, that he was hard and haughty in character, that he was afraid of the country being inhabited, and that he was the means of entirely preventing the settlement of colonists in Acadia for many years.

Acadia, large as it was, was not large enough for two such ambitious men as Charles La Tour and d'Aulnay Charnisay. The two were entirely dissimilar in disposition and character, and each saw in the other qualities which excited his resentment. La Tour, although trained in the hardest school of adversity, and although he had spent the better part of his boyhood and youth among the Indians, exposed to all the hardships incident to a savage life, had all the qualities of a polished courtier and politician. Where he got that wonderful suavity of address which enabled him to gain the favor of all whose aid he sought, is perhaps a useless inquiry, for the school in which he was taught was not one in which such accomplishments were in vogue. Under happier auspices, and in a country where his talents could have had scope, Charles La Tour could scarcely have failed to make a conspicuous figure in his nation's history, but in Acadia the rugged might of nature neutralized his talents, and almost reduced him to the level of commoner men. He might, perhaps, have lived and died in obscurity, but for the misfortunes which have linked his name with one of the most romantic chapters in Acadian history.

Charles La Tour's fort at the river St. John was a structure of four bastions, one hundred and eighty feet square, and enclosed by palisades, after the fashion of that age. It was placed on the west side of the harbor of St. John, on a point of land opposite Navy Island, commanding at once the harbor to the south of it and a considerable stretch of the river to the northward. Here he dwelt in state, like a feudal baron, with a large number of soldiers and retainers in garrison, who, besides their martial occupations, were made useful in the Indian trade which he conducted. Here the painted savages, not only from the St. John and its tributaries, but from the rivers in the interior of Maine, came to dispose of the furs which were the spoils of the chase. Here the yearly ship from France brought him goods suitable for the Indian trade, supplies of ammunition, and such provisions as the wilderness did not afford. A welcome sight her arrival must have been to those exiled Frenchmen, as she came freighted with guerdons and memories of their native land.

A rude abundance reigned at the board around which gathered the defenders of Fort Latour. The wilderness was then a rich preserve of game, where the moose, caribou and red deer roamed in savage freedom. Wild fowl of all kinds abounded along the marsh and intervale lands of the St. John, and the river itself—undisturbed by steamboats and unpolluted by saw mills—swarmed with fish. La Tour, as Denys informs us, had a stake net on the flats below his fort, where he took such abundance of gasperaux as sometimes to break the net, besides catching salmon, shad and bass. And so those soldier-traders lived, on the spoils of forest, ocean and river, a life of careless freedom, undisturbed by the politics of the world, and little crossed by its cares.

Within the fort Lady La Tour led a lonely life, with no companions but her domestics and her children, for her lord was often away ranging the woods, cruising on the coast, or perhaps on a voyage to France. She was a devout Huguenot, but, although Claude La Tour had been of the same faith, Charles appears to have professed himself a Roman Catholic about the year 1632. Policy probably had quite as much to do with his profession as conviction, for he seems to have troubled himself little about points of theology, and was more concerned for the profits of the fur trade than the discussion of doctrinal questions. After the fashion of the times, and to show his conformity with the religion of the court and King, he usually kept a couple of ecclesiastics in his fort, one of whom frequently accompanied him on voyages along the coast. The difference of religion between the husband and wife, if any sincere difference really existed, seems never to have marred the harmony of their relations. He never attempted to make her conform to his professions of religion; she remained a Huguenot to the last, although the religion of his wife was one of the main charges brought against him by the enemies who sought his ruin.

The differences between Charles La Tour and Charnisay seem to have commenced very soon after the occupation by the former of Fort La Tour at St. John in 1635. It is not necessary to enter into any minute examination of the causes of the quarrel, for nothing could be more natural than that men, situated as La Tour and Charnisay were, should have disputes. Both held large territories in Acadia; both had commissions from the King of France as his lieutenants; both were engaged in the same trade. To complicate matters still further, Charnisay's fort at Port Royal was in the middle of the territory which had been placed under the government of La Tour, while the fort of the latter, at the mouth of the St. John, was in the territory which was under the government of Charnisay. Although the territory attached to this fort was only fifty square leagues in extent, it enabled La Tour to command the whole trade of the St. John river, which was then incomparably the best river in Acadia for the fur trade. In fact, the trader who held the mouth of the St. John river was in a position to do most of the Indian trade from the Gulf of St. Lawrence to the Penobscot. It was impossible, therefore, that Charnisay could look upon the advantages possessed by his rival without jealousy, and, having some influence at the French court by the favor of Cardinal Richelieu, he set himself diligently to work to supplant La Tour, who, having spent most of his life in Acadia, was comparatively a stranger in France.

The first results of Charnisay's efforts at the French court were not very encouraging. They are embodied in a royal letter addressed to him on the 10th of February,

1638. This document, which was signed by King Louis himself, after setting forth his desire that there should be a good understanding between Charnisay and La Tour, and that the limits of the places where each was to command should not be the subject of controversy between them, declared the will of the King to be that Charnisay should be his lieutenant-general on the coast of the Etchemins, "beginning from the centre of the firm land of the French Bay, thence towards Virginia," and that La Tour should be his lieutenant-general on the coast of Acadia, "from the middle of the French Bay to the Strait of Canso." Charnisay was told that he was not empowered to change any arrangement in the settlement at the River St. John, made by La Tour, who was to direct the economy of his people according to his judgment; and La Tour, on the other hand, was not to attempt to change any thing in the settlements of Charnisay at La Have or Port Royal. The fur trade was directed to be conducted in the same maner as in the time of commander Isaac De Razilly. Charnisay was further directed to redouble his care for the preservation of the places within the bounds of his authority, and to permit no foreigners to settle within "the countries and coasts of New France."

This very plain and explicit statement of the wishes of the French king failed entirely in its object, for the very excellent reason that Charnisay's interests were altogether opposed to the arrangement which it contemplated. He soon found means to defeat it. The justice of a cause at that period in France had but little influence on its success or failure, and truth and integrity were of comparatively no account when balanced against that species of pressure which a person high in favor at court could bring against their possessor. Richelieu, although enfeebled with age,

J

was still master of France, and to have influence with him was to be strong indeed. That Charnisay had much influence with the great Cardinal is certain, but at this day it is not so easy to see precisely from whence that influence was derived. It has been conjectured that he was a relative, but that consideration might have had less weight with Richelieu than others which could be suggested. The connection of Richelieu with the Company of New France, and Charnisay's purchase of the territorial rights of the Cardinal's relative, Isaac De Razilly, would naturally bring him under his notice, and Charnisay seems to have lacked neither boldness nor perseverance in the pursuit of gain or of revenge. His father, who resided in Paris, and who is styled, in a document which still exists, " Councillor of the King in his state and private councils," no doubt was intimate with Richelieu, and probably did much to forward his son's interest at court, while La Tour had no agent at court, and no friends in France, except the men of Rochelle, who were the last sort of people likely to gain Richelieu's ear. It was not so many years before that he had been directing all his energies, backed by all the power of France, to the reduction of that rebellious city, and it was a still shorter time since he had issued the fatal edict which destroyed its independence for ever. The friends of La Tour in Rochelle were all Huguenots, and therefore doubly odious to the man who was the real master of France.

La Tour, on his part, seems to have been quite unaware of the plans which Charnisay was laying to destroy him. Had he known that accusations of the gravest character were being preferred against him in France by the agents of Charnisay, he would certainly have taken some pains to set himself right before the government, for, weak as he was at court, Charnisay was no match for him in those accomplishments which make men successful courtiers. Had La Tour been in France in the year 1640, he would no doubt have been able to maintain himself in the favor of the King, and his doing so at that time might have changed the whole current of Acadian history. But it was not fated so to be. While long and wordy documents, filled with accusations of treason and other crimes against La Tour, were being presented to Richelieu, the man most vitally interested in those documents was quietly pursuing the ordinary routine of his life in New France. In that year he appears to have been in Quebec, for his name is still to be seen on the registers there as sponsor for the son of a Scotchman named Abraham Martin. The incident would scarcely be worthy of mention were it not for the fact that this Abraham Martin was the owner of the plains of Abraham, and gave his name to one of the most famous battle fields in the history of the world. His son, Charles Amador Martin, La Tour's godson and namesake, became a priest and a canon of the Quebec cathedral.*

In 1641 the long impending blow fell. On the 13th February of that year an order was issued by the King, directed to La Tour, commanding him to embark and return to France immediately, to answer the charges which had been made against him. A letter was likewise sent by the King to Charnisay, directing him that, if La Tour failed to obey the order of the King, he was to seize his person and make an inventory of his effects. To accomplish this, Charnisay was ordered to employ all the means and forces at his disposal, and to put La Tour's forts in the hands of persons well disposed to the King's service.

* Abraham Martin was pilot for the King on the St. Lawrence. His wife's name was Margaret L'Anglois. Their son, Eustache, christened 24th October, 1621, was the first child born in Quebec of white parents.

La Tour, in short, was at one blow to be stripped of his property, deprived of his liberty, and sent a prisoner to France. A few days after this order was issued, the King in council revoked the commission of governor which Charles La Tour had held for ten years—a commission which he had honorably won and manfully defended.

To facilitate the carrying out of these orders against La Tour, a vessel, named the St. Francis, was sent by the King to Acadia to carry the deposed governor to France. This vessel appears to have reached Acadia early in August, but when the letters she carried were presented to La Tour, he utterly refused to obey them, stating that the orders of the King had been obtained by misrepresentation, which was, no doubt, perfectly true. His fort at St. John was in such a state of defence that Charnisay did not venture to attack it, and he was obliged to content himself with ordering his secretary, Capon, to prepare and forward to France the necessary papers, setting forth La Tour's refusal to embark in the St. Francis, and his disobedience to the King's orders in other respects. These papers were sent to France in the same vessel which was to have borne the proscribed La Tour.

The mere disobedience of a royal order in a distant colony, which few people knew anything about, and still fewer cared anything for, would probably have passed with little notice, and might have been in a short time forgotten, but for the persevering conduct of Charnisay. He seems to have had very accurate information of the course of government in France, and he knew also that without assistance from France he could not hope to dispossess La Tour, who would doubtless defy the King's orders as long as he had force enough at his command to enable him to do so. A governor who had been maintaining himself in

Acadia, by the aid of his sword alone, for so many years, was not likely to pay much heed to any of those documents which the legal gentlemen of Paris regarded as all-powerful, and which, doubtless, were so where there was an army to enforce them. But a writ of ejectment served in Acadia required something more than the King's seal to make it effectual, where the man on whom it was to be served had a strong fort armed with cannon and a garrison of armed retainers at his command. Charnisay, therefore, towards the close of the year 1641, went to France to strengthen himself at court, and to obtain such material assistance as would enable him to effectually destroy his rival La Tour.

La Tour was well aware that Charnisay had powerful friends at court and that he was not likely to rest quiet after one defeat, especially where he could make any action forward his own interest which might be taken by the government of France to vindicate its authority. La Tour therefore began to prepare for the struggle which appeared inevitable, and to enable him to do so successfully, it was necessary for him to call in some outside aid. His first thought seems to have been to obtain help from his neighbors of New England, with whom he was on good terms, and who had sufficient force to assist him effectually. Accordingly, in November, 1641, he sent a messenger to Boston to see what could be done there to aid his cause. This messenger, who was a Huguenot named Rochette, from Rochelle, had called at Pemaquid on his way and there left his boats. Mr. Shurt, the principal resident of that place, received him courteously and gave him a letter to Richard Bellingham, the governor of Masachusetts Bay. Rochette proposed that the people of Massachusetts Bay should enter into a treaty with La Tour. The proposed treaty, as Winthrop informs us, was to embrace three points: first, liberty of free commerce; second, assistance against d'Aulnay Charnisay, with whom he had war; third, that he might make return of goods out of England by the merchants of Boston. The first condition with reference to trade was immediately granted. The Massachusetts authorities excused themselves from entertaining the other two, on the ground that Rochette had brought with him no letters or commission from La Tour. This might have been an excellent reason for not making any treaty whatever with Rochette, but why such an objection should be applied to two propositions out of three, is not so clear. If Rochette was a competent agent for La Tour as regards one condition, he was certainly a competent agent with respect to the others. But causistry was a thing not unknown in New England at that time. However, Rochette, although he did not obtain all he asked, was most courteously entertained by the people of Boston, and, after remaining with them for some days took his departure again for Fort La Tour.

La Tour was so little discouraged by the refusal to treat with his messenger, Rochette, that in October of the following year (1642) he sent his lieutenant to Boston with a shallop and fourteen men. He carried letters from La Tour to John Winthrop, the governor of Massachusetts Bay, filled with compliments and desiring assistance from the people of New England against his enemy, Charnisay. La Tour's people remained about a week in Boston, and were well treated by the hospitable New Englanders, but no measures were taken then to grant the assistance asked for, although there was no question as to the lieutenant's authority to treat on behalf of La Tour. Winthrop records the fact that, although all these Frenchmen were Papists, they attended the Church meetings in Boston, and the lieutenant professed to be greatly affected at what he saw, and at the order which was kept in those solemn assemblies. One of the elders gave him a French testament, with Marlorat's notes,* which he gratefully accepted and promised to read. Altogether, the intercourse between the Frenchmen and the people of Boston was of the most agreeable nature, and they seem to have parted with the best feelings towards each other.

La Tour's lieutenant, while in Boston, became acquainted with several merchants, and made proposals to them with regard to the opening up of a trade with his master. The Boston merchants of that day were not wanting in enterprise and boldness, and some of them immediately sent a pinnace to the St. John river, laden with suitable goods, to trade with the French governor. He gave them a very courteous welcome, and their trade seems to have been mutually satisfactory, for it was the beginning of a connexion with the Boston merchants which lasted as long as he remained in Acadia. He sent letters by them to Governor Winthrop, in which he related the state of the controversy between himself and Charnisay, and in which he thanked the people of Boston for the handsome manner in which they had entertained his lieutenant. On their voyage back to Boston the merchants stopped at Pemaquid, which was then a common place of call between Acadia and Boston. There they met Charnisay himself, who, learning that they had come from La Tour at St. John, took great pains to inform them that the latter was a rebel, and exhibited a copy of an order which he had procured in France for his arrest. Charnisay sent a printed copy of this order of arrest to Governor Winthrop, and accom-

*Marlorat was a French Protestant divine, who was executed at Rouen by the orders of Montmorency, after the capture of that city in 1562. Several of his tracts, which were chiefly commentatorial in their character, were translated into English.

panied it with the threat that, if any of the merchants of Boston sent their vessels to trade with La Tour, he would seize them as lawful prize.

This order of arrest was the result of Charnisay's voyage to France a few months before. It was dated the 21st of February, 1642, and was substantially a confirmation of the orders which had been made just one year previous. It directed Charnisay to seize La Tour's forts and person, and to send him to France as a rebel and traitor to the King. Without an armed force to carry it out, it was merely a dead letter, for La Tour was as little disposed as ever to give up his fort, even at the command of the King. Charnisay, while in France, had gone through the legal formalities of an arrangement which had been substantially executed long before, and secured a transfer to himself of all the estates which the late Isaac De Razilly had possessed in Acadia. The deeds by which this transfer was made were executed by Claude De Razilly, and were dated the 16th January, 1642. They conveyed to Charnisay both Isaac De Razilly's Acadian property and his rights in the Company of New France, the consideration of the transfer being the sum of fourteen thousand livres, which Charnisay agreed to pay in seven years. This wholly inadequate consideration for the transfer of such an enormous property, shows that it was then made for some other purpose than merely to confirm to Charnisay what he already possessed. The fact was, that Charnisay was sadly in need of money to enable him to equip a sufficient force to dispossess La Tour, and to obtain the sum he required, it was necessary that he should have a perfect title to his possessions in Acadia. Then, and at subsequent periods, he obtained on this property large sums from Emmanuel Le Borgne, the sums thus obtained amounting in 1649 to the enormous aggregate of two hundred and sixty thousand livres, most of which was wastefully expended in an absurd crusade against a fellow countryman with whom he might have lived in peace; for Acadia was large enough for both, and both might have been enriched by its trade had Charnisay chosen to let La Tour alone, whereas, as matters turned out, both were ruined.

The supreme effort which Charnisay was about to make for the destruction of his rival demanded abundant means, and money must have been liberally supplied, for it enabled him to arm and equip such a force as had seldom before been brought by any one private individual against another. No less than five vessels and five hundred armed men were provided by him for this Acadian war, a force which, humanly speaking, should have been able to sweep everything before it, and to bear down any opposition which La Tour could offer.

But while Charnisay was thus preparing for the conflict, La Tour was not idle. He sent Rochette to France to represent at Rochelle the desperate straits in which he was likely to be, and to obtain aid, if possible, to enable him to maintain himself in Acadia. Rochelle, although stricken down and deprived of its ancient privileges, was still the home of an energetic and wealthy Huguenot population, who hated the very name of Richelieu, and who were ready to befriend any who dared to resist his commands. The Rochellois seem to have embraced La Tour's cause with a warmth and heartiness which would be regarded as surprising in modern times among men who have never felt the edge of a sword at their throats on account of their faith. It was enough for them to know that a persecuted brother in Acadia was in distress, and was in danger of being destroyed by an enemy, who was also the enemy of their religion. They felt that they could do no less than rush to his rescue. Accordingly, they fitted out a large armed vessel named the Clement, loaded her with ammunition and supplies, and, putting on board of her one hundred and forty armed Rochellois, sent her to the aid of La Tour in Acadia. Thus was the civil war in that distant region fed on both sides from France, and swords were being sharpened at Rochelle and in Paris, destined to clash in fratricidal strife, and to be stained with blood needlessly spilt. Darkly and ominously the clouds of fate were gathering over Fort La Tour.

CHAPTER IX.

THE SIEGES AND CAPTURE OF FORT LA TOUR.

ON the 12th June, 1643, the people of Boston were considerably amazed, and not a little frightened, at the sudden appearance of an armed French ship in their harbor. She came in so unexpectedly and so swiftly that scarcely any one observed her until she passed Castle Island, when she thundered forth a salute which echoed over the little Puritan town. But it was not returned, because the castle was deserted, the General Court having, in a fit of economy, withdrawn the small garrison which had formerly held it, and so this French stranger had Boston at his mercy had his designs been hostile. As the vessel sped up the harbor a boat filled with men was seen to leave her side, and was rowed rapidly to Governor's Island, landing at Governor Winthrop's garden. The Governor and two of his sons came forward to meet the strangers, who proved to be La Tour and a party of his men. The Acadian governor was not long in explaining the cause of his visit. Early in the Spring his enemy, Charnisay, had suddenly made his appearance before Fort La Tour with two ships and a galliot, besides several small craft, manned by five hundred men. Being unable to carry the fort by assault, as he had hoped, he proceeded to blockade it, knowing that want of provisions would eventually compel La Tour to surrender. In the meantime the Clement from Rochelle, laden with supplies for the fort, arrived off St. John, but was unable to enter the harbor owing to the blockade. At this juncture La Tour, ever fertile in resources, bethought him of his Boston friends, whose trade he was beginning to cultivate. Accordingly, he and his wife stole silently out of St. John harbor in a shallop, under cover of the darkness, and boarded the Clement, which immediately set sail for Boston. They had been favored with a fair wind and had made a rapid passage, and they had taken a pilot out of a boat from Boston which they met at sea, leaving a Frenchman to supply his place. La Tour had now come to obtain such aid as would enable him to return to his fort, which was sadly in need of the ammunition and provisions which the Clement contained.

Governor Winthrop declined to give any pledge of assistance, until he had conferred with the other magistrates, but next day he called together such of them as were at hand, and gave La Tour a hearing before them. The captain of the Clement produced a parchment, dated the previous April, under the hand and seal of the vice-admiral of France, authorizing him to carry supplies to La Tour, who was styled in this document his majesty's lieutenant-general of Acadia. He also produced a letter from the agent of the Company of New France, addressed to La Tour, informing him of the attempts which Charnisay was making against him, and advising him to have a care for his own safety. In this letter, also, La Tour was called lieutenant-general for the King. These documents, being of later date than the order of arrest produced by Charnisay, satisfied Governor Winthrop that La Tour was still regarded in France as the governor of Acadia. The truth was that in France, in April 1643, the government was in a transition state. Richelieu had died four months before, and the sceptre was about to fall from the feeble hand of Louis XIII., who was stricken with a mortal disease. Some confusion in the various departments of the administration was the inevitable result of such a state of affairs, and, in view of this the recognition of La Tour as governor of Acadia, even after the proceedings which had been taken against him, is not so difficult to understand. Governor Winthrop and his associates accepted the documents presented by La Tour as evidence that he stood on good terms with the Company of New France, and also with the French government. Therefore, although they could not grant him aid against Charnisay without the advice of the other commissioners of the New England confederacy, they gave him permission to hire such ships and men as were in Boston, so that he might return to Acadia with force enough to enable him to reach his fort in safety. La Tour, who had many warm friends among the merchants of Boston, lost no time in taking advantage of the permission thus granted to him. However reluctant the General Court might be to give active aid, the traders of Boston were shrewd enough to see the great injury which would result to them from the destruction of La Tour, and an increase in the power and importance of Charnisay. The former was friendly to the people of New England, and both willing and anxious to trade with them. The latter hated the New Englanders cordially, refused to trade with them, and omitted to take advantage of no opportunity of giving them annoyance. All their interests led them to support La Tour's cause, and had they done wisely they would have continued to sustain him to the end, notwithstanding the remonstrances of some very enlightened gentlemen among the Puritans, who were horrified at the idea of extending any assistance to a Papist.

La Tour hired from Edward Gibbons and Thomas Hawkins, of Boston, four vessels—the Seabridge, Philip and Mary, Increase, and Greyhound—with fifty-two men and thirty-eight pieces of ordnance. He also enlisted ninety-two soldiers to augment the force on board his vessels, and provided them with arms and supplies. Two years later La Tour was obliged to mortgage his fort in Acadia to Gibbons and Hawkins for the sum of two thousand and eighty-four pounds to secure them for the money advanced for supplies in 1643, a large sum for those days, which will convey some idea of the ruinous character of the strife which Charnisay and La Tour were waging against each other. The terms on which the ships were hired do not seem to have contemplated their participation in any offensive operations. They were required to go as near to La Tour's fort as they could conveniently ride at anchor, and to join with the Clement in the defence of themselves and of La Tour against Charnisay's forces in case they should unjustly assault or oppose La Tour on his way to his fort. Any further assistance was to be a matter of mutual agreement between La Tour and the agent of the owners of the ships, who was to accompany the expedition. No doubt the wily Frenchman thought that, in case of a conflict in which the English vessels took part against Charnisay, they would forget the strict terms of the agreement and assist him in annihilating his enemy. The result proved that he was not far wrong in his calculations.

But a more formidable danger than even Charnisay's forces menaced La Tour's enterprise in its very inception. The news of the doings at Boston had been spread far and wide throughout New England, and had excited in some quarters great alarm. Thomas Gorges wrote from his home in Piscataqua to warn Governor Winthrop of the danger into which he was leading the colony by taking sides against Charnisay. He represented that the latter had long waited, at a charge of eight hundred pounds a month, to destroy La Tour, and that, if his hopes were frustrated by the people of New England, he would seek satisfaction. Mr. Endicott, afterwards Governor of the colony, wrote from Salem to express his fears at the Governor having anything to do with "these idolatrous French." Many others, whose names Winthrop does not record, joined in these remonstrances against giving aid to La Tour; several ministers referred to the matter in their sermons, and one even went so far as to prophecy from his pulpit that because of this alliance with the French governor the streets of Boston would yet run red with blood. It became necessary for Governor Winthrop to write and publish the true state of the proceedings between himself and La Tour, which seemed to be much misunderstood. Finally, to give all parties a chance to be heard, the Governor appointed another meeting, to which all the magistrates, deputies and elders were invited, and the whole matter was again fully debated.

The Puritans regarded the Old Testament as a safe guide in matters of public policy, and the arguments against and in favor of giving aid to La Tour were all drawn from its pages. One party endeavored to show by the examples of Jehoshaphat, Josias and Amaziah, that it was wrong for righteous men to be associated in any way with the ungodly. The other side contended as stoutly that the censure on those kings for aiding the wicked only applied to the particular instances under which it was given, and could not be applied to every case, or it would be unlawful to help any wicked man in any case, even though he were a brother or a father, and in danger of losing his life. These and other arguments—some of which strike the modern reader as being rather sophistical—engaged the attention of the meeting for the better part of a day; but the friends of La

Tour seem to have had the best of the argument, for the former decision to permit him to hire ships and men in Boston was not interfered with, and the expedition intended for the relief of his fort was allowed to proceed.

La Tour, with his fleet of auxiliaries, set sail from Boston on the evening of the 14th of July, parting on the best of terms with the chief men of the town, who accompanied him to his boat. He had made himself so agreeable to all that he had entirely disarmed those who at first were jealous of his presence, and as he sailed away, he carried with him the best wishes of the people. The quest upon which he had gone was one of danger and difficulty, and, as if to mark it with this character from the very outset, his flotilla sailed out of Broad Sound, where, as Winthrop tells us, no vessels of such tonnage had gone before. But there was reason for haste, for Fort La Tour had all this time been blockaded by the ships of Charnisay, who looked forward to a speedy triumph over his rival. He did not dream that La Tour had escaped from his grasp, and was organizing a force to overwhelm him.

When La Tour's fleet of five ships and a pinnace came in sight of St. John, Charnisay seems for the first time to have suspected the truth. His vessels were lying beside Partridge Island, but he did not wait to measure his strength against his enemy, but hoisted sail and stood right home for Port Royal. La Tour pursued, but Charnisay got his vessels into Port Royal Basin in safety, and ran them aground opposite his mill. He and his men then betook themselves to the shore, and commenced to put the mill in a posture of defence. Captain Hawkins, who commanded the New Englanders, sent a messenger ashore with a letter which Governor Winthrop had addressed to Charnisay. This letter was a sort of apology for the presence of the Boston people in aid of La Tour, and professed a desire to bring about a reconciliation between him and Charnisay; but the latter refused to open it because it did not address him as lieutenant-general for the King in Acadia. He exhibited the original of the order of arrest against La Tour, and sent Captain Hawkins a copy of it, but refused to come to any terms of peace. The messenger reported that there was great terror and confusion among the French, but that all, friars included, were putting forth their best efforts to fortify themselves.

La Tour, upon this, urged Captain Hawkins to send a force ashore to attack his enemy. Hawkins refused to give any orders to his men, but signified that any who chose to go ashore with La Tour might do so. About thirty of the New Englanders took advantage of this permission, and the united force attacked Charnisay's position, driving his men from the mill where they had fortified themselves. Three of Charnisay's men were killed and one prisoner taken in the mill. La Tour had three men wounded, but the New Englanders suffered no loss. The Boston vessels then returned to Fort Latour, which had been so suddenly freed from its perilous blockade. While they were lying there a pinnace belonging to Charnisay fell into their hands. This craft was laden with four hundred moose and four hundred beaver skins, and was, therefore, a valuable prize. The booty was divided between the crews and owners of the Boston vessels and La Tour—for Captain Hawkins, although unwilling to fight against the enemies of La Tour, was quite ready to rob them where it could be done without danger. When the time for which the ships had been hired was nearly expired, they were paid off by

K

La Tour,* and returned to Boston, which they reached on the 20th of August, having been absent but thirty-seven days. They had certainly made good despatch, and their return without loss was fortunate; but the elders were offended and grieved at some of their actions, especially at their piratical seizure of Charnisay's pinnace. They saw readily enough that such an act would provoke the enmity of the revengeful Frenchman, who was none too well disposed toward the people of Boston at any time, and who would now have a substantial grievance against them. They had, in fact, done either too much or too little. They should either have remained neutral in the war between Charnisay and La Tour, or, having taken any part in it, they should have given the latter such effectual aid as would have enabled him to destroy his rival.

As it was, Charnisay was more resolute than ever to compass the object upon which he had set his heart. As a preliminary to further proceedings, he commenced the erection of a new fort at Port Royal† which would be capable of making a good defence in case he should again be attacked. As soon as it was fit for occupation he set sail for France, to protect his interests at the French court and to obtain further aid against La Tour. While in France he heard of the arrival there of the person whom he hated above all others. This was the lady La Tour, who had gone to Rochelle to further her husband's interests there and to procure supplies for the fort. A generous rival would have seen in her a noble and devoted wife

---

*Winthrop says that the pinnace went up the St. John river some twenty leagues and loaded with coal. This statement shows that the coal mines of Queen's County were known and worked at a very early period.

†Winthrop is the authority for this statement. Although it is scarcely susceptible of proof, I assume that Charnisay's old fort was on the site of that of Champlain, opposite Goat Island, and that the new fort was built on the site of the now ruined fortifications of Annapolis.

whose heroic constancy deserved his respect; but Charnisay had nothing generous in his nature to any that bore his great enemy's hated name. He procured an order for the arrest of the lady La Tour on the ground that she was, equally with her husband, a traitor to the King. Fortunately she had friends, who forewarned her of the danger which impended, and before the order could be executed she fled to England, which, even in those days of civil war, was a safer retreat for a Huguenot lady than France. In England she found friends, and by their aid was able to communicate with her husband, and inform him of the danger he was in from Charnisay. As for herself, she lost no time in freighting a ship from London with provisions and munitions of war for Fort Latour, and had the energy of those on whom she relied for service been equal to her own, would doubtless have reached it in time to ward off any attack which might threaten.

La Tour, bereft of his wife's counsel and companionship, and oppressed with the sense of coming disaster, waited wearily by the shores of the St. John for her return. Months passed, but still she came not, and then, almost despairing of her safety, and perplexed by a hundred doubts and fears, he started for Boston, where he arrived in July, 1644. John Endicott was then the Governor of Massachusetts, and La Tour speedily made known to him the difficulties with which he was surrounded, and besought his aid. The Governor appointed a meeting of the magistrates and elders of Boston, before which the distressed Frenchman appeared, and made known his case. He was careful to give due prominence to his father's grant of territory in Acadia from Sir William Alexander, and to assert his long possession of that territory and of Fort Latour. The men of Boston were impressed by the strength of his case. Most of the magistrates and some of the elders were clear that he should be relieved, both on the ground of charity, as a distressed neighbor, and also in point of prudence, so as to root out, or at least weaken, such a dangerous neighbor as Charnisay. But as many of the elders were absent, and, as three or four of the magistrates dissented, it was agreed that the rest of the elders should be called in, and that another meeting should be held at Salem to discuss the matter further. At this second meeting, after much disputation, it was found that some of the magistrates and elders still remained unwilling to aid La Tour, and the majority who favored him were indisposed to take action without the consent of all. This being so, a third method was suggested, to which, as it involved no risk, all gave a ready assent. This was simply to send a letter of remonstrance to Charnisay. In this letter very little was said about La Tour or his wrongs, but a great deal was said against Charnisay's interference with the merchants of Boston, who had gone to Fort Latour to trade. Some apologies were made for the conduct of those who had gone from Boston to aid La Tour the previous year, and satisfaction was demanded for the taking of Penobscot by Charnisay, an event which had occurred eight years before. The grim Frenchman, if he had any sense of humor at all, must have smiled at the perfunctory manner in which La Tour's New England friends were pleading his cause. Such a letter was, in fact, an invitation to him to proceed to all extremities against La Tour, for it showed that the latter had nothing further to hope for from the people of Boston. La Tour, however, had to be satisfied with what he had obtained, and on the 9th September he left Boston, where he had spent two months to very little purpose. It was training day, and all the train bands made a guard for him to his boat, and as his ship sailed out of the harbor he was saluted by all the English vessels lying at anchor. He was accompanied by a Boston vessel, laden with provisions, and here fortune, which had sometimes proved adverse, favored him, for Charnisay, with an armed ship was cruising off Penobscot, and waiting to capture him. Had La Tour gone forward with the fair wind with which he left port, he would surely have fallen into the hands of his enemy, but he delayed at several places by the way, until Charnisay concluding he had escaped, put into port, and then he passed on unmolested to Fort Latour.

Scarcely had the white sails of La Tour's vessels sunk on the eastern horizon when a stout ship from London came sailing into Boston harbor. She had been fitted out by Alderman Berkley and Captain Bailey, and she brought among her passengers Roger Williams, the founder of the Providence plantation. But her chief passenger was that heroic and devoted wife, whose memory will never perish from Acadian history, the lady La Tour. They had left England six months before, and their destination was Fort Latour, for which they had a cargo of goods. But the master of the vessel spent so much time in trading by the way, that they did not reach Cape Sable until September, and as soon as they got into the Bay of Fundy they fell in with one of Charnisay's vessels, which was cruising to intercept and capture them. The master of the ship was forced to hide the lady La Tour and her people in the hold and to conceal the identity of his ship, which he pretended was bound direct to Boston. Charnisay, who little suspected how great a prize he had in his hands, let the vessel go, merely contenting himself with sending a civil message to the governor of Massachusetts, in which he professed his desire to be on good terms with the people of that colony, and expressed his intention to communicate further with them with regard to his differences with La Tour. The vessel was therefore obliged to abandon her voyage to Fort Latour and go to Boston instead. This change in the voyage, added to the unreasonable delay which had already taken place, was a great loss and inconvenience to the lady La Tour, and she sought her remedy by bringing an action on the charter party against the persons who freighted the ship. The cause was tried at a special Court in Boston before all the magistrates and a jury of the principal men who gave her a verdict of two thousand pounds damages. On this judgment she seized the cargo of the ship, which was appraised at eleven hundred pounds, and hiring three vessels in Boston to convoy her home, at length arrived safely at Fort Latour, to the indescribable relief of her husband, who had almost despaired of her safety. She had been absent from him more than a year.

While the lady La Tour was still in Boston a messenger arrived from Charnisay in the person of Monsieur Marie, whom the men of Massachusetts supposed to be a friar, although he was attired like a layman. He was accompanied by ten men, and brought letters of credence and a commission from Charnisay. The object of his mission was to prevent the people of New England from giving any further aid to La Tour, and to obtain, if possible, their assistance for his master against the truculent Frenchman who persisted in holding Fort Latour against the mandate of the King himself. Marie had with him a commission from the King, under the great seal of France, with the privy seal annexed, in which the former proceedings against La Tour were verified, and in which he was condemned as a rebel and a traitor. Attached to this was an order for the apprehension of La Tour and his lady, the latter, among her other crimes, being charged with having fled out of France against the special order of the King.* M. Marie, after exhibiting these documents, complained of the aid given to La Tour in the previous year, and proffered terms for a league of peace and amity. He also proposed that the people of Massachusetts should assist Charnisay against La Tour, or, at all events, that they should give the latter no further aid. The magistrates said that some of the ships and many of the men which La Tour had employed to aid him were strangers to them, and that none of them had any commission from them nor any permission to commit any acts of hostility. They urged strongly that Charnisay should become reconciled to La Tour. Marie replied to this that if La Tour would voluntarily submit and come in, he would assure him of his life and liberty, but if he was taken, he was sure to lose his head in France, and, as for his lady, she was known to be the cause of his contempt and rebellion, and therefore Charnisay was resolved to capture her to prevent her from reaching her husband. The end of these negotiations was that an agreement was made between the governor and magistrates of Massachusetts on behalf of the colony, and M. Marie, on behalf of Charnisay, governor and lieutenant-general for the King of France in Acadia. This document, which was signed on the 8th October, 1644, mutually bound the people of Massachusetts and Charnisay to keep firm peace

* Among the documents preserved by the Menou family are letters from Charnisay, charging lady La Tour with being of low origin and dissolute manners. The most infamous charges are made against La Tour himself. One memoir preserved by the Menou family says: "After the death of Biencourt La Tour lived a wandering life in the woods with eighteen or twenty followers, mingling with the Indians, leading licentious and infamous lives, like brutes, without any exercise of religion, not even causing their children, born of Indian women, to be baptized; on the contrary, abandoning them to their mothers, as they still continue to do." As Charnisay was not in Acadia at the time of which he writes, nor for years afterwards, he probably drew on his imagination for most of his facts.

with each other. It made it lawful for all persons, both French and English, to trade with each other, the people of Massachusetts reserving the right to trade with any other persons they chose, whether French or not, wherever they dwelt. This agreement, it will be observed, effectually prevented the Massachusetts people from giving any open aid to La Tour, but it did not hinder them from trading with him. The main advantage which most of the magistrates saw in it was that it freed the colony from the fear that Charnisay would take revenge on them for the harm he had sustained from the force which went from Boston to aid La Tour the year before. Marie, having finished his business with great despatch, left Boston the same evening, two days before the lady La Tour set sail for her fort. No doubt his haste was partly due to the hope of giving Charnisay warning in time to enable him to intercept her; if so, it was a delusive hope, for long before the commissioner reached his master, the lady La Tour was safe within her fort at St. John.

When Charnisay heard that the lady La Tour had escaped from Boston and arrived at Fort Latour, his rage was boundless. The treaty of peace which his agent had made with the people of Massachusetts seemed to him but a poor equivalent for the escape of his most hated enemy from his vengeance. He wrote a most angry and insulting letter to the governor of Massachusetts, in which he charged the people of that colony with being responsible for her escape, and he wildly threatened them with the vengeance of his master, the King of France. The cheeks of the stern Puritan governor burned with anger as he read this menacing epistle, in which the honor of the magistrates was called in question and the whole colony insulted in their persons.

Charnisay soon had an opportunity of proving in a practical manner how much he was provoked. La Tour had gone to Boston early in the winter for supplies for his fort, and sent forward a small vessel to Fort Latour, laden with provisions. Charnisay—who was cruising off the mouth of the St. John to intercept La Tour—captured this craft, and turned her crew, all of whom were English, upon Partridge Island, in the midst of deep snow, without fire, and with only a sorry wigwam for their shelter. He kept them there ten days, and then gave them an old shallop in which to return home. But he took from them most of their clothes, and refused them either gun or compass, so that they had neither the means to defend themselves nor to navigate the seas in safety. They, however, contrived to reach Boston, where the ill treatment they had received provoked great indignation. A vessel was immediately despatched to Charnisay, with letters from Governor Endicott, remonstrating against the gross breach of the treaty which he had committed, and likewise answering the charges which he had made in his letter, relative to the aid given to the lady La Tour. The Puritan governor declared with spirit that his people were not to be coerced by threats, and that, while they did what was right according to their consciences, they did not fear even the vengeance of the King of France. For even should he attempt to destroy them, New England had a God who was able to save and who would not forsake His servants.

When this pious letter was delivered at Port Royal to Charnisay, he was already in a most unamiable temper, and it added fuel to his anger. He told the messenger, Mr. Allen, that he would return no answer, nor would he permit him even to enter his fort, but he lodged him in his gunner's house without the gate. He, however, treated him with no personal discourtesy, for he went daily to dine and sup with him, thereby giving him to understand that it was simply as the bearer of Governor Endicott's letter that he was unwelcome. At length, after some delay, he wrote an answer to the Massachusetts governor in very high language, requiring satisfaction for the burning of his mill in 1643 by the New England auxiliaries of La Tour, and threatening revenge in case his demands were not granted.

Charnisay indeed had some reason to be angry, for he had just met with a most disastrous and humiliating defeat. At the very time when the crew of the Boston vessel, whom he had put on Partridge Island were maintaining an arduous struggle against cold and hunger, two friars hailed his ship from the mainland and asked to be taken on board. The lady La Tour had discovered that these men were plotting against her and in league with Charnisay, and, instead of hanging them as spies and traitors as she might have done, she contented herself with simply turning them out of the fort. When they were received on board Charnisay's vessel they told him that his opportunity for vengeance had come. They said that La Tour was absent, that his fort contained but fifty men, that there was but little powder in the fort, and that little much decayed, and that he might easily capture the place. Filled with high hopes of triumph, Charnisay entered the harbor of St. John and ranged his vessel in front of Fort Latour, in the expectation of seeing the flag which waved above it hauled down at his summons. But he was grievously disappointed. The lady La Tour had an heroic soul, and was not disposed to yield without a struggle. She inspired her little garrison with a spirit equal to her own. From one of the bastions she directed the attack on Charnisay's ship, and a fierce cannonade commenced which resulted disastrously to the besiegers.

Their vessel was so vigorously assailed by the ordnance of the fort, and so much shattered, that, to keep her from absolutely sinking beneath them, Charnisay's men were obliged to warp her ashore behind a point of land where she was safe from the guns of the fort. Twenty of the besiegers were killed and thirteen wounded in this affair, which terminated in a manner so different from Charnisay's expectations.

This repulse took place in February, 1645, and in the following April Charnisay again attacked Fort Latour— this time from the land side. Unfortunately it stood in no better position for defence than it was in before, and La Tour was still absent in Boston, unable to reach his fort owing to the armed cruisers with which Charnisay watched the Bay of Fundy, and denied any aid from the people of New England, who had formerly assisted him. Fortune, which for years had alternately frowned and smiled on the proscribed Governor of Acadia, now seemed to avert her face; the shadow of destiny was upon him, and in a little while he was to be deprived of all his possessions, and of those who were far dearer to him than any earthly treasures. How strange were the fortunes of this man, whose whole life reads like a romance, who made ordinary men the pliant instruments of his will, whose spirit no adverse fate could subdue, and who, although apparently crushed to the earth, lived to triumph over all his enemies!

It was on the 13th April, 1645, that Charnisay began his last attack on Fort Latour. The lady La Tour, although hopeless of making a successful resistance, resolved to defend her fort to the last. For three days and three nights the attack proceeded, but the defence was so well conducted that the besiegers made no progress, and Charnisay was compelled to draw off his forces with loss.

Treachery finally accomplished what force could not effect. Charnisay found means to bribe a Swiss sentry who formed one of the garrison, and on the fourth day, which was Easter Sunday, while the garrison were at prayers, this traitor permitted the enemy to approach without giving any warning. They were already scaling the walls of the fort before the garrison were aware of their attack. The lady La Tour, in this extremity, opposed the assault at the head of her men, and repulsed the besiegers with so much vigor that Charnisay—who had lost twelve men killed and many wounded—despaired of taking the fort. He therefore proposed terms of capitulation, offering the garrison life and liberty if they would consent to yield. The lady La Tour knew that successful resistance was impossible, and she desired to save the lives of those under her command. She therefore accepted the terms which Charnisay offered, and permitted him to enter the fort. No sooner did he find himself in possession of the place, to the capture of which all his efforts had for years been directed, than he disclosed the full baseness of his nature. He caused all the garrison, both French and English, to be hanged, except one man, to whom he gave his life on the dreadful condition that he became the executioner of his comrades in arms. But even the murder of these poor soldiers did not satisfy Charnisay's desire for vengeance. No doubt he would have assassinated the lady La Tour also, had he only dared, but the court of France, venal as it was, would scarcely have tolerated such an outrage as that. But he did what was almost as bad. He compelled the heroic lady to be present at the execution of her soldiers, with a rope round her neck, like one who should have been executed also, but who by favor had been reprieved. But it mattered little to her what further plans of vengeance her great enemy might design; they had little power to touch her. Her great heart was broken. She was severed from the husband, to whose fortunes she had been so faithful, and could scarcely hope to see his face again, except as a captive like herself. She felt that her work in life was done, for she was not born for captivity. So she faded away, day by day, until her heroic soul left its earthly tenement, and in three weeks from the time when she witnessed the capture of her fort, she was laid to rest by the banks of the St. John, which she loved so well, and where she had lived for so many years. Thus died the first and greatest of Acadian heroines—a woman whose name is as proudly enshrined in the history of this land as that of any sceptred Queen in European story. As long as the sons and daughters of this new Acadia take an interest in their country's early history, they will read with admiration the noble story of the constancy and heroism of the lady La Tour.

This noble wife and mother left behind her a little child, which was sent to France in the care of one of the lady's gentlewomen. What became of this unfortunate infant is not known, but as no further mention is made of it in the genealogies of the family of La Tour, it probably died young. The booty taken by Charnisay in Fort Latour was very large, and was valued at ten thousand pounds sterling, an estimate which will serve to show the extent of the trade which was carried on by La Tour in Acadia, for all this wealth was the result of the Indian trade. The loss of so much property was ruinous to La Tour, whose affairs were already much embarrassed by the cost he had been put to in his warfare with Charnisay. Nor had the latter, although he had succeeded in ruining his rival, greatly improved his own fortunes. For he had become deeply involved in France, in consequence of the large forces he had been obliged to maintain in Acadia, and his success was dearly purchased. The civil war, in which these rivals had engaged, was in fact destructive to both. But for Charnisay's vindictive jealousy and ambition, both might have lived in Acadia in peace, and acquired great wealth by trade. The result of the war was that La Tour lost all, and became an outcast, and almost a beggar, while Charnisay incurred such an enormous indebtedness, as no man could hope to liquidate by trade in Acadia, large and profitable as its trade undoubtedly was.

CHAPTER X.

THE DEATH OF CHARNISAY.

La Tour was in Boston when the tidings of the capture of his fort and the death of his wife reached him, and the heavy news must have dashed even such a strong spirit as his, for it involved both the breaking up of his domestic hearth and the loss of his estate. But the feelings of the inner heart are seldom inscribed on the pages of a book; the strongest natures suffer in silence, and therefore we can only conjecture the measure of the grief which oppressed the bereaved and despoiled lord of Acadia. But La Tour had a hopeful spirit and a ready mind to design means for relieving himself from his difficulties. He seems also to have had the faculty of imparting the same confidence in his fortunes to others which he felt himself. No man ever had firmer friends than La Tour made in Boston. Although the result of their transactions in some instances involved their own ruin as well as his, they appear never to have doubted him or to have lost faith in his integrity. In his greatest straits he never wanted for money or friends in the capital of New England, and this fact alone is a complete refutation of the calumnies which some New England writers have heaped upon his memory. The men of Boston, who were his contemporaries, knew La Tour better than those obscure scribes whose attempts to blacken his character were made after he had been dead for a hundred years.

On the 13th May, 1645, La Tour gave a mortgage of his fort and property at St. John to sergeant major Edward

Gibbons of Boston. This instrument was made to secure the payment of the full sum of £2,084 which he owed Gibbons for money and supplies advanced, and the condition was that this sum was to be repaid, with interest, on the 20th February, 1652. As this mortgage was made nearly a month after the capture of Fort Latour, we may presume that event was known in Boston when it was executed, and that it was the first act of La Tour towards securing his New England creditors after he had heard of the great loss which had overtaken him. He probably thought also that the fact of a leading citizen of Boston having a large interest in the property which Charnisay had seized, would force the people of New England out of their neutral attitude and induce them to take an active part against that truculent governor. This very matter was, in fact, brought up before the Commissioners of the United Colonies, who met at Boston in the following August, but they decided that the mortgage having been made after the commission from the King of France to Charnisay was made known, it was of no effect against the latter, especially after the fort had been seized into the hands of the King of France by authority of the said commission. Thus any expectations of aid which La Tour might have formed on that basis were doomed to disappointment, the people of New England being more anxious for peace than for money, or even for the maintenance of their own honor. The only warfare which they were disposed to wage was that which they constantly maintained against all whose religious views differed from their own, or who felt inclined to protest against the gloomy theological despotism which they had established on the shores of the New World.

La Tour, finding that there was no prospect of his

receiving any further help from the authorities of Massachusettts, resolved to go to Newfoundland, where Sir David Kirk was Governor, thinking that he, being almost a Frenchman, would be likely to take a livelier interest in his fortunes than a man of alien race. He accordingly took shipping in a Boston fishing vessel bound to Newfoundland, and on his arrival there, was very courteously received by Kirk, who made him many fair promises; but he soon discovered that Kirk, even if he had the will, had not the means to aid him effectually, so he returned to Boston in one of Kirk's vessels. He spent most of the following winter in Boston,* but towards Spring a number of the merchants of that place furnished him with supplies to the value of five hundred pounds for a trading voyage to the eastward, and he set forth again in the same little craft in which he had returned from Newfoundland. The master of this vessel was a stranger, and her crew consisted of five of La Tour's Frenchmen and five English of Boston. In May, 1646, the latter returned to their homes with a pitiful story of wrong and suffering. They told that, when La Tour reached Cape Sable, which was in the heart of winter, he conspired with the master and his own Frenchmen, and forced the English sailors out of the vessel, shooting one of them himself in the face with a pistol. They said that, after wandering up and down for fifteen days, they found some Indians, who gave them a shallop and victuals and an Indian pilot, so that they were enabled to reach Boston.

It is impossible at this distance of time to determine what degree of credit is to be given to this story, which, if true, would prove La Tour to have been one of the basest of men. It rests on the authority of Governor Winthrop,

* Winthrop says that during the winter La Tour was entertained by Mr. Samuel Maverick, at Nottles Island.

one of the most faithful and conscientious gentlemen of his age, but he, of course, had to rely on the statements of the sailors themselves, who alleged that they had been the victims of La Tour's cruelty. There is nothing to be said in favor of this story, except that it rests on direct evidence. Against it may be put the previous character of La Tour, who had so conducted himself during the forty years of his residence in Acadia, that even when he appeared to be absolutely ruined, the merchants with whom he traded in Boston, did not lose confidence in his integrity. Add to that, that for many years after this alleged outrage he lived in Acadia, that he stood so high in the favor of the English government as to receive almost unparalleled gifts at its hands, and we are forced to conclude that this sailors' story of outrage and piracy, which has given some writers an opportunity of blackening La Tour's character, was merely invented by the sailors to justify their own mutinous conduct, and to win sympathy for the sufferings they had brought upon themselves by their own acts.

La Tour arrived at Quebec on the 8th August, 1646, and on his landing on the following day was received with great honor by the governor, M. Montmagny. Salutes were fired; he was lodged in the fort, and the Governor gave him precedence, a distinction which he accepted the first day, but afterwards declined. Nothing, perhaps, could better illustrate the looseness of the French system of administration than the fact that such honors were given by the governor of Canada to a man who, in Acadia, had been declared an outlaw by royal edict. But in France it was not merit, but influence and the use of money, which won the favor of those in authority, and the bastile stood always open to receive men whose only crime was that they had become distasteful to some great personage with influence enough to obtain an order for their imprisonment.

For the next four years La Tour was absent from Acadia, and during two of them at least he was in Canada. We get glimpses of his life from time to time in the journal of the Jesuit Superior,* which has been preserved in the archives of the seminary at Quebec. In one entry he is recorded as accompanying father De Quen to baptize M. de Chavigry's child. In another, he is mentioned as conveying father Bailloquet to Montreal in his shallop. He was one of those who took part in the procession of the feast of the Holy Sacrament in 1648. In that year he is also mentioned as having gone forth to engage in the war which was being waged against the Iroquois. Those were exciting years in Canada, and there was abundant scope there for the talents of a man so bold and enterprising as La Tour. He continued to engage in the fur trade, and in the prosecution of that profitable pursuit he is said to have visited the shores of Hudson's Bay, that vast ocean gulf which afterwards gave its name to the great Company by which for two centuries the fur trade of North America was mainly controlled.

Charnisay, having succeeded in driving his rival out of Acadia, may be said to have attained the summit of his hopes. He had the whole of Western Acadia to himself, and with establishments at Port Royal, Penobscot and St. John, could control the entire fur trade of a region nearly half as large as the kingdom of France. The territory in the possession of Denys was but a narrow strip on the Gulf of St. Lawrence; all the rest of Acadia was Charnisay's own. The proper occupation and defence of his three forts required him usually to maintain three hundred

* This interesting journal was published in 1871.

men, and demanded likewise large supplies of food and ammunition. His principal establishment was at Port Royal, where most of the inhabitants, brought out from France by Isaac De Razilly, as well as those brought by Charnisay himself, were settled. There he had built mills for the grinding of grain, and had dyked the marshes to increase their fertility by the exclusion of the tide. He had two large farms at Port Royal, which were cultivated on his own account, and he also engaged somewhat in shipbuilding. During his occupation of Port Royal he built there two vessels of about seventy tons each, besides five pinnaces and several shallops. These were probably the first vessels built in Acadia. These enterprises, together with the care of such small outlying settlements as La Have and St. Anne, must have kept Charnisay fully employed while in Acadia, and made him the very reverse of an idle man. Yet he might have done far more for Acadia than he did, had he only been content to relinquish warlike pursuits and devote himself wholly to the work of trade and colonization.

In the Autumn of 1645 Charnisay paid another visit to France, where he carried to the Queen Regent the news of his success in Acadia. He was received by her with great favor, and received from her a letter acknowledging his great zeal in opposing La Tour, who was accused in it of a desire to subvert the King's authority in Acadia. Accompanying it was another letter, purporting to come from the King himself—then a mere child—in which La Tour was charged with a design to deliver up his fort to foreigners. The King ordered a vessel to be equipped to bring Charnisay to Acadia, to which he returned laden with princely favors and cheered by the smiles of royalty.

The treaty which the authorities of Massachusetts had

made in 1644 with M. Marie, Charnisay's agent, had never been ratified by the latter, although it had received the sanction of the Commissioners of the United Colonies. When Captain Bridges was sent by them in 1645 to Charnisay for his confirmation of the articles of peace—although he entertained the messenger with all state and courtesy—he refused to subscribe the articles until certain differences between himself and the people of New England were composed. He accordingly wrote back a letter, in which he accused the Commissioners of desiring to gain time, and said that if their messenger had been furnished with power to have treated with him, he had no doubt that they could have come to an agreement. He, however, added that he would postpone any further action towards redressing his wrongs until the Spring, when he expected to hear from the Commissioners again. When the General Court of Massachusetts next met, they took this answer into consideration, and agreed to send the deputy governor, Mr. Dudley, Mr. Hawthorne and Major Denison to meet Charnisay at Penobscot, with full power to make a treaty which should cover all the points in dispute between them and the governor of Acadia. But when Charnisay was informed by letter of this resolution, he sent back word that he was now convinced the people of New England seriously desired peace, as he did himself, and that he accounted himself highly honored that they should propose to send such principal men of theirs to him. But he desired to spare them that labor, and he would send two or three of his men to Boston in August to make a treaty. This proposal was not ungrateful to Governor Winthrop and the magistrates of Boston, for the deputy governor, Mr. Dudley, owing to his advanced age, was scarcely counted fit for the voyage to Penobscot, yet his experience and closeness at a bargain were deemed desirable in dealing with Charnisay.

On Monday, the 20th August, 1646, M. Marie, M. Louis and Charnisay's secretary arrived at Boston in a pinnace, and were met at the water side by Major Gibbons, who conducted them to his residence, where they were to lodge. After public worship was over, the Governor sent a guard of musketeers to attend them to his house, where they were entertained with wine and sweetmeats, and he afterwards accompanied them home to their lodgings. The next morning they repaired to the Governor and delivered him their commission, which was in the form of an open letter delivered to the Governor and magistrates. Although they lodged with Major Gibbons, their diet was provided at the ordinary, where the magistrates were accustomed to eat when attending the court, and the Governor always honored them with his presence at meals. Every morning they called at the house of the Governor, who attended them to the place of meeting, and in the evening either he or one of the commissioners accompanied them to their lodgings. Thus everything was done with due form and ceremony. It was the third day at noon before the commissioners of the United Colonies could be got together, but from that time to the close of the negotiations the work was carried on with all diligence. Charnisay's representatives laid before them the great injuries which he had sustained from Captain Hawkins and his men when they went to aid La Tour, and sought to make the commissioners responsible for the damage. But they denied that they had given Hawkins any commission, or even permission, to do what he had done. They said they had only given La Tour assistance to conduct his ship home, according to the request contained in the commission of the vice-admiral of France. And, as for what Hawkins and his men had done beyond their commission, in palliation of that they produced Charnisay's own letter, sent by Captain Bailey, in which he stated that the King of France had laid all the blame on the vice-admiral for those occurrences, and that the King had enjoined him not to break with the people of New England because of what Hawkins had done. The commissioners also pleaded the peace formerly made with M. Marie, without any reservation of these things. The Frenchmen answered that, although the King had remitted his own interest, yet he had not intended to deprive Charnisay of his own private satisfaction. For two days the commissioners battled over this point, and it looked at one time as if the negotiations would break off altogether; but in the end the Puritans proved the better hands at a bargain. The French commissioners at first claimed eight thousand pounds as damages, but afterwards they said they did not stand upon the value. They were willing to accept a very small sum in satisfaction of the claim if the commissioners for New England would acknowledge any guilt on the part of their government. Finally, a compromise was reached, to which both parties were willing to agree. The New England commissioners agreed to accept the French commissioners answer in satisfaction of those things which they had charged upon Charnisay. The French commissioners, on their part, accepted the answer of the New England commissioners, so as to clear the government of Massachusetts of what had been charged against them. But, as they could not excuse what Captain Hawkins and the other volunteers from New England had done, the commissioners agreed to send a small present to Charnisay in satisfaction of that, and so all injuries and demands were to be remitted and a final peace to be concluded.

Fortunately for the thrifty Puritans they were not required to disburse any money on this occasion, nor did the present to be given to Charnisay come from the general fund, but from the private estate of Governor Winthrop. Some months before a certain Captain Cromwell, one of those redoubtable rovers of the sea, trained in the school of Drake, had visited Boston. He had just come from a cruise in the Spanish Main, where he had captured several Spanish vessels bound to Spain from Mexico. In one of them was a sedan chair of very elegant make, which the Viceroy of Mexico was sending home to his sister in Spain. Cromwell had presented this chair to Governor Winthrop, and the Governor now offered it to Charnisay's commissioners, and it was accepted as a satisfaction of all claims against the people of New England. Winthrop was almost as well pleased to get rid of this chair as M. Marie was to receive it, for it was altogether too fine an article to be of any use to him. The grave Governor of Massachusetts would have cut but a sorry figure in a vehicle made for the use of some ancient Spanish duenna.

The agreement between the representatives of Charnisay and the commissioners of the United Colonies having been signed by both parties, M. Marie and his companions took their departure under a salute from Boston, Charlestown and Castle Island. They had been treated most courteously during their stay, but were glad enough, no doubt, to get away from a place where a man did not dare to appear on the streets on the Sabbath, unless he chanced to be going to public worship. The peace thus concluded was an excellent measure in all respects, and removed any apprehensions of further trouble. It enabled the people of New England to pursue their peaceful avocations without apprehensions of being molested, and it gave Charnisay—

if he so desired—an opportunity of improving his Acadian possessions in safety. Yet, although the peace was kept, an event took place the very next year which put its continuance in some peril. In March a vessel of eighty tons was fitted out at Boston by one Captain Dobson for a trading voyage to the eastward. Her papers were made out for the Gulf of St. Lawrence, but being caught in a storm, and having lost a boat, they put into harbor at Cape Sable, and commenced to trade with the Indians. Charnisay heard of their presence, and sent twenty men overland from Port Royal, who succeeded in capturing the vessel and her crew. Both vessel and crew were taken to Port Royal. The ship and her cargo, which were worth a thousand pounds, were confiscated, and the men were put into two old shallops and sent home, arriving at Boston in May. The merchants, who had lost by this venture, were very indignant, and complained to the court for redress, offering to fit out an armed ship to attack Charnisay's vessels, but the court thought it neither safe nor expedient to begin war with the French, especially as they could not charge any manifest wrong upon Charnisay, for they had told him that if any New Englanders traded within his territory, they should do so at their own peril. The seizure of the ship was therefore not an unlawful act, but in accordance with the common practice of the times among civilized nations. Besides, Governor Winthrop thought there must be an overruling providence in the affair, otherwise Charnisay could not have seized a ship, so well fitted, for she was double manned, nor could wise men have lost her so foolishly.

In February, 1647, Charnisay received another mark of the royal favor. A commission was issued to him under the sign manual of Louis XIV., confirming and re-establishing him in the office of governor and lieutenant-general for the King in Acadia. This commission recites the services of Charnisay in Acadia, stating that he had for fourteen years been employed in the conversion of the Indians and in the establishing of the royal authority. It credits him with having built a seminary, carried out Capuchins from France to teach the Indian children, and with expelling foreign religionists from the fort of Penobscot, and with recovering by force of arms and placing under obedience the fort of the River St. John, which La Tour had occupied, and, by open rebellion, was striving to retain against the royal will. This commission, besides making him governor of Acadia from the St. Lawrence to Virginia,* gave him the exclusive privilege of the fur trade over all that vast territory, and the use of the mines and minerals to him and his heirs. Thus Charnisay, after his long struggle with his enemies, stood the undisputed master of Acadia, both by possession and by the highest documentary title which his King could give him. He was more absolutely a ruler in Acadia than even the French King was in his own dominions, for he had no council to trouble him with advice, no Mazarin to govern him, no Queen Mother to impose her wishes upon him. Well may his breast have swelled with pride as he contemplated his own sudden rise to fame, fortune and authority.

Only one thing more was needed to complete the work he had begun, and that was the expulsion of Nicholas Denys from Acadia. Denys had come to Acadia in 1632 with Isaac De Razilly, and for some time had been engaged in the shore fishery at La Have. When Isaac De Razilly

---

*Virginia in this commission meant the British possessions in North America generally. The territòry between 34 and 45 north latitude was all termed Virginia in the grants made by King James I. to the North and South Virginia Companies in 1606.

died he was nominated by the Company of New France Governor of the whole coast of the Bay of St. Lawrence and the isles adjacent, from Cape Canso to Cape Rosiers. Being a man of much enterprise and business capacity, he speedily built up a profitable fishing business and erected two small forts, one at Chedabucto and the other at St. Peter's, in the Island of Cape Breton. He also had a fishing establishment at Miscou, at the entrance of the Bay Chaleur, where the Jesuits had established a mission in 1635. Charnisay, armed with his new commission from the King, captured Denys' forts, seized his goods, broke up his fishing establishments, and ruined his settlers. Denys and his family had to leave the country, and seek refuge in Quebec. He deserved better treatment at the hands of Charnisay, for they had been companions in youth and friends. But all those early associations were forgotten. Any one who ventured to carry on trade in Acadia, Charnisay counted an enemy, and treated him as such, and so La Tour, Denys and the New England colonists necessarily fell under his displeasure, and felt the weight of his resentment.

But there is one enemy which no man can escape, and that is Death. The most formidable walls and battlements will not keep him out. His footsteps are sometimes heard, even in the palaces of Kings, and the sword falls from the hand of earth's greatest conquerors when he appears. And so Charnisay, the victor in the struggle against his mortal enemies, was vanquished at length by a mightier hand than his own. In 1650 he was drowned in the river of Port Royal. Neither history nor tradition give us any further particulars of his fate than is contained in these few words. But if it is true, as some say, that a man who goes down to death through the dark waters sees before him in an instantaneous mental vision a panorama of his whole life, then surely deep anguish must have smitten the soul of the dying Charnisay—for he had been hard and cruel and revengeful. He had shown himself to be destitute of pity for his kind. No generous thought for his enemies had ever found a place in his heart. And above the shadowy forms of those he had wronged and murdered, the face of one victim must have impressed him with a deeper remorse than all the rest, that of the heroic, noble and faithful lady La Tour.

If Charnisay had any friends when living, none of them were to be found after his death. Most men like to speak gently of the dead, but no one had anything but evil to tell of him. Denys, his contemporary—who knew him well—only speaks of his rapacity, tyranny and cruelty. His influence at the French court, which must have been great, rested on such a slender foundation of merit that it did not survive him for a single day. He who had stood so high in the royal favor was, a few months after his death, branded as a false accuser in an official document signed by the King's own hand. The whole fruits of his life-long contentions and schemes were either wasted or were gathered by his enemies.

CHAPTER XI.

LA TOUR RETURNS TO ACADIA.

THE news of Charnisay's death seems to have reached La Tour very soon after the event took place, and the exiled lord of Acadia lost no time in taking advantage of an occurrence which again placed wealth and honor within his grasp. He made all haste to reach France, where for so many years he had not dared to show his face, and went vigorously to work to undo all that his dead rival had done in regard to the affairs of Acadia. At the French court in these days a living man with a good cause was not always certain of success; but La Tour, no doubt, wisely judged that such a man ranged against a dead rival, whose cause was bad, could scarcely fail. Nor was he deceived, for he speedily obtained from the French government an acquittal of the charges which had been preferred against him by Charnisay, and, what was of more value, he obtained a new commission as governor and lieutenant-general for the King in Acadia. This document, which was in the form of letters patent from the King of France, was dated the 25th February, 1651. It recited that La Tour had been appointed and established governor by Louis XIII., and had for forty-two years devoted himself there to the conversion of the savages, and the establishment of the royal authority; that he had constructed two forts, and contributed to the extent of his power to the instruction of the savages, had by his courage and valor driven the foreign sectaries from these forts, which they had taken possession of to the prejudice of the rights and authority of the Crown, and would have continued to do so had he not been hindered by Charles De Menou, Sieur d'Aulnay Charnisay, who had favored his enemies in accusations and pretences, which they had not been able to verify, and of which the said La Tour had been absolved. The commission then proceeded to confirm to him the government of Acadia and all his territorial rights in it. It gave him power to appoint officers, to enact laws and ordinances, and to make peace and war. It gave him all the mines and minerals in the country, reserving only a royalty to the Crown, and gave him also the exclusive right to the fur trade. Finally, it empowered him to seize and confiscate to his own use the vessels and merchandise of any who sought to infringe upon his exclusive privileges. Thus, with his character cleared of the clouds which had rested upon it, and endowed with the amplest powers that his sovereign could bestow, La Tour stood once more the absolute master of Acadia.

Armed with this patent, La Tour returned to Acadia, and in September, 1651, took possession of his old fort at the mouth of the St. John, and resumed the trade with the Indians, which had been so profitable in former years. The widow of Charnisay was still living in Acadia with her children, and she seems to have made no opposition to La Tour's re-occupation of his fort, but it was impossible that she could view without alarm his pretensions to the governship of the whole Province. In June, 1651, the King had issued a letter and commission to the Sieur de La Fosse, authorizing him to administer the property and government of Charnisay, but his widow seems to have thought that some more powerful protector was necessary, in order to enable her to enjoy her estates in peace. Accordingly, in February, 1652, she entered into an arrangement with the

Duke De Vendome,* grand master and superintendent of the navigation and commerce of France, by which she sought to enlist his rank and influence in her cause. By this it was agreed that Vendome should aid in recovering her forts from La Tour, Denys and others, who had usurped possession of her territory, and, in consideration of the expense to which he would be put in carrying out this arrangement, she agreed that Vendome, his heirs and assigns should be co-seigniors of Acadia with her and her children. This agreement was confirmed by the King by letters patent, dated December, 1652, but as Vendome never paid anything under it, the claims of his heir to territorial rights in Acadia were set aside by a judgment of the French Council of State in 1703.

In fact, almost before this agreement was completed—certainly before there was any opportunity of it becoming operative—another arrangement had been made which rendered the interposition of Vendome wholly unnecessary. On the 24th February, 1653, a document was signed at the fort of Port Royal which put an end at once and forever to the strife between the families of La Tour and Charnisay in Acadia. This was a marriage contract which was entered into between Charnisay's widow and La Tour, the end and principal design of the intended marriage being, as the contract expressed it, "The peace and tranquillity of the country, and concord and union between the two families." This contract was drawn with elaborate care, as was fitting in a document which was intended to reconcile and settle so many conflicting claims and interests, for both parties to this marriage had children by their former mar-

* Cæsar Duc de Vendome was a reputed son of Henry IV. by his mistress, Gabrielle d'Estrees. He was born in 1594, and in 1598, on his betrothal to Françoise de Lorraine, daughter and heiress of the Duc de Mercœur, was made legitimate and created Duc de Vendome.

riages.* The creditors and associates of Charnisay had to be provided for, and the children which might be the result of the new union had also to be taken into account. La Tour endowed his future wife, for her lifetime, with his fort and habitation on the River St. John, and also gave her for a marriage present the sum of thirty thousand livres tournois, which circumstance shows that he was then in easy circumstances, and turning his monopoly of the fur trade in Acadia to profitable account. The marriage contract was witnessed by father Leonard de Charteres, vice-prefect and custos of the mission, by brother Jean Desnouse and by three other witnesses, so that no formality seems to have been wanting to give the alliance that solemn character which the importance of the interests involved appeared to demand.

Thus, after so many years of conflict, the two families, whose feuds had been so disastrous to Acadia, were united, and their differences disposed of in such a way that it was impossible they should ever again become occasion for strife. La Tour had then passed his sixtieth year, and after a life of much viscissitudes must have rejoiced at the prospect of peace, which his changed circumstances seemed to offer. But fortune had still something left in store for him as surprising as anything that he had before experienced at her hands.

Hitherto the wars in Acadia had been conducted by soldiers who, whatever their other qualities, were at least at

*La Tour had two or more sons by his first marriage, but they seem to have been educated in France, and they never took any part in Acadian affairs. La Tour's oldest daughter was born in 1626, so that these sons were probably grown up at the time of his second marriage. We may presume that they were brought up by the Huguenot relatives of their mother at Rochelle, and that, as by the marriage contract their father's property in France was especially set apart for them, they lived and died in that country. Charnisay's eldest son was Joseph de Menou, who was born in 1636, and was killed in the service of the King prior to 1686. Charnisay was twice married.

home in the tented field and accustomed to the sounds of battle. La Tour and Charnisay had contended against each other like nobles of the medieval times, with hundreds of armed retainers and for a princely prize. But it was reserved for this period to see a new element introduced into the wars of Acadia, and to behold a man who, without warlike experience or the courage of a soldier, undertook to paralyze the might of the sword by writs of ejectment, and to expel the bold nobles who occupied the forts of Acadia by the efforts of catchpoles and constables. Such attempts would have been ridiculous a few years before, when the sword was in every man's hand, and when even a royal mandate was of no effect unless backed by sufficient force to compel its execution. But the times had changed since those brave days, and a long exemption from the evils of civil war had produced its effects even on the bold and vigilant La Tour. His fort at St. John had become merely a trading post, and he himself a merchant. Port Royal was similarly held by La Verdure on behalf of the children of the deceased Charnisay, and trading posts were maintained by La Tour at Penobscot and Cape Sable.

It was at this period that Emmanuel Le Borgne first appeared in Acadia. He had been a merchant of Rochelle, and had made advances to Charnisay to the extent of two hundred and sixty thousand livres prior to 1650. He appears to have obtained judgment from the Courts in his favor for that sum, and, armed with this authority, came out to Acadia in 1653 to take possession of Charnisay's estate. When he arrived at Port Royal he appears to have became impressed with the idea that he might seize the whole of Acadia, Charnisay having claimed nothing less. Filled with this design, he commenced active operations against Nicholas Denys, who was carrying on the shore fishery at La Have. Denys in that same year had obtained a grant from the Company of New France of all the territory from Canso to Cape Rosiers. By virtue of the authority contained in this grant he was busily engaged in founding a settlement at St. Peter's, in the Island of Cape Breton, when Le Borgne attacked him. Denys states that his people were then on shore clearing land, but that he himself had gone to St. Anne's to see the harbor, when sixty of Le Borgne's men landed and made his people at St. Peter's all prisoners. They also took possession of his vessel, and of all it contained. Then twenty-five of Le Borgne's men were sent to lie in ambush on the road, which Denys would take on coming from St. Anne's. Denys, who had only three unarmed men with him, was captured by this detachment and carried to Port Royal. As they passed La Have, on their return with their booty and prisoners, Le Borgne's men burnt down the establishment which M. Denys had there, not even sparing the chapel, which, with the fort and buildings, was destroyed. Denys was placed in irons and confined in a dungeon at Port Royal; but he was liberated before the end of the year, and returned to France, to complain of the outrages of which he had been made the victim. On the 30th January, 1654, he received a commission from the King, confirming him in the grants made to him by the Company of New France, and appointing him King's governor and lieutenant-general "in all the country, territory, coasts and confines of the great Bay of St. Lawrence, beginning from Cape Canso unto Cape Rosiers, the Islands of Newfoundland, of Cape Breton, St. John and other islands adjacent." In the Spring of 1654 Denys returned to St. Peter's, where he found his fort in charge of an officer, whom Le Borgne had placed there a short time before, and this person quietly surrendered it to Denys on the King's commission and the grant of the Company being produced. Denys then sent these documents by a trusty messenger to Port Royal, so that Le Borgne might be informed of their contents and govern himself accordingly.

Le Borgne, while these things were passing at St. Peter's, had his mind fixed on another exploit—no less than the capture of Fort Latour. La Tour himself—whose trade relations were rather with New England than with France—had been considerably embarrassed by a prohibition of the General Court of Massachusetts in 1653 against the transport of provisions either to the French or Dutch. La Tour complained of this prohibition being applied to him, and the order was so far relaxed in his favor that a small vessel was allowed to go from Boston with flour and provisions for his fort at St. John. In the summer of 1654 he was again short of provisions, and his supplies from Boston had not arrived. Of this fact Le Borgne was aware, and he conceived the idea of making the necessities of La Tour the means of capturing his fort. He went to Fort Latour with two vessels filled with men, intending to seize that place, under pretence of carrying La Tour provisions. But before he had been enabled to put this nefarious design into execution a shallop arrived from Port Royal in hot haste to inform him of what Denys had been doing at St. Anne's. Le Borgne was utterly confounded by this intelligence, and, learning that the messenger of Denys was still at Port Royal with the original grant and commission in his possession, he resolved at once to return and rob him of them by force, so that Denys might have no authority to show for his presence at St. Anne's when he next went to attack him, which he proposed to do at once. Such was the plan which Le Borgne conceived for the purpose of circumventing M. Denys, and an attempt would, no doubt, have been made to carry it out had not the French in Acadia, in the midst of their petty quarrels, been suddenly summoned to face the greatest danger that had ever menaced their colony.

On the very next day after the departure of Le Borgne from Fort Latour, an English fleet appeared in front of it, and summoned it to surrender. Two years before, the English Parliament had declared war against the Dutch, and the first blow was struck by Blake at the naval power of Holland. The jealousies between the English colonists of Massachusetts and the Dutch of New York, suggested the idea of transferring the scene of warfare from the Old World to the New, and the lord protector, Oliver Cromwell, sent out four armed vessels to Boston, with a view to organize an expedition against the Dutch of Manhattan Island. These vessels did not arrive at Boston until the beginning of June, 1654, and a few days later news came that peace had been concluded between England and Holland. Preparations had, however, by that time been well advanced, and five hundred men enlisted in Massachusetts, under the command of Major Robert Sedgwick, of Charleston, a military officer of some reputation in the colony. Those who had the expedition in charge thought that it would be a pity to let so fine an armament go to waste for want of employment, and where could such a force be employed to better advantage than against the French in Acadia? The men of Massachusetts were not long in deciding that it was their duty to dispossess their Popish neighbors to the north-east, and Sedgwick and the commander of the fleet readily fell in with their plans. This was the reason why the English fleet so suddenly appeared before Fort Latour.

La Tour had already received so many buffets from fortune, that even his patience must have been exhausted by this last blow. But he accepted the inevitable with dignity and firmness; his fort was entirely unprepared for an attack; he was short of provisions, and so he yielded gracefully to his fate and surrendered the stronghold which he could not defend. Almost before Le Borgne's ships had reached Port Royal the English flag was waving over Fort Latour.

Le Borgne, in the midst of his plans for the recapture of Denys, was suddenly startled by the appearance of the English fleet in Port Royal Basin. To a real soldier the prospect of an encounter with an enemy, however superior in strength, is seldom unwelcome, but to a man like Le Borgne, who was waging war by writs and ejectments, and undertaking the capture of fortresses on commercial principles, such a sight was sufficiently alarming. Still, when summoned to surrender, he replied with a boldness which he could scarcely have felt, and placed the English under the necessity of attacking him. The men that he sent out against them were repulsed and put to flight, and Le Borgne, finding that his vocation was not that of a soldier, resolved to capitulate. Advances to that end were made on the 15th August; on the 16th the articles were completed and signed on board the Admiral's ship, Auguste, and on the following day Port Royal was surrendered.

Le Borgne's ship, the Chateauford, had been lying in the Basin when the English appeared, and was promptly captured. Her armament made it impossible to mistake her character, yet in the articles of capitulation, Le Borgne, who, before and afterwards, claimed the lordship of all Acadia, sought to appear merely as a private citizen and merchant, and in that capacity endeavoured to obtain the restoration of his ship and property. Sedgwick was not to be so easily imposed upon, and, although he promised to take the matter into consideration, he restored Le Borgne nothing. La Verdure, by whom the capitulation was made as commandant for the King, obtained honorable terms for his soldiers and transportation for them to France. He also received favorable consideration for the children of Charnisay, who had much property at Port Royal. The inhabitants were permitted to remain, with liberty of conscience, and to enjoy their property, or to sell it, and return to France. The missionary priests were also permitted to remain in the country, if they chose, provided they lived two or three leagues from the fort. Most of the inhabitants appear to have availed themselves of this permission to remain in Acadia, which now, with all its forts, passed into the hands of the English. Sedgwick returned to Massachusetts with his booty, leaving Captain John Leverett at Port Royal as governor and commander of the forts of St. John, Port Royal and Penobscot.

CHAPTER XII.

THE ENGLISH IN ACADIA.

THE seizure of Acadia was very gratifying to the people of New England, who had looked with alarm on the growth of a foreign power on their northern borders, and their consciences do not seem to have been troubled by the fact that there was no state of war existing between England and France at the time to justify the act. Cromwell, who was then in the zenith of his power, seems to have approved the measure, and the officers by whom it had been accomplished appear to have been filled with a zealous desire to make Acadia a permanent English colony. A government had been promptly organized for the new Province, one of its first regulations being that no one should trade with the savages but such as were deputed to do so by those in authority, it being considered that those who enjoyed this trade should pay enough for the privilege to maintain the garrison. The General Court of Massachusetts was asked to enforce this law, so that persons convicted of any breach of it should be punished in Massachusetts, as if they had been taken in Acadia. It was also asked to pledge itself to furnish assistance to the English in Acadia, in case they were attacked and needed help.

At this time Cardinal Mazarin, then the virtual ruler of France, was endeavoring to conclude a treaty of commerce with England, and such a treaty was made at Westminster on the 2nd November, 1655. The twenty-fifth article of this treaty stated that the forts of Penobscot, St. John, Port Royal, and La Have were claimed by France as forts in Acadia, and the matter was referred to the consideration of commissioners whose appointment was authorized by the treaty. No commissioners were named under this authority until 1662.

La Tour, in the mean time, finding himself at the age of sixty-two without a home in Acadia, bethought himself of a bold move for the purpose of retrieving his fortunes. He hastened to England, and with all the plausibility and address of which he was master, laid his case before Cromwell, showing that as co-grantee and heir of his father he was entitled to a large territory in Acadia under the English Crown, through Sir William Alexander. The result was a triumphant success for the Acadian diplomatist. On the 9th August, 1656, La Tour in conjunction with Thomas Temple and William Crowne, received from Cromwell a grant of an immense tract of territory in Acadia, extending from what is now known as Lunenburg in Nova Scotia, to the River St. George in Maine, including the whole coast of the Bay of Fundy on both sides and one hundred leagues inland, a territory considerably larger than the island of Great Britain.* As the language of this grant seemed to make a distinction between the boundaries of Acadia and Nova Scotia, it opened the way to all the disputes which followed as to the proper limits of that Province.

In making this grant, Cromwell seems to have had in view the restoration to La Tour of the very territory

* The words of the grant are as follows:—" The country and territory called Acadia and part of the country called Nova Scotia, from Merliguesche on the east coast to the port and Cape of Laheve, along the sea coast to Cape Sable, and from thence to a certain port called Port Latour, and now named Port L'Esmeron, and from thence along the coasts and islands to Cape Forchu, and from thence to the Cape and River St. Mary along the sea coast to Port Royal, and from thence along the coast to the head of the Bay, and from thence along the said Bay to the fort of St. John, and from thence all along the coast of Pentagoet and the River St. George in Mescourus on the confines of New England on the west coast, and one hundred leagues inward."

granted to him and his deceased father by Sir William Alexander, and while he was able thus to avail himself of La Tour's knowledge of the country to advance its settlement, he was also free to reward Temple and Crowne for their services to his cause.* The only consideration exacted from the grantees in return for so rich a heritage was the payment of a small annual rental in beaver skins. The grantees had the absolute control of the whole trade of the country, and might confiscate all vessels found trading without their permission. No person could be appointed governor of a fort who had not been approved by the Protector, and none but Protestants were to be permitted to reside in the territory granted. This last provision seems never to have been enforced against the French Acadians.

Temple received the appointment of governor of the forts at St. John and Penobscot, and early in 1657 arrived in Acadia with an order to Captain Leverett for their delivery to him. Temple then commenced those large expenditures for the improvement of his territory, which involved him so deeply that they ended in his ruin. La Tour sold out his rights in Acadia to Temple and Crowne and retired into private life, leaving to other shoulders the burthen of an authority which he had borne so long. No doubt he was sagacious enough to foresee that serious disputes were certain to arise between England and France with regard to the possession of Acadia.

The first movement came from the Company of New France, which was deeply interested in the question. In January, 1658, they sent Le Borgne to England to urge the immediate restoration of Acadia, and King Louis wrote

---

*Temple was a Colonel in the army. In the Memoirs of Thomas Hollis he is called a brother to Sir William Temple, but I doubt the statement. Crowne was a minister, and the father of John Crowne the Dramatist, who was born in Acadia.

to Bourdeaux, his Ambassador in London, requesting him to support this demand. The time seemed propitious for such a step, for in the previous March, France and England had concluded an alliance against Spain. But Cromwell would not listen to any proposal to surrender Acadia, and the negotiations fell to the ground.

But Le Borgne did not trust to negotiation alone. In February, 1658, he sent his son Emmanuel to Acadia with fifty men, with orders to occupy La Have and rebuild the fort there. With young Le Borgne went one Guilbaut, a trader of Rochelle, who was his partner in business. They reached La Have safely, and in a short time constructed a small palisaded fort. But the English soon got notice of their arrival, and a force was sent to dislodge them. Le Borgne, who seems to have resembled his father in character, fled to the woods panic stricken, and left his partner to bear the brunt of the English attack. Guilbaut, however, speedily became conscious that the fort could not be held, and offered to surrender it and leave Acadia on condition that he and his men should be allowed to carry off their property. Soon after this agreement was carried out, Le Borgne was constrained by hunger to emerge from the woods and surrender himself to the English. They carried him off to Boston, and from thence to London. The King of France, through his ambassador, complained of the treatment Le Borgne had received, and demanded his release and reparation for the injury done to him. Before this remonstrance reached England, the Lord Protector had breathed his last. Le Borgne was released and permitted to return to France, but his goods were not restored.

Temple made the fort at Penobscot his headquarters in Acadia, but maintained garrisons at St. John and Port

Royal. Fort Latour, at St. John, seems to have been abandoned at this time, and a smaller fort erected at Jemseg, up the St. John River, that position being regarded as more convenient for the Indian trade. The peltry trade of Acadia was then very large and profitable, and a large amount was also obtained for fishing and trading licenses on the coast. No doubt his speculations in Acadia would have turned out well, had the life of Cromwell been spared; but his death involved him in no end of trouble. Charles II. was restored to the throne in May 1660, and Temple's possessions in Acadia were at once made the subject of attack by two sets of claimants—the Crown of France and private parties in England. The most dangerous of the latter was one Thomas Elliot, whose claims to Acadia were reported on by the Council of State in 1661, and with him Temple was finally obliged to compromise by an annual payment of six hundred pounds. He was obliged, also, to go to England to defend his interests, one Captain Breedon being appointed governor of the Province in December, 1661. We have a glimpse of Breedon's administration in the report of a meeting of the Commissioners of the United Colonies of New England at Boston in September, 1662. He made his appearance before them and exhibited a complaint against certain Mohawk Indians for killing some of his trading Indians and taking others captive, to the number of about eighty persons, and also for killing the cattle and robbing the storehouses of the colonists. He asked the commissioners for aid against such outrages, and they permitted him to enlist such a number of volunteers as might be necessary to enable him to obtain satisfaction.

Breedon's term of government was brief, for the same year Temple returned to Acadia with the commission of the governor of Nova Scotia in his possession. On that visit he also obtained what was of considerably less value, the title of knight baronet. He appears to have received these favors from the weak and worthless Charles, more by reason of his wit than from the justice of his claims. A very characteristic anecdote of the intercourse of Temple with the King is told in the Memoirs of the venerable Thomas Hollis, whose name will be ever dear to the students of Harvard. During the Protectorate, the Massachusetts authorities had coined a quantity of silver money —the well known pine-tree shillings. Charles was highly incensed at this invasion of his prerogative, and in the course of a conversation with Temple on the affairs of Massachusetts, abused the colonists roundly. Temple presented some of the money to the King, who, observing the device of the pine-tree on the coin, asked him what tree it was. Temple wittily replied that it was the Royal Oak, which had preserved his majesty's life. This explanation quite mollified the King, and he dismissed the affair, calling his presumptuous subjects in Massachusetts "a parcel of honest dogs."

In 1661 the French King renewed his demands for the restoration of Acadia. In the following year M. d'Estrates, the French Ambassador in London, desired that commissioners might be named, agreeably to the 25th article of the treaty of 1655, to discuss the title to Acadia, and this was done, but no immediate result was attained. The people of New England were bitterly opposed to the restoration of Acadia, and used all their influence to prevent such a result. Negotiations on the subject of Acadia were still in progress between the two Crowns in 1665, when the war between England and Holland commenced, which was shortly followed by a war with France.

In 1664, while these negotiations were going on, Charles II. granted to his brother, the Duke of York, all the territory from the St. Croix westward to Pemaquid, and from the head of the river of that name northward by way of the Kennebec to the St. Lawrence. This grant, which was termed the "Duke of York's property," or "the territory of Sagadahock," was a serious infringement on the rights of Temple and Crowne, whose territory extended westward to the River St. George. As matters turned out, the making of this grant had no practical effect on Temple's rights, but the circumstance must have warned him how little he could depend on the good faith of the English King.

The Company of New France, which, as we have seen, had been founded by Richelieu in 1627, had by this time fallen into decay. The results it had achieved bore no sort of proportion to the magnificent promises with which it had commenced its work. More than half of the original hundred partners were dead, and it was evident that those that survived were not in a position to do much for New France. For these reasons M. d'Avaugour, Governor of Canada, persuaded the King to dissolve the Company of New France. Accordingly, in February, 1663, the Company surrendered all its rights and property in New France to the King, while he, by an edict made the same year, revoked all grants made by the Company of lands which had not been cleared, or should remain uncleared, six months from the date of the edict.

But while one huge monopoly was thus got rid of, another far more powerful and dangerous was brought into existence. This was the Company of the West Indies, which was established by a royal edict of the 24th May, 1664. Its domains extended over both hemispheres, and included Acadia and the whole of New France. It had a monopoly of trade granted to it for forty years, and was endowed with most of the privileges of sovereignty, including the power to wage war and to make peace. A singular instance of the rights assumed by this powerful Company is furnished by the fact that, in 1666, it undertook to arrange with the English West India Company and the proprietors of lands in America for the liberty of trade and neutrality during the war between the two Crowns.

In this year, 1666, Charles La Tour breathed his last.* He had reached the ripe age of seventy-two, and after much hardship and many changes of fortune, he had enjoyed a period of prosperous tranquillity in his declining years. He died and was buried in that beloved Acadia which had been his home from boyhood.

The inglorious war which England was waging with France and Holland, was brought to a close by the treaty of Breda, which was signed July 31st, 1667. By this treaty it was agreed that the English half of the Island of St. Christopher, of which they had been dispossessed by the French, should be restored, and that England in return should give up Acadia to France. Thus was one of the richest pieces of territory on the American continent bartered for one half of a paltry island containing an area scarce a thousandth part as great as that of the country so inconsiderately surrendered.

*La Tour had five children by his second wife, Madame Charnisay, viz., Marie, born in 1654, and married to Alexander Le Borgne de Belleisle; Jacques, born in 1661, married to Anne Melançon; Charles, born in 1664: Anne, also born in 1664, married to Jacques Muis, sieur de Poubomcou; Marguerite, born in 1665, married to Abraham Muis. The D'Entrements, who are still numerous in the western part of Nova Scotia, are many of them the descendants of Anne and Marguerite La Tour. There are several other families, both in Nova Scotia and New Brunswick, that have some of the blood of La Tour in their veins, such as the Girourds, Porliers and Landrys.

The French were in great haste to resume possession of their restored Province, the West India Company taking the lead in the steps necessary for that purpose. In the summer of 1668 they sent Morillon Du Bourg to Acadia. He carried with him a commission from the King of France, an order from the King of England to Temple to deliver up Acadia to Du Bourg, and very ample instructions as to the arrangements he was to make for the restitution of the Province. He was accompanied to Acadia by Alexander Le Borgne, a son of the soldier-merchant whose career in Acadia had been so unfortunate. This son, who was then but twenty-four years of age, had assumed the title of Belleisle, and from this period until his death, he figures prominently in Acadian history. Du Bourg, instead of proceeding direct to Boston, where Temple was residing, followed the whole length of the coast of Acadia, beginning at La Have, and visited all the places marked in his instructions. At Port Royal he left Belleisle, investing him with authority to act as governor, and finally reached Boston late in October.

The order of Charles II. to Temple for the surrender of Acadia, was in the same terms as the Act of Surrender of February, 1668, and required him to deliver up "all that country called Acadia," specifying "the forts and habitations of Pentagoet, St. John, Port Royal, Laheve, and Cape Sable." Temple on being served with this order, took the ground that several of the places specified were in Nova Scotia and not in Acadia, and that His Majesty must have granted the order under a misapprehension as to the facts of the case. He maintained that of all the places named in the order only Laheve and Cape Sable were in Acadia, the rest of the places named, viz: Port Royal, St. John and Pentagoet being in Nova Scotia. He, therefore, signified his resolve to hold on to these places until His Majesty's intentions were further known. He also objected that St. Christopher had not been restored to England, and that Du Bourg had invaded Acadia in a hostile manner. Four days after Temple had communicated this determination to Du Bourg, and while the latter was still detained in Boston, a ship arrived from England bearing an important letter from King Charles to Temple, in which he was commanded not to deliver up Acadia until His Majesty's further pleasure was known. Why this order was sent can now only be conjectured, but it was probably the result of some representations previously made by Temple to the King. Temple having communicated this last order to Du Bourg, the latter took his departue for St. Christopher. In the meantime Temple sent an armed force to Port Royal to drive Belleisle from that place. Temple, in subsequent letters to the Lords of Trade and to the Earl of Arlington, endeavoured to strengthen his position relative to Acadia, and to induce the King to retain the country. He pathetically pleads his old age, his poverty, the great expense at which he has been to preserve and improve the territory, and the ruin which must follow in case he is dispossessed of it. None of these arguments, however, moved King Charles. He was too much under the influence of the French Monarch to have any consideration for his own subjects where their interests clashed. By an order of 8th March, 1669, subsequently confirmed by a second order made in the following August, he ordered Temple peremptorily to deliver up Pentagoet, St. John, Port Royal, Cape Sable, and La Have to the person appointed by the French King to receive them. This order was delivered to Temple in Boston in July, 1670, by Hubert d'Andigny, Chevalier de Grand-fontaine, who bore a commission from Louis

XIV., dated the previous July, empowering him to receive possession of Acadia. Temple at once obeyed this order, and being unable to carry it out personally in consequence of ill-health, issued his order to Captain Richard Walker, his deputy-governor, then actually present in Acadia, to surrender it to Grand-fontaine. Accordingly, the fort at Penobscot was surrendered on the 5th August, Jemseg, on the St. John River, on the 27th of the same month, and Port Royal, September 2nd. The small post at Port Latour was immediately afterwards delivered up under an order from Walker to Rinedon, who was in command there. Grand-fontaine received the surrender of Penobscot in person, and at once established himself there. The task of taking possession of the other posts and forts in Acadia was entrusted to his lieutenant, Soulanges. A careful inventory was taken of the forts and their contents, with a view, it would seem, of establishing a claim for indemnity on Temple's behalf. He estimated his expenditures in Acadia at £16,000, but neither he nor his heirs were ever able to recover any part of this large sum from the English Crown. Thus Acadia passed once more into the possession of France.

CHAPTER XIII.

FROM GRAND-FONTAINE TO MENNEVAL.

GRAND-FONTAINE, as we have seen, had established himself at Penobscot in August, 1670, as commandant for the King of France in Acadia. He was not wanting in zeal for the service of the King, and he required it all in order to rise superior to the depressing influences by which he was surrounded. The fort which he had made his residence was a paltry work, incapable of resisting any serious attack, and only fit to be used as an Indian trading station. Its garrison numbered but twenty-five, all told. But bad as it was, it was the only fortification in Acadia, with the exception of the fort at Jemseg, which was still more contemptible in its armament. Fort Latour had been long abandoned, the fortifications at Port Royal had crumbled away, Fort St. Louis, at Port Latour, had degenerated into a mere fishing station, the fort at La Have had no other tenants but the wild beasts from the forest which surrounded it.

Such was the military aspect of Acadia. Its civil condition was, if possible, worse. Grand-fontaine had a census of the Province taken in 1671, which exhibits in a striking manner its poverty and weakness. The total number of people in Acadia was but four hundred and forty-one, including the twenty-five soldiers which garrisoned the fort at Penobscot. At Port Royal were sixty-eight families, numbering three hundred and sixty-three souls, of whom two hundred were under twenty years of age. At Pubnico there were fourteen persons, and the same number at Cape

Negro. At Musquodoboit there were thirteen souls; at St. Peter's, in Cape Breton, seven, and three at Riviere aux Rochelois. In all Acadia there were but four hundred and thirty-nine arpents of land under cultivation, and the live stock of the colony consisted of eight hundred and sixty-six horned cattle, four hundred and seven sheep, and thirty-six goats. This was a small result for so many years of colonization and such vast expenditures to yield.

At this period, however, a greater degree of vigor was infused into the work of colonizing Canada, and Acadia shared in the benefits of it. Colbert, the French minister of that day, was a man of great ability, and he interested himself in the work of peopling the French possessions in North America. Courcelles, the Governor of New France, and Talon, the Intendant, were filled with zeal for the advancement of the colony, and spared no efforts to that end. Talon appears to have had views of public affairs far in advance of his age, and even in advance of those of Colbert. He pointed out to the latter the great injury which was likely to be done to New France by giving the West India Company a monopoly of its trade, and the revocation of the privileges of the Company in 1674 may be largely traced to his influence.

In 1671 a vessel named L'Oranger brought sixty passengers to Acadia, five of whom were females. Talon desired to open communication with Penobscot by way of the head waters of the Penobscot river, and some of the new colonists were intended to settle on that interior line of communication with Canada, but most of them were sent to Port Royal. In the letter in which Grand-fontaine informs the French minister of the arrival of these colonists, we get some glimpses of the routine of his duties as commandant in Acadia, and of the difficulties which he had to face. He was then about to send his ensign to the River St. John, to establish Fort Latour and guard it until he could have the cannon brought down from the fort at Jemseg. The same ensign was charged with the duty of telling the people at Port Royal to live in peace until some one could be sent to command them. It would seem that there had been much disorder at that place in consequence of Belleisle attempting to exercise authority over the inhabitants. Belleisle and Molin, the priest, had been carrying matters with a high hand, having caused a negro to be hung without any trial, killed an Indian, and banished three inhabitants. Grand-fontaine had also been obliged to put his lieutenant, De Marson, under arrest for disrespect to himself. He was embarrassed for want of officers fit to command, and desired the minister to send him half-pay officers to put in charge of the trading posts and fishing stations in his territory. He pointed out the desirability of occupying the River St. George, which bounded the English settlements. He stated that if the King could obtain from the Duke of York the restitution of Kennebec and Pemaquid, the English settlers of these places would be contented, as they did not wish to recognize the authority of the Massachusetts government, and only asked for liberty of conscience. It is remarkable that in the course of this same year the Massachusetts authorities ordered another survey to be made of the eastern limits of their patent, and the new surveyor succeeded in satisfying his employers so well that he advanced the frontier of Massachusetts as far east as Penobscot Bay, within a few miles of the French fort at Penobscot. Evidently the question of boundaries between Acadia and Massachusetts was soon likely to reach a more interesting stage.

During Grand-fontaine's administration, one more was

added to the settlements of Acadia. Jacob Bourgeois, a resident of Port Royal, took a few colonists to Chignecto, where an enormous area of marsh land awaited but the care of man to yield its riches. He was followed soon afterwards by Pierre Arsenault, who took more settlers to the colony, and thus the beginnings were made of what afterwards became a large and flourishing settlement. These marsh lands had been known to the French as early as the year 1612, when they were visited by Biencourt and father Biard.

A few years later a settlement was commenced at Mines. Its principal founder was a rich inhabitant of Port Royal, named Pierc Theriot, and Claude and Antoine Landry and Réné LeBlanc were associated with him. This settlement became a favorite outlet for the surplus young men of Port Royal, and finally grew to be the richest and most populous in Acadia.

Grand-fontaine did not remain long in Acadia, being recalled to France in May, 1673, Chambly, who had been an officer of the Carignan Saliéres regiment, being appointed commandant in Acadia in his stead. One morning, in 1674, as Chambly and his little garrison of thirty men were engaged in their usual duties about the fort at Penobscot, they were startled by the appearance of a Dutch war vessel in the river. Louis XIV. was then engaged in a war with Holland, and while his generals were winning glory for him in Europe, the Dutch thought that they might safely attack the ill-guarded Provinces of France in America. The Hollander carried one hundred and ten men, and was heavily armed, while Chambly was in no condition to defend the place successfully. But a soldier, who had fought against the Turks, could not be expected to yield without bloodshed, and so Chambly undertook the hopeless task of driving off his assailants, but after several of his men had been killed, and he himself shot through the body, he was obliged to retire, and the fort was surrenderd at discretion. The commander of the Hollanders at once sent a detachment to the St. John River, where De Marson was in command at Jemseg with a few soldiers. He was speedily captured, and the fort ruined. The amount of plunder as the result of this expedition was not large, and the Dutchman made no attempt to hold on to the forts which he had so easily captured. But it had one important result; the French government from that time made no further attempts to occupy the fort at Penobscot, and it fell into decay.

In December, 1674, the French West India Company, which had been created ten years before, was dissolved by royal edict, and the lands, which had been granted to it, reverted to the Crown of France. This was an act of wise statesmanship, and had it been followed up by entire liberty of trade on the coasts of Acadia, the consequences would have been most important. But, unfortunately, neither Louis XIV. nor his minister seemed capable of understanding that any sort of commerce could benefit Acadia which was not a monopoly.

In May, 1676, Chambly received a new commission from the King appointing him Governor of Acadia. In this document he was directed to uphold the arms of his majesty in the way of aggression as well as of defence; to maintain good order and discipline among the soldiers who were to be given him for the defence of the fort; to urge the Colonists to trade in skins and devote themselves to commerce, and to allow entire freedom to the French merchants to trade in Acadia, in virtue of the passports from his majesty, of which they were the bearers. These manifold duties were quite out of proportion to Chambly's means of carrying them out, for he was without soldiers or ships, and was merely living in Acadia on sufferance. A curious proof of the defenceless state of the country is furnished by the fact that the Dutch at this time again occupied Penobscot, and undertook to restore and garrison the fort. The French were in no condition to resist this second invasion of their territory, but the English colonists who had just succeeded in getting rid of the Dutch Province to the south of them, were not disposed to see a Dutch colony established on their northern borders. Accordingly, two or three vessels were sent from Boston, and the Dutch driven from Penobscot, the English, with incredible generosity, leaving the fort unoccupied as soon as they had dispossessed the intruders from the Netherlands.

Pentagoet, as the Penobscot fort was called, was however not suffered to remain long without a tenant, but was immediately occupied by the Baron de St. Castin, one of the most picturesque characters in Acadian history. Castin was a native of Oloron in the Basses Pyrenees and had been an officer of the Carignan Salières. When that famous regiment was disbanded he threw himself among the savages of Acadia, whose language he speedily learned. He married a daughter of Matakando,* the principal chief of the Penobscot Indians, and soon became more influential in their councils than any of their natural leaders. He acquired an immense fortune by trading with them, and was thus able to attain the attachment of his savage allies by handsome presents, as well as by the ties of affection. His presence at Penobscot was eminently useful to the French in Acadia, for it kept the savages of all that coast faithful

* The English called this chief Madockawando, while the French called him Matakando. I spare the reader the extra syllable.

to their cause and prevented them from making peace with the English. There was no man of his day that the border settlers of New England were less disposed to quarrel with than the Baron St. Castin.

But Castin was not the only member of the *Noblesse* who came from Canada to Acadia. In 1676 Michael Le Neuf sieur de La Valliére, a scion of the Potherié family, arrived from Quebec. The same year he obtained a large grant of territory at Chignecto, and established a fishing station at St. John. Soon after his arrival Chambly left Acadia to assume the government of Grenada, and Soulanges, who was appointed to command in Chambly's place, died before he had held that commission very long. The latter was grantee of two extensive seigniorial estates on the St. John, Nashwaak, and Jemseg. His death threw the appointment of Commandant in Acadia into the hands of La Valliére, who received a commission from Count Frontenac, then Governor of Canada, dated the 16th July, 1678.

La Villiére had come to Acadia mainly for the purpose of making money, and he was disposed to view his new office as a ready means of attaining that end. Evidently there was an opportunity for a thrifty commander to better his fortunes without doing the King any great injury. He was a fisherman and trader; the English who came upon the coast were fishermen and traders also, and he saw a way of making such arrangements with them as would be mutually advantageous. Former commanders had vainly endeavoured to prevent the English from fishing on the coast; he recognized at once the fruitlessness of such efforts, and permitted all to fish, provided they paid him a license fee of five pistoles for each vessel. Former commanders had also endeavoured to prevent the English from trading on the coast. He was willing they should trade as much as they pleased, provided they traded with him. So La Vallière encouraged the English to come to the coast of Acadia, and for several years they came and went, and fished and traded as much as they wished.

This, however, was too good to last. A merchant from Rochelle, named Bergier, came to Acadia, and saw at once its immense resources and the profitable use to which they might be put. He allied with him three citizens of Paris, named Gautier, Boucher and De Mœntes, and formed a Company for the prosecution of the shore fishery in Acadia. In February, 1682, the King made a grant to these persons of such lands as they might find suitable along the coast of Acadia and on the St. John River, for the purpose of forming an establishment for the inshore fishery, extending six leagues round the settlements they should make. They had also permission to engage in trade with the French islands of America and in New France in fish, oil, timber and other goods. Under this authority they commenced operations by erecting a small fort and fishing establishment at the head of Chedabucto Bay, on the site of the present town of Guysborough, and brought out a number of men from France to fish and cultivate the soil. From that time there was no peace in Acadia. La Vallière's interests clashed with those of the fishing company, and Bergier and his associates were incessant and clamorous in their complaints against him. They accused him not only of permitting the English to fish and trade on the coast, but of robbing the Indians, and of other acts of rapacity. They also represented that he was a poor man, with but a small settlement of eight or ten men, with no force sufficient to enforce the authority of the King, and therefore obliged to trade with the English for a living. All this and much more was said of the commandant in numerous memorials, which were supported by elaborate documents in proof of the statements advanced. The same memorials which contained these accusations against La Valliére, were also filled with complaints of the conduct of the English of Boston and Salem, who were accused of acts of piracy on the coast. The people of Port Royal had fitted out six small fishing vessels, and these were captured by some freebooters, whom Bergier speaks of as English, one Carter of Salem being the instigator of this outrage. At this period, and for twenty years afterwards, acts of piracy were frequent on the coast of Acadia, and caused great annoyance and loss to the inhabitants. Although many of these outlaws were English, many also were French, but no government was willing to be made responsible for their acts because of their nationality. The Governor of Massachusetts, to whom Bergier complained of these outrages, promised to punish the parties who committed them if they fell into his hands, and told Bergier to do the same. The latter actually succeeded in capturing a man named Tailer, who had piloted the buccaneers that captured the Port Royal vessels, but instead of hanging him promptly, detained him a long time in his fort, with a view to sending him to Quebec for trial.

The representations of Bergier and others were so far successful that the appointment of La Villiére was cancelled by the King, almost at the very time when he was on the point of being promoted to the office of Governor. He had made himself so acceptable to Count Frontenac and his successor, La Barre, that, on their representations, the King, in August 1683, sent La Barre a despatch signifying his intention of appointing La Villiére Governor. But before he received this commission, Louis had changed his mind, and in April, 1684, M. Perrot was appointed

Governor of Acadia, and Bergier was commissioned as lieutenant of the King under Perrot. La Villiére was at the same time strictly forbidden to act as commandant in Acadia, or to grant fishing licenses to foreigners.

Perrot at the time he received this appointment was Governor of Montreal. A more unsuitable man for Governor of Acadia could scarcely have been found, for all the bad qualities of which La Valliére had been accused were exaggerated in him. His conduct at Montreal had been so scandalous that it had caused his imprisonment in Quebec for nearly a year, and in the Bastile for a shorter term. That he was reinstated as Governor of Montreal and afterwards made Governor of Acadia must be attributed to the fact that he was related to Talon, the former Intendant, who was high in favor at the court of the King. Perrot conducted himself in Acadia precisely as he had done at Montreal. He engaged in illicit trade, sold brandy to the Indians, and attempted to monopolize the whole peltry traffic of the country. He also continued the practice, for which La Valliére had been so much censured, of allowing the English to fish on the coast.

Fortunately for the shore Fishery Company, Perrot did not arrive in Acadia for some time after his appointment, and in the meantime Bergier proceeded to carry out his instructions with the zeal of a man, whose self-interest coincided with his duty. In the course of the summer he captured eight English vessels for fishing and trading on the coast of Acada, and sent them to France to be condemned. Even this achievement was not without its drawbacks, for two of the vessels taken had licenses from La Valliére, and Bergier was obliged to restore them and to indemnify their owners. La Valliére, who had retired to his farm at Chignecto, continued to give the Fishery

Company much trouble. He entirely disregarded Bergier's commission, and on one occasion went so far as to send a force to attack Bergier, who was then trading on the coast of Cape Breton. Beaubassin, La Valliére's son, who was the leader in this attack, entered Bergier's cabin in the night with a party of armed men, bound his servants, and robbed him of all his goods. Bergier considered himself lucky in escaping with his life. An unfortunate Indian, who was on his way to Chedabucto with a canoe load of skins, was also captured by Beaubassin and robbed of the whole. These outrages were duly complained of to the minister, but the booty was never returned, and neither La Valliére nor his son received any punishment for their piratical conduct.

At this period there was a strong disposition on the part of many of the Acadians to become rangers of the woods (coureurs de bois) rather than cultivators of the soil. This was an evil which had reached enormous proportions in Canada, and against which the most stringent laws had been enacted, the penalty for bush-ranging being no less than death. The fascinations of forest life must have been strong, indeed, when men would brave such risks for their sake, but a coureur de bois, as he sat by his camp fire in the wilderness, could feel that he was, at least for the time, a free man, and pity his too much governed brothers in the settlements. Freedom is of some value after all, even if it can only be gained by flying from civilization. Several of the most noted bush-rangers of Canada had come to Acadia. Among them were four sons of Councillor D'Amours, of Quebec, who had been arrested for bush-ranging in Canada. Three of them received grants of land in Acadia in 1684, and they commenced a trade with the Indians of the St. John River, giving them brandy and

French goods for their furs. The vast unsettled wilderness through which this river flowed was a paradise to the coureur de bois.

When Perrot arrived in Acadia he was dismayed to find that coureurs de bois were doing most of the trade of the Province. This cut him to the soul. True, when Governor of Montreal, he had done his best to encourage bush-ranging, but he took care to reap the profits of the illicit trade which he encouraged. He was the more angry because he was utterly powerless to prevent other traders from participating in the profits of a traffic which, as Governor, he thought should have been wholly his own. He had thirty soldiers in Port Royal quartered on the inhabitants, but they could not aid him much in his attempt to make himself the only merchant in Acadia. St. Castin, who did the largest trade of any private person in the Province, was, for that reason, more detested by Perrot than any other man in Acadia, and was made the subject of many complaints in his despatches to the Minister. Perrot also looked with jealousy on the operations of the Fishing Company at Chedabucto, and desired to erect a rival establishment at La Have, of which he requested a grant, with a frontage of twelve leagues on the sea coast and ten leagues in depth inland. In order to enable him to settle his proposed seigniory, he demanded fifty soldiers in addition to the thirty already in garrison, a corvette of ten guns, and a large supply of tools and material for re-building the fort. He also asked for authority to seize the inhabitants who were not engaged in cultivating the soil, or who had not settled establishments, so that he could compel them to work for him at La Have. These and a number of other requests equally modest are contained in a memorial which he forwarded to the Minister in 1686, but they received no attention. Indeed, by the time his memorial reached France, the resolution to replace him by a more honest Governor had already been taken.

At this period we get an interesting view of the state of Acadia from the census taken by De Meulles, the Intendant of Canada, which visited all the Acadian settlements in 1685 and 1686, and prepared a memorial on the state of the Province and a census of its inhabitants. Their total number at this period, exclusive of soldiers, was 851, the population having more than doubled since the enumeration of fifteen years before. Port Royal, although it had in the meantime established new settlements at Chignecto and Mines, had increased its population from 363 to 592. At Chignecto there was a settlement of 127 persons and 57 at Mines. The progress of the latter settlement had been retarded by the claims made by La Valliére to seignorial rights there. But Belleisle who was seignior of Port Royal and who claimed Mines also, succeeded in having his rival's pretensions set aside by the Intendant, and from that time Mines prospered rapidly in population. After making the largest allowance for natural increase it is evident that a considerable proportion of the gain in population between 1671 and 1686 must have been due to immigration, and as a further proof of this, the number of surnames in the colony had doubled in the interval. In another chapter I purpose to deal more at length with this matter of Acadian population.

In April, 1687, M. De Menneval was appointed Governor of Acadia, and Perrot was ordered to return to France, an order which he totally disregarded. Before Menneval arrived to replace him he had an opportunity of taking a petty revenge on St. Castin, his hated rival in trade. Castin was visiting Port Royal and seems to have committed some act of imprudence in the way of gallantry for which Perrot kept him under arrest for seven weeks, long enough to interfere seriously with Castin's trading arrangements for that season. He was naturally disgusted at this trick of his rival, and in a letter to Governor Denonville, complaining of his arrest, he gives a most unflattering description of Perrot's doings in Acadia, even accusing him of selling brandy by the pint and half-pint before strangers in his own house. Perrot was not the last governor of Acadia against whom similar charges were made.

Menneval, on succeeding to the government, was furnished with a letter of instruction which contained elaborate directions for his guidance in the conduct of affairs. He was informed that the principal object of the King was the propagation of the Catholic faith, and therefore he was ordered to maintain the observances of religion among the inhabitants and repress all licentiousness and immorality. He was to prevent the inhabitants from going into the woods under pretence of trading, and to restore to the royal dominions those granted lands which had not been occupied. Inhabitants guilty of excesses, or who refused to conform to the laws against bush-ranging, were to be sent back to France. He was also ordered to prevent foreigners from fishing or trading on the coast, and to aid him in this he was supplied with a frigate—La Fripoune—under the command of M. De Beauregard. Thirty additional soldiers were also to be sent to him, and he was instructed, with their help, to rebuild the fort at Port Royal, which he was to make his principal place of residence. Finally, he was told that the prohibition against licentiousness and bush-ranging applied likewise to St. Castin, who was to be given to understand that he must give up the vagabond life he was leading with the savages, and the trade which he carried on with the English, and commence without delay a substantial settlement. He was further to be told that if he did as he was commanded and acted as became a gentleman, the King would give him tokens of his favor. Lest Louis XIV. should be accused of hypocrisy in thus rating St. Castin for his immoral conduct, it should be remembered that the King, after spending all his youth and strength in licentiousness, had reformed at the age of forty-seven, married Madame De Maintenon, become extremely pious, and was then engaged in the task of wholly extirpating heresy from his dominions.

Perrot had represented to the Minister that Boudrot, the Judge at Port Royal, was so old as to be unfit for duty, and that D'Entremont, Procureur du Roi (Attorney General) was an ignorant man. Both were displaced in 1688, Des Goutins being appointed Judge, and Du Breuil Attorney General. The directions to the former show the paternal interest which the King was taking in Acadia. He was to discourage lawsuits and act rather as an arbitrator than as a Judge. He was told to examine into the resources of the colony, to report where new settlements might be made, to give an account of the land fit for cultivation, and the best fishing stations, and to ascertain the number of inhabitants who might find a subsistence in the colony. He was to encourage the inhabitants to sow all sorts of grain, and to plant all kinds of trees brought from France, in order that those which were the most useful and profitable might be selected. Amongst his other duties was the preparation and transmission to France of an annual census of the colony. The nature of these directions shows what a lively interest Louis and his minister were taking in colonial affairs. It was well that such a spirit was abroad, for the colonies of France were threatened by enormous dangers, and events of dreadful import to France were about to transpire in Europe. Louis, who had kept England his subservient ally for twenty years, by making pensioners of two of her Kings, was soon to see the resources of England employed against him by his life long enemy, William of Orange.

The position of St. Castin at Penobscot was one which exposed him to peculiar dangers, for it was a debatable land which was claimed by both nations. James II. of England regarded it as a part of his ducal territory under his grant of 1664, and in 1686 Messrs. Palmer and West, the Commissioners appointed by Dongan, Governor of New York, to superintend the affairs of the ducal province of Sagadahoc, were directed to lay claim to the country as far west as the St. Croix. In pursuance of this claim they seized a cargo of wine which had been landed at Penobscot, and confiscated it for non-payment of duties, on the ground that it should have been entered and paid duty at the Custom House at Pemaquid, their head-quarters. This act gave offence both to the French and the people of Massashusetts, for the wine belonged to Mr. John Nelson, a popular young gentleman of Boston, nephew of Sir Thomas Temple, and the people of Boston looked with no sort of favor on the erection of such a Province to the eastward of them. However, for the present, the dispute was settled amicably, for after some correspondence on the subject the wine was restored.

The difficulty was revived in 1688 when Andros became royal governor of New England, under a commission from James II. He resolved to seize upon Penobscot, and went there in the Rose frigate in the course of the Spring of that year. The frigate anchored opposite Castine's residence and Andros sent a lieutenant ashore to inform the Baron that he desired to see him on board his vessel. St. Castin, who had not a very high idea of the good faith of Andros declined the interview, and retired with his family to the woods, leaving most of his goods and household effects behind him. Andros landed with a party of officers and entered Castin's dwelling, which they robbed of a quantity of arms, ammunition, iron kettles and cloth. They even carried off his chairs, and Andros claimed great credit for his generosity for not interfering with the altar and the pictures and ornaments attached to it. Andros returned to Pemaquid in triumph with his booty, but it proved a costly prize, for it was the means of bringing on another Indian war.

The Indians commenced hostilities in the following August, and no one doubts that they were urged on by St. Castin, although they had some grievances of their own which furnished them with an excuse for going to war. Andros marched against the Indians with a large force, but they entirely eluded him, and he neither killed nor captured a single savage. Before he had an opportunity of taking the field again in the Spring of 1689 a revolution had taken place in Massachusetts, and he had been removed from office. His master, James II., had been driven from the throne and was a fugitive in France, and in May William of Orange now become William III. of England, declared war against Louis. In America, French and Indians were at once banded together for the destruction of the English Colonies. The war was to be carried on along the whole line from Niagara to the Penobscot. Frontenac had been reappointed governor of Canada, and the programme of operations intrusted to him was bold enough to satisfy even his ambition. New England was to be ravaged and laid under coutribution, New York was to be captured and its Protestant population banished from its soil.

The Eastern Indians renewed the war in June, 1689, by the destruction of Dover, New Hampshire, where Major Waldron and twenty-two others were killed and twenty-nine taken captive. Waldron richly deserved his fate, for more than twelve years before he had been guilty of a base act of treachery towards the Indians, which has, doubtless, since caused the spilling of much innocent blood. In 1676, towards the close of King Philip's war, Waldron, then commander of the militia at Dover, had made peace with four hundred Indians, and they were encamped near his house. Two companies of soldiers soon after arrived at Dover, and by their aid Waldron contrived a scheme to make the Indians prisoners. He proposed to the savages to have a review and sham fight after the English fashion, the militia and soldiers to form one party and the Indians another. After manœuvring for some time, Waldron induced the Indians to fire the first volley, and the instant this was done they were surrounded by the soldiers, and the whole of them made prisoners. Some of them were set at liberty, but over two hundred were taken to Boston, where seven or eight were hanged, and the rest sold into slavery. It was to avenge this despicable act that Waldron was slain in 1689.

The destruction of Dover was soon followed by other attacks. In July a number of men were killed by the Indians at Saco, and in August the fort at Pemaquid, garrisoned by Captain Weems and fifteen men, was taken and the settlement destroyed. A number of St. John River Indians were in that expedition, and John Gyles, whose interesting account of his nine years captivity contains much valuable information with regard to them, was one of the prisoners taken. Thury, a Jesuit missionary, stationed on the Penobscot, was with the Indians when they attacked Pemaquid.

New England was aroused to action by these attacks, and sent a large force of volunteers into the field to drive the Indians to their fastnesses. Major Church, who had won reputation in King Philip's war, was placed in command of the forces of the United Colonies. The only operation of importance in which he took part that year was a fight he had with the Indians at Falmouth, in which he suffered considerable loss. After ascending the Kennebec for some distance, he turned back, and, leaving sixty soldiers in Fort Loyal, returned to Boston. This ended the operations for the year, and the border settlers of New England welcomed the approach of winter as likely to give them a respite against their savage foes.

While these events were transpiring on the frontiers of Acadia, Port Royal, the capital and heart of the Province, was the scene of a series of petty quarrels between Menneval and Des Goutins, who, instead of loyally supporting each other, and endeavoring to perfect the defences of the place, spent their time in writing long letters to the Minister full of complaints against each other. Menneval, it would seem, was walking in the path of his predecessors in office, and carying on a trade with the English for his own profit. He was also accused of tyrannical conduct, and of interfering with the functions of the Judge, while the priests were accused of being his partners and assistants in the unlawful trade with the English, their houses being made the receptacle for English goods, which were carried on shore at night under the noses of the sentinels, who were forbidden to cry, "Who goes there?"

The French Government had sent two war vessels to the coast of Acadia in the Autumn of 1688, which captured six English ketches and a brigantine, which were engaged in fishing. Menneval had the brigantine brought to Port Royal, where he proposed to fit her up as a war vessel to drive away the English fishermen and guard the coast from pirates. If, however, he was as deeply concerned in English trade as the accusations of his enemies would seem to indicate, he would probably have been able to put the vessel to a more profitable use.

The war between the French and English in America opened early in 1690 by a series of attacks planned by Frontenac on the English colonies. Three war parties were formed at Montreal, Three Rivers and Quebec, their destination being respectively New York, New Hampshire and Maine. The Montreal force consisted of two hundred and ten men, of whom about one half were Indians, converts of the Iroquois tribe settled near Montreal. The leaders were d'Allebout, de Mantet and Lemoine de Sainte-Hélène. They had intended to attack Albany, but, when after a terrible winter journey through the wilderness they reached its vicinity, the savages objected, and Schenectedy was attacked instead. This peaceful village was assailed at midnight on the 4th February, and many of the inhabitants massacred in their beds—old men, women and little children all shared the same fate. Sixty persons were killed, of whom ten were women and twelve were children ; all the houses in the village were burnt down, with the exception of two, and twenty-seven persons were led captive to Canada. Many of those who escaped the massacre and fled towards Albany, lost their limbs from frost. This attack may be considered a specimen of what the chivalry of Canada was capable of, for besides the leaders who were members of the Noblesse, d'Iberville, Bienville, and other Canadian gentlemen took part in it. The victors, although they carried away a great quantity of plunder, did not escape unmolested, for they were pursued by a party of Mohawks, and a number of them killed or taken.

The Three Rivers expedition consisted of forty-nine men, of whom twenty-five were Indians, under the famous Hopehood. The commander of the force was François Hertel, a resolute man, who in his youth had been captured and tortured by the Mohawks. After a journey which occupied two months, and was attended by great hardships; this party attacked Berwick on the morning of the 28th March, before daybreak. Thirty-four persons were killed, and more than fifty taken prisoners. After setting fire to the houses, barns and other buildings, Hertel's party retreated to the woods, pursued by one hundred and forty persons hastily collected from the neighboring towns. Hertel made a stand at Wooster River, checked the pursuit, and at nightfall continued his retreat unmolested.

The third war party, sent out by Frontenac, left Quebec on the 28th January. It consisted of fifty Canadians and soldiers, and seventy Abenaquis Indians, all under the command of Porteneuf and his lieutenant, Courtemanche. On the Kennebec they were joined by Hertel and his party, now reduced to thirty-six men, and a number of Kennebec Indians also reinforced them. A still larger reinforcement of Indians from St. John and Penobscot, under Matkakando and St. Castin, swelled the total force to about five hundred men. This expedition differed from the others, by reason of the fact that the English were not surprised, but the overwhelming numbers of the enemy made the result the same. Falmouth was attacked on the 26th May, and all the people who were unable to reach the fortified houses were slain. During the night the inhabitants retired to Fort Loyal, where there was a small garrison under Captain Davis. The French and Indians besieged this place for four days, and finally Davis was forced to surrender. Porteneuf promised the inmates of Port Loyal quarter and a guard to the next English town, but when the place was given up, all the conditions of the surrender were violated. The French allowed the Indians to murder the whole of the prisoners, who numbered about one hundred, men, women and children, with the exception of Captain Davis and three or four others, who were carried off to Quebec. Fort Loyal was destroyed, and the dead bodies of the unfortunate people of Falmouth were allowed to lie unburied about the ashes of their homes. All that summer their ghastly corpses remained exposed to the elements and to the wild animals of the forest; but in October, Major Church, then on an expedition to the eastward, gathered their bones together and buried them.

While the people of Maine were thus suffering from the attacks of savages, important events were taking place in Acadia. The war had been proclaimed at Boston on the 17th December, 1689, and the New England people, mindful of what they had suffered from the French in times past, resolved to attempt the reduction both of Port Royal and Quebec. The Port Royal expedition sailed from Boston on the 9th May, 1690. It consisted of seven vessels, a frigate of forty guns, two sloops of sixteen and eight guns, and four ketches, and a complement of seven hundred men. The command was given to Sir William Phips, a native of Maine, who had brought himself into notice by his recovery of the cargo of a Spanish treasure-ship which had been wrecked near the Bahamas fifty years before.

Phips and his squadron arrived off Port Royal on the 19th May, and the alarm was at once given to the fort by the guard stationed at the entrance of the Basin firing off a mortar. At eleven the same night they arrived at the fort, and reported to Menneval the number of the enemy. Menneval at once perceived that an attack was intended, and summoned the inhabitants into the fort by the firing of a cannon. Only three of them obeyed the signal, and they advised Menneval to give up the idea of defending the fort, and to retire with his garrison and stores to a place two leagues further up the river, where the English would be unable to follow him. Menneval consented to abide by this advice, as the fort was evidently incapable of a successful defence; he had only seventy men in garrison, the fortifications were in an unfinished state, and the eighteen cannon which he had were not mounted. Measures were at once taken to carry this programme into effect. The brigantine, which was lying in the river, was brought near the fort, and the soldiers commenced to load her with provisions and ammunition, to be taken to the post up river. While this was going on, the two priests—Petit and Trouvé—arrived, and induced Menneval to change his plan. They persuaded him that he would only increase his difficulties by abandoning the fort, and that as matters stood he might make an advantageous capitulation, which Petit himself undertook to negotiate. Accordingly, when the English squadron entered Port Royal Basin on the following day, and Phips sent his trumpeter to summon the garrison to surrender, Menneval detained him, and sent Petit to Phips to arrange a capitulation. The terms finally agreed upon were that the garrison should be conveyed to France, with their arms and baggage; that the inhabitants should remain unmolested on their lands, enjoying the free exercise of their religion, and that their church should not be injured. On these conditions Port Royal was surrendered.

While Menneval was on board the English flag-ship ratifying these terms, some soldiers and inhabitants broke into the storehouse of M. Perrot and took out some goods. Phips made this a pretext for violating the terms of the capitulation. His soldiers rifled the church, broke the altar ornaments, and plundered the houses of the two priests, robbed Menneval of his personal property, and carried him and most of his soldiers and the two priests off to Boston, where they were thrown into prison. Before he left Port Royal, Phips called all the inhabitants together and made them take the oath of allegiance to the crown of England, which they did without much demur. He also organized a sort of provisional government of which Chevalier, a sergeant of the garrison, was made President, with a council of six inhabitants. They bound themselves to administer the affairs of the settlement under the crown of England and the government of Massachusetts.

Phips returned to Boston with his plunder, but sent one of his Captains named Alden to reduce La Have and Chedabucto. The only place where any resistance was offered was Chedabucto, where Captain Montorgueil had a garrison of fourteen men, who were finally compelled to surrender. All the goods belonging to the Fishing Company were taken, and their losses there and at Port Royal were very large, amounting to upwards of fifty thousand crowns.

CHAPTER XIV.

VILLEBON ON THE ST. JOHN.

A FEW days after the departure of the English, a French ship, the Union, came sailing into Port Royal Basin. She was from France direct, and was laden with merchandize, provisions for the garrison, ammunition for the Indians, and presents to keep them faithful to the cause of France. She also brought ten recruits to complete the complement of the Acadian garrisons, fifty stand of arms for the soldiers, Saccardie, an engineer officer, to direct the rebuilding of the fort at Port Royal, and Villebon, a brother of Menneval, who had been one of his officers in Acadia, who now came to place himself at the head of the Indians of the Kennebec, for the purpose of continuing the war against New England. Perrot, ex-Governor and trader, came on board almost as soon as the Union dropped anchor, and told Villebon the doleful story of the capture of the place by Phips. Des Goutins, the Judge, also came, and further explained the situation, and a consultation was held to decide what was the best course to pursue. As the English were still on the coast, and might return if they heard of Villebon's arrival, it was decided that his safest plan was to proceed to the River St. John and occupy the old fort at Jemseg. There the effects of the Crown and of the Company could be stored in safely, and a sufficient number of soldiers collected to guard them. Villebon immediately proceeded to carry this programme into effect. He crossed to St. John, and went up that river to prepare Fort Jemseg for the arrival of the goods entrusted to his care. The Union was directed to follow in a few days. But the Union never came, and when Villebon returned to Port Royal in high anger at the neglect of his orders, he learned that a misfortune even greater than the first had overtaken the cause of France. Two pirate ships had made their appearance in his absence, and finding Port Royal defenceless, their ruffianly crews had landed and engaged in their congenial work of pillage and murder. At the Cape, near the entrance of the Basin, on the Granville side, they burnt sixteen houses, and then proceeding to the fort they burnt twelve houses in its vicinity, including one in which was a woman and her children. Two of the other inhabitants they hanged, and then seizing all the plunder they could gather, including the Union and her cargo, they sailed away. They took with them Saccardie and Perrot, the latter of whom they ducked almost to the point of death, in order to force him to tell where his money was buried. He survived the operation, however, and got back to France, where, in the following year, he was writing memorials on the state of Acadia and seeking to be re-appointed its Governor.

Villebon, in the trying position in which he was placed, acted with prudence and vigor. He returned at once to Jemseg, and there assembled as many of the savage chiefs as he could collect. He told them how the presents intended for them had been seized by the English, but said that he was about to return to France to get better presents for them than those which had been lost. He begged them to make no peace with the English until his return, but to continue the war and to meet him there in the following Spring. They promised to carry out his wishes, and expressed their determination to remain faithful to the cause of their brothers—the French. Villebon, bidding them farewell, took his departure for Quebec, from which he proposed to take ship for France.

Quebec was at this time threatened by an attack from the English. The easy success of Phips at Port Royal emboldened the people of the United Colonies to prepare an expedition for the capture of Quebec, the seat of Frontenac's government and the place where all the murderous assaults against their settlements had been planned. Phips was placed in command of the Quebec expedition, which consisted of thirty-two vessels and upwards of two thousand men. It left Boston on the 19th August, but did not reach Quebec until the middle of October. Phips summoned the garrison to surrender, but his proposal was treated with contempt by Frontenac, and several ill-planned attacks, which he made upon the place, made no impression. After losing many men, he was forced to retire, and the misery of his position was aggravated by the small pox, which had broken out violently among his men. Phips returned to Boston late in November, to tell the story of his failure.

Villebon had been detained in Quebec by the English invasion which prevented vessels from leaving the St. Lawrence, but before the winter set in he returned to France in the ship which carried Frontenac's despatches announcing the failure of the attack on Quebec. He explained the situation of affairs in Acadia to the minister, and being a favorite of Count Frontenac, from whom he had high letters of recommendation, he was appointed to command in Acadia. He received very full instructions in regard to his duties; the necessity for keeping the Indians hostile to the English being specially pressed on his attention. He reached Quebec in July, but the vessel which was to carry him to Acadia was detained there for some time, and he did not reach Port Royal until late in September. Bonaventure, the officer who carried him to his new charge however effected a fortunate capture in the seizure of Colonel Edward Tyng, who had been appointed governor of Port Royal by the Massachusetts authorities, and who was being conveyed to that place by Mr. John Nelson who was well acquainted with Acadia. Both were carried to Quebec and from thence to France, where Tyng died a prisoner. Nelson, after several years captivity, was restored to his family.

Villebon, after pulling down the English flag at Port Royal, and informing the inhabitants that they were once more to consider themselves subjects of France, established himself at Fort Jemseg, on the St. John. He had with him fifty soldiers, a garrison sufficient to ward off any attack that was likely to be made upon him at that remote post. He had with him his brother, Porteneuf, the daring leader of the attack on Fort Loyal.

During Villebon's absence from Acadia the savages had done but little for the common cause. Indeed, in December, 1690, six Abenaquis chiefs had signed a five months' truce with the English, and had promised to meet them in the following May to surrender their prisoners and make a lasting peace. They did not come at the time appointed, but in June, Moxus, one of the signers of the truce, attacked Wells with two hundred Indians. This place was defended by a strong garrison, under Captain Converse, and the savages were repulsed. They went away, vowing vengeance against Converse, and during the remainder of the Autumn roamed about the country like a pack of wolves, killing and destroying.

The presence of Villebon at Jemseg was soon felt. He put himself in communication with Thury, the priest of the Penobscot tribe, and incited them to a winter attack on the English settlements. One hundred and fifty of that tribe and a large band of Kennebec Indians made an attack on York in February, 1692. The place was surprised, one of the five fortified houses which it contained, taken, and all the inhabitants, who were unable to gain the others, killed or captured. About seventy-five persons were slain, among whom was the venerable Mr. Dummer, the minister of the place. The captives numbered nearly one hundred. Several aged women and a number of children were released and allowed to go to the garrisoned houses to requite the English for sparing the lives of some Indian women and children at Pejèpscot a year and a half before. This proves that the savages were not wholly destitute of gratitude, and that they had rather a nice sense of honor, for it is worthy of note that at Pejèpscot, Church did not spare all the squaws and children, but only the wives of the two Sagamores, their children and two or three old squaws. All the other Indian women and the children, of which there was a large number, this squaw-killer Church slew in cold blood.

In the following Spring, another great war party was organized by Villebon, composed of Micmacs, Malicites from the St. John, and the tribes of the Penobscot and Kennebec, to the number of four hundred warriors. Porteneuf was with the party, and several other officers and Canadian soldiers, St. Castin and all the principal chiefs of the tribes engaged. Their rendezvous was Penobscot, and from there they went in canoes to attack Wells. The principal garrisoned house at this place was occupied by Captain Converse, who had some thirty men with him. He defended his post bravely, and repulsed his assailants, the French being unable to induce their savage allies to make a determined assault. A French officer named La

Brognarie was killed in this attempt. In revenge for his death the savages put John Diamond—whom they had taken captive before attacking the fort—to the torture. Having thus wreaked their fury on a helpless prisoner, they dispersed and returned to their homes.

Sir William Phips had this year been appointed Governor of Massachusetts, under a new royal charter granted by William and Mary. He commissioned Church, and gave him a force to clear the eastern frontier, and went in person with him to carry out what had long been a favorite plan of his own, the erection of a strong fortress at Pemaquid. There, near the site of the old stockade built by Andros, rose a formidable work, built of stone, which cost the Province upwards of twenty thousand pounds. It mounted eighteen guns, and was garrisoned by sixty men. Phips gave it the high-sounding name of Fort William Henry. Both Phips and Church had long desired to capture St. Castin, whom they regarded as the chief cause of the hostility of the Indians. Accordingly, Church went to Edgemoragan Reach, a little to the eastward of Penobscot, where two Frenchmen named Petipas and St. Aubin resided, and carried them with their families to Boston. Phips thought to make them the means of capturing St. Castin. Petipas and St. Aubin were sent to Penobscot with two French soldiers named Du Vignon and Albert, who had deserted from the garrison at Quebec, to surprise St. Castin and bring him away. They were told to pretend that they were escaped prisoners, so that the Baron would be thrown off his guard. The wives and children of Petipas and St. Aubin were in the meantime detained in Boston as hostages for the faithful performance of the treacherous mission with which they had been entrusted. Instead of betraying the Baron, they disclosed to him the plot of which he was to be made the victim, and the two deserters were seized and sent to Quebec, where they were tried, condemned and shot. Petipas and St. Aubin, in consideration of their fidelity, afterwards received a sum of money from Villebon to enable them to ransom their families from imprisonment.

The two deserters who met such a well-merited fate, had been the bearers of a letter from Nelson, who was then a prisoner at Quebec, which probably saved Fort William Henry from capture. Matakando had gone to Quebec to visit Count Frontenac, and informed him of what the English were doing at Pemaquid. He resolved to drive them from that position before they had time to establish themselves; and as there were two war vessels available, the Poli and Envrieux, under the command of d'Iberville and Bonaventure, there seemed to be no difficulty in executing that design. It was arranged that they should co-operate with Villebon and take on board a party of Indians at St. John and Penobscot, and then assail Pemaquid. But the design miscarried. When they reached their destination, the English were on the alert, the news of the attack having been carried to Boston by the deserters, whom Nelson had bribed. D'Iberville found an English vessel riding at anchor under the guns of the new fort, and declined to make the intended attack. He was much censured for pursuing this course, and the Indians were so dissatisfied that the affair threatened to cause a breach between them and the French.

This year Villebon removed his garrison from Jemseg to Nashwaak, where he commenced the erection of a new fort on a point of land on the northern bank of that river at its junction with the St. John, nearly opposite the city of Fredericton. The change was made because Fort

Jemseg was subject to inundations, and because it was insufficient in size. Fort Nashwaak was a palisaded work of four bastions, similar to the majority of those in Acadia. It had one great advantage over the fort at Jemseg in its nearness to the Indian villages. The winter of 1692-3 was spent at the new fort in the midst of this vast Acadian forest.

During 1693, Frontenac was waging war against the Mohawks of New York, and Acadia had a season of repose. The Acadian Indians, who—like all the Indian races—were fickle and changeable as children, were already weary of the war, especially since the failure of the attempt to surprise the fort at Pemaquid. That stronghold annoyed them to an extent which can scarcely be appreciated, except by those acquainted with their habits. Standing out far into the ocean, it prevented them from making canoe voyages along the coast, and cut off the Indians of the Androscoggin and Kennebec from sea communication with those of the Penobscot and St. John. Many of them began to think seriously of making peace with the English, and in August thirteen chiefs, representing all the tribes from Passamaquoddy to Saco, concluded a treaty with the English Commissioners at Pemaquid, by which they declared their submission to the Crown of England, renounced the cause of France, agreed to release all captives without ransom, and live in perpetual peace and friendship with the English. They left five hostages at Pemaquid as pledges of their good faith.

The making of this treaty caused much rejoicing in New England, which had suffered greatly from Indian attacks, but the French regarded it with dismay, and soon found means to render it a nullity. Fortunately for them, they possessed a mode of influencing the savages, to which

P

the English could not pretend. Missionaries of the Order of Jesus had long resided among the Abenaquis tribes, and they had become converted to the Christian faith, after a fashion. At this period the two Jesuit missionaries, Bigot on the Kennebec, and Thury on the Penobscot, were active in their opposition to the English peace. Villebon also spared no effort to produce a breach of the treaty. The Malicites, among whom he lived, and the Micmacs of the Peninsula, had taken no part in the alliance, and he employed their powerful influence to renew the war. Porteneuf, his brother, had been withdrawn from Acadia, and replaced by Villieu, an officer of some reputation, who came nominally as commander of a detachment of Marines in Acadia, but in reality was intended to be employed to lead the savages in a new crusade against the English settlements.

After spending the winter at Fort Nashwaak, Villieu on the 1st May started for the Penobscot, taking Medoctec on his way, and travelling by the usual route up Eel River and down the Mattawamkeag to his destination. There he met the chief Taxous, Thury the Jesuit, and Bigot, the missionary from Kennebec. After some conferences with the Indians, he returned with a party of them to Nashwaak for presents and to obtain soldiers from Villebon. The latter was only able to give him two soldiers, none of the others being capable of managing a canoe, an indispensable accomplishment for such an expedition. Even these two left him at Medoctec, and returned to the fort. Villieu sought to create the impression that Villebon was indifferent to the success of the expedition, but all the probabilities are against such an inference. On June 3rd Villieu was once more at Castin's house, on the Penobscot, in conference with Taxous and the priests. Again the Indians were assembled, but at this juncture Matakando arrived with the news that the English intended to deliver up the prisoners on the 5th July, according to the terms of the treaty. This set the Indians talking of peace, and it required all Thury's eloquence to prevent them from at once returning to their homes. It was only by working on the jealousy of Taxous and other chiefs, and representing to them that Matakando had no right to make the treaty without their being parties to it, that anything like a warlike spirit was kept up. Every argument was made use of, which it was thought would serve to prejudice them against the English. They were told that the invitation to go to Pemaquid to obtain prisoners was only a snare for the purpose of killing or capturing all their principal warriors, and Waldron's treachery at Dover was cited as a specimen of English faith. Finally, on the 27th June, a dog feast was held, at which all the Indians sang the war song, except Matakando and thirty of his party, and they, after much persuasion and ridicule and many presents, at length were won over. The great war party now increased to two hundred and fifty warriors by bands from the Kennebec, and commanded by Matakando, Bomaseen and Taxous, attacked Dover, captured five of its twelve garrisoned houses, killed upwards of one hundred persons, and carried twenty-seven into captivity. Twenty houses were burnt, but Thury took possession of the meeting house and prevented the savages from doing it any injury. After this exploit the savages divided themselves into smaller bands and killed several persons at Groton, Piscataqua, York, Kittery, and other places. Villieu went to Montreal to receive the applause of Count Frontenac, to whom he presented a string of English scalps—a fine gift for one French gentleman to bestow upon another. Villieu had done his work well; he had broken the peace with the English, and sowed such seeds of distrust between them and the savages as to make it almost impossible for a lasting peace to be made.

The Fishing Company of Acadia were still in existence at this period, although they had experienced many vicissitudes. In 1687 they had increased their colony at Chedabucto to one hundred and fifty persons, of whom eighty were fishermen. That year their troubles commenced. The ship which was coming to carry their fish to France got blown off the coast, and next Spring when another vessel arrived, most of the fish were spoiled. Then they had their largest vessel wrecked at Rochelle. In August, 1688, a pirate attacked Chedabucto, plundered it and captured the two vessels of the Company then anchored in front of it. In 1690, when Port Royal was taken, the Company lost all the goods in their storehouse there, and their establishment at Chedabucto was broken up and plundered by an English war vessel immediately afterwards. After Villebon's return to Acadia, the Company assisted in re-establishing the colony by furnishing supplies in the shape of provisions and goods to the French settlers and savages. Each year they sent a vessel to the St. John river with goods, and on more than one occasion the assistance they were able to give proved very acceptable to the King's troops.

In the midst of their rejoicings over the destruction of the English settlements, the savages of Acadia were stricken with a mortal plague which swept them away by hundreds. The war parties which went from the St. John river in September were turned back at Penobscot, and the warlike operations of the year were brought to a close. The Chief of the St. John Indians died of this disease, and its ravages were so severe that Medoctec was abandoned by the savages for the time. Upwards of one hundred and twenty persons, including many of the best warriors of the tribe, died on the St. John river alone.

Villebon kept a diary during his command in Acadia, and by its aid and that of the many despatches sent by himself and others to the Minister, we obtain a clearer idea of life in Acadia in his time than at almost any other period in its history. His principal causes of concern were to keep the Indians at war with the English, to prevent the latter from fishing on the coast, and to guard his fort from attack. His means were very inadequate, but he made up in vigilance and activity what he lacked in strength. Some of the orders which he gave will strike the people of this day as being cruel in the extreme, but it was an age of cruelty, and wars are always cruel, especially wars in which savage tribes are enlisted.

To keep the coast of the Province clear of English fishermen, Bonaventure cruised pretty constantly in a war ship for several years. He was aided by a number of French privateers, who found sufficient profit in the occasional capture of an English fishing vessel to induce them to keep the sea. The English of Massachusetts generally had a war vessel on the Acadian coast, and several privateers, fitted out at Salem and elsewhere in New England, were generally cruising in these waters. All these private armed vessels the French were accustomed to designate as "pirates." Besides them there were genuine pirates on the coast sometimes, who plundered with strict impartiality, irrespective of nationality. Between war vessels, privateers and pirates, the coast was pretty thoroughly patrolled at this period. One of the most famous French corsairs of the period was Robineau, who, after taking many English prizes, was, in 1694, driven into the harbor of St. John by an English ship, and forced to burn his vessel. Another famous privateer was Baptiste, Captain of the corvette La Bonne, which vessel was captured in 1695, in Musquash harbor, after a severe fight, by an English war vessel; a third was François Guyon, who was connected with two of the d'Amours by marriage, and who was also captured in the Spring of 1696. These and other French privateers did very effectual work in driving English fishermen and traders from the coast.

The management of the Indians was a mattter which caused Villebon constant anxiety; indeed, at that period, had it not been for the efforts of the priests, it is doubtful if they could have been kept faithful to the French. The English were prepared to trade with them on much more advantageous terms than the French had ever done, and the French private traders, such as the d'Amours, while they debauched the Indians with brandy, undersold the Company. The excessive prices charged by this Corporation for their goods kept the Indians so miserably poor that they could scarcely supply themselves with ammunition and sufficient clothing. When the Indians found that the English would trade with them on terms so much more favorable, it greatly cooled their regard for the French. It was expecting too much of human nature that they would consent to spill their best blood and keep their families in constant danger for the sake of a people, who were daily over-reaching them in trade.

It therefore became necessary for Villebon to put a stop to the extortionate conduct of the Company, and to arrange a tariff for the sale of beaver, and the purchase of goods that would satisfy the Indians. In June, 1695, a grand gathering of the savages was held at Fort Nashwaak for the purpose of arranging this important matter. They came from the Kennebec and Penobscot, and from the two great settlements of the St. John, Medoctec and Madawaska, to be entertained by Villebon, and to have "a great talk" with him about their grievances. There were fourteen chiefs in all—among them Matakando, of Penobscot, who had become the chief of the St. John river tribe, and Taxous, the adopted brother of Villebon. There, too, was Thury, the missionary priest, the friend and adviser of the Indians, to interpret between Villebon and his guests.

Villebon entertained them for three days. First came the giving of presents, an important and somewhat difficult matter to manage satisfactorily, and when that was over a great council was held. The chiefs proved to be severe sticklers for ceremony, and they were a long time deciding who should speak first. At length it was agreed that the chiefs of the Kennebec should do so, and their orator commenced a harangue, which is thus reported by Villebon:—
"It is a long time since we anxiously desired to assemble as we now do, but the distance of our settlements, and the fear of exposing our families to our enemies during our absence has caused us to defer our assembling together until the present time. We know that you have been vexed at the parleys we have had with the English, and that you feared we would make peace with them, but we assure you that we never entered into such parleys without informing Count Frontenac, and receiving his approval. We, from Kennebec, are too far removed from you to give you information of what was going on, but those from Penobscot could have done so. The reason which forced us to seek the English arose from our necessities, for we were in want of everything, and grieved to see our families destitute. But it will depend only upon yourself whether we

shall have the same reasons in future, and therefore you must tell us at what price the goods will be sold upon this river, and when you have settled the price with us, we promise you to cease all parleys with the English, and to prevent our young men from having any intercourse with them. You know already from the first savages that came from our quarter that we talked with the English at Pemaquid a few days ago, and brought them seven prisoners of their nation, in order to get ours, who are in Boston. They have promised to give them up to us at the end of this month at Pemaquid. If they fail to do so, we shall no longer give them any quarter, but shall consider our prisoners as dead."

Villebon replied to this speech by telling them that if he had been grieved at their conferences with the English, it was not because he suspected that they would speak of peace with them, after all the treachery of which they had been guilty, but he feared that, under the pretext of trade, the English might take them unprepared and give them no quarter. He had heard from the Frenchmen who came from Boston that this was their intention, and if they had deferred the blow at that time, it was because they wished to collect together a larger number of savages. He then spoke of the tariff of goods which was to be in force while the war lasted, and went on to impress the chiefs with the obligations they were under to continue their attacks upon the English. The tariff of goods was then arranged, and was very satisfactory to the savages; the conference broke up, and Villebon had all the chiefs to sup with him that evening. Early next day they took the route homeward, more resolute than ever to continue the war. The conference which had been arranged at Pemaquid at the end of June, for an exchange of prisoners, only deepened the resentments of the Indians. They attended punctually, but found that the English Commissioners refused to treat until the English prisoners whom the Indians had were produced. The chiefs thought this an unfair condition, for they said, "You have not brought Bomaseen, Robin, Doney and our friends, who are your prisoners. We'll talk no more." And so without further parley they departed. From that time until the end of the year the savages continued to prowl around the forts and kill all who ventured beyond their limits. So closely were the forts watched, that ten men were killed or wounded within cannon shot of Pemaquid. The Indians, however, although reinforced by Micmacs from the Peninsula, and by the tribes of Richibucto and St. John, attempted no important operation that year. Those Indians also went to Cape Sable, and did good service to the French by capturing and driving away English fishermen from that coast. Des Isles, Villebon's brother, led a party of savages to Penobscot in October, but the weather became cold, and the Indians could not be persuaded to keep on the war path. Accordingly, they returned home without accomplishing anything, but promised to meet the French again in the Spring.

Villebon had, at this period, in his mind a scheme no less daring than the capture of Boston, which he conceived might be taken by a simultaneous attack by such land and sea forces as the French could bring against it. This plan was, however, exchanged for one less bold and more feasible, the reduction of the fort at Pemaquid, which was a constant source of annoyance to the savages. Arrangements were made during the winter in Acadia and at Quebec to effect this object. Villieu and Montigny arrived from Quebec in November, and wintered at Fort Nashwaak. Villebon had also with him such useful aides as Neuvillette and Des Isles.

During the winter the English were guilty of an act of treacherous folly, which more than justified all that Villebon had said as to their real intentions towards the Indians, and which greatly exasperated the latter. Stoughton, the Governor of Massachusetts, sent a message to the Indians, telling them to bring in their prisoners for exchange. Some of the tribes returned a haughty refusal, but the Penobscot tribe were extremely anxious to get back five of their number who were confined in Boston; so, in February, 1696, they went to Pemaquid with five English prisoners to effect an exchange. Captain Chubb, the commander of Pemaquid, received them with much show of kindness, and induced them to give up the five English prisoners, promising to send to Boston at once for those they desired in return. He even promised to make them some presents, and the savages were so charmed with the good treatment they were receiving, that they had almost concluded to "bury the hatchet." Chubb proposed a conference within sight of the fort, and it was agreed that nine of the English and nine Indians should meet without arms at the place selected. The Indian party consisted of three chiefs—Taxous, Egeremet, Abenquid and six others; the English, of Chubb and eight of his garrison, who had come with pistols concealed in their bosoms. The Indians had partaken rather freely of Chubb's liquor, which had been lavishly bestowed, and being somewhat intoxicated did not observe that a party of English soldiers had surrounded them at some little distance. When everything was ready, Chubb gave the signal. Egeremet, Abenquid and another Indian were instantly killed, the bold and athletic Taxous was seized by four English, who endeavored to bind him;

but another powerful Indian seizing at this moment a musket from one of the soldiers, bayoneted three of Taxous' assailants, and enabled the chief to escape. Another Indian, after killing three English, was shot down. Four Indians were killed in this affray, and three made prisoners, Taxous and the savage who rescued him alone escaped. It is unnecessary to enlarge upon the character of this scandalous transaction, further than to observe that it was a crime not only against the Indians, but also against the English settlers, who in the end were the greatest sufferers by all such treacherous acts. By the light of our present knowledge of the influences which worked upon the Indians, nothing is more clear than that an honest and just course of policy towards them after the close of King Philip's war, would have made them friends of the English, to whom they were well disposed by reason of the advantages they derived from their trade. But such inexcusable crimes against faith and honesty as those of Waldron and Chubb, made it impossible for the Indians to believe that the English would keep any truce with them; for those instances of English treachery were told at the camp fires of every tribe from Cape Breton to Lake Superior, and they were repaid in kind in after years.

In June, 1696, the tribes of Acadia began to assemble for the intended expedition against Pemaquid. Many went direct to Penobscot, while others, including the Micmacs from Richibucto and Mines, met Villebon at the mouth of the St. John, where two French war vessels, under the command of d'Iberville and Bonaventure, were coming from Quebec to meet them. Villebon had to wait nearly a month there with his Indian allies before the vessels arrived, and would have had hard work to keep them together but for the presence of two English war vessels—the Sorling and Newport—whose crews made several attempts to land. D'Iberville's vessels left Quebec in June, and after calling at Cape Breton, where they took on board thirty Indians, proceeded to St. John. There they encountered the two English vessels, and after a sharp engagement, the Newport, of twenty-four guns, was captured, the Sorling and her tender escaping in the fog. At St. John, the Profond and Envieux took on board fifty more Micmacs and father Simon, the Recollet Missionary of the St. John. At Penobscot, where they arrived August 7th, they found Villieu and Montigny with twenty-five Canadians, Thury, St. Castin and three hundred savages waiting for them. On the 14th August the whole party commenced the investment of Fort William Henry, at Pemaquid, by land and sea.

This fortress, which had been erected at an enormous cost, and was believed to be very strong, mounted fifteen cannon, and was manned by ninety-five soldiers, under the command of Captain Chubb. D'Iberville immediately summoned Chubb to surrender, but he replied grandiloquently: "I will not give up the fort, though the sea be covered with French vessels and the land with wild Indians." This was an excellent answer, provided it had been followed up by corresponding deeds. But almost as soon as he had given it utterance, Chubb found his courage leaving him. The French and Indians surrounded the fort that night, after plying it for some time with musketry, and long before daylight next morning d'Iberville had landed cannon and mortars. These were placed in battery before noon, and early in the afternoon they commenced to fire. Two or three shells fell into the fort, and produced much consternation among the garrison, in the midst of which a letter was received from St. Castin, informing

Chubb that if he did not surrender without an assault, he must expect no mercy from the Indians, who were so exasperated at his former treacherous conduct that they would give no quarter. Chubb at once decided to give up the fort, only stipulating that he and his men should have their lives spared, and be taken to Boston and exchanged. To enable him to keep this compact, d'Iberville found it necessary to remove them all to an island near the fort, and place them under a guard, for the Indians were so incensed against them that their lives were not safe. Their rage was not lessened by the discovery of one of the Indians, captured in February, lying half starved in the fort, and so heavily ironed that it took father Baudouin two hours hard work to set him free. Thus fell Fort William Henry, the strongest fortress in New England, almost without resistance, owing to the incapacity and cowardice of its commander.

The French and Indians lost no time in demolishing the fort, blowing down its walls with gunpowder and burning its buildings. When the work of destruction was over, the French sailed away in triumph. D'Iberville, after sending Chubb and his garrison to Boston, sailed for Newfoundland to engage in an expedition for the reduction of that island. Villieu, whose share in the capture of Pemaquid was not inconsiderable, was so unfortunate as to be captured with his detachment of Canadians, by an English squadron of three ships, which reached Penobscòt just in time to see the French leave it.

A few days later an expedition started from Boston to strike a blow against the French and avenge the fall of Pemaquid. Church was commissioned by the Governor of Massachusetts to command a force of English and Indians against the French. He received his commission in August, on the very day that the French left Penobscot to invest Fort William Henry; but the expedition was considerably hastened by the tidings of the fall of that fort. Church had about five hundred men, including some Indians, embarked in open sloops and whale boats, which were the most convenient vessels for ranging the coast. After visiting the Penobscot, where he killed four or five Indians and wasted their corn-fields, he sailed for Chignecto at the head of the Bay of Fundy. The whole population of the settlement three years before was only one hundred and twenty-six, of whom but seventeen were male heads of families. It is not probable that at the time of Church's visit there were twenty-five men capable of bearing arms in the settlement. To meet this handful of peasants, Church landed four hundred men. Of course there was no resistance, but one of the inhabitants named Bourgeois took a paper to Church, showing that when Phips visited Acadia, the inhabitants of Chignecto had taken the oath of allegiance to the British Crown, and were considered to be under its protection. The production of this document prevented Church from allowing the inhabitants to be murdered by his soldiers, but he permitted unlimited plunder, and most of the people, fearing their throats would be cut, fled in terror to the woods. After a stay of nine days at Chignecto, in the course of which he and his men burnt down all the buildings, including the chapel, and killed most of the cattle in mere wantonness, he gathered up his booty and returned down the Bay.

He landed some of his men at the mouth of the St. John, where Villebon had a small guard of observation under the command of an ensign named Chevalier. The French soldiers retired to the woods when the English landed, and Chevalier sent a messenger to Villebon to inform him of their presence. On returning to the mouth of the river the French fell into an ambuscade which had been made by Church's Indians, Chevalier being killed, and his two soldiers made prisoners. The latter revealed to Church that twelve cannon were buried in the sand near the old fort; and they were dug up and seized by the English. Church thought this was glory enough for one expedition, so instead of going up the river to attack Villebon's fort, he embarked his men to return to Boston. At the St. Croix, however, he met three Massachusetts vessels with two hundred additional men under Colonel Hawthorne, who being senior to Church, deprived him of the command which he had disgraced. Church acquired some reputation in King Philip's war, but in his Eastern expeditions he always took care to be absent when there was any serious fighting to be done.

Hawthorne turned the expedition back, and announced his intention of besieging Villebon's fort on the St. John. That officer had, however, been already warned of his danger, and the attack, which might have succeeded if attempted a month before, was now doomed to failure. Villebon had one hundred men with him in his Nashwaak fort, and its position was such that it was not easily assailed. He warned the inhabitants below the fort to come in, and sent to Aukpaque, where father Simon had a mission, for as many of his warriors as he could muster, and that zealous ecclesiastic brought thirty-six warriors with him into the fort on the 14th October. On the 16th Villebon heard that the English were in force below Jemseg, and on the evening of the 17th, knowing the enemy to be near, he addressed the garrison in stirring terms, and encouraged them to resist to the last. The same night Renè and Mathieu d'Amours, and Baptiste, the privateer, came into the fort with ten other Frenchmen, and were assigned the task of operating with the Indians. Next morning the English made their appearance in three armed sloops, and effected a landing on the south side of the Nashwaak River, opposite the fort. They at once commenced the erection of a battery, and had two guns mounted, and a little later a third of larger calibre. A lively cannonade then commenced, which was only ended by the approach of night. Villebon prevented the English from lighting fires that night by discharges of grape, and they suffered much from cold. Next day the cannonade was renewed, but one of the English guns was dismounted after a short time, and the others had to be abandoned. That night the English lighted fires over a large extent of ground, and then broke up camp and retreated down the river. On the morning of the 20th their camp was found deserted, and a small party, under Neuvillette, which was detached to follow them, found them embarked some leagues below the fort, and going down the river with a fair wind. No one has ever been able to explain why the English force made such a poor attempt, but it is said there were dissentions between Church and Hawthorne, which marred the harmony of the expedition. The French list of killed and wounded amounted to but three in all; the English lost twenty-five men, of whom eight were killed.

This ended the operations of 1696, which had been wholly favorable to the French. Villebon, however, felt that he had run much risk of capture, and that the strengthening of his fort by a new line of palisades was necessary. A large part of the winter was spent in cutting palisades for the fort and placing them in position, for until this was done, the French commander did not feel secure from attack.

In the following summer the Indians were again on the war path, and large bands went from Mines and the River St. John to Penobscot. They were accompanied by their priests, St. Cosme, Simon and Chambault, and likewise by Porteneuf and René d'Amours. Their orders were to burn and destroy, and to give no quarter. Although they attempted no great enterprise, they annoyed the English settlements greatly. At Kittery they killed Major Frost, who was concerned in Waldron's treachery. They also killed a number of people in the vicinity of Wells, and they had a severe skirmish near Pemaquid with the force of Major Marsh, who, with five hundred men, was ranging the eastern coasts. The English lost twenty-five in this affair, and the Indians seven. This was probably the last blood shed by the Indians of Acadia during the war, for a treaty of peace between France and England was signed at Ryswick in September, 1697, and the Indians, no longer openly assisted by the French, were forced to make peace with the people of New England in January, 1699.

Not long after Villebon had established himself at Nashwaak, he had represented to his government the necessity for the erection of a fort at the mouth of the St. John, as a more convenient place for supplying the settlers with goods, and also because it would give the French privateers and war vessels a secure place of shelter in case of attack. The Minister looked upon the project with favor, and as early as 1696, some measures were taken towards rebuilding the old fort, which was a work with four bastions, and which needed little else than that new palisades should be erected and the ditches deepened. During 1697 no work was done, but in the following year the reconstruction of the fort went on with great vigor, and in the Autumn of that year the garrison was removed from

Nashwaak and taken to Fort Latour, which had been abandoned for so many years.

France and England now being at peace, Villebon had no warlike enterprises to engage his attention. His energies were chiefly directed to keeping the English fishermen off the coast, and confining the ambitious colony of Massachusetts within its proper bounds. Villebon claimed the Kennebec as the boundary of Acadia, and threatened to seize all vessels fishing or trading to the eastward of it. But those under his command gave him almost as much trouble as foreigners, for Belleisle and Abraham d'Entremont, who had married daughters of La Tour, claimed to be Seigniors at Port Royal, and granted fishing licenses to English vessels at fifty livres a vessel. These were not Villebon's only troubles. During his term of office, and especially the latter part of it, he seems to have been on very bad terms with some of his officers, especially with Des Goutins, the Judge. Their letters to the Minister were filled with complaints and accusations against him; but fortunately it is not necessary to believe them all, for it is certain that many of the charges made against those in authority in Acadia must have been slanders. The French government disregarded the quarrels among its subordinate officers in Canada and Acadia; too much harmony was evidently not thought desirable, as that would have prevented the officers from watching each other.

In 1700, it was decided by the French government to abandon the forts on the St. John, on the ground that its harbor was too small, and that the difficulties of navigation made a permanent establishment there inadvisable. Fontenu, the engineer who made the report on which this action was based, had been sent out by the King to examine into the affairs of Acadia, and he must have seen it with curious eyes. It was the fate of France in its schemes of colonization to commit a series of stupendous blunders, but the greatest of all was, perhaps, the abandonment of the largest river and most fertile territory in Acadia, on such shallow pretences. The harbor, which d'Iberville alleged would not hold three vessels, has many a day since seen more tonnage anchored on its bosom at one time than the government of France sent out to Acadia in any fifty years that it possessed the country. But it is of little moment now to comment on the folly of the French in abandoning the St. John, for it was inevitable that this river and the whole of Acadia would fall into the possession of the English whenever they chose to make an effort to take it.

The order went forth to remove the garrison and establishment to Port Royal, but before it could be carried out Villebon died. He was the most capable commander, probably, that the French ever had in Acadia—great both in peace and war, and wholly devoted to the interests of France. His influence over the Indians was powerful, for he was one of those grandly made men, whom barbarous peoples look upon as their natural chiefs. Men in these days, will find it difficult to excuse the cruel acts which he permitted the Indians to commit, such as the torturing and maiming of prisoners on his orders to give no quarter to the enemy. These are serious blots on the character of a man otherwise admirable, who deserved well of his country and his King. Yet, after making allowance for such faults—which after all were rather the faults of the age than of the man—it must be admitted that Villebon deserves to take a high place among the sons of New France.

CHAPTER XV.

THE CAPTURE OF PORT ROYAL.

THE death of Villebon left Villieu in the temporary command of Acadia. He caused the fort at Nashwaak to be demolished, and continued the re-building of that at Port Royal. Like his predecessor, he endeavoured to put a stop to trading with the English, and failing in that, he urged upon the home government that St. Castin and the missionaries—who were accused of being engaged in this trade—should be sent back to France.

In June, 1701, Villieu was relieved of his command by the arrival of M. de Brouillan, who came to assume the government of Acadia. Brouillan had been governor of Placentia, where he had the misfortune to meet with the gay and witty La Hontan, who has pilloried him and handed him down to the contempt of posterity in his book of "Voyages." Brouillan was both brave and diligent, but he had a bad temper and was deficient in judgment. In Newfoundland he acted the part of a cruel and vindictive tyrant, and in Acadia he added to the bad reputation which he had acquired in his former government.

Brouillan commenced his administration in Acadia with a great show of zeal and activity. His first exploit was the demolition of the fort at the mouth of the St. John River, which had just been completed. He razed it to the ground, tore down the buildings, and removed the guns to Port Royal. He desired to have a fort built at La Have, and thought it should be the principal place in the Province, and he recommended that the fort at Port Royal should be built of stone. He advocated the erection of a redoubt at the entrance of Port Royal Basin for the accommodation of a guard to give notice of an enemy's approach. He was also anxious to have the whole eastern coast of the Province granted into seignories, and did not forget to name two which he wanted for himself. In fact, Brouillan's whole term of office was a succession of requests and complaints, which must have greatly wearied the French Secretary of State, who had to read his letters.

More important events were now at hand than even the complaints and recommendations of an Acadian Governor, who boasted of his Gascon blood. James II., the dethroned King of England, died at St. Germain in September, 1701, and before he expired received the promise of Louis XIV. that he would recognize his son, the Prince of Wales, as King of England. Diplomatic relations between France and England were immediately suspended; but in March, 1702, William III. died before war had been formally declared. The formal declaration of war was issued by the government of Queen Anne on the 15th May. Then commenced the war of the Spanish succession, in which England, Holland, Savoy, Austria, Prussia and Portugal were arrayed against France, Spain and Bavaria. By Englishmen, this war is chiefly remembered by the victories of Marlborough, and the original causes of the quarrel have become merely of antiquarian interest.

The Indians had been at peace with the people of New England since January 1699, and the latter were extremely anxious to avoid another Indian war, which seemed almost a necessary accompaniment of the renewal of hostilities with France. Accordingly, in June, 1703, Governor Dudley of Massachusetts met the Eastern Indians at Falmouth, for the purpose of having a conference with them and confirming them in their pacific conduct. The result of this meeting was so satisfactory that the English were flattered by the hope that, whatever they might have to fear from the French, the Indians would remain neutral.

All these hopes proved to be illusive. Vaudreuil, the Governor-General of New France, exerted all his influence to prevent the Indians from becoming reconciled to the English, and the fact that all the Abenaquis tribes had not taken part in this conference, aided him to break up the compact. The Indians of Saco, Kennebec and Penobscot had alone joined in it, and neither the tribes of the St. John and St. Croix, nor the Micmacs, had been represented or consulted in the negotiations. He was aided also by an outrage which a party of Englishmen committed at Penobscot in plundering the residence of St. Castin. This transaction was skilfully used as a lever to detach the Penobscot tribes from the English alliance.

In August, a body of five hundred Indians and French divided into several parties, and under French leaders, fell upon the Eastern settlements of New England. Wells, Saco, Scarborough, Casco, and three or four other places in Maine, were attacked simultaneously, and the destruction of property and loss of life were very great. At Casco, the leader was Beaubassin, the son of La Valliére, and the fort there would have been captured but for the timely arrival of Captain Southwick with an armed ship. About one hundred and fifty-five English were killed or taken in these several attacks, which alarmed the whole frontier settlements from Casco to the Connecticut River.

This was but the beginning of the destruction. The Indians thronged the Eastern seaboard of New England like wolves, ready to kill any unarmed parties of white men, or capture any weakly manned vessel they could find.

Terror and confusion filled all the settlements. Militia men were gathered in haste and sent to drive back the wily savages. The Legislatures of Massachusetts and New Hampshire offered a bounty of twenty pounds for every Indian prisoner under ten years of age, and twice that sum for every older prisoner, or for his scalp. As scalps were much more easily taken care of than prisoners, it was but reasonable to expect that under a premium list so arranged the number of prisoners would be few; but even these liberal terms failed to yield many scalps. It then occurred to the authorities of Massachusetts that to retaliate on the French settlements might prove, in the end, the easiest way of protecting their own.

Accordingly, in May 1704 an expedition against Acadia was fitted out at Boston and placed under the command of Benjamin Church, now raised to the rank of a Colonel. He was furnished with a force of five hundred and fifty men, besides officers, and provided with fourteen transports, thirty-six whale boats and a shallop, and he was convoyed from Boston by three war vessels of forty-two, thirty-two and twelve guns respectively. At Penobscot he killed and took several French and Indians, among the captives being a daughter of St. Castin and her children. At Passamaquoddy he took some French settlers prisoners, and killed others who had made no resistance. When he reached the Bay of Fundy he sent his war vessels to Port Royal, while he went farther up the Bay and engaged in the more congenial task of plundering and destroying the French settlements at Mines. At this place he caused the dykes to be cut, so as to destroy the marsh lands, burnt down the dwellings of the inhabitants, and captured as many prisoners as he could secure. Then he returned to Port Royal, where the fleet had, in the mean time, been lying, but without making any serious approach to capture it. The barbarous Church, who had no stomach for real fighting, while so much more was to be obtained by the plundering of unarmed peasants, contrived to get the officers of the expedition to sign a paper to the effect that it would not be prudent to attack that place. When this was done he hastened away to Chignecto, which he had so mercilessly visited eight years before. There he burnt twenty houses, killed one hundred and twenty horned cattle, destroyed and wasted the settlement, and did the unfortunate settlers all the damage in his power. Then he returned to Boston to receive the thanks of the Legislature of Massachusetts for his eminent services.

Brouillan went to France in December, 1704, to recruit his health, and Bonaventure, who had been captain of one of the King's ships, and afterwards lieutenant for the King in Acadia, was left in command at Port Royal. Much of Brouillan's time in France seems to have been employed in writing letters to the Minister to justify his own conduct while in Acadia, and in making accusations against others. It was an unprofitable employment, for he was destined never to see Acadia again. He died at sea off Chebucto in September, 1705, on board the war ship Profond. His body was committed to the deep, but his heart was carried to Port Royal for burial, where it was interred with military honors. The hatred which this man seems to have excited among those who had dealings with him in Acadia was so intense, that it followed him to the very grave. Des Goutins, writing to the Minister after his death, says that "the public were unable to conceal their joy at his loss."

The garrison of Port Royal at this time consisted of one hundred and eighty-five men, and while some of them were invalids, others had been guilty of acts of insubordination.

Bonaventure had great difficulty in preventing them from killing the cattle of the inhabitants, or stealing their effects. Desertions were very frequent among the soldiers, and this was attributed to the irregular periods at which the provision ships arrived, leaving the men without their usual supply of food. Some of the provisions supplied were of bad quality, and this also had a bad effect on discipline. The fortifications, too, were in a bad state, owing to some original imperfection in their mode of construction, and, although a large amount of money had been expended on them, they were far from being secure from attack.

In 1706, M. de Subercase was appointed Governor of Acadia, and arrived at Port Royal. He was a man of great capacity, of amiable manners, and was as much beloved as Brouillan had been detested. Although Bonaventure had expected the appointment, he, nevertheless, supported Subercase most loyally, and for the first time for nearly twenty years, something like harmony reigned in the colony.

The ponderous volumes which contain the correspondence from Acadia at that period, and from which most of the history of the colony has necessarily to be derived, afford a curious illustration of the condition of a small community, isolated from the rest of the world, outside of the great movements of the age, and whose main business seems to have been to plot against and slander each other. The French minister, who had charge of Acadian affairs, received letters from all sorts of people in the colony, governors, judges, officers, priests and private citizens, and there is scarcely one of these letters from the time of Menneval to the time of Subercase, which is not filled with complaints of the conduct of others. One of the most common complaints against the governors of Acadia was that they traded secretly with the English. Menneval, Villebon, and Brouillan were all accused of this, although probably falsely. Iu the case of Villebon and Brouillan, tyrannical and arbitrary conduct were added to the list of charges brought against them, and many other accusations were preferred, some of which must certainly appear to a modern reader frivolous and absurd. Des Goutins, who filled the office of Judge in the colony, was one of the principal accusers of others, and in his turn had a double share of accusations preferred against him. The complaints of his bad conduct extend from Menneval's time to that of Subercase, but still he was not removed from office, and the last mentioned governor gave it as his deliberate opinion that he had been grossly slandered. Bonaventure figures for several years in the correspondence, most unenviably in connection with a liason which he had formed with the widow of Mathieu d' Amours, and in other ways the reverse of complimentary; yet Subercase states, that—except in being a little too fond of gallantry—he was an estimable person. But no class of men in Acadia had more charges preferred against them than the priests. All the governors, even Subercase, who accused no one else, had something to say against them. They were accused of rapacity, of insolence, of disobedience to the civil authority, of engaging in illicit trade, and of raising cabals in the colony. No doubt a false zeal frequently led them to mingle in temporal affairs with which they had no concern, but every one will desire to believe that their conduct was generally exemplary, and that they had the real interests of their people at heart.

At this period there was great activity among the privateers, both French and English, and the number of prisoners on each side became burthensome. Frequent voyages were made between Boston and Port Royal for the exchange of prisoners, and from the small number sometimes returned, it was thought that the exchange of prisoners was frequently made a pretext for carrying on unlawful trade with the enemy. Even Governor Dudley of Massachusetts did not wholly escape censure, for he was accused of being implicated in this trade, but the Legislature declared him innocent. Others were not so fortunate, and bills of pains and penalties were passed for the punishment of those who were supposed to be guilty, but they were very properly disallowed by the English government, as being an interference with the ordinary course of justice.

Governor Dudley now determined to show his zeal for the interests of New England, by making an attempt to capture Port Royal, and all Acadia with it. In the Spring of 1707 he induced Massachusetts, New Hampshire, and Rhode Island to raise two regiments of militia, and gave command of them to Colonels Hilton and Wainwright. Colonel March, who had won some reputation in frontier service against the Indians, was given the chief command, and the transports which carried the force to Acadia were convoyed by two ships of war. They reached Port Royal on the 6th June, and the alarm was carried to the fort by a guard which Subercase had stationed at the entrance. The Governor af Acadia was taken by surprise, and was very ill prepared for an attack, but he concealed his fears, and inspired his people with a confidence which he scarcely shared. He sent out messengers to order the inhabitants into the fort, and as fast as they arrived he embodied them into skirmishing parties and sent them to the right and left, so as to retard the approach of the enemy. It was a fortunate circumstance for Subercase that sixty soldiers from Canada had arrived at the fort a short time before the

English made their appearance, and that St. Castin, the son of the old baron, was there to command the Indians and the inhabitants. For, although the English had landed upwards of one thousand men to invest the place, they were so well met at all points that March became discouraged, and finding he was making no progress, abandoned the seige after it had lasted for eleven days. The only exploits of his army had been the burning of some houses and the killing of some cattle about the fort. March stated that his officers and men refused to assault the place, a statement which, if true, spoke very little for their courage or discipline, or for the qualities of their commander.

March wrote from Canso of the failure of the expedition, which had already been announced to Governor Dudley by straggling parties of troops which had reached Boston. There, nothing but the capture of Port Royal had been anticipated, and preparations had even been made for celebrating the event, so that the dissapointment at March's want of success was very great. Governor Dudley was determined that another attempt should be made before so fine a body of troops was permitted to disperse. He gave strict orders to allow none of the soldiers to land from the transports, on pain of death; and, sending Colonel March one hundred recruits and some who had disbanded themselves in Boston, with three Commissioners to supervise the conduct of the expedition, he ordered him back to Port Royal.

This bold stroke might have insured the capture of the place had the spirits of the leaders of the expedition been as high as that of Governor Dudley, for the French were far from anticipating a second visit. But March was sick and declined the command, and Wainwright, the next senior officer who was appointed to it, does not appear to have had any qualifications for the position. The second seige began on the 20th August and lasted until the end of the month, but the English were repulsed at all points, and if their commander's letters are to be believed, reduced to a very miserable condition. It would be tedious to enumerate the petty skirmishes which distinguished this unsuccessful affair, which reflected so little credit on the New England troops. The French seem never to have been really pressed by their besiegers, for the losses on both sides were too small to have involved much hard fighting. The French only admitted a loss in the second seige of three men killed and wounded, so we must put down Charlevoix accounts of desperate hand to hand fighting as largely fabulous. On the 1st September the New England troops embarked, and sailed away from Port Royal, where they had met with such a mortifying want of success.

During this year the Indians, incited by the French, continued their attacks on the English frontier settlements, and killed a number of persons. But beyond the terror which these marauding expeditions occasioned, they had no effect whatever on the war, except to make the English more resolute than ever to capture Port Royal, where the Indians received the arms and ammunition with which they carried on these attacks.

France was at this time waging war with much ill successs in Europe; her treasury was so exhausted, and the nation so impoverished, that she had neither men nor money to spare for Acadia. No doubt this was why the King's ships, which arrived at Port Royal after the siege, brought no merchandise either for the use of the inhabitants or the Indians. The latter were only to be kept faithful by constant presents, and even the inhabitants were not always so loyal as was to be desired. Their loyalty to France wonderfully increased under the English régime, when it was no longer their duty to practice it. Before that they were frequently supine enough when the French King's interests were involved. Many of the inhabitants had, however, suffered severely during the siege, in the loss of their cattle, dwellings and goods, and some of them were even reduced to a condition of great misery in consequence. Subercase had promised these people that they would be rewarded for their efforts to repel the enemy, and that the goods they had lost by the siege would be paid for by the King. Yet the negligence or poverty of the French government put it out of his power to keep these promises.

Notwithstanding these discouragements, the Governor continued to strengthen himself at Port Royal, and the capture of a prize laden with valuable goods by one of the men-of-war, enabled him in some measure to keep faith with the Indians and inhabitants. He employed the crew of the Venus to aid in repairing the works of the fort, as well as the soldiers of the garrison, and such of the inhabitants as he could induce to engage in the task. During the whole summer of 1708 he thus employed two hundred and fifty extra hands, and greatly improved the defences of the place, finishing the barracks, erecting a bomb proof magazine, and building a chapel and quarters for some of the officers. He was anxious to fortify La Have also, and to fit out more vessels to cruise against the English; but want of money prevented his wishes from being carried out. Failing to obtain sufficient war vessels to answer his demands, he encouraged the fitting out of privateers, and they captured many English prizes, which were of much service in meeting the wants of the colony. During this year he was greatly disturbed by rumors of invasion, but all proved false, for although the English meditated a descent upon the place, they were not then prepared to engage in it.

During that year, however, Captain Vetch, who had been frequently to Acadia on trading voyages, went to England to represent the condition of the French colonies, and to solicit aid for their reduction. He returned to New England in 1709, with the promise that a fleet would be sent out in the Spring to aid the colonists in an expedition against Quebec, and bearing to them the commands of Her Majesty that they should enlist men for that purpose. The arrangement was that a squadron of ships was to be at Boston in May, and that five regiments of regular troops were to be sent out from England, to be joined by twelve hundred men, who were to be enlisted in Massachusetts, New Hampshire and Rhode Island, and this force was to attack Quebec. Fifteen hundred men were to be enlisted by the Colonies south of Rhode Island, and they were to march by way of the lakes to attack Montreal. In America everything was prepared for the enterprise, the southern contingent, under General Nicholson, advanced to the place of rendezvous on the shores of Lake Champlain, while the New England forces were assembled at the appointed time, and awaited but the order to embark. But the promised English fleet did not appear. It had been got ready, and the British troops were on the point of embarking, when the exigencies of the war, which England was maintaining in Europe, diverted the troops to another destination. The disappointment of the colonists was great, for the expense of the proposed expedition had been heavy, and the finances of several of the colonies were so low, that they had to issue bills of credit to defray the cost which they had incurred.

This did not prevent the colonists from making another attempt to interest the Mother Country in the invasion of

New France. A Congress of governors and delegates from the legislatures met at Rhode Island in the Autumn of 1709, and resolved to send home agents to assist Colonel Nicholson, who was then in England representing the state of the country and soliciting a new expedition against Canada in the Spring. The British ministry then thought the invasion of Canada too great an enterprise to be undertaken, especially as the governor, Vaudreuil, had been warned of the previous expedition, and had made great preparations to defend himself against invasion. It was thought that the weak state of Port Royal and its proximity to Boston, made its capture a much more feasible enterprise than that of Quebec, and the smaller undertaking was therefore resolved upon.

Nicholson returned to New England in July 1710, with several war ships, and preparations were immediately made for the expedition against Port Royal, which was to be under his command. It was ready to sail in September, and on the 24th of that month was before Port Royal. Considering the weakness of that place, it was scarcely possible that Nicholson could fail, with the force at his disposal. His fleet consisted of six frigates and a bomb vessel, and his land forces were on board of thirty transports, all of which arrived safely at Port Royal except one, which was driven ashore at the entrance of the basin and lost, with twenty-six men. Nicholson's troops consisted of a regiment of royal marines from England under Colonel Redding, and four regiments of New England troops, commissioned by the Queen, and armed at her cost. His adjutant-general was Samuel Vetch, who had been promoted by the Queen to the rank of Colonel. The four Colonels of the New England land forces were Hobby and Tailer of Massachusetts, Whiting of Connecticut, and Walton of New Hampshire. The land forces were estimated by the French at 3,500 men; but as some of the regiments were quite weak, this was probably an overestimate. But, after all deductions had been made, it was much more than sufficient to accomplish the work with which it was charged.

No man knew better than Subercase the extreme weakness of his garrison, and the bad condition of his fort to stand a siege. He had less than three hundred men, yet he seems to have thought at first that the soldiers he had would stand by him, and that the inhabitants were also well disposed. But the harvest had been bad, and provisions were scarce among the Acadians. For two years the French government had left him on his own resources, and he was without money to purchase provisions, even if they had been abundant about Port Royal, while his credit was exhausted. Under these circumstances, and with a fort ill supplied with the very necessaries of life, at a season when they should have been most abundant, the soldiers naturally looked with despairing eyes on their prospects for the coming winter. Three-fourths of the soldiers at Port Royal were natives of Paris, who had been sent abroad by their parents in consequence of their bad conduct, and severe military virtue was not to be expected among such men. Almost as soon as the English forces appeared at Port Royal, they began to murmur and to say that they had been abandoned by their native country. Desertions rapidly followed, and would have been much more numerous, had not Subercase taken the precaution to remove the canoes in which the soldiers usually escaped. The evil effects of this want of confidence in his garrison became more apparent when the English landed, for Subercase was neither in a position to attempt to oppose their landing, nor to obstruct their movements, as he feared to send out any detachments of his men, lest they should desert to the enemy in a body.

Although part of Nicholson's fleet had been lying at the entrance of Port Royal Basin since the 24th September, he did not summon Subercase to surrender until October 3rd, and his vessels did not go up to the fort until the 5th. On the 6th the English troops were landed, and on the following day, under cover of the attack of a bomb-vessel, they succeeded in conveying a quantity of cannon and ammunition past the fort in boats. The English continued to work at their trenches, although continually cannonaded by the French, until the evening of the 10th, when they began to fire bombs, two of which fell into the fort, doing some damage. The same night fifty of the inhabitants and several soldiers deserted, and on the following day the remaining inhabitants presented a petition to Subercase, asking him to surrender. He paid no attention to this request, but on the followiug day, when he found that the soldiers were as much demoralized by the English fire as the inhabitants, he resolved to summon a council of his officers to consult as to what should be done. A council of war never fights, and the advice Subercase received from this one was that it was necessary to surrender. Subercase accordingly sent one of his officers to General Nicholson to propose a capitulation, and the latter authorized Colonel Redding to go to the fort and treat with Subercase as to the terms. These were finally arranged, after considerable debate, and on the 13th October the capitulation was signed. Three days later the garrison—two hundred and fifty-eight in number—miserably clad, and bearing all the marks of privation and distress, marched out of the fort with their arms and baggage, drums beating, and colors flying, according to the terms of the capitulation. The

French flag was hauled down, which had floated there as the emblem of authority for more than one hundred years, but which was never more destined to wave above that fortress, so dear to the hearts of the people of Acadia.

The soldiers of the garrison, under the terms of the capitulation, were sent in English vessels to France. Subercase sent the Baron St. Castin* to convey the tidings of the fall of the fort to Vaudreuil, Governor of New France. He was accompanied by Major Livingston, who was the bearer of a letter from Nicholson to the French Governor, in which he stated that all the inhabitants of Acadia, except those within cannon shot of the fort, were residing there on sufferance, and that he would make reprisals on them if the barbarities practiced by the savages on the frontiers of New England were not discontinued. Vaudreuil returned a haughty answer, in which he stated that any retaliatory measures which might be adopted by the English would be amply avenged by the French, denying at the same time that the French treated their captives with inhumanity, or were accountable for the behavior of the Indians. He added that a truce, or even a neutrality, might have long before terminated the miseries of the war, had the English desired it. Nicholson did not venture to carry his proposals of retaliation into effect.

The work of the expedition being done, it returned to Boston. Colonel Vetch was left in charge of the new conquest, which was re-named Annapolis Royal, in honor of the reigning Sovereign, Queen Anne. A force of two hundred marines and two hundred and fifty New England

---

* This was St. Castin, the younger, the Baron's half breed son. St. Castin, the elder, went to France about the year 1701, and must have died soon afterwards, as Subercase, writing in 1708 of his son's efforts to prove his legitimacy, so that he could obtain his father's estate, uses expressions which show that St. Castin must then have been dead for several years.

troops was detailed to garrison the place, which had been so cheaply won and so improvidently lost. The cost of the expedition to New England was £23,000, which was afterwards repaid by the British Parliament. The English loss in men did not exceed fifteen, besides those who were drowned in the wrecked transport. The French loss was smaller, but it was hunger and insubordination, and not fighting, which reduced Port Royal, which thenceforth vanishes from Acadian history.

The success of the expedition against Acadia encouraged Nicholson to attempt one on a larger scale against Canada. He went to England to solicit the aid of the government, and an armament was got ready proportioned to the magnitude of the enterprise. Nicholson returned to Boston in June, 1711, for the purpose of hurrying forward the preparations of the colonies, and later in the same month the British fleet, under Sir Hovenden Walker, arrived. It brought seven veteran regiments of the Duke of Marlborough's army and a battalion of marines under the command of Brigadier General Hill. The forces of New York, Connecticut, and New Jersey, to the number of four thousand, including nearly one thousand Indians, were collected at Albany, and, late in August, under the command of General Nicholson, marched towards Canada. The New England troops were embarked with the regulars, and sailed for the river St. Lawrence on the last day of July. The fleet consisted of sixty-eight vessels, and the troops they carried numbered six thousand four hundred and sixty-three, a force quite sufficient to have subdued Canada. But the unskilfulness of the pilots caused eight or nine of the transports to be driven ashore on the north shore of the St. Lawrence, and nearly a thousand men were drowned. This disaster caused Admiral Walker to relinquish his design, and he bore away for Cape Breton, and thence sailed directly for England. General Nicholson waited at Lake George for news of the fleet, and learning that it had miscarried, retreated to Albany. So, French domination in Canada had a respite from the great danger which had menaced it, and even the Acadians began to believe that they might succeed in driving the intrusive English from the country.

The Acadians about Annapolis had, indeed, shown great impatience of the presence of the English, and only a month after the capture of the place, they sent Renè d'Amours to the Governor of Canada, asking his assistance to enable them to withdraw themselves from the country. They complained that Colonel Vetch treated them harshly and kept them in a condition of servitude. These representations, and the statement that the Acadian Indians were growing cool in their attachment to the French alliance, caused Vaudreuil to send two trusty agents to Acadia, who were required to visit all the settlements, assure the inhabitants of his assistance in expelling the English, and exhort them to patience. Letters were also sent to the priests, pointing out to them the necessity of their keeping the Indians in an attitude of hostility to the English. But, as it was evident that some secular person having authority over the Indians, and at the same time in good understanding with the French, should be appointed to manage them, the Baron St. Castin, the younger, was entrusted with a commission for the regulation of Indian affairs, and made commandant of Penobscot and lieutenant of the troops in the country.

At this time the French Secretary of State, whose neglect of Acadia was the main cause of the capture of Port Royal, began to evince a laudable anxiety to effect its restoration. In a letter written to M. de Beauharnois he expresses his great desire to reconquer Acadia before the English should have an opportunity of establishing themselves there, and his belief that the enterprise could be easily accomplished by the sending of a detachment from Canada during the winter. In the same communication he requests his correspondent to put himself in communication with Bonaventure, Du Vivier and Subercase, and to advise as to the most certain and rapid means of success. Unfortunately, Vaudreuil was himself expecting an attack, and could therefore spare no Canadians to recapture Acadia, and the French treasury was at so low an ebb that no war vessels could be fitted out to co-operate in an attack on the English in Acadia. Louis XIV., in his quest for glory, had reduced his country to a condition of bankruptcy, and his colonies were left to shift for themselves, for he could send neither men nor money for their defence.

Under these adverse circumstances, the Acadians might have been disposed to remain quiet had it not been for the conduct of the Indians, who were now wholly under the control of St. Castin. He had sent forty of his Penobscot Indians to Annapolis to collect the savages in that vicinity and incite them to insurrection. Excuses for an outbreak were not wanting, and the circumstances of the garrison were such as to encourage an attack. The New England troops, unaccustomed to the close confinement of the fort, became the prey of disease, great numbers of them died, while others, longing for a life of freedom in the forest, so far forgot their honor and their flag as to desert. The garrison was thus left in a state of great weakness, and the fortifications were also much out of repair. Colonel Vetch had gone to Boston to take part in Nicholson's expedition to Canada, leaving Sir Charles Hobby in command, when the threatened outbreak took place. The English commandant was engaged in repairing the fortifications, and required the inhabitants to supply timber for that purpose. The Indians opposed themselves to the furnishing of timber to the English, and induced the Acadians to refuse to comply with the Governor's demands. The latter resolved to punish both French and Indians for their disobedience, and sent a detachment of sixty men under Captain Pigeon to seize some of the Indians and inhabitants who were up the river. These troops fell into an ambuscade of Indians, and thirty of them were killed, and the rest made prisoners. This success was the signal for a general rising of the inhabitants and Indians, and the garrison being greatly weakened by the loss of so many men, they were able to invest the place and keep it in a state of siege for several weeks. The inhabitants within cannon shot of Port Royal sent word to the Commandant that they considered he had violated the terms of the capitulation, to their prejudice, and that they regarded themselves absolved from the oath which they had taken not to bear arms. They then withdrew from their dwellings and joined the rest of the French in blockading the garrison. Gaulin, a missionary priest, who took an active part in inciting this revolt, wrote to Costabelle, governor of Placentia, for arms and ammunition, and afterwards proceeded there himself to obtain an experienced officer to conduct the siege. Costabelle sent a large quantity of ammunition to the insurgents in a privateer, and intended to send L'Hermite, an engineer officer, to conduct the siege, but before this could be done, Annapolis had been relieved by a reinforcement of two hundred men from Boston, and the Acadians were compelled to disperse. The privateer with the ammunition was also captured on the coast, and St. Castin—who had been most active in this Indian rising—was pressed so hard by a force under Colonel Waldron, that he had to fly from Penobscot and regain Quebec by a perilous journey through the wilderness.

Both England and France were by this time weary of the war, which had lasted with but one intermission for twenty years. Secret negotiations had been going on for some time through subordinate agents—Ménager, member of the Board of Trade for France, and the poet Prior for England—when, on the 29th June, 1712, the general conferences of the powers which had been engaged in the war, were opened at Utrecht. After more than a year had been spent in propositions and counter-propositions, on the 11th April, 1713, a treaty of peace was concluded, to which France, Great Britain, Savoy, Portugal, Prussia and Holland were parties. Whether this treaty was a prudent one or not on the part of England, may be an interesting question for speculative statesmen, but it does not much concern the present generation. The territorial questions which it was supposed to have settled had afterwards to be referred to the arbitrament of the sword. But for the time at least it gave, or was supposed to give, all Acadia to England, for its twelfth article declared that "all Nova Scotia, or Acadia, comprehended within its ancient boundries, as also the City of Port Royal, now called Annapolis," were yielded and made over to the Queen of Great Britain and to her Crown for ever. No one doubted at the time this treaty was made that its terms were explicit enough, or thought that there would be any difficulty in determining what really were the ancient limits of Acadia. But in the course of time the limits of Acadia became a great national question, and led to differences of opinion which could never be reconciled, so widely were they apart. For, while

England claimed that Acadia included all the territory east of a line from the mouth of the Kennebec to Quebec, including the whole south shore of the St. Lawrence, Gaspè, the Island of St. John, and Cape Breton, the French contended that Acadia only included the southern half of the peninsula of the present Province of Nova Scotia. But these are matters which will be treated more fully in their proper place.

CHAPTER XVI.

THE ACADIAN PEOPLE.

THE larger part of the written history of every country is taken up with accounts of changes of administration, wars with foreign nations, and personal details of the lives of its rulers. It is but seldom that we get a glimpse of the common people, upon whose prosperity the fabric of national greatness must mainly rest, for most historians seem to regard it as beneath the dignity of history to invite us to enter into the homes of the masses, to witness their daily life, and listen to the opinions which pass current among them. But in treating of the History of Acadia it is impossible to leave out of sight the origin and character of its people, whose fidelity to a lost cause overwhelmed them with misfortunes. In the preceding portion of this history they occupy but a secondary place, being overshadowed in importance by the representatives of the French Government, the great Seigniors, and the Companies, who monopolized the trade of Acadia. In the portion which is to follow they will take the leading position in the story,— a position due to them as the real upholders of French influence in Acadia after the King of France had abandoned them to their fate.

The people of Acadia are mainly the descendants of the colonists who were brought out to La Have and Port Royal by Isaac de Razilly and Charnisay between the years 1633 and 1638. The former brought out some forty families of colonists, and the latter twenty families, most of whom appear to have remained in Acadia, and commenced the cultivation of the soil. These colonists came from Rochelle, Saintonge and Poitou, so that they were drawn from a very limited area on the west coast of France, covered by the modern departments of Vendee and Charente Inferrieure. This circumstance had some influence on their mode of settling the lands of Acadia, for they came from a country of marshes, where the sea was kept out by artificial dikes, and they found in Acadia similar marshes, which they dealt with in the same way that they had been accustomed to practice in France. The uplands they almost wholly neglected, so much so that in 1734 Governor Philipps wrote to the Lords of Trade that in almost a century they had not cleared more than three hundred acres of forest lands. After making considerable allowance for exaggeration in this statement, it may be accepted as a fact that the Acadians at a time when their population was quite large had made scarcely any impression on the forests of Acadia. They found the cultivation of the marsh lands more profitable, and therefore they are not to be blamed for directing their energies to reclaiming them.

Charnisay seems to have set the example of diking the marshes at Port Royal, and Denys, whose book was published in 1672, is authority for the statement that these diked lands produced wheat in great abundance. Diereville, who visited Acadia in 1699-1700, tells his readers that the Acadians stopped the current of the sea by erecting large dikes which they called "Aboteaux." Their method was to plant five or six rows of large trees in the places where the sea enters the marshes, and between each row to lay down other trees lengthwise on top of each other, and fill up the vacant spaces with clay, so well beaten down that the tide could not pass through it. In the middle they adjusted a flood-gate in such a way as to allow the water from the marsh to flow out at low tide without permitting the sea water to flow in. He adds that these works were very expensive and demanded much labor, but the abundant harvest obtained the second year repaid them for their outlay. As the marshes were owned by many persons, they worked at the erection of dikes in concert. Diereville's account of the method of diking marsh lands pursued by the Acadians two hundred years ago might very well answer for a description of the same operation as practised at the present day in this modern Acadia.

Up to the year 1671 most of the Acadian families resided at Port Royal. The first census of Acadia was taken in that year, and it gives us a good view of the progress which had been made in the thirty-five or more years since these people had come to the country. In all Acadia there were but four hundred and forty-one people, but, omitting soldiers and fishermen, the total of actual settlers in the colony was reduced to four hundred and one, comprising seventy-four families, of which sixty-eight, numbering three hundred and sixty-three souls, were at Port Royal. The people at Port Royal had four hundred and seventeen arpents of land under cultivation, and had harvested five hundred and twenty-five barriques and fifty-seven minots of grain,—an amount which may be roughly stated to represent four thousand three hundred bushels. The Port Royal people had eight hundred and twenty-nine horned cattle, and three hundred and ninety-nine sheep, so that as a farming community they were fairly well off. The surnames of the families at Port Royal were Aucoin, Babin, Belliveau, Baiols, Belou, Bertrand, Blanchard, Boudrot, Bourc, Bourgeois, Breau, Brun, Commeaux, Cormiè, Corporon, Daigle, Douçet, Dugast, De Foret, Gaudet, Gauterot, Girrouard, Gougeon, Grangè, Guillebaut, Hébert,

Kuessy, Labathe, Lanaux, Landry, Lebland, Martin, Melanson, Morin, Pelerin, Petipas, Poirié, Pitre, Richard, Rimbaut, Robichaut, Scavoye, Sire, Terriau, Thibéadeau, Trahan, Vincent,—or forty-seven names in all. The other Acadian names of that census were Mius or D'Entremont at Pubnico, Lalloue at Cape Negro, and Poulet at Riviére au Rochelois.

The next census of Acadia of which we have full particulars was taken in 1686, and in the fifteen years that had elapsed since the former census, the population had more than doubled. A considerable portion of this increase was due to immigration, Grand-fontaine having brought out sixty persons in 1671, of whom five were females. Most of these immigrants had gone to Port Royal, which had increased its population to ninety-five families, numbering five hundred and ninety-two persons. Notwithstanding this large increase, there was less land under cultivation than at the previous census, and the number of horned cattle had also decreased by nearly two hundred. This may be taken as an indication that the people of Port Royal were at that time devoting themselves more to fishing and other pursuits than merely to agriculture. In the interval between the two enumerations, two important settlements had been founded by colonists from Port Royal—that of Chignecto, which at the census of 1686 contained seventeen families, numbering one hundred and twenty-seven persons, and Mines, which had ten families and fifty-seven persons. The people of Chignecto had four hundred and twenty-six arpents of land under cultivation, a larger area than was cultivated at Port Royal, and they possessed two hundred and thirty-six horned cattle and one hundred and eleven sheep. At Mines there were eighty-three arpents under cultivation, and the settlers had ninety horned cattle and twenty-one sheep.

This census gives us nearly fifty new names not found in the census of 1671. At Port Royal there were Arsenault, Barilost, Basterache, Benoit, Brossard, Leblanc, Leborgne, Brien, Colson, Como, Douaron, Dugas, Fardel, Garault, Guillaume, Goho, Godet, Godin, Henry, LaVoye, Lort, Leuron, Margery, Peltict, Prijean, Leprince, Leperriere, Toan and Tourangeau, none of which had been in Acadia at the previous census. All the other settlements contained persons who had evidently reached Acadia after the census of 1671. At Chignecto the new names were Mirande, Labarre, Mignault, Cochin, Cottard, Mercier, Lavalle, Lagasse, and Blon. At Mines were Laboue, La Roche, Pinet and Rivet. At La Have were Provost, Labal, Vesin, Lejeune, Michel and Gourdeaux.

In addition to these new names of settlers, there were at this time in Acadia a number of persons whose families did not become permanent residents of the country. At Penobscot, the Baron St. Castin resided with his family and servants. At Chignecto, La Valliére had an extensive establishment, and cultivated sixty arpents of land. At Miramichi resided Richard Denys, a son of Nicholas Denys, then in France. At Nepisiquit was Enaud, who had married an Indian woman. On the River St. John resided Martin D'Aprendistigué, a son-in-law of La Tour, his wife Jeanne, then sixty years old, and his daughter Chariane. On this river also resided three of the d'Amours family, Louis, Mathieu, and René, the first two being married. Mathieu d'Amours resided at Freneuse, on the east side of the St. John, opposite the Oromocto; Louis had his residence at Jemseg.

None of the La Tour family appear in the census of

1671, but in 1686 Jacques La Tour, the oldest son of La Tour by his second marriage, was living at Cape Sable, and was married to Mariè Melançon, probably a daughter of the La Verdure who appears as a witness in his father's marriage contract. Charles La Tour was also at Cape Sable at this time, but was unmarried. At the same place were his sisters, Anne and Marguerite, married to two of the D'Entremont family, Jacques and Abraham Mius. The oldest sister, Mariè, was at Port Royal, and was the wife of Alexander LeBorgne, better known as M. de Belle-isle. All of La Tour's children by his second marriage, were therefore in Acadia in 1686. None of the name are now left in either of the Provinces which formed Acadia. Jacques La Tour's only son retired to the French dominions after the English occupation of the country, as did also Charles La Tour, who died some time prior to 1732.

The next census of which we have details was taken in 1693, the population of all Acadia being then one thousand and nine, of which five hundred persons, divided into eighty-eight families, resided at Port Royal. The population of the Province had increased in seven years by one hundred and. twenty-four, which is probably about what the natural rate of increase should have been, but Port Royal had lost ninety-two of its population. Chignecto also had reduced its population from one hundred and twenty-seven to one hundred and nineteen. These losses are easily accounted for. The progress of the Chignecto colony had been retarded by the seigniorial claims of La Valliére, who claimed the whole of that fine territory. Port Royal had ceased to be the seat of government, which was then administered by Villebon at Fort Nashwaak, and its people had gone in large numbers to Mines, which afterwards became the most flourishing settlement in Acadia.

Mines had in 1693 a population of two hundred and ninety-seven persons, who had three hundred and sixty arpents of land under cultivation, and possessed four hundred and sixty-one horned cattle, three hundred and ninety sheep, and three hundred and fourteen swine. Port Royal also, though it had lost in population, had gained in other respects, for it had thirteen hundred and fifteen arpents of land under cultivation, and possessed eight hundred and seventy-eight horned cattle, twelve hundred and forty sheep, and seven hundred and four swine. Chignecto had one hundred and fifty-seven acres of land under cultivation, and owned three hundred and nine horned cattle, two hundred and eighty sheep, and one hundred and forty-six swine. The other settlements at this period were insignificant. At Cape Sable there were thirty persons, at Port Razoir twenty, at River St. John twenty, and twenty at Penobscot.

A partial census taken in 1695 gives us details of the settlements on the St. John river, which then contained ten families, numbering forty-nine persons. There were one hundred and sixty-six acres of land under cultivation and seventy-three in pasture. The crop of the year was one hundred and thirty bushels of wheat, three hundred and seventy of corn, thirty of oats, and one hundred and seventy of peas. The live stock consisted of thirty-eight horned cattle and one hundred and sixteen swine. In 1698 there was another partial census of Acadia, when Port Royal had five hundred and seventy-three inhabitants, and Chignecto one hundred and seventy-five. Port Royal had twelve hundred and seventy-five arpents of cultivated land, fifteen hundred and eighty-four fruit trees, nine hundred and eighty-two horned cattle, and eleven hundred and thirty-six sheep. Chignecto had been sacked by Church two years before, but still it had held its ground pretty well. It had two hundred and ninety-eight arpents under culture, three hundred and fifty-two horned cattle, and one hundred and seventy-eight sheep. Church had boasted that in 1696 he left their "cattle, sheep, hogs and dogs lying dead," but as the only live stock which had diminished were the sheep, he must have wreaked his vengeance mainly on them.

In 1701 there was another census of Acadia, which shows Port Royal with its population reduced to four hundred and fifty-six persons, and a still greater reduction in its live stock and cultivated acreage. Mines, however, had increased its population to four hundred and ninety, and Chignecto had a population of one hundred and eighty-eight. In 1703 Port Royal had a population of four hundred and eighty-five, and Chignecto two hundred and forty-five; but the population of Mines had fallen to four hundred and twenty-seven; and in this census Cobequid appears for the first time with a population of eighty-seven souls. Evidently this settlement had been included in previous enumerations of Mines, or there had been a large emigration from Mines to Cobequid in the interval.

In 1714 a census of Port Royal and Mines was taken by Felix Pain, a missionary priest, and is preserved in the archives of Paris. By that census it appears that Port Royal, including the Banlieu, the Cape and the residences close to the fort, contained eight hundred and ninety-five French inhabitants. Mines, under which designation were included the residents on the rivers Gaspereaux, Piziquid, Habitants and Canards, had eight hundred and seventy-eight inhabitants. Many new names appear in this census, showing that some immigrants had come to Acadia from Canada, or from France, and that many soldiers of the garrison had settled in the country, married and founded families. The names in this census list which are not to be found in the lists either for 1671 or 1686, are Abraham, Alain, Barnabé, Beaumont, Beaupré, Bernard, Blondin, Bonappetit, Baguette, Babet, Bourg, Breau, Bodart, Boutin, Boucher, Boisseau, Brasseau, Cadet, Carne, Champagne, Clemenceau, Cosse, Chauvet, D'Amboise, Debert, Dubois, D'Arocs, Emmanuel, l'Etoile, Gentil, Gouselle, Jean, Jasmin, Labaune, Langlois, La Liberté, Laurier, La Rosette, Lafont, La Montagne, Lavergne, Le Basque, Lésperance, Le Breton, Lemarquis, Lionnais, Maillard, Moire, Mouton, Nantois, Oliver, Paris, Parisien, Perrinè, Potier, Raimond, Rieul, Roy, Samson, Savary, Sellan, Surette, Saunier, St. Louis, St. Scenne, Toussaint, Villate, Voyer, Yvon. Here we have sixty-nine names of families which must have come to Acadia subsequent to the census of 1686. It is possible that some of these names are not new, but are merely the old names spelled differently, such as Bourg, which may be merely Bourc, with the final letter changed. But after making allowance for such alterations, the fact remains that at least half of the one hundred and twenty names of families residing at Port Royal and Mines in 1714 did not exist in Acadia prior to 1686. Indeed the development of new names in Acadia was quite remarkable, for in 1730, after the English had been in possession of the country for twenty years, among the signatures to the oath of allegiance are several names not to be found in any previous census.

Having in the foregoing pages gone over the progressive stages in the growth of the Acadian settlements with some degree of minuteness, the result may be summed up in a few words—that the Acadian people are descended in the first place from some sixty families, brought from Rochelle and its vicinity between 1633 and 1638, from sixty other individuals brought also from Rochelle in 1671, and from sixty or seventy others, most of them disbanded soldiers, mainly from Paris, who settled in the country between 1686 and 1710. A few settlers from Canada, such as the d'Amours, came to Acadia at various times, but they nearly all went back again, so that the Canadian element had little or no influence on the Acadian population. The Acadians were, therefore, a homogeneous people to a greater degree than almost any other race that can be named. Very few women came out from France after the first immigrations prior to 1638, so that, although new families were founded, the mothers were in most cases Acadians of the original stock, and so the unity of race was preserved. Grand-fontaine brought out four girls and one woman among his sixty immigrants of 1671, and these seem to have been the only females brought to Acadia by the French Government. A further proof of this fact is furnished by the remarkable scarcity of marriageable women in Acadia at all times. By the census of 1686, it appears that there were three hundred and forty-two unmarried males in Acadia and only two hundred and forty-five unmarried females. These figures include the children of every age, and even after deducting twenty-five unmarried fishermen at Chedabucto and Miramichi, indicate a positive dearth of unmarried young women at the settlements. The census of 1693 shows three hundred and eighty-three unmarried males and only two hundred and seventy-five unmarried females. Fortunately in this census the ages are given. There were two men between thirty-one and forty unmarried, but no single women of that age. There were fourteen unmarried men between twenty-one and thirty, but only four unmarried women of the same age. There were forty-seven youths between sixteen and twenty, but only seventeen girls of corresponding ages. There were seventy-seven boys between eleven and fifteen, and fifty-five girls of the same age; there were two hundred and fifteen boys of ten years and under, and one hundred and eighty girls of the same age. Thus, while the normal proportion of boys to girls was as one hundred and nineteen to one hundred up to the age of ten years, in consequence of early marriages among the girls, the proportion changed between eleven and fifteen to one hundred and sixty-nine boys to one hundred girls, and between the ages of sixteen and twenty to two hundred and seventy-six boys to one hundred girls. It is, therefore, clear that about twenty per cent. of the Acadian girls were married before they had reached their sixteenth year, and that scarcely any were left unmarried at twenty. This excess of males continued as long as Acadia was a French Province. In 1698, in the two settlements of Port Royal and Chignecto, the unmarried males exceeded the unmarried females by sixty-eight in a total population of seven hundred and forty-eight. In 1701, at Port Royal, Chignecto and Mines the unmarried males numbered four hundred and seven, and the unmarried females three hundred and fifty-one. In 1703, the numbers were four hundred and forty-eight males to three hundred and ninety-two females, and in 1714, at Port Royal and Mines, there were six hundred and sixteen unmarried males and only five hundred and sixty-three unmarried females. An attempt has been made to disprove the scarcity of women in Acadia by citing the case of Marie Salé, an old maid, who was living at Port Royal in 1686. This venerable female was then eighty-six years of age, and was not in Acadia at all when the census of 1671 was taken. She must have passed her three-score years and ten before she came to the country, and therefore her case proves nothing, except that none of the Acadians desired to marry a woman old enough to be a great-grandmother.

Probably it was the scarcity of white women that caused some of the Acadians to marry Indian females. M. Rameau, the talented author of "La France au Colonies," has been fiercely attacked for ascribing the great friendship which existed between the Acadians and the Indians to these marriages. Nevertheless, that such unions took place is susceptible of as clear proof as any fact in Acadian history. There are four undoubted marriages of Acadians to Indian women recorded in the official census returns prepared for the information of the French government, three of which were fruitful. The marriages in question are those of St. Castin at Penobscot, Pierre Martin at Port Royal, and Martin Lejeune at La Have. A most absurd attempt has recently been made by a descendant of the Acadians to get rid of the issue of these three marriages by driving St. Castin's children off among the Indians, sending Martin and his family to La Rochelle or Louisburg in 1710, and conveying Lejeune and his progeny to some unknown and unnamed region whence they could never return to defile the pure blood of the Acadians. Unfortunately the facts are against such a disposal of these families. The sons of St. Castin by his Indian wife did not remain in Acadia and found families; but two of his daughters married in Acadia in 1707. Anastasia St. Castin became the wife of Alexander Le Borgne, son of M. de Belleisle, and grandson of Charles La Tour. He appears to have gone to reside among the Indians, but he returned to Port Royal, and was residing there in 1734 and up to the time of the invasion of Annapolis in

1744. Frances, his daughter, married an inhabitant named Robicheau, between 1741 and 1744, and her descendants are now doubtless in Acadia. Belleisle himself, or his eldest son, was living on the St. John river in 1754. Therese St. Castin, who married Philip D'Entremont, also remained in the Province. The fact that these marriages took place shows that such alliances were not regarded as disgraceful, for both the bridegrooms had the best blood in Acadia in their veins—both were grandsons of La Tour. And scarce as young women were in Acadia, the fact that Anselme St. Castin, the young Baron, was a half-breed, did not prevent him from marrying one of the best born maidens in the Province, for Charlotte, daughter of Louis d'Amours, became his wife.

The name of Pierre Martin appears in the census of 1771. He was then forty years of age. His wife was a squaw, Anne Oxihnoroudh, and he had four children, the eldest of whom was ten years of age. In the census of 1714, four years after Port Royal was taken, and after all the inhabitants who left the Province in consequence of the English occupation had departed, the name of Pierre Martin figures in the list of inhabitants of Port Royal. There is also Pierre Martin, the younger, evidently one of the half-breed sons, who has no less than eleven children, eight sons and three daughters, suggesting frightful thoughts as to the capacity of the Martins for spreading Indian blood among the Acadians. The Martins continued to increase and flourish, notwithstanding the English occupation. The oath of allegiance of 1730 was signed by no less than seven Martins then residing at Annapolis, viz., Batist, Pierre, Charles, Etienne, Michell, and two Martins named René. It is a little singular that the third signature to this oath should have been that of Pierre

HISTORY OF ACADIA.   295

Martin, no doubt a direct descendant of the original Pierre.

In the census of 1686 the name of Martin Lejeune occurs. He resided at La Have; his wife was an Indian woman, and they had two children. The La Have colony was broken up in 1690 by the English, and the inhabitants sought homes in other parts of the Province. Fugitives from La Have would naturally make their way to Port Royal or Mines, either being within three days journey of La Have. In fact, one of the sources of the La Have can be traced to the same chain of lakes which feed the Gaspereaux flowing into the Basin of Mines. Accordingly, among the inhabitants of Mines residing on the Piziquid river in 1714, were two men named Lejeune, one with a wife and one son, the other with a wife, three sons and three daughters. To strengthen the supposition that these Lejeunes were from La Have, it may be stated that a man named Michel was a resident of La Have in 1686, and that in 1714 a Michel was residing at Piziquid, near the Lejeunes. On the other hand, it is just possible that Lejeune did not leave the neighborhood of La Have, notwithstanding the attack of the English. There was a man named Lejeune living at Petite River, a short distance west of La Have, in 1745, and he had the honor of being mentioned in a letter written by Governor Beauharnois to the Count de Maurepas. It is, therefore, pretty clear that the descendants of Lejeune, of La Have, and his Indian wife are still in Acadia.

It is abundantly clear, however, that three marriages between Acadians and Indian women two centuries ago could have no influence whatever, after eight generations, on a race as numerous as the Acadians. These marriages, therefore, became matters rather of antiquarian interest

than as bearing on the origin of the Acadian people.
Whether there were other marriages of a similar character
prior to 1714, is a matter which it is, perhaps, not worth
while to inquire into, for the census of that year supplies no
information on the subject. Colonel Vetch, in a letter
written to the Lords of Trade in that year, states that Acadians had intermarried with the Indians, and to this and
to their being of one religion he ascribes the influence
which the French had over the latter. Vetch had an
opportunity of knowing the truth with respect to this if he
chose to tell it, for he had traded with the Acadians before
Port Royal fell, and had prior to the time he wrote been
for some time commander at that place. A minute of
council written by Paul Mascerene, then Lieutenant-
Governor, in January 1745, supplies another interesting
contribution to the literature of this subject. This minute
states that a letter was laid before the Council from the
inhabitants of Grand Pré, River Canard, and Piziquid,
stating that they had been informed that several armed
vessels had arrived from New England, that they had
pressed several of the inhabitants of Annapolis to serve as
pilots to go against the Indians, and that they had heard
they were "coming up the Bay to do the same, and to
destroy all the inhabitants that had any Indian blood in
them and scalp them." They then went on to say, that
as there were "a great number of Mulattoes amongst them
who had taken the oath, and who were allied to the greatest
families, it had caused a terrible alarm." They therefore
prayed for the protection of the Lieutenant-Governor. The
minute then goes on to relate that the three inhabitants
who were chosen by the three districts named to bring this
letter were called in and assured by Mascerene of his protection, and told also that "in regard to the notion that the

inhabitants had amongst them that all who had any Indian blood in them were to be treated as enemies, it was a very great mistake, since if that had been the design of the New England armed vessels, it might very well be supposed that the inhabitants of this (Annapolis) river, many of whom have Indian blood in them, and some even who live within reach of the cannon, would not be suffered to live peaccably as they do." This minute would seem to show that it was rather a matter of notoriety that there were Acadians with Indian blood in them at Grand Pré, Piziquid, River Canard and Annapolis, in the year 1745.

La Mothe Cadillac, who lived in Acadia for several years, writing in 1693, gives a description of the Acadians of that day, which shows that in the earlier days of the colony marriages with the Indians could not have been common. He says: "The natives of the country are well made, of good figure, and well proportioned. They are robust, and can stand much fatigue. *They generally have light hair.*" This certainly is not a description of a people who had Indian blood in their veins, and where the Acadians of the present day have preserved this type, we may conclude that the few marriages with Indians, which are recorded, have made no impression upon the race. Although the Acadians are a darker people than the majority of their ancestors were, that fact proves nothing with regard to the purity of their blood. Different modes of living and differences of food are potent influences in changing the complexions of a people. The Anglo-Saxon in America loses the flaxen hair and ruddy complexion, which marked his ancestors, without exciting any suspicion of being of mixed blood. The per centage of Indian blood in the veins of the Acadians is too small to be worthy of being taken into account, and in modern times marriages between Acadians and Indians have been exceedingly rare.

The world is indebted to the Abbé Raynal for that picture of the mode of life and character of the Acadians, which was accepted so long without question, and which served to make their misfortunes appear so cruel and undeserved. It represents them as a people without quarrels, without litigation and without poverty, "where every misfortune was relieved before it could be felt, without ostentation on the one hand, and without meanness on the other." Whatever little differences arose from time to time among them were amicably adjusted by their elders. "They were," says Raynal, "a society of brethren, every individual of which was equally ready to give and to receive what he thought the common right of mankind. So perfect a harmony naturally prevented all those connexions of gallantry, which are often so fatal to the peace of families. This evil was prevented by early marriages, so that no one passed his youth in a state of celibacy." We are also told by the same authority that "their habitations, which were constructed of wood, were extremely convenient and furnished as neatly as substantial farmers' houses in Europe."

This is but a part of the elaborate and highly colored description which Raynal has given of the Acadians. It was written for the purpose of drawing a sharp contrast between the condition of the Acadians and that of the miserable peasantry of France, who before the Revolution were reduced almost to the condition of slaves. So long as the picture of the Acadian peasants was made sufficiently striking to point the contrast, Raynal cared nothing for its truth. Indeed, such a condition of things as he imagined in Acadia, never existed anywhere, and never can exist so long as human passions and human motives remain unchanged. There is no reason to believe that the Acadians differed materially in character from any other peasant class of their race. They were intensely patriotic, much more so than the peasant of their metropolitan state, and this, no doubt, was largely due to the influence of their priests, who were always wedded to the interests of France. But there was another cause for this feeling. Their ancestors had left France when she was great and powerful under the master hand of Richelieu, when the memory of the first and greatest of its Bourbon kings was still fresh and glorious. A century passed away, and France had become debauched and ruined by the follies and vices of her kings, yet to the Acadian she was still the France of his forefathers, and he could not understand why the relations between the nations should so change, that England should acquire the ascendant in America.

The Acadians, living as they did remote from the centres of thought, escaped the malign influence of that form of scepticism which passed for philosophy in the eighteenth century. They accepted without question the teachings of their ecclesiastics, and were largely guided by them in the conduct of their affairs. The influence of the priests was, no doubt, generally employed for proper and beneficial purposes, but when they became political emissaries, their influence became evil and even ruinous to the Acadian people. Still, apart from that, the aspects in which they presented themselves in their relations to the people was sometimes very different from what they should have been. The French Governors of Acadia were constantly complaining that the priests sought to rule the people, and infringed on the civil authority. These complaints began with Grand-fontaine in 1671, and continued as long as the

French had Governors in the country. The ecclesiastics were accustomed to defy the authority of the French Governors just as they sought to defy the authority of the English Governors in later times. Some of the priests were accused of very unclerical conduct both by the French commandants and other officers connected with the administration of affairs. There was scarcely one of the priests in the larger settlements who was not accused of engaging in illicit trade with the English. In Menneval's time the priests' houses at Port Royal were said by Des Goutins to be the receptacles of smuggled goods. Charges of a graver character were preferred against them. Trouvé, one of the priests at Port Royal, is charged with putting improper questions to several women at the confessional. These women went to Des Goutins, the Judge, asking him to receive their complaints against Trouvé, and stating that this priest, by the questions he asked, wished to awaken in their minds wrong feelings towards their husbands. Des Goutins adds: "Some scandal of this kind occurred in the case of a young lady of quality, who, tired out and annoyed by questions of this sort, rose and left the confessional, saying that she would not come again and confess to him. The said Trouvé was seen to come out very much excited and scolding, and he went immediately to perform mass." He must have been in an excellent frame of mind for this solemn duty. This same Trouvé was also charged with refusing to receive the confession of Dominick Garreau, Sergeant Royal, when on his death-bed, because Garreau refused to resign his office. Jeoffry, another priest, was accused of refusing to bury the son of one of the settlers. In consequence of this last difficulty, a number of the settlers refused to pay their tithes, and the priests had to go to law to obtain the twenty-sixth part of the produce, which they claimed.

St. Cosme, the priest at Mines, was charged with very unbecoming conduct in 1694. The wife of Pierre Theriot, the principal colonist there, had been accused by a man named Le Baume, Theriot's servant, of being too intimate with Jean Theriot, who was a nephew of Pierre and lived at his house. Le Baume was brought up on a charge of slander before the Judges at Port Royal, who gave sentence against him and condemned him to make a public apology to the parties he had slandered, and to pay the costs of the suit. This sentence was carried out, but the priest, instead of acquiescing in it and rejoicing in the vindication of an innocent woman, pronounced sentence of excommunication against her on three successive Sundays, and on the fourth expelled her from the church, reiterating the disproved charges which had been made against her. A community where such things could happen must have differed considerably from that depicted by Abbé Raynal.

The Acadians themselves were frequently spoken of in terms far from flattering by the writers of the despatches to the Minister. Perrot, writing in 1686, says that many of them did nothing but hunt and wander away from their superiors, under pretence of owning grants that they did not improve. If we are to believe this authority, the inhabitants neglected their land in order to go hunting, and that some of them led dissolute lives with the savage women. At this period, he states that there were many lawsuits and much disorder in the colony. The orders sent to Menneval by the King relative to the government of the country are not such orders as a monarch would be likely to send with reference to a people who were above reproach. The King, it would seem, had been informed that there were continual divisions among the settlers, and that bush-ranging was the only occupation of part of them. He had been informed also that many of them were leading dissolute lives with savage women, and this Menneval was instructed to prevent. It might perhaps be presumed by those who wished to give the Acadians the benefit of every doubt, that these instructions applied to St. Castin, the d'Amours, Enaud, and one or two other Seigniors, who, although then residents of Acadia, were certainly not Acadians in the ordinary meaning of the term. But this view of the subject is entirely disproved by what follows, for the letter of instructions goes on to say—" What His Majesty has explained concerning his plans for the prevention of licentiousness and ranging the woods, which forms the only employment of those living in five or six of the old and principal settlements, and to compel those who are there to cultivate the ground and fish, applies also to the Sieur de St. Castin." This addition shows clearly that the King, when referring to the prevailing licentiousness, was speaking of the inhabitants in general, and not merely of a few lawless men of rank.

The united testimony of all the Governors of the Province—French and English—goes to show the litigious disposition of the Acadians. As they had no commerce worth naming, and very little barter of any kind, they had very few subjects to go to law about; but such as they had they eagerly took advantage of. The most fertile causes of litigation with them were disputes as to the boundaries of their grants, and they pursued these quarrels sometimes with such zest as to carry appeals to the Council at Quebec, which was harder to reach than Australia is at the present day. The English Courts in Nova Scotia would not entertain their civil causes, because to have undertaken to adjudicate upon the boundaries of their lands would have involved the admission that they were entitled to hold them. But this did not prevent them from quarreling. Governor Lawrence, writing in December, 1753, to the Lords of Trade, says: "The French inhabitants are tolerably quiet as to government matters, but extremely litigious among themselves." This scarcely agrees with the Abbé Raynal's account of the Acadians. At the very time when he represents them as having no differences among themselves but what were amicably adjusted by their elders, they were clamorous to have their causes tried before the English Courts.

The gentle and peaceful character of the Acadians has been much insisted on, and given as a reason against their forcible removal from the Province. The people within reach of the guns of Port Royal were tolerably obedient, but in the settlements where there was no military force to coerce them, they exhibited very different traits. When Governor Brouillon visited Mines in 1701, he found the people extremely independent, not acknowledging royal or judicial authority. The judgments of the Judge at Port Royal they entirely disregarded, and Bonaventure had to use considerable pressure to bring them to order. Nor was their patriotism at that time very strong. They expressed their fears to Brouillon that the Province was about to be put under the control of a Company, and declared that in that case they would do nothing for its defence, but would rather belong to the English. This testimony of a French Governor as to the disposition of the people of Mines agrees precisely with that of Paul Mascerene, a French Huguenot in the British service, who wrote to the Lords of Trade in 1720 as follows: "The inhabitants of this place" * * * "are less tractable and subject to command.

All the orders sent to them, if not suiting to their humors, are scoffed and laughed at, and they put themselves upon the footing of obeying no government." Governor Armstrong, writing of the Acadians in 1731, says: "It will be a difficult matter to bring these people to any reasonable terms of obedience to His Majesty's government, or even to any manner of good order and decency among themselves; for though they are a litigious sort of people, and so ill-natured to one another as daily to encroach upon their neighbors' properties, which occasions continual complaints, yet they all unanimously agree in opposing every order of government, though never so conducive to their own interests."

This may be regarded as the account of an enemy of the Acadians, and therefore colored by prejudice. But it is somewhat unfortunate that very unflattering accounts of their condition and character have been written by men of their own race. Costabelle, the Governor of Placentia, writing to the French Minister in regard to the proposed removal of the Acadians to Cape Breton for the purpose of strengthening that colony, says that the Acadians are half Indians in disposition, and that they could never be relied on. "Without money," he says, "one can expect nothing from the good will of the people, who will be always more disposed to go back into foreign territory on the smallest discontent, than to be subjected to the nation from which they draw their origin, which they have for the most part forgotten." And in 1745, Beauharnois, Governor of Canada, in a letter to Count De Maurepas, says of the Acadians: "The Acadians have not extended their plantations since they have come under English dominion; their houses are wretched wooden boxes, without conveniences and without ornaments, and scarcely containing the most necessary furniture. But they are extremely covetous of specie. Since the settlement of Isle Royale, they have drawn from Louisbourg—by means of their trade in cattle and all the other provisions—almost all the specie the King annually sent out. It never makes its appearance again; they are particularly careful to conceal it."

These extracts from the letters of contemporaries of the Acadians, French and English, are not given for the purpose of showing that the Acadians were worse than other people in point of morality, but merely to prove that they were not so much better than their neighbors as to be above the laws which apply to ordinary mortals. The enemies of British power have industriously labored to invest the Acadians with a certain halo of sanctity, so that their expulsion in 1755 might be made to appear an awful and inexcusable crime. The readers of this book, as they trace the course of events from the fall of Port Royal to the capture of Beauséjour, will have an opportunity of judging for themselves as to the morality or necessity of that extreme exercise of power. If they have a turn for historical comparisons, they may wish to measure it with the treatment of the Huguenots after the revocation of the Edict of Nantes by Louis XIV. But the act must not be judged by any parallel supplied by that cruel and vain-glorious King. One evil deed does not excuse another, and the enforced exile of the Acadians must be justified or condemned on its own merits. It is a subject in regard to which a modern writer can well afford to deal impartially, for there is no reason that national prejudices should warp our judgment of events which happened a century and a quarter ago.

The modern Acadians are, no doubt on the whole, a better people than their ancestors, less violent in their animosities, and less visionary as to the glory of the nation from which they sprung. Indeed a modern Acadian would find it difficult to find in the France of the present day any of the lineaments of the old France from which his forefathers came, and for which they cherished such a deep affection. Here alone has been preserved with fidelity the type of the French peasant of two centuries and a half ago. Here again a portion of old France survives under happier conditions and with better hopes, preserving the picturesque and homelike aspects of the Mother Land without those drawbacks which made the French peasant of ancient times little better than a slave. Nearly one hundred thousand of the descendants of the ancient Acadians now people the Maritime Provinces of Canada, a loyal, frugal, industrious and contented peasantry, a people of strong religious convictions, and of high moral character. Instead of being an element of political weakness, as their ancestors were, they form one of the bulwarks of the state, and there is no race of men in the Dominion whose loyalty is more to be depended on. And they have beyond all other races in Canada that strong element of patriotic feeling—the love of the soil upon which they were born. This is still to them the Acadia of their fathers; the land well beloved and without a peer, and they are proud to call this spot of earth their home. Long may the Acadians flourish and increase in a land which their forefathers subdued, and which they hold so dear.

CHAPTER XVII.

THE ENGLISH AT ANNAPOLIS.

THE treaty of Utrecht, by which Acadia was given to England, also ceded Newfoundland wholly to that power, but France retained the Island of Cape Breton and the other Islands of the Gulf of St. Lawrence, including, of course, the Island of St. John, now known as Prince Edward Island. The way was thus left clear for France to erect new and powerful establishments on the very borders of Acadia, and to retain for herself the rich fisheries of the Gulf of St. Lawrence, and the practical control of the whole of the coasts washed by that mighty sea. That was what France immediately proceeded to do. The French garrison, withdrawn from Placentia, was removed to Cape Breton, which was re-named Isle Royale, and there on the shores of English Harbor began the erection of a great fortress, from which France might look forth and defy her enemies, the widely-famed and potent Louisbourg.

It was evident from the first that the French intended to interpret the cession of Acadia in as restricted a sense as possible, and that it was their aim to neutralize the power of England in the colony, by confining it within the narrowest limits. The inhabitants numbered some two thousand five hundred at the time of the treaty of Utrecht, divided into three principal settlements at Port Royal, Mines and Chignecto. The priests at these settlements during the whole period from the treaty of Utrecht to the expulsion of the Acadians were, with scarcely an exception, agents of the French Government, in their pay, and resolute opponents of English rule. The presence of a powerful French establishment at Louisburg, and their constant communications with Canada, gave to the political teachings of those priests a moral influence, which went far towards making the Acadians continue faithful to France. They were taught to believe that they might remain in Acadia, in an attitude of scarcely concealed hostility to the English Government, and hold their lands and possessions as neutrals, on the condition that they should not take up arms either for the French or English. In other words, they were to enjoy all the advantages of British rule, and have all the privileges of British subjects, without being liable to any of the drawbacks which such an allegiance implied.

When Port Royal was taken, a certain number of the French inhabitants, such as lived within a league of the fort, were by the terms of the capitulation, permitted to remain upon their estates, with their corn, cattle and furniture, for two years, on taking the oath of allegiance. No provision whatever was made for the other residents of Acadia. By the fourteenth article of the treaty of Utrecht, it was stipulated "that the subjects of the King of France may have liberty to remove themselves within a year to any other place, with all their movable effects. But those who are willing to remain, and to be subject to the King of Great Britain, are to enjoy the free exercise of their religion according to the usages of the church of Rome, as far as the laws of Great Britain do allow the same."

On the 23rd June, 1713, nearly three months after the treaty of Utrecht was signed, Queen Anne wrote to Nicholson, the Governor of Nova Scotia, as follows: "Whereas our good brother, the Most Christian King, hath, at our desire, released from imprisonment on board his galleys, such of his subjects as were detained there on account of their professing the Protestant religion. We, being willing to show by some mark of our favor towards his subjects how kind we take his compliance therein, have therefore thought fit hereby to signify our will and pleasure to you, that you permit such of them as have any lands or tenements in the places under your government in Acadia and Newfoundland, that have been or are to be yielded to us by virtue of the late Treaty of Peace, and are willing to continue our subjects, to retain and enjoy their said lands and tenements without any molestation, as fully and freely as other of our subjects do or may possess their lands or estates, or to sell the same if they shall rather choose to remove elsewhere. And for so doing this shall be your warrant."

The status of the Acadians in 1714 can be easily gathered from the article of the treaty and the royal letter above quoted. They were entitled to sell their property, real and personal, and remove from the Province if they so desired, or if they chose to remain in the Province, they might do so, and were to be permitted to reside upon their lands and enjoy their property as fully and freely as other subjects of the British Crown, and likewise the free exercise of their religion. But the language of both treaty and letter shows that it was as British subjects only these privileges were to be enjoyed. (It was never contemplated that the Acadians should establish themselves in the country a colony of enemies of British power, ready at all times to obstruct the authority of the government, and to make the possession of Acadia by England merely nominal.) A letter from father Felix Pain, missionary at Mines, to Costabelle, written in September, 1713, shows clearly enough what were the views of the Acadians at that period. Father

Felix reports them as saying: "We shall answer for ourselves and for the absent, that we will never take the oath of fidelity to the Queen of Great Britain, to the prejudice of what we owe to our King, to our country, and to our religion." In this same letter they declined to remove to Cape Breton, as was desired by some of the French authorities, but gave Costabelle to understand that while they remained in Acadia, they would be faithful and devoted subjects to the King of France.

Queen Anne died in August, 1714, and in January, 1715, Messrs. Capoon and Button were commissioned by Governor Nicholson to proceed in the sloop of war Caulfield to Mines, Chignecto, River St. John, Passamaquoddy and Penobscot, to proclaim King George, and to tender and administer the oaths of allegiance to the French inhabitants. The French refused to take the oaths, and some of the people of Mines made the pretence that they intended to withdraw from the colony. Lieutenant-Governor Caulfield—to whom Messrs. Capoon and Button made their report—wrote to Secretary of State Stanhope for instructions how he should proceed. A year later the people of Mines notified Caulfield that they intended to remain in the country, and at this period it would seem that most of the few French inhabitants who actually left the Province had returned. Caulfield then summoned the inhabitants of Annapolis, and tendered them the oath of allegiance, but with no better success than his deputies had met at Mines and Chignecto. His successor as Lieutenant-Governor, Doucette, in the autumn of 1717 summoned the people of Annapolis to sign a declaration acknowledging the King of Great Britain to be sole King of Acadia, declaring him their Sovereign King, and promising to obey him as his true and lawful subjects. The French of Annapolis sent in a written answer to this request, stating that they were ready to comply with the demand as soon as the King had provided them with some means of shelter from the savage tribes; but unless they were protected from these savages, they could not take the oath demanded. They, however, expressed their readiness to take an oath that they would take up arms neither against the King of England nor against France, nor against any of their subjects or allies.

This statement, that they feared the Indians, was of course a mere pretext, for the loyalty of the savages to the French Government was something that required to be constantly stimulated by presents, and the Micmacs were not so learned in oaths as to be able to make nice distinctions between an oath of neutrality and one of fidelity. And if the inhabitants of Annapolis, who had an English garrison to defend them, could assume such an attitude, what measure of protection was likely to satisfy the inhabitants of Chignecto and Mines, who had no soldiers near them?

General Phillips, who became Governor of Nova Scotia in 1717, and who arrived in the Province early in 1720, had no more success than his predecessors in persuading the Acadians to take the oaths. Every refusal on their part only served to make them more bold in defying the British authorities. The third day after his arrival at Annapolis, Governor Phillips was visited by father Justinian Durand, the priest of the settlement, attended by one hundred and fifty young men, his object evidently being to impress the Governor with the force he could command. On being asked to take the oaths, these people refused, through their priest, in the same terms which they had before employed, alleging their fear of the Indians, and stating that in Governor Nicholson's time they had bound themselves to remain subjects of France, and to retire to Cape Breton. A proclamation, which the Governor sent to the various settlements, demanding that the inhabitants should take the oaths, only drew forth another refusal, father Justinian in the meanwhile being despatched to Louisbourg with a letter, asking the assistance of M. St. Ovide de Brouillan, the Governor of that place. In this letter they say: "We have up to the present time preserved the purest sentiments of fidelity to our invincible monarch. The time has come when we need his royal protection and assistance."

The British Government, and those who administered their affairs in Acadia, undoubtedly exhibited great lenity, not to say weakness, in dealing with these people, who naturally became possessed of the idea that they might safely defy British power. The garrison at Annapolis was weak, and there was no British force in any other part of the Province to keep them in awe. They held themselves in readiness to take up arms against the English the moment war was declared between the two Crowns, and to restore Acadia to France. But as there was a peace of thirty years duration between France and England after the treaty of Utrecht, there was no opportunity of carrying this plan into effect.

Vaudreuil, Governor of Canada, however, continued to keep the Acadians on the alert by means of his agents, and the Indians were incited to acts of hostility against the English, both in Acadia and Maine. The first difficulty occurred at Canso in 1720, by a party of Indians assailing the English fishermen there. The Indians attacked the fishermen in their beds, killed three or four of them, and robbed them of everything. A number of French fishing vessels from Cape Breton came next night, and took away the fish and property belonging to the English, but the master of a sloop, who chanced to arrive the following morning, pursued the French vessels, and captured six or seven of them, recovering the property they contained. The Indians were incited to this attack by the French of Cape Breton, who were annoyed at one of their vessels being seized at Canso by a British war vessel for illegal fishing. Eleven of the Indians engaged in the robbery at Canso returned home by way of Mines, and there found a New England trading sloop belonging to Mr. John Alden. This vessel they plundered under the very eyes of the French inhabitants, who made no effort whatever to prevent them. Governor Phillips, in his indignation at these outrages, wrote to Secretary Craggs that it would be more for the profit and honor of the Crown to give back the country to the French than to be contented with the name only of government, while the French made it subservient to the support of their settlement at Cape Breton, which could scarcely subsist without the grain and cattle carried there from Mines. One immediate result of the Canso outrage was the sending of a company of soldiers there, under Major Armstrong, to take possession of a small fort, which the fishermen had erected. Very strong remonstrances were addressed by the Governor to the people of Mines regarding their conduct in permitting Alden's vessel to be robbed, and they finally promised to make good the damage.

It was at this period that the plan of having deputies elected annually to represent the French inhabitants was adopted at the suggestion of Governor Phillips. These deputies were elected every 10th of October, and their duties were to act on behalf of the people in communicating with the Governor, and to publish the orders of the latter. The number of deputies varied from four to eight in each settlement. They were invested with no judicial powers, but were often appointed arbitrators for the decision of small cases. The Government of the Province then consisted of the Governor or Lieutenant-Governor, and a number of Councillors, most of them officials or connected with the garrison. This was substantially the form of government which existed up to the year 1758, when the first Assembly of the Province of Nova Scotia was convened. Indeed the fewness of the English settlers and the hostile attitude assumed by those of French origin rendered any more elaborate system of administration impossible.

Governor Phillips, who had accurate information with regard to the attempts of the French to incite the savages to hostilities, endeavored to counteract these schemes by a policy of friendship towards them. He had nine of the principal chiefs of the St. John Indians brought over to Annapolis, where they were handsomely entertained, and had presents distributed among them. They went home apparently pleased with their reception. Phillips also encouraged the Indians of the Peninsula to visit him frequently, and never permitted them to depart without presents. No doubt, if they had been left to themselves, they would have continued at peace with the English, but it was not to the interest of France that this should be. And they had a most powerful means of influencing these children of nature, in the missionary priests who had spent their lives among the Indians, learning their language, and teaching them the doctrines of their religion. The Indians had indeed some reason to be disquieted, for the progress of the English settlements east of the Kennebec filled them with apprehensions. Unfortunately the English had not been always so just in their dealings with them that they could rely entirely on their forbearance. The Indians claimed their territorial rights in the lands over which the English settlements were spreading; the French encouraged them in this claim, alleging that they had never surrendered this territory to the English. While these questions were in controversy the Massachusetts authorities were guilty of an act which did not tend to allay the distrust of the Indians. This was nothing less than an attempt to seize the person of father Ralle, the Jesuit missionary at Norridgewock. He, whether justly or not, was blamed for inciting the Indians to acts of hostility, and was therefore peculiarly obnoxious to the English. In December 1721 a party of armed men was sent under Colonel Westbrook to Norridgewock to capture this priest. They arrived at the Indian village where he lived, without being discovered, but before they could surround his house he escaped to the woods, leaving his books and papers behind him. The English alleged that these papers contained his correspondence with the Governor of Canada, and implicated Ralle in the attempts to stir up the Indians to war. This attempt to take Ralle, and the seizure of the young baron St. Castin who was taken to Boston about the same time, deeply exasperated the Indians and caused them to decline another conference with the English. They were resolved upon war, and accordingly in the summer of 1722 a war commenced, in which all the Indian tribes from Cape Canso to the Kennebec were involved. The French could not openly take part in the war, but such encouragement and assistance as they could give the Indians secretly they freely supplied.

The first blow was struck in June, when a party of sixty Indians captured nine families at Merry Meeting Bay, but let all go except five men, who were retained as a compensation for four hostages held by the English. At Damariscove, six Indians attacked a fishing vessel commanded by lieutenant Tilton, but got the worst of the encounter, for three of them were killed by the fishermen. They next attempted to surprise the fort at the River St. George, but failed, and in revenge, burnt a sloop and took several prisoners. They renewed their attempt on this fort a few weeks later, and tried to undermine it, but a heavy rain caused the sides of their trenches to fall in on them, and they gave up the attempt. Their next exploit was the capture of Mr. Newton, the collector at Annapolis, John Adams, son of one of the Council of the Province, and Captain Blin, a Boston trader. They were going in a vessel from Annapolis to Boston, and touched at Passamaquoddy for water. On going ashore they were surprised by a party of Indians, with whom were some French, and made prisoners. The Indians were preparing to attack the vessel when those on board cut the cable, hoisted sail and put to sea, where no canoe could follow them.

This attack was speedily followed by others. A number of trading vessels were taken in the Bay of Fundy, and no less than eighteen in the various harbors on the Atlantic coast of the Peninsula, including a sloop which Governor Phillips had sent with bread for the garrison of Annapolis. The capture of this vessel seems to have emboldened the Indians to attempt to starve out Annapolis, but this attempt was frustrated by the Governor, who sent several armed vessels from Canso with food for the beleagured fortress. Doucett, who was in command there, succeeded in capturing twenty-two Indians, and the rest fled. They were next heard of on the coast near Canso, cruising on the fishing banks with the vessels they had captured, and compelling their prisoners to serve as mariners. They threatened to attack Canso in force, and there was much consternation among the owners of valuable fishing establishments; but fortunately Governor Phillips was there, and he succeeded in fitting out two armed sloops, placing an officer and a detachment of soldiers on board of each. These two vessels did such effective service, that in three weeks they re-took all the vessels and prisoners except four. Phillips states that many Indians were killed, among others four chiefs who had been with him but a month before receiving the King's presents and assuring him of their intention to live at peace with the English. All the Indians captured agreed in stating that they had been incited to go to war by the French Governors. This check relieved the Province from any further attacks during that year.

In Maine, however, they continued active. The fort at Casco neck was threatened, and one man found outside of it killed. The settlement at Brunswick was destroyed, but the party engaged in this operation was followed by Captain John Harmon, of Kennebec, with a company of thirty-four men, and fifteen of the Indians killed, as they slept by their camp fires. Georgetown was attacked in September by four or five hundred Micmacs and Abenaquis, but it was too well guarded, and the Indians retired, after killing fifty head of cattle and burning twenty-six houses.

In February, 1723, Colonel Westbrook, with two hundred and thirty men, ascended the Penobscot, and destroyed a fort which the Indians had there, including the chapel and priest's residence. As the savages had deserted it, no great lustre attached to the enterprise. During this year about thirty persons were killed or captured in Maine, in various attacks, but the Indians nowhere appeared in great force. In Acadia they did but little damage, and many of the chiefs professed a willingness to make peace. The only bloodshed recorded for the year in the Province was the killing of a man named Watkins, who was on a fishing voyage to Casco, and who, together with two other men, a woman and child, were attacked and slaughtered by the savages.

In 1724 the war was resumed with renewed fury. The Indians commenced their depredations in March, by attacking a man at Cape Porpoise. In April they shot a man who was working in his field at Black Point, and carried off his two sons. They captured a sloop at Kennebunk, and put the whole crew to death. They then killed three men in a saw mill up that river. In May they killed two men at Berwick, and scalped a man named Stone, who afterwards recovered and lived to old age, a maimed and crippled proof of Indian ferocity. The same month Captain Josiah Winslow and sixteen men fell into an ambuscade on the St. George River, and, after a desperate resistance, were all killed. Winslow was a great-grandson of Governor Edward Winslow, of the Plymouth Colony, and a brother of General John Winslow, who, in 1755, removed the Acadians from the Province. In June, a party of Indians consisting of thirty Malicites and fifty Micmacs, gathered at Isle Haut, with a view to attack either Annapolis or Canso. From there they proceeded to Mines, where two English trading vessels were at anchor, but they were on the alert, and the Indians did not venture to attack them. They were so much divided in opinion as to which was the best place to attack, that they separated, some of the Micmacs going home, while the Malicites and twenty-six of the Micmacs went to attack Annapolis. In a few days they appeared before it, and repulsed a party from the fort that sallied out to drive them away, killing and scalping a sergeant and private of the garrison, and wounding four others. In revenge for this, one of the Indians, who had been captured at Annapolis by Doucett two years before, was shot and scalped by order of the Council, on the very spot where the sergeant had been killed. This was simply a wanton murder, and quite in keeping with the mingled weakness and ferocity which occasionally distinguished the administration of the Province at that period. Father Charlemagne, the priest of Annapolis, had been at Mines when this war party gathered there, and could have easily warned the Annapolis garrison of the intended attack upon them, which was, indeed, publicly talked of at Mines. As he had failed to do so, and had evidently endeavored to prevent intelligence of the attack from reaching the English, he was put into custody and sent to Louisbourg. Father Isadore, the priest of Piziquid, who had sent a warning to Annapolis, although it arrived too late, was thanked and highly commended, and made Curè of Mines. This will serve to show that the priests differed widely from each other in sentiment and conduct towards the English. Isidore, unfortunately, was not allowed to remain at Mines, being obliged to give place to Gaudin, who was very far from being a friend of the English.

While the English in Acadia pursued a purely defensive policy, they were actively aggressive further to the westward. Father Ralle was an object of intense hatred to the people of New England, and an expedition was planned for the destruction of his village at Norrigdewock. Two hundred and eight men, attended by three Mohawk Indians, ascended the river late in August, and having obtained accurate information as to the condition of the place, made a fierce and sudden attack upon it. The Indians, entirely taken by surprise, made scarcely any resistance; all who could escape, fled, and those who could not were shot down without mercy. Father Ralle, who was in his wigwam, was killed, scalped, and his remains barbarously misused. The killing of this old man, who was sixty-seven years of age and very feeble, was a despicable and cowardly act, utterly unworthy of the civilization which New England boasted. But some allowance should perhaps be made for men who had seen their homes ravaged, and their wives and children murdered, and who believed Ralle to be the cause of these atrocities. The destruction of Norridgewcok was a blow from which the Kennebec Indians never recovered, for the number of slain was large, and included Mog, Bomaseen, and many of their most noted warriors. Ralle, their missionary, who had been with them for twenty-six years, was greatly beloved by the tribe. He was a man of good family and of rare attainments, an excellent classical scholar, and familiar with several Indian languages. He was buried by the Indians on the site of the altar of his church, which had been robbed of its sacred vessels and ornaments, and burnt by the English. In recent years, a monument has been erected to his memory on the spot where he fell.

The death of Ralle caused great rejoicing in Massachusetts, and when Harmon, who was senior in command, carried the scalps of his victims to Boston—this string of bloody trophies, including the scalps of several women and of an aged priest—he was received as if he had been some great general fresh from the field of victory. A certain Captain John Lovewell, emulous of Harmon's fame as a taker of scalps, and his patriotism fired by the large bounty offered by Massachusetts for that kind of article, gathered a band of thirty volunteers in December 1724, and commenced scalp-hunting on the borders of New Hampshire, killing one Indian, for whose scalp the company received £100. He started again in February 1725 with forty men, and at Salmon Falls River surprised ten Indians asleep by their camp fire, and killed them all, their scalps netting him and his companions £1000. Here he should have paused and not trusted too much to fortune, but the prospect of gain and glory opened to him, induced him to make a third venture, which ended in the loss of his own scalp. He and thirty-four of his men fell into an Indian ambuscade on Saco River and more than half of them were killed, Lovewell himself being among the slain.

Fortunately for New England and for Nova Scotia the Indians were growing tired of the war, and were disposed to treat for peace. A preliminary conference was held at St. George's fort in July, at which the Indians displayed a pacific disposition, and in November four of the principal Sagamores of the country, Loron, Arexus, François Xavier, and Meganumba, representing the tribes of the Penobscot, Norridgewock, St. John and Cape Sable, met in Boston to negotiate a treaty of peace. After discussions which lasted more than a month an agreement was arrived at, the Indians engaging to abstain from further hostilities, and to give up their prisoners. They acknowledged the sovereignty of King George to the Province of Nova Scotia or Acadia. This treaty was ratified at Annapolis by the chiefs of Cape Sable and St. John, and at Falmouth in the following August, where it was signed by twenty-six chiefs, Paul Mascarene being present to represent Nova Scotia. Thus, happily, closed a conflict which was extremely dangerous to the weak English colony in Nova Scotia, and which would have been fatal but for the fact that the French were obliged to preserve the appearance of neutrality.

At this time Canada experienced two severe losses in the death of Governor Vaudreuil and in the drowning of a ship load of passengers bound for Quebec. The Chameau, a sixty gun ship, was driven on the rocks near Louisbourg in a fearful August gale, and every soul on board perished. Among her passengers were Chazel the new Intendant, Louvigny the Governor of Three Rivers, and many officers, ecclesiastics and colonists.

Lieutenant-Governor Armstrong, having got the Indian war off his hands, began to devote himself anew to the task of inducing the Acadians to take the oath of allegiance. He succeeded better than his predecessors had done, for in the Autumn of 1726, the deputies and inhabitants of Annapolis River took a qualified oath of allegiance, with a clause not requiring them to take up arms. But at Mines and Chignecto the inhabitants still persisted in their refusal to take any oath, and sent back an insolent answer. They would take no oath, they said, but to "our good King of France," a reply which had far from a soothing effect upon Armstrong's temper, which was none of the best. To punish them for their insolence it was resolved by the Council that no vessel should be permitted to trade with the inhabitants of Chignecto and Mines until they took the oath required.

George I. died in 1727, and his death was known at Annapolis in September. This rendered it necessary to require the inhabitants of Annapolis to take the oath of allegiance again. They were therefore ordered to assemble for that purpose; but, instead of doing so, they sent in a written answer refusing to take the oath except on certain conditions, which were deemed by the Council insolent.

This was the more singular as they had taken the oath the previous year, and Armstrong asserts in his letters to the Secretary of State that their refusal was entirely due to the deputies, who, instead of persuading them to take the oath, frightened them from it, by representing it as extremely binding. Three of the deputies, Landry, Bourgeois and Richards, were put in prison for their share in this refusal, and the fourth, Abraham Bourg, in consideration of his advanced age, was permitted to leave the Province, which, however, he seems not to have done. An ensign named Wroth was sent to Mines and Chignecto in a vessel with a company of soldiers to proclaim King George II., and administer the oaths of allegiance to the people there; but he granted such concessions to the inhabitants as were regarded as unwarrantable and dishonorable by the Council, and his proceedings were treated as null and void. The embargo with respect to trade which had rested on these places for more than a year, was, however, removed.

The return of Governor Phillips to the Province in the Summer of 1729 gave an entirely new turn to affairs. The French inhabitants gave him a joyful welcome when he arrived at Annapolis, and in a short time he induced all the male inhabitants from sixteen years of age and upwards to take the oath of allegiance, without any condition as to not bearing arms. In the course of the following Spring he visited Chignecto, Mines and the other French settlements, and administered the oath of allegiance to all the inhabitants, so that in November 1730 he was able to write to the Lords of Trade that there were "not more than five or six scattering families on the eastern coast to complete the submission of the whole Province." Phillips regarded this achievement with considerable complacency, although he candidly expressed his belief that it did not insure the peace of the country longer than the union between the two Crowns lasted. The Acadians afterwards maintained that when they took this oath of allegiance, it was with the understanding that a clause was to be inserted, relieving them from bearing arms. The statement was probably accurate, for that was the position they always assumed, but the matter seems to have been lost sight of, and so for the time the question of oaths, which had been such a fertile cause of discord in the Province, appeared to be set at rest.

The question of the seigniorial rights of the grantees of the King of France at this time came into prominence. The three largest settlements in Acadia were all on the territories of seigniors, that of Chignecto being on lands granted to La Vallière, while Mines and Port Royal were on lands held by the La Tour family and their branches. Lieutenant-Governor Armstrong, who now—in the absence of Governor Phillips, who had returned to England—administered the Government, was perplexed by the conflicting claims of the seigniors, who now made their appearance, and demanded to be put in possession of their property. He was instructed by the Lords of Trade to recognize the rights of those who had remained in the country after the treaty of Utrecht, but not of those who had then gone to France, and afterwards returned to Acadia. Among the seigniors then in Acadia was Belleisle, grandson of Emmanuel Le Borgne and of Charles La Tour. The seigniors of the La Tour family got into litigation on the subject of their titles, Madame Belleisle (Marie La Tour) and her son being ranged on one side, and Mrs. Agatha Campbell and the D'Entremonts representatives of Jacques, Anne and Marguerite La Tour, on the other. Charles La Tour, the younger, having retired to

France, seems to have taken no part in these lawsuits. Finally, about the year 1732, Mrs. Campbell,* who seems to have had a good deal of her grandfather's cleverness, succeeded in buying out the other claimants, and sold the seigniorial rights of the La Tour family to the Crown for three thousand guineas. The Provincial Government appointed persons to collect these rents at Mines, Chignecto and Annapolis, but the amount realized from them was small, even when calculated in New England money, which was not worth more than a fourth of its nominal value in sterling.

The Indians, although they had made peace, were guilty of occasional acts of robbery, which were usually disavowed by the tribes, and which were probably committed by lawless vagabonds, who bore the same relation to other savages that modern criminals bear to the masses of the people. Occasionally a trading sloop was robbed by these strollers, but it was rarely that any violence was done to the persons plundered. Of a different character was the attack made on a vessel sent to the St. John for a load of limestone for Annapolis. The Indians opposed the landing of the people, pretending that the land and quarries belonged to them, and should be paid for; they also boarded the vessel and took a quantity of clothes and provisions which they found on board. This affair became the subject of remonstrance, and induced the Annapolis authorities to cultivate closer relations with the Indians of the St. John.

Very soon after the treaty of Utrecht, claims had been made on behalf of France that the St. John and the territory north of the Bay of Fundy had not been ceded to

* Agatha La Tour, oldest daughter of Jacques La Tour, who was the oldest son of Charles La Tour by Madame Charnisay, was married in 1714 to Lieutenant Edward Bradstreet, of the Annapolis garrison. On his death she married Ensign James Campbell.

England, and did not form a part of Acadia. As early as 1718, Governor Vaudreuil wrote to the Lieutenant-Governor at Annapolis: "I request you also not to permit your English vessels to go into the River St. John, which is always of the French dominion." The same statement was made in letters written to some of the French inhabitants in Acadia by the French Governors, any who desired to remove to the St. John being told that they might have lots of land on applying to father Lejard, the Jesuit missionary there. About the year 1730, a number of French families went to settle there, and a census taken in 1733 for the government of France, gives the number of inhabitants on the St. John as one hundred and eleven, divided into twenty families. Fifteen of these families, consisting of eighty-two souls, resided "au dessous du village d' Ecoupay" (Aukpaque), probably on the site of the present city of Fredericton. Two families lived at Freneuse, and three at the mouth of the River St. John. In 1736 two of the inhabitants who visited Annapolis gave the Lieutenant-Governor a list of the people settled at St. John, which comprised seventy-seven persons, divided into fifteen families. There is reason to believe that only those at the mouth of the river are included in this enumeration. The names are Bellefontaine, Bergeron, Roy, Dugas, Pair and Robert, some of which do not occur in any previous Acadian census list. These people made their submission to the English Crown that year. But as there was no force there to sustain its authority, the submission was merely nominal, and the St. John river afterwards became a place of refuge for hosts of political exiles from the rest of Acadia.

The relations of the inhabitants of Acadia to the government from 1730 down to the close of Governor Armstrong's administration, although marked by several petty quarrels, had on the whole been tolerably harmonious. The Indians had indeed prevented the erection of a garrison house at Mines, and were believed by the Lieutenant-Governor to have been instigated by the French to that act. Some of the French had refused to pay their rents, and there were occasional instances of disobedience to English authority. The priests occasionally proved difficult to deal with, and some of them had been ordered out of the Province in consequence of disobedience. But on the whole, considering the peculiar views held by the Acadians as to their rights, considering also that nearly all their trade was with the French at Louisbourg, and bearing in mind that their priests were in the pay of the French government, and under the jurisdiction of the Bishop of Quebec, it is remarkable how small were the grounds of difference which existed between the Acadians and the Provincial government when Lieutenant-Governor Armstrong died in 1739. Perhaps if a man less peevish in temper, and less disposed to take a serious view of trifling difficulties, had been at the head of affairs, the differences between the Acadians and the Government might have been greatly decreased; for there is reason to fear that for some time prior to the melancholy event which ended his career, the Lieutenant-Governor was not in a proper mental condition to administer the affairs of the government. He died by his own hand in December 1739 under the influence of an insane melancholy which had long affected his health and impaired his judgment.

Paul Mascerene, who succeeded to the lieutenant-governorship in 1740, was a very different sort of person. He was a French Huguenot, and with his parents was driven out of his native country by the events which followed the revocation of the Edict of Nantes. His whole life was spent in the military service of England, and he proved himself a most efficient officer, rising by his merit, unaided by patronage, to the rank of Major General. He assumed the administration of affairs in Acadia at a time when serious difficulties and dangers were imminent, and showed his capacity by the manner in which he discharged the duties of his position. It was well that at such a crisis in the history of the country the reins of government were in strong hands.

CHAPTER XVIII.

THE CAPTURE OF LOUISBOURG.

THE long peace between France and England, which had been maintained for thirty years, was now about to be broken. Frederick the Great, of Prussia, the most unprincipled of modern kings, had ascended the throne, and, like the royal brigand that he was, seized Silesia, then a Province of the Austrian empire. Europe was plunged into another war, in which France and England were ranged on opposite sides, France supporting Frederick, while England came to the rescue of Maria Theresa with sword and purse. Frederick, in the meantime, patched up a peace with the latter, and left his allies to their fate, France, as d'Argenson wrote at the time, "with her armies in the middle of Germany, beaten and famine-stricken." In June, 1743, the British and French crossed swords at the battle of Dettingen, and another was added to the long list of British victories. In the following March, France and England mutually declared war against each other, and the bloody drama, in which they had so often taken part, was renewed both in Europe and America.

The French in Louisbourg had for a long time been preparing for the event, and were not slow to take advantage of it. The state of Acadia was such as to invite atttack, there being only two garrisoned places in the Province, Annapolis and Canso, and the garrisons in both extremely weak. In 1735, M. Du Vivier, a great-grandson of Charles La Tour, prepared an elaborate Memoir upon

Acadia, and offered with a very small force to restore it to France. In this paper he discloses the methods which were employed to keep the Province in a state of disquiet, how the missionaries were "incessant" in keeping the inhabitants loyal to France, and how even the most influential of the people, on whom the English blindly relied, were secretly their enemies. If Du Vivier's statements are to be believed, the D'Entremonts, his grandfather and his uncle—at a time when the English at Annapolis believed them to be wholly passive—were engaged in secretly stirring up the other inhabitants to acts of hostility. Du Vivier's Memoir, disclosing, as it did, the weakness of English rule in the Province, and the forces which could be used to destroy it, no doubt made a strong impression on the French authorities, to whom it was addressed, and it was but natural that he should be selected to command any expedition for the reduction of Acadia.

The news of the declaration of war reached Louisbourg in April, six weeks before it was known in Boston, and although Duquesnel, the Governor, had received general orders to stand on the defensive until he was reinforced, the weakness of the Acadian garrisons and the zeal of Du Vivier caused him to disobey his orders. Du Vivier had undertaken to recapture Acadia with but one hundred men. Duquesnel gave him three hundred, besides several armed vessels, and told him to make good his promise. With this force he immediately sailed for Canso, which he reached on the 11th May, and where he was joined by two hundred Indians, who had received early notice to rendezvous there. Canso was incapable of making any defence. Although there had been a garrison stationed there for several years, the soldiers had no better defence than a block-house, built of timber, which the fishermen had erected a long time before. The commander and his garrison of eighty men, therefore surrendered, the conditions being that they should be taken to Louisbourg, and at the expiration of a year sent either to Boston or to England. Du Vivier then took possession of the place, burnt down the block-house and buildings, and sent his prisoners and plunder back to Louisbourg.

Had Du Vivier, after taking Canso, marched immediately to Annapolis, it must have fallen, almost without resistance. The fort was in a most ruinous condition. Being originally built of sandy earth, it was liable to wear away after heavy rains, or in thaws after frost. An order had been given to rebuild it in brick and stone, but the workmen had done little more, in the two summers they had been employed, than to prepare the material. It had only about one hundred and fifty men in garrison, and there chanced to be an unusually large number of women, wives of the officers and soldiers, at Annapolis. Their presence would have materially impaired the defence of the fort. But Du Vivier delayed at Louisbourg to make more elaborate preparations for capturing Annapolis, and in the meantime Mascerene was warned of his danger. On the 18th of May a sudden panic seized the lower town, where the families of several officers and soldiers were quartered, and they commenced removing their goods into the fort. This panic was due to a rumor that Morpin, a famous commander of a privateer in the former war, was up the river with five hundred French and Indians. Mascerene could not discover the author of this report, and next day all were assured that it was false; yet the impression which it made could not be effaced. Soon after this the Massachusetts galley arrived from Boston with the chief engineer of the fortifications, and brought them the intelligence that a Boston newspaper had published the statement that war had been declared against France, although the Government had received no official information on the subject. This caused several of the officers to resolve to send their families to Boston, and the galley took as many on board as she could conveniently carry. Two other vessels were freighted with part of the remainder, yet even then more than seventy women and children were left, who could not be sent to a place of safety until late in the year.

As there was no possibility of making the new work of the fort serviceable in case of an immediate attack, Mascerene urged the engineer to direct all his energies to the work of repairing the old fortifications. The assistance of the French inhabitants was called for and they responded with alacrity, not only geting the necessary timber, but working at the repairs on the fort itself. They continued at this labor cheerfully until a party of Indians made their appearance, and then they all withdrew to their dwellings.

The Indians, three hundred in number, and consisting both of Malicites and Micmacs, emerged from the forest on the 1st July. They were under the guidance of two or three white men, one of their leaders being young Belleisle, who himself had Indian blood in his veins, being the son of Anastatia St. Castin. Belleisle had been active in inciting the Indians to war in the hope that by expelling the English he would obtain the restoration of the seigniorial rights of his family. With these savages was a man whose name fills a large place in our Acadian annals, La Loutre, a missionary priest, who had been officiating among the Indians about the Basin of Mines. He was probably the most dangerous and determined enemy to British power that ever came to Acadia. A considerable portion of this band of Indians had been with Du Vivier at Canso, and it was agreed that they should rendezvous at Mines and wait until Du Vivier's force arrived there, but the impatience of Belleisle to win the glory of the capture of Annapolis for himself and leave his cousin Du Vivier nothing, caused a premature attack, and spoiled the whole plan.

No force of Indians that ever was gathered has ever shown itself capable of making a sustained assault upon a fort armed with cannon and bravely defended. Belleisle's party proved no exception to this universal rule. The Indians in their first onset killed two men who were straggling in the gardens, and came near capturing a party of officers and men who were engaged in pulling down a house on the Governor's grounds. The Indians then got under cover of some barns at the foot of the glacis, and kept up a steady fire of musketry upon the fort until they were dislodged by its cannon. They then set fire to some houses in the lower town, a quarter of a mile from the fort, which placed the block-house there—which was held by a sergeant and a guard—in danger of being burnt. The guard withdrew from their dangerous station, but Mr. How and a party of workmen, with a detachment of soldiers, dropped down the river in the ordnance tender, and, supported by her cannon, drove off the Indians, replaced the guard, and tore down the houses and fences which threatened the block-house with destruction. They then pulled down all the houses that obstructed the fire of the fort, and the Indians, not being able to approach within the distance of a mile, gave no further trouble, except by stealing some sheep and cattle. On the 5th July, the Massachusetts galley arrived with seventy auxiliaries, which Governor Shirley had promptly sent to strengthen the garrison. The Indians immediately became disgusted with the siege, and the very same day marched off towards

Mines. The vessel was despatched back to Boston immediately, and soon returned with forty additional men. These, with the seventy already in Annapolis, the soldiers —of whom one hundred were serviceable—and the workmen who had come to rebuild the fort, most of whom had volunteered for service, formed a very respectable force, and Mascerene, by the exercise of great dilligence, succeeded in arming and equipping them quite respectably.

In the meantime Du Vivier was making his way towards Annapolis with two hundred soldiers. Instead of coming direct by sea, the vessels which carried him from Louisbourg had landed his little army at Baie Verte, from which it had marched to Chignecto. There he expected to receive substantial assistance and sympathy, but although some of the inhabitants joined his standard, the majority were disposed to act cautiously, and the requisitions he made upon them were not responded to with any degree of cheerfulness. From Chignecto he proceeded to Mines where he found the Indians encamped, in extremely low spirits, and in very bad humor over their repulse. Here he issued peremptory orders to the inhabitants for supplies, and created a most unfavorable impression on their minds. Any who refused to comply with his demands were to be handed over to the tender mercies of the savages. Notwithstanding this threat he found the people of Mines very unwilling to give him any assistance, and his bright hopes of a spontaneous rising of the Acadian people against British power vanished before the chilling reality. A new generation had grown up in Acadia who knew nothing of war, and who were not disposed to welcome those who would bring it to their doors.

Du Vivier, who had now some four hundred and fifty Indians with him, took the route for Annapolis, which he did not reach until the latter part of August. Having no artillery, he was obliged to resort to night attacks, his men keeping up a continual fire upon the parapets and wearying the garrison with constant alarms. After this had gone on for several days, Du Vivier sent in a flag of truce by his brother, and a letter stating that he expected three war vessels of seventy, sixty and forty guns, and a transport with two hundred and fifty more men and a supply of cannon, mortars and implements of war. He sought to persuade Mascerene to sign a capitulation conditioned on the arrival of this armament, but the brave commander steadily refused, although some of his officers, who had a great dread of becoming prisoners of war, gave countenance to the proposal. Mascerene succeeded in persuading them that the Frenchman's only object was to sow dissensions among them, and the spirits of his men being high, all negotiations were broken off. Du Vivier then renewed his night attacks and kept them up for about three weeks, but they daily grew more contemptible, and resulted in scarcely any loss to the garrison. A very timely reinforcement then arrived from Boston. An armed brigantine and sloop brought fifty Indian Rangers, whom Shirley thought would prove serviceable for skirmishing purposes. A few days after they came, one of them was captured, and he told Du Vivier that he heard Mascerene say he intended to pay him a visit at his camp. The French commander concluded not to wait for his visit, but immediately broke up camp and started with his force in the midst of a heavy rain for Mines. There he proposed to remain for the winter with his soldiers, but the inhabitants sent in such a strongly worded remonstrance against this plan, that he was constrained to withdraw. At Chignecto he found the people equally averse to his remaining with them for the winter, and he was finally obliged to return to Louisbourg to meet the reproaches of his Commander for his bad management of the campaign.

Du Vivier had not been gone many days when a large French frigate, an armed brigantine and a sloop appeared in the Basin. This was a portion of the sea force intended to assist in the reduction of the fort. Finding the land force gone, the Captain of this squadron concluded not to make any attack, and sailed away. In these operations, the French were extremely unfortunate. Had Du Vivier persevered a little longer until the squadron arrived, Annapolis must have fallen. As it was, Mascerene breathed freely, for he felt that the greatest danger was past, and resolved that another year would not find him so unprepared. But while he and his soldiers and auxiliaries deserve all credit for their bravery, vigilance and good conduct during the siege, no small share of Mascerene's success in defending Annapolis was due to the attitude of the Acadians, who with a few exceptions, gave no willing aid to the invaders. The Deputies of Mines wrote to the French Commander, " We live under a mild and tranquil government, and have all good reason to be faithful to it." Mascerene manfully acknowledges how much he owed to this conduct on their part, for in a letter to Governor Shirley he says, " To the breaking up of the French measures, the timely succor received from the Governor of Massachusetts, and our French inhabitants refusing to take up arms against us, we owe our safety." Had they only been permitted to preserve this attitude, what a sea of difficulties they would have escaped!

Mascerene diligently employed the remainder of the Autumn and the Winter in strengthening the defences of his fort, and before Spring he had greatly improved its condition. Rumors reached him from time to time of another attack, and in March he learned that an officer, named Marin, and a number of Canadians had spent the winter at Chignecto, and were coming to Annapolis in the Spring. In May, Marin arrived at Mines with three hundred troops, chiefly Canadians, who had been sent from Louisbourg, and three hundred Indians, which had been collected by the diligence of La Loutre, their missionary. Some of the people of Annapolis, it seems, had been informed of Marin's movements, and a clandestine correspondence with Mines had been maintained by means of two boys—Charles Raymond and Peter Landry—who had made three journeys between the two places during the Winter and Spring. Marin presently made his appearance at Annapolis with his motley force, and spent three weeks in making feeble night attacks, which produced no impression on its defences. He captured two Boston trading vessels and burnt some houses, but beyond that accomplished nothing. Possibly he might have remained longer making requisitions on the inhabitants and threatening the direst vengeance on the disobedient, but at this juncture he received a very peremptory summons to return to Louisbourg, which was then in great peril.

Louisbourg, after thirty years of labor and a vast expenditure of money, had grown to be a mighty fortress, a constant menace to New England, and the rallying place of a swarm of privateers which in time of war preyed upon English commerce. The name "the Dunkirk of America," which it received from the people of Massachusetts, well illustrates the hate and suspicion with which it was viewed, and the disfavor with which its growth was regarded. Its gloomy walls, behind which the Jesuit, the gay soldier of France, and the savage of the Acadian woods found shelter,

v

were looked upon by the descendants of the Puritans as the bulwarks of a power which they dreaded and a religion which they abhorred. Louisbourg was indeed a potent fortress for this continent and for that age. The town which was more than two miles in circuit, was surrounded by a rampart of stone from thirty to thirty-six feet high, and the ditch in front of it was eighty feet wide. There were six bastions and three batteries containing embrasures for one hundred and forty-eight cannon and six mortars. On an island at the entrance of the harbor was planted a battery of thirty twenty-eight pounders, and at the bottom of the harbor, opposite to the entrance, was the grand or royal battery of twenty-eight forty-two pounders. The entrance of the town on the land side was at the west gate over a draw-bridge, near which was a circular battery mounting sixteen twenty-four pounders. Such was Louisbourg when Governor Shirley conceived the bold project of capturing it with an army of rustics from Massachusetts, New Hampshire and Connecticut.

Shirley had written to the British ministry in the autumn of 1744, asking assistance for the defence of Nova Scotia and the capture of Louisbourg. In January 1745, before there was time for him to receive any answer from England, he placed his plan for the reduction of Louisbourg before the General Court, the members having previously taken an oath of secrecy. The scheme appeared so visionary to most of the members that it was at first rejected, but at that moment a petition arrived from the merchants of Boston, Salem and Marblehead, complaining of the great injuries they suffered from the French privateers which harbored at Louisbourg, and this enabled Shirley to have his proposal reconsidered, and finally carried by a majority of one vote. Circular letters were immediately despatched to all the English colonies, requesting their assistance, but all excused themselves from taking part in so desperate an enterprise, except Connecticut, New Hampshire and Rhode Island. The latter State, unfortunately, missed its share in the glory of the affair by the tardy arrival of the three hundred soldiers, which it had undertaken to contribute.

Four thousand and seventy troops were enlisted and assembled in Boston early in March, of which Massachusetts furnished three thousand two hundred and fifty men, Connecticut five hundred and sixteen, and New Hampshire three hundred and four. The naval force for the expedition consisted of thirteen armed vessels, furnished by the four colonies, and mounting in all two hundred cannon. Shirley sent to Commodore Warren, the commander of the fleet on the station, asking him to assist in the proposed enterprise, but he declined to do so without special orders from England. His refusal, which reached Boston as the expedition was preparing to sail, was made known by Shirley to General Pepperell, the commander-in-chief, and to Brigadier-General Waldo, and to them alone. It was a severe disappointment, but neither of the three brave men, who knew the secret, dreamed of making it the cause of postponing the expedition for a single hour. Indeed, the affair had been inaugurated in a manner so extraordinary, and rested so much on fortune for its success, that the absence of the ordinary conditions on which success might be supposed to depend, scarcely excited remark.

General Pepperell, who was at the head of this extraordinary crusade, instead of being a battle scarred veteran, was a merchant of Kittery, who had never witnessed any more serious warlike enterprises than a few skirmishes with the Indians. He had never seen anything of civilized warfare, and had never heard a cannon fired in anger.

Most of those under him were equally inexperienced, but there was no lack of courage nor of enthusiasm, and both were required, for the task which they had undertaken was one from which brave men might well have shrunk, considering the inadequate means at their command. The expedition set sail from Boston late in March, freighted with the hopes of New England and blessed by its prayers. From every pulpit rose the supplication that the God of battles would go forth with this host of His chosen people, and point their way to victory.

Fortune smiled on them from the start. They arrived at Canso, which was the place of rendezvous, early in April, and found the whole coast of Cape Breton surrounded by a barrier of floating ice. It was certain that no news of their enterprise could have reached Louisbourg. While waiting at Canso they built a block-house to replace the one destroyed by Du Vivier, and placed in it a garrison of eighty men. One of their vessels captured a richly laden brigantine from Martinique, which was thus early bound for Louisbourg. A few days later, four war vessels were descried far out at sea, but apparently making towards Canso. There was great excitement and some alarm, and the vessels in the harbor were got ready for action. Who could the strangers be? What if they were a French squadron bound for Louisbourg? These and other questions were speedily set at rest as they drew near, and the broad pennant of Commodore Warren was seen flying from the Superb, the flagship of the squadron. Warren, soon after he despatched his letter of refusal, had received orders from England to proceed to the assistance of the expedition, and learning from a fisherman that it had left Boston, made all haste to join it at Canso. After a conference with Pepperell, it was arranged that Warren should cruise in front of Louisbourg, and intercept all vessels going there. There he was joined in the course of a few weeks by six more war ships, so that he had quite a powerful fleet under his command.

Louisbourg was thus cut off from all succor before its garrison or inhabitants dreamed of danger. Two sloops were despatched to Baie Verte to intercept any vessels going from that place with supplies, and to make the surprise of Louisbourg complete, the fort at St. Peter's was seized and its occupants held as prisoners. These measures were so effectual that, when on the 30th April the New England flotilla arrived in Gabarus Bay, they were so entirely unexpected, that the alarm and confusion were extreme. Cannon were fired, bells were rung, and officers and soldiers ran hither and thither in the greatest dismay.

As the English threatened to land, an officer named Boulardiere was detached with one hundred and fifty soldiers to prevent them, but Pepperell deceived him by a clever ruse, and landed a detachment higher up the Bay, which drove the French party into Louisbourg. That day the English landed about two thousand men, and on the following day the remainder and a large quantity of stores. Colonel Vaughan, of New Hampshire, marched round the harbor in the night with four hundred trooops to the rear of the grand battery north of the city, and setting fire to the storehouses behind it, which were filled with pitch and tar, frightened its garrison out of it. This battery was immediately occupied, and its thirty cannon turned on the town with deadly effect. Then commenced the landing of cannon from the ships, which took a whole fortnight, and was effected with incredible labor, the men dragging the heavy guns on sledges over the rough ground and through a morass to their camp. Du Chambon, the Governor, was summoned to surrender, but returned a haughty refusal, and the New Englanders directed their energies to the erection of batteries to demolish the landward defences of the place. An unsuccessful night attack was made on the island battery, but a safer plan of silencing it was devised by the erection of a battery on Light House Point, which enfiladed the Island battery, and made it almost untenable. The Vigilant, a sixty-four gun ship, laden with stores for Louisbourg, had been captured by the English fleet, and Pepperell, by means of a flag of truce, had this information conveyed to the French Governor. The knowledge of this misfortune, the weak and mutinous condition of his garrison, and the firm hold that the besiegers had acquired of the outworks essential to the successful defence of the place, disposed Du Chambon to surrender; and finally, on the 15th June, the terms of a capitulation were agreed upon, and on the 17th, the flag of England floated over Louisbourg, after a siege of forty-nine days, which, on the part of the besiegers, had been conducted with a degree of courage, enterprise and activity which left nothing to be desired. The garrison, numbering six hundred regulars and thirteen hundred militia, with the crew of the Vigilant and many of the inhabitants, numbering in all upwards of four thousand persons, were sent back to France. A swift sailing schooner carried the news to Boston of the glorious triumph which the sons of New England had won. Then such joy was seen on the faces of all ranks as can only be witnessed in a free State among a people who have escaped a great danger and won a noble victory. And well might they rejoice, for the capture of Louisbourg was one of the most wonderful achievements that is recorded in the world's history. Even the victors themselves rejoiced with trembling as they saw the amazing strength of its defences, and the deadly peril they would have had to brave had an assault been demanded of them. That a band of untrained artizans and husbandmen, commanded by a merchant, should capture a fortress that it had taken thirty years to build, and which was defended by veteran troops, was something so wonderful that the news of the event was received in Europe with incredulous surprise. Had such a deed of arms been done in Greece two thousand years ago, the people of England would have made it the theme of innumerable commentaries, the details of the achievement would have been taught to the children in the schools generation after generation, great statesmen would have written pamphlets on the subject, and great poets would have wedded it to immortal verse. But as the people who won this triumph were not Greeks nor Romans, but only colonists, the affair was but the talk of a day and then dropped out of sight. Most of the books that are called Histories of England ignore it altogether. And even the descendants of the captors of Louisbourg have been too busy celebrating later triumphs to remember Pepperell and his band of heroes, whose daring was only equalled by their success.

CHAPTER XIX.

THE CAPITULATION AT GRAND PRÉ.

MARIN, who was recalled by Du Chambon from Annapolis to go to the relief of Louisbourg, was chased near Cape Sable by three New England cruisers, and forced to land, and did not reach Cape Breton until Louisbourg had fallen. He returned to Quebec to console the Governor of Canada for the loss of that place, by informing him that all the inhabitants of Acadiá, with the exception of a very small portion, desired to return under the French dominion, and that they would not hesitate to take up arms as soon as they saw themselves at liberty to do so. He said that "the day he left Annapolis all the inhabitants were overpowered with grief. This arose from their apprehension of remaining at the disposition of the enemy, of losing their property, and being deprived of their missionaries." It was resolved by the Governor of Canada to make another attempt to drive the English from Acadia.

Meanwhile Mascerene was engaged in disciplining the Acadian deputies and some of the inhabitants for the aid and comfort which they had given to the enemy. Some of them probably had acted under duress, but in the case of others there seems to have been a great deal of alacrity and readiness to help Marin and his associates. In other respects the Acadians about this time began to show themselves unfriendly to the British authorities. They had been long accustomed to supply Louisbourg with provisions, sending some four hundred head of cattle every year to that place for the use of the garrison, and large quantities of produce. This trade had been declared illegal at the beginning of the war, but still it went on. But when the English captured Louisbourg the Acadians refused to send supplies to it, and the Commissariat authorities were put to great inconvenience. These acts show the hostile spirit that was beginning to actuate the Acadians, for the trade was an advantageous one to them.

The year 1746 was one of great projects both on the part of England and France, none of which turned out according to the expectations of their originators. Governor Shirley, whose energy was extreme, was resolved on nothing less than the conquest of Canada, and probably if he had been seconded heartily by the British Government, the achievements of thirteen years later would have been anticipated. More than eight thousand men were enlisted in the New England States, and in New York, New Jersey, Pennsylvania, Maryland and Virginia, but the fleet from England, which was to co-operate with them, did not arrive, and the troops were finally disbanded in the autumn of the following year. The French were equally resolute to recover what they had lost. A great fleet was got ready at Brest to attack Louisbourg, Annapolis and Boston, and a large body of Canadian Rangers was collected at Quebec to be reinforced by a large number of Indians, and to co-operate with the fleet in its operations in Acadia. This detachment was under the command of an officer named Ramezay, who arrived at Chignecto in June with six hundred Canadians, and was joined there by three hundred Malicites, under Lieutenant St. Pierre, and a large body of Micmacs, under Marin. Two French frigates from Brest were then lying in Chebouctou (Halifax) Harbor awaiting the arrival of the fleet. They had been sent out in advance to communicate with Ramezay's forces, and to keep them on the alert. In the meantime the latter did not consider his force strong enough to attack Annapolis. While he waited for the Brest fleet the Governor of Canada had been alarmed at the rumors of invasion from New England, and sent word for him to return. He had started to return to Quebec, when late in September he was overtaken by a messenger, who arrested his march with the thrilling intelligence that the Brest fleet was in Chebouctou Harbor.

The French fleet was indeed there, but in a sorry plight. When it left Brest on the 22nd June it formed by far the most powerful armament that had ever essayed to cross the Atlantic. It consisted of seventy sail, of which eleven were ships of the line, twenty frigates, five sloops and brigs, and thirty-four transports, tenders and fireships,—manned by more than ten thousand sailors, and carrying a land army of upwards of three thousand men. It was under the command of the Duke d'Anville, and his orders were to capture and dismantle Louisbourg, to take Annapolis, and to attack and burn Boston. The approach of this fleet was viewed with great alarm by the people of New England, and the militia were gathered in haste from the inland towns and held in readiness for an attack. These precautions proved to be needless. Soon after it left the coast of France the fleet was scattered by a tempest; four ships of the line and a transport were disabled and forced to put back. When d'Anville reached Chebouctou on the 10th of September he had but three ships of the line and a few transports. A terrible mortality prevailed among his men, and on the 16th he himself sickened and died. Four more ships of the line, with the Vice-Admiral d'Estournelle, arrived the same day, but Conflans, who was expected with four ships from the West Indies, had not been heard of; in fact, he had arrived at Chebouctou in August, and not finding d'Anville there, had returned to France. A council of war was held, at which the Vice-Admiral advocated the abandonment of the expedition, seeing that so many of the vessels were missing and that twenty-five hundred men had already died of fever. Jonquière, the newly appointed Governor of Canada, who was on board, vehemently opposed this proposal, saying that Annapolis at least could be taken. Most of the officers were with Jonquière in this view, and the Vice-Admiral finding himself overruled, committed suicide. This left Jonquière at the head of the expedition, and he, after allowing the men to remain some time ashore to recruit, re-embarked them, and on the 13th October set sail for Annapolis. There were still forty-two vessels left, of which thirty were ships, but the strength of the land forces had dwindled away to one thousand efficient men. Still, it was thought that Annapolis must surely fall; and to insure the safe arrival of every vessel, a large number of the French inhabitants who were familiar with Annapolis Basin, had come over from Mines to pilot the ships. But the hand of destiny was upon this fleet. Off Cape Sable another tempest arose and damaged the ships, and news was received that there was a strong English fleet at Louisbourg, and a squadron in Annapolis Basin. It was unanimously agreed to abandon the attack on Annapolis, the Acadian pilots were landed, and the fleet bore back to France. Thus ignobly ended an enterprise which, according to all human calculations, should have accomplished at least the reduction of Louisbourg and Annapolis, and which perhaps might have done much more towards weakening the power of England in America, if well conducted and favored by fortune. The people of New England were so sensible of their escape from a great peril that they attributed their deliverance to nothing less than the direct

interposition of Divine Providence. In every church and by every fire-side, venerable ministers and pious maidens read with exulting voices Deborah and Barak's song of triumph and thanksgiving: "They fought from heaven; the stars in their courses fought against Sisera. The river of Kishon swept them away, that ancient river, the river Kishon. O my soul, thou hast trodden down strength."

Ramezay, who had been recalled by the arrival of the fleet at Chebucto, arrived in front of Annapolis with seven hundred Canadians and Indians late in September. Mascerene's garrison was, however, too strong to be attacked, and in October, when he learned that the fleet had returned to France, he withdrew his force to Mines and afterwards to Chignecto, where he proposed to spend the winter. His presence there alarmed Mascerene, who was in constant communication with Governor Shirley, and he represented to the latter the necessity of having at least a thousand more men in the Province to overawe the Acadians and check the attacks of the detachments from Canada. Shirley accordingly enlisted five hundred troops in Massachusetts, and despatched them to Mascerene in December. They were intended to occupy Mines during the winter, but it was too late in the season to get into the Basin of Mines, and therefore they had to land on the south shore of the Bay of Fundy and march on foot to their destination to the south of the River Gaspereaux. There they were quartered in the houses of the inhabitants in February, when an attack was made upon them which was most fatal in its results.

Ramezay, who was resting at Chignecto, was informed by a messenger from Mines of the arrival of the English and of the manner in which they had disposed themselves. He saw at once that their scatttered condition and the carelessness of their guard offered an admirable opportunity for cutting them off. To do so would involve a winter march of great difficulty through a wilderness, but it was in such enterprises as this that the Canadian coureur de bois was most at home. So the adventure was resolved upon. Ramezay was himself disabled and incapable of making such a journey, but he found a worthy substitute in De Villiers, the same officer that forced George Washington to capitulate at Fort Necessity in 1754. He received the command of the detachment, and he had with him such able lieutenants as Lusignant and La Corne. On the 23rd January 1747 he set out from Chignecto with three hundred and fifty Canadians and sixty Indians on his arduous journey. By the ordinary route in summer the distance between Chignecto and Grand Pré would not exceed seventy miles, but at that season the Basin of Mines could not be navigated by canoes, so that he was obliged to make a long detour around its shores, and to cross the many rivers on his route, above the influence of the tide. It takes now but a few hours to pass by rail from the Misseguash to the Gaspereaux. De Villiers and his band thought they had done well to accomplish the distance in eighteen days.

While the Canadians on their snow shoes were pressing on in defiance of cold and storm, dragging their food behind them on sledges, through the weary passes of the Cobequid mountains, and along the banks of the Shubenacadie, the English were resting in fancied security. Some of the inhabitants told them that the French were coming, but they ridiculed the idea, and made no change in their arrangements, so that when they were attacked in the early morning of the 10th February, they were utterly taken by surprise. De Villiers had been joined by a number of Acadians at Piziquid, and was informed by them of the exact position of the English. They were quartered in twenty-four houses, from which the inhabitants had prudently retired, when whispers of the coming of the French were first heard. De Villiers resolved to attack ten of them, in which the principal officers lodged, with such an overpowering force that failure would be impossible; and having thus disposed of the leaders of the English, he judged that the others would be obliged to yield. Fortune favored him in his perilous undertaking. A terrific snow storm had been raging for a day and night, and while there was four feet of snow on the ground the air was still thick with the fast falling flakes. As the French, divided into ten detachments, approached the ten houses singled out for attack, the blinding storm prevented the English sentries from discovering them until it was too late. They had barely time to give the alarm when the French were upon them, and they were bayoneted where they stood. The English officers and soldiers thus suddenly attacked leaped from their beds and made a desperate resistance. But the struggle was very unequal, for most of them were undressed, many were unarmed, and they were outnumbered by the enemy. Colonel Noble, who commanded the English, was killed fighting in his shirt, and with him fell four other officers and seventy non-commissioned officers and soldiers. Sixty of the English were wounded and sixty-nine were made prisoners. The French only lost seven killed, and fourteen wounded, so unequal were the conditions of the struggle, but De Villiers and Lusignant were among the latter.

The English who remained were in an extremely difficult position. They were outnumbered by the French and Indians; they were cut off from their store of provisions; their principal officers were captured, and they were without snow-shoes, so that they could not travel. The snow in fact imprisoned them more effectually than a whole army could have done. They, however, made a desperate attempt to retrieve their fortunes, and tried to fight their way to their stores and vessel, but the snow defeated their efforts. At noon a suspension of arms was agreed on, and finally a capitulation was arranged between Captain Goldthwaite, on behalf of the English, and La Corne, who had taken command of the French. The terms were, that the English were to depart for Annapolis within forty-eight hours, with their arms and six days provisions, and not to bear arms at Mines, Cobequid, or Chignecto for six months. The prisoners taken were to remain prisoners of war, and the English wounded were to be conveyed to River Canards, and lodged there until they were in a condition to be removed to Annapolis. Among the wounded prisoners was Mr. How, of the Council, who had gone to Mines as Commissary General. He was released on parole, and afterwards exchanged for a French officer.

The people of Grand Pré having thus got rid of the English, informed the French officers that they were very short of provisions, and on their representations they decided to return to Chignecto, taking their prisoners with them. They had achieved a great triumph, which was only rendered possible by the extreme negligence of the English commander; but that does not detract from the merits of the French, for men who take all the chances in war should not be robbed of their laurels when they succeed. The moral influence of this victory was powerful on the minds of the Acadians, who saw a strong English detachment defeated and compelled to surrender to a less numerous body of French and Indians, without, perhaps, considering too closely the causes which brought about such an occurrence. It was therefore a misfortune in every way that such a chance should have befallen the English, for it was probably one of the causes which lured the Acadians to their ruin.

In May of this year a terrible misfortune happened the French, which deprived them of any hope of recovering either Louisbourg or Annapolis. Jonquière set sail from Rochelle with six line of battle ships and a number of transports, bound for Canada, in company with a frigate and six large merchantmen, bound for the East Indies. There were thirty-eight sail in all, and Admirals Anson and Warren followed them with thirteen line of battle ships and two frigates, and brought them to action off Cape Finisterre. The action was very unequal, and the English won a complete victory, capturing the six line of battle ships, the six East Indiamen and many of the transports. The frigate was the only war vessel which escaped to tell how the French flag had been driven from the seas. Jonquière, who was thus baulked in his second attempt to get to his seat of government, said, as he gave up his sword to Anson, "Sir, you have conquered the Invincible, and Glory follows you," pointing to the two ships of that name which had been captured. Anson had done more than that; he had broken the naval power of France.

One of the results of the aid and comfort which De Villiers had received from the Acadians was a proclamation, proscribing as guilty of treason twelve of the French inhabitants. The men who were thus declared outlaws were Louis Gautier and his sons Joseph and Pierre, Amand Bugeau, Joseph Le Blanc, Charles and Francis Raymond, Charles and Phillips Le Roy, Joseph Brossard, Pierre Guidry and Louis Hebert. A reward of fifty pounds sterling was offered for the capture of each of these persons.

Mascerene wrote in severe terms to the Deputies of Mines in August, 1748, accusing them of contempt of orders and disrespect to His Majesty. It appears from his letter that they had opposed the publication of the proclamation above referred to, and thrown the packet, which contained a duplicate of it for Chignecto, into the fire. It appears also that they were then harboring and concealing those whom the proclamation proscribed. He accuses them also of receiving and entertaining deserters from the Annapolis garrison, and furnishing both them and the Indians with arms. He implored them not to suffer such proceedings amongst them, and added, "Let me, therefore, prevail on you, if you have any love for yourselves, or regard for your posterity, to recollect my repeated advice, and avoid these mischiefs which that banditti, through hope of assistance from France, are endeavoring to draw you into." This was sound advice, and it would have been well for the Acadians if they had been endowed with sufficient firmness to follow it.

The detachment of Canadians was withdrawn from Chignecto in the Spring and Summer of 1747, and no operations of any importance were undertaken from that time until the end of the war. Marin was indeed sent down from Quebec in the Summer of 1748 with forty Canadians, under orders to collect a party of Indians, harrass the English, and prevent them from forming any new settlements; but beyond burning some firewood and capturing a few non-combatants, he accomplished nothing. The truth was that the power of France to achieve the re-conquest of Louisbourg and Acadia had departed. She had neither money nor ships sufficient for such extensive enterprises.

The treaty of Aix-la-Chapelle, which was signed on the 18th October, 1748, brought the war to a close. By it

w

France and England mutually restored the conquests they had made during the war, and under this arrangement England had to cede the Island of Cape Breton and the fortress of Louisbourg to France. The people of New England were chagrined to see this stronghold, which had been such a menace to them, and which they had so bravely captured, given up, as if it was a worthless prize. To restore Louisbourg was, indeed, an act of extreme folly, considering how aggressive the French had become in America, and that the peace was not likely to be lasting. The peace—to use the words of Lord Macaulay—was "as regards Europe nothing but a truce; it was not even a truce in other quarters of the globe."

CHAPTER XX.

LA LOUTRE AND HIS WORK.

The English, after a possession of Acadia which lasted nearly forty years, had not succeeded in founding a single English settlement, or adding to the English speaking population of the Province. The French Acadians, on the other hand, had gone on increasing and spreading themselves over the land. They were strong and formidable, not only by reason of their number, but because of their knowledge of wood-craft, of the management of canoes, and of many other accomplishments which are essential to those who would live in a forest country, and which were almost indispensable qualifications for soldiers in such a land as Acadia. All that the English had to show for their thirty-nine years occupation of the country were the fortifications of Annapolis and a ruined fishing station at Canso. All the substantial gains of that time belonged to France, for the Acadians were nearly three times as numerous as they were when Port Royal fell, and they were quite as devoted to the interests of France as their fathers had been. Acadia in 1749 was as much a French colony as it had been forty years before. The only difference was that the English were at the expense of maintaining a garrison instead of the French, and that they sometimes issued orders to the inhabitants which the latter very seldom chose to obey.

Many schemes had been devised for the purpose of giving Acadia an English population, but none of them had come to anything. One of the best was, perhaps, that of Governor Shirley, who proposed to scatter English settlers among the French in all the principal settlements in sufficient numbers to maintain something like a balance of power. This, no doubt, was quite feasible, and had the right kind of settlers been obtained—hardy pioneers from the borders of New England—the problem which so greatly perplexed successive Governors of Nova Scotia would have been solved, and the Acadians kept quiet, or their influence at least neutralized. In 1749 a plan of a simpler character, but less likely to be immediately effective, was adopted. This was to bring settlers from England to a portion of the coast not already occupied, and to found a town and establish a strong English colony. General Philipps, although he had not been in the country for many years, was still Governor of the Province, the government being administered by the Lieutenant-Governor of the fort of Annapolis. The commission of Philipps was now revoked, and the Hon. Edward Cornwallis was appointed Captain-General and Governor-in-Chief of Nova Scotia. He arrived in the Province in the summer of 1749, and established at Chebouctou, a colony of some two thousand five hundred persons, many of them disbanded officers, soldiers and sailors. A town arose as if by magic on the soil which had been covered by a dense forest a few weeks before, and to it Cornwallis gave the name of Halifax, out of compliment to the Lord then at the head of the Board of Trade. Here the government of the Province was reorganized, fortifications erected, and the beginnings made of the large military and naval establishments which have grown up on the shores of the old Chebouctou.

At the very first Council held in Halifax, which was on the 14th July, three French deputies appeared to pay their respects. These were Jean Melançon from Canard River,

Claude LeBlanc from Grand Prè, and Philip Melançon from Piziquid. They were presented with a declaration, which Governor Cornwallis had previously prepared, defining the rights and duties of the Acadian people. In this declaration it was stated that the many indulgences which the King and his royal predecessors had shown to the inhabitants had not met with a dutiful return; but, on the contrary, that several of them had openly abetted, or privately assisted, His Majesty's enemies. "Yet His Majesty, being desirous of showing further marks of his royal grace to the said inhabitants, in hopes thereby to induce them to become for the future true and loyal subjects, is graciously pleased to allow that the said inhabitants shall continue in the free exercise of their religion, as far as the laws of Great Britain do allow the same, as also the peaceable possession of such lands as are under their cultivation, provided that the said inhabitants do within three months from the date of this declaration take the oaths of allegiance appointed to be taken by the laws of Great Britain, and likewise submit to such rules and orders as may hereafter be thought proper to be made for the maintaining and supporting of His Majesty's Government; and provided likewise that they do give all possible countenance and assistance to such persons as His Majesty shall think proper to settle in this Province." A fortnight later ten deputies, representing the settlements of Annapolis, Grand Prè, River Canard, Piziquid, Cobequid, Chignecto and Shepody arrived in Halifax, and delivered a written answer to the Governor's declaration, asking that they be permitted to have priests and the public exercise of their religion, and demanding an exemption from bearing arms in case of war, even should the Province be attacked.

In response to this the Governor issued a second declaration, granting the Acadians priests and the free and public exercise of their religion, provided that no priest should presume to officiate without having obtained the permission of the Governor and taken the oath of allegiance. The declaration stated that the King was not willing that any of his subjects, possessing habitations and lands in the Province, should be exempted from an entire allegiance, or from the natural obligation to defend themselves. Accordingly, it was stated that all must take the oath of allegiance before the 26th October, and that officers would attend at the several settlements to administer it. The deputies, on hearing this second declaration read to them, inquired if any that desired to leave the Province would have leave to sell their lands and effects, and were told that if they retired, they must leave their effects behind them, the year allowed them for that purpose by the treaty of Utrecht having long expired. They were also warned that if they did not take the oath of allegiance before the 26th October, they should forfeit all their possessions and rights in the Province. This declaration was issued on the 1st August, and on the 6th September the Acadian deputies returned with an answer in writing, signed by upwards of one thousand persons. In this they stated that "the inhabitants in general over the whole extent of the country have resolved not to take the oath;" but they offered to take the old oath, taken in 1730, with an exemption against bearing arms. They added that if the Governor was not disposed to grant them this, they were resolved, one and all, to leave the country. Governor Cornwallis replied to this, by telling them that by the treaty of Utrecht all who remained in Acadia became subjects of the Crown of England, and that they were on the same footing as other Catholic subjects. They therefore deceived themselves if they supposed that it lay with them whether they would be subject to the King or not. He told them, also, that it was only out of pity for their situation and their inexperience in the affairs of government that he condescended to reason with them; "otherwise, the question would not be of reasoning, but of commanding and being obeyed." He reproached them for not having given a better return for the privileges they had enjoyed for the past thirty-five years, and ended by enjoining them to act as good subjects, and to do all in their power to assist the new colony. There the question rested, for that year Cornwallis took no steps to deprive them of their property, or compel them to leave the country, but simply wrote home for instructions as to what course he should pursue towards them the following Spring.

Meanwhile, the Governor of Canada had already anticipated the movements of the English at Halifax by sending an officer named Boishebert and thirty men to the St. John River in the Spring, to take possession of the territory at its mouth and prevent any English from settling there. They occupied a little fort on the northern bank of the Nerepis, at its junction with the St. John, which had been erected by the Indians in Villebon's time. La Corne was also sent from Quebec with a stronger detachment of soldiers and Canadians to Shediac to hold Chignecto and prevent any English from settling in that vicinity. These measures were consistent with the claim which France was making, that the territory north of the Isthmus of Chignecto was not part of Acadia, and therefore not ceded to England by the treaty of Utrecht. In July, Cornwallis sent Captain Rous in the Albany to the St. John to order the French away. He found that Boishebert and one hundred and fifty Indians gathered there under the French flag, and in explanation of his presence he showed orders from the Governor of Canada, ordering him to prevent the English from settling at St. John. The same vessel brought back to Halifax Chiefs and Deputies of the St. John River, Passamaquoddy and Chignecto tribes of Indians to renew the treaty of peace and submission made in 1726. They renewed the treaty and made great professions of friendship, which La Loutre took care that they did not keep.

In September, Captain Handfield was detached from Annapolis, with one hundred men, to occupy Mines, and he established himself and erected a block-house at Grand Prè. This act was looked upon with great disfavor by the French emissaries in the Province, and the Indians were excited to acts of hostility, almost before the ink of their treaty was dry. Their first attack was at Canso, where they took twenty Englishmen prisoners, most of whom had come there in a vessel from Boston to cut hay. They were taken to Louisbourg, and afterwards released by the French Governor Desherbiers. The next attack was made at Chignecto, where the Indians endeavored to surprise two trading vessels belonging to Messrs. Daniel and Winniett. Three English were killed, but the Indians lost seven men and were beaten off. In October the Indians attacked six men who were cutting timber for a saw mill near Halifax, killing four of them and capturing one. This act called forth a proclamation from the Government, offering a reward of ten guineas for the capture of each Micmac Indian, or for his scalp. In December three hundred Micmacs and St. John Indians suddenly appeared at Mines, and captured lieutenant Hamilton and eighteen men, whom they surprised outside the fort. They prowled about the fort itself for seven days and made several attempts upon it, but were foiled and obliged to retire.

Eleven of the French inhabitants of Piziquid assisted them in their assault on the fort, and an attempt was made to arrest them, but they abandoned their dwellings and fled to Chignecto, which had become the place of refuge for all the outlaws of the Peninsula. They carried with them three Englishmen who had ventured to settle among them. The author and instigator of all these attacks was well known to Governor Cornwallis to be La Loutre, the missionary to the Micmacs, who held the office of Vicar-General of Acadia under the Bishop of Quebec. This priest came to the Province as early as 1740, and it was not long before he commenced to plot against the English. He was in close and constant communication with the French Governors of Canada for many years, and was the prime mover in all the schemes for the subversion of English authority up to the fall of Beauséjour. Indeed his spiritual functions seems to have been made entirely subservient to his political mission, and there is excellent evidence to show that the Bishop of Quebec was very far from approving of his conduct. Perhaps there is a standpoint from which La Loutre's acts can be justified, but the Acadian people will scarcely be able to feel much affection for the memory of a man who brought such misfortunes on their fathers. It may have been pure patriotism which moved him in all his schemes, but many ascribed his conduct to personal vanity. Nor was he so single-minded as not to have an eye to temporal advantages, for M. Franquet states that, in 1751, La Loutre kept a shop at Baie Verte on his own private account. The plan which he pursued consistently from first to last with the Acadians, was to threaten them with the vengeance of the savages if they submitted to the English, and to refuse the sacraments to all who would not obey his commands. It was by such threats as these that he induced the inhabitants of Chignecto to take the oath of allegiance to the King of France in 1749, and that he afterwards caused so many of them to withdraw from the Peninsula. Cornwallis thought that if he could capture this arch plotter, he would be doing the Acadians a service and materially lightening the cares of his government. He went so far as to commission Captain Sylvanus Cobb to enlist a party to capture La Loutre; but the affair became advertised in Boston, owing to the stupidity of the agents who had it in charge, and the plan was abandoned.

In January, 1750, La Loutre was at Cobequid with a party of Indians, and at the church door, in the presence of both priests, he forbade the inhabitants to pass the River Shubenacadie on pain of death. This menace was intended to prevent them from having any further communication with the English at Halifax, and especially to prevent any of the inhabitants of Cobequid from going to Halifax to work, which some of them had done. Thirty Indians remained at Cobequid all winter, and some of the inhabitants were in league with them, for they captured and sent to Chignecto a messenger that Cornwallis had sent to Gerard, the priest. The Governor was indignant at his messenger not returning, and at the presence of the Indians; and in February Captain Bartalo was sent to Cobequid with one hundred men to surprise the Indians, and bring Gerard and the deputies to Halifax to answer for their conduct. Bartalo returned in March without the Indians, who had taken their departure, but he brought the priests and deputies, and they were detained for a time. Gerard finally took the oath of allegiance, and was sent to officiate at Mines.

The lawless conduct of some of the inhabitants of Piziquid induced Cornwallis to send a detachment there in

March, under the command of Captain John Gorham. After an engagement with the Indians on the St. Croix, in which he and some of his men were wounded, he established himself on an eminence between the Piziquid and St. Croix, and commenced the erection of Fort Edward, which from that time became one of the regular garrison stations of the Province. In April, Cornwallis and his Council resolved to erect a block-house at Chignecto, which was the focus of most of the intrigues which were hatched against English authority. Major Lawrence was entrusted with this work, and furnished with four hundred men, nearly half of whom were regulars. He marched to Mines, and there took shipping to Chignecto, which he reached on the 1st May. There, on the southern side of the Misseguash, which the French pretended to be the boundary of Acadia, was a large village named Beaubassin, consisting of one hundred and forty houses. The inhabitants were rich and prosperous, for the territory upon which it stood, and the surrounding marshes, formed, and still forms, one of the most fertile regions in Acadia. The French had early notice that the English were coming, and the wily La Loutre persuaded the inhabitants of this populous settlement, numbering more than a thousand souls, to abandon their dwellings, and, with their cattle and household effects, to cross the Misseguash, and come under the protection of the French troops on its northern bank. Then, to make the step irrevocable, he ordered his Indians to set fire to the village, and it was totally destroyed, not even the chapel being spared. The statement that such an act of wanton devastation was committed on the French inhabitants by the orders of a priest of their country and their faith, would be incredible, were it not well authenticated. More than a thousand persons were embraced in this forced emigration, and the number was increased later in the year, as La Loutre's fulminations and threats took effect. About eight hundred Acadians were residing at Port la Joie, the site of Charlottetown, P. E. I., in August 1750, and were being fed on rations furnished from Quebec. There they lived miserably, like Indians in the woods, and suffered many hardships. A large number of them remained on the isthmus, scattered at various points between Baie Verte and the head of the Bay of Fundy. For several years these poor refugees, flattered by hopes that were destined never to be realized, lived in voluntary exile in sight of the fields that had been their own, and to which they might have had liberty to return, on embracing the easy conditions which they were offered. Yet they were restrained by the influence of a wicked priest, who had a band of savages, which he employed to coerce them.

The French were now gathered in great force north of the Misseguash, there being a considerable body of regulars, a larger body of Canadians, several hundred Indians, and many able-bodied Acadian inhabitants. La Corne sent word to Lawrence that he intended to hold the north bank of the Misseguash as French territory until the boundary question was settled by the two Crowns, and the scope of Lawrence's orders did not embrace any instructions to drive La Corne away. As the removal of the French inhabitants had made the erection of a block-house unnecessary, and as he had not the means for the construction of a regular fort, Lawrence resolved to take his force back to Mines until measures were perfected for the larger enterprise which the changed attitude of the French had rendered necessary.

La Loutre, by means of his agents in the various settlements, had been unremitting in his efforts to induce the

HISTORY OF ACADIA. 365

inhabitants to withdraw from the isthmus, and from under English rule. In April, deputies arrived at Halifax from River Canard, Grand Prè and Piziquid, asking for leave to evacuate the Province, and to carry off their effects. They also announced their determination not to sow their fields. Cornwallis replied in a most kind and conciliatory strain. He said—

"I am not ignorant of the fact that since my arrival in the Province every means has been employed to alienate the hearts of the French subjects of His Britannic Majesty. I know that great advantages have been promised you elsewhere, and that you have been made to imagine that your religion was in danger. Threats even have been resorted to, in order to induce you to remove into French territory. The savages are made use of to molest you. The savages are to cut the throats of those who persist in remaining in their native country, attached to their own interests, and faithful to the Government. By the manner in which this scheme has been carried out, you yourselves will judge of the character of the directors, and of their designs. You will judge whether those deserve your confidence, who sacrifice their own honor, the honor of their Sovereign, and of their nation, to lead you to your ruin. You know that certain officers and missionaries, who came from Canada to Chignecto last Autumn, have been the cause of all our troubles during the winter. Their entrance into this Province and their stay here are directly contrary to the treaties which exist between the two Crowns. Their conduct has been horrible, without honor, probity or conscience, and such as they dare not acknowledge themselves. They are doing everything by underhand dealings, and by means of the savages, whom they will disown in the end. It was these, gentlemen, who induced the savages of the

River St. John to unite with the Micmacs the day after a solemn treaty. They induced the Micmacs to commence their outrages, and furnished them with everything necessary for their war. Finally, since the peace, they have been engaged in intrigues and enterprises, for which an honest man would have blushed, even during the war. These same, gentlemen, are doing their best to cause you to leave the country, and to transfer yourselves to French territory. They have endeavored to give you very false ideas, which you would not fail to declare to us. Their aim is to embroil you with the Government." Cornwallis concluded by telling the deputies that they were the subjects of Great Britain, and not of France; that it was ridiculous for them to say that they would not sow their fields; that no one could possess lands or houses in the Province, who refused to take the oath of allegiance, and those who left the Province would not be permitted to take their effects with them.

Five weeks later, deputies from Annapolis, Grand Prè, River Canard and Piziquid, came with petitions from the inhabitants, asking permission to leave the Province. Cornwallis replied, that as soon as tranquillity was re-established he would furnish those who wished to leave the Province with passports. In the meantime, considering that the moment they crossed the Misseguash they would be compelled to take up arms against the English, he declined to grant them permission to depart at that time. There was something almost touching in the terms in which the Governor expressed his regret at the determination of the Acadians to withdraw from under English rule. He thus expressed himself—

"My friends, the moment that you declared your desire to leave and submit yourselves to another government, our determination was to hinder nobody from following what he imagined to be his interest. We know that a forced service is worth nothing, and that a subject compelled to be so against his will, is not very far from being an enemy. We frankly confess, however, that your determination to leave us gives us pain. We are well aware of your industry and your temperance, and that you are not addicted to any vice or debauchery. This Province is your country; you and your fathers have cultivated it; naturally you ought yourselves to enjoy the fruits of your labor. Such was the desire of the King, our master. You know that we have followed his orders. You know that we have done everything to secure to you not only the occupation of your lands, but the ownership of them for ever. We have given you also every possible assurance of the enjoyment of your religion, and the free and public exercise of the Roman Catholic faith. When we arrived here we expected that nothing would give you so much pleasure, as the determination of His Majesty to settle this Province. Certainly nothing more advantageous to you could take place. You possess the only cultivated lands in the Province; they produce grain and nourish cattle sufficient for the whole colony. It is you that would have had all the advantages for a long time. In short, we flattered ourselves that we would make you the happiest people in the world. We are sorry to find in our government persons whom it is impossible to please, and upon whom our declarations have produced nothing but discontent, jealousies and murmurings. We must not complain of all the inhabitants. We know very well that there are ill disposed, interested and mischievous persons among you who corrupt the others. Your inexperience and your ignorance of the affairs of government, and your habit of following the counsels of those who have not your real interests at heart, make it an easy matter to seduce you." This may be the language of tyranny and oppression, but it sounds wonderfully like the tone of gentle and kindly remonstrance. Unfortunately, the Acadians were not permitted by their advisers to believe in the sincerity of anything which an English Governor might say. It was the policy of the agents of the French King to fill them with distrust, and to compel them to withdraw from their lands and submit to all the privations which such a course involved.

The establishment of a Fort at Chignecto was the next object which engaged the attention of Cornwallis and his Council. Lieutenant-Colonel Lawrence arrived at the Isthmus in September 1750, with a strong force, consisting of the 48th regiment and three hundred men of the 45th regiment. The Indians and some of the French inhabitants were rash enough to attempt to oppose the landing of this formidable body of troops, but they were driven off after a sharp skirmish, in which the English lost about twenty killed and wounded. On an elevation, a short distance south of the Misseguash, Lawrence commenced the erection of a picketed fort, with block-houses, which was named after himself. Here a garrison of six hundred men was maintained until the fall of Beauséjour. The two Crowns were supposed to be at peace when Fort Lawrence was erected, but on that border land there was something very nearly akin to war.

CHAPTER XXI.

THE FALL OF BEAUSÈJOUR.

On the northern bank of the Misseguash, less than a mile from that river, which now forms the boundary of two Provinces, the Intercolonial Railway winds round a remarkable hill, which, rising suddenly from the marsh, runs back in a high narrow ridge towards the north east. The traveller, as he gazes listlessly at the landscape, suddenly has his attention fixed by the sight of a ruined magazine and the ramparts and embrasures of an ancient fortress, and turns to his guide-book to discover what this may be. These wasting battlements, which now seem so out of place in the midst of a peaceful pastoral scene, have a sadder history than almost any other piece of ground in Acadia, for they represent the last effort of France to hold on to a portion of that Province, which was once all her own, which she seemed to value so little when its possession was secure, yet which she fought so hard to save. This ruin is all that remains of the once potent and dreaded Beausèjour.

The erection of Beausèjour was commenced in 1750 by La Corne, and it was scarcely completed when it passed out of the possession of the French five years later. It was a fort of five bastions, capable of accommodating eight hundred men, and provided with casemates. It mounted thirty guns. In connexion with Beausèjour, the French constructed a complete system of defence for the northern portion of Acadia. At Baie Verte they had a small fort, which they named Fort Gaspereaux. It was close to the sea shore, on the northern side of the Bay, and was used as a depôt for goods coming to Beausèjour, from Louisbourg and Quebec. It mounted six guns, and had a garrison of from fifteen to thirty men. At Pont a Buot there was a block-house garrisoned by thirty men, and there were guards at Shepody, Shediac, and one or two other points. At the River St. John there was a detachment of seventy or eighty men, besides Indians. This line of posts formed a continuous chain from the Gulf of St. Lawrence to the St. John, and Beausèjour could at any time be reinforced, either by way of the Gulf or from the River St. John, without the English at Annapolis or Halifax having any notice of it. At Beausèjour, La Loutre made his headquarters, and issued his edicts to the Acadians, who trembled at his frown. He had the Indians under as complete control as it was possible for these wayward people to be kept; yet even he found them sometimes difficult to manage. In a letter written to Bigot, the Intendant of Canada, in August 1750, La Loutre says: "If all our savages were Frenchmen, we should not be embarrassed; but the wretches get tired, and will perhaps leave us in our greatest need." This sentence throws a flood of light on the crooked policy of the agents of France, and shivers to atoms the pretence that the Indians of themselves would have attacked the Acadians if they had taken the oath of allegiance to England. It was only when persuaded to it by such men as La Loutre, that the savages made even a pretence of threatening the Acadians. The pressure placed upon the latter all came from men of their own race.

To preserve his influence with the savages, La Loutre was prepared to go all lengths. Among the gentlemen of the garrison of Fort Lawrence was Captain Edward How, a person well acquainted with the Indians, and who had been employed in several negotiations to which they were parties. He was sent to Chignecto by Governor Cornwallis in consequence of his familiarity with the country and its people, not without the hope that he might persuade the savages to abandon La Loutre and the French interest. The unscrupulous priest soon discovered his mission, and marked him for destruction. How had been accustomed to meet French officers at the Misseguash with flags of truce when there was any communication to be made between one fort and the other. La Loutre, taking advantage of this circumstance, dressed up an Indian named Cope like a French officer, and sent him down to the river with a white flag. This signal brought How down to the Misseguash to meet the pretended French officer, and when he got within range, a party of Indians which lay concealed behind the dike rose, and firing a volley, shot him dead. The indignation of Cornwallis at this outrage was extreme. In a letter to the Duke of Bedford, he characterized it as "an instance of treachery and barbarity not to be paralleled in history." It has been paralleled since, but we have to go to the subjects of that dagger-haunted tyrant, the Russian Czar, to find another case as flagrant.

La Loutre kept his Indians busy intercepting the messengers of the Governor and cutting communication between Halifax and the various garrisoned posts. Dartmouth, which was much exposed, was attacked by them in the Spring of 1751, and a number of persons killed and scalped. These attacks seem to have been made in mere wantonness, for it was not to be supposed that a settlement as strong as that around Chebucto harbor would be seriously injured by such efforts. One effect of the danger from the Indians was, however, to prevent solitary settlers from going into the forest after the approved Anglo-Saxon fashion, and there making homes for themselves.

In August of this year Franquet, an engineer officer sent by the French Government to report on the forts in Acadia and the Island of St. John and suggest measures for their improvement, visited Beausèjour, and instructed St. Ours, the commander, as to the proper mode of making it defensible. There were then one hundred and forty-two Acadian refugees living at Baie Verte, and eleven hundred and eleven at Beausèjour and in its vicinity.* Most of these people were from the villages immediately south of the Misseguash, although some of them had come from Mines and Cobequid. Some of these poor people became very ill satisfied with their position as dependents on the bounty of the French government, and asked permission of the government at Halifax to return to their lands. They always received the same answer, that they might go back to their lands and cultivate them as before, provided they were willing to take the following oath of allegiance:
" Je promets et jure sincèrement que Je serai fidèle, et que Je porterai une loyauté parfaite vers Sa Majestè le Roi George Second."

There was no time up to the capture of Beausèjour when these "deserted inhabitants," as they were termed,

* Franquet gives a list of the villages these people had come from. I preserve the spelling he adopts, but the places will be readily recognized.

Villages of Acadia.	Men.	Women.	Children.	Total No. of Persons.
Menoudy,	29	26	114	169
River Heberts,	20	21	71	112
Mankane River,	12	13	61	86
Nampane River,	18	20	104	142
Weschkok,	17	19	79	115
La Butte,	14	13	59	86
Les Planches,	11	6	39	59
Beaubassin,	32	30	128	190
Mines, Cobequid and other places,	25	23	107	155
	178	171	762	1111

might not have returned to their lands on complying with this condition, and they were also promised by the Government the free exercise of their religion, a sufficient number of priests, and all the other privileges granted by the treaty of Utrecht. All La Loutre's power was freely  used to prevent them from returning to the territory under the English flag. He caused them to demand conditions that he knew could not be granted, and that were even insulting in their character, and therefore calculated to bring all negotiations to an end. In his sermons he told them that if they returned to the English they would be allowed neither priests nor sacraments, but "would die like miserable wretches." To prevent, as far as possible, any further communications between them and the English, he succeeded in sending a large number of them to the St. John River, and many of them to the Island of St. John, with a view to their settling there. Still, after all these emigrations, eighty families were living under the guns of Beauséjour in 1754. In that year they sent two deputies to the Governor of Canada, asking permission to return to their lands, but these messengers of a people, who had sacrificed everything for their loyalty, were very badly received, and treated almost as if they had been criminals.

In the portions of Acadia not claimed by the French, the attitude of the inhabitants continued unfriendly to the English government. Cornwallis left the Province in 1752, and was succeeded by Governor Hopson, but he had no better success in tranquillizing the inhabitants than his predecessors. It was the policy of La Loutre to keep the Acadians hostile to the English, and, as most of the missionary priests were in sympathy with him, he had abundant success in that direction. His ability to annoy and harass the English was very great, for the garrisons in the various settlements were dependent to a large extent on the good will of the people. Governor Hobson, with a view to remove all causes of complaint, issued stringent orders to the commanders of the forts at Mines and Piziquid to make no requisitions on the inhabitants, and if they refused supplies, not to redress themselves by military force, but to lay the case before the Governor and wait his orders. The provisions and fuel furnished by the inhabitants were to be paid for according to a free agreement between buyer and seller, and not at a fixed price. This piece of lenity had no effect whatever in improving the disposition of the Acadians, but gave La Loutre's agents an opportunity to create difficulties for the English which they did not fail to embrace. The Acadians ceased to bring any supplies to the English forts, carrying all their surplus provisions to the French establishments at Beauséjour and St. John, and finally at the instance of Daudin, one of the priests, the inhabitants of Piziquid refused to furnish any wood to the garrison at that place. It became necessary to issue peremptory orders to the people to supply the wood required, and Daudin, who had acted most insolently in the matter, threatening the English with the direst vengeance, was carried off to Halifax a prisoner, and not permitted to return to his charge until he had made a very humble submission, and promised to amend his conduct.

At this time it also became necessary to pass a stringent order in Council forbidding the exportation of grain from the Province without a permission in writing signed by the Lieutenant-Governor. This was done for the purpose of preventing the French inhabitants from supplying grain to the Indians and French on the north side of the Bay of Fundy, and also in the hope that the supply of grain for the Halifax market might thereby be increased.

One of the evils produced by the contempt for authority which distinguished the French inhabitants was that the German settlers who had been brought to the Province in 1753, and who were settled at Lunenburg showed a disposition to rebel, and soldiers had to be sent among them before they could be quieted. Some of these Germans went off among the French and gave them their countenance in their rebellious attitude towards the government. It was evident that some vigorous measures must be taken if Acadia was to be saved to England, for the authority of the government was not respected in those places where there was no armed force to maintain it. This was very plainly demonstrated in the autumn of 1754, when about three hundred inhabitants went to Beauséjour, in spite of the orders of the government, to work on the aboteau which La Loutre was erecting. These men were offered work by the government at Halifax, and the certainty of good wages, but they chose to run all the risks which their disobedience entailed, and to go without passes rather than to work for the English.

England and France were now on the verge of a war which was destined to end in the humiliation of the latter power, and the loss of the greater part of her possessions in America. The attempt made to settle the limits of Acadia by means of a commission had failed, as it was evident it must do from the first, considering how conflicting were the claims of the two powers. Governor Shirley, who had been the English Commissioner, was now returned home, and was revolving in his active brain many schemes for the destruction of the power of France in Acadia and Cape Breton. He had in Lieutenant-Colonel Lawrence, who, in the absence of Governor Hopson, had become Lieutenant-Governor of Nova Scotia, an active and energetic assistant, and one whose firmness was to be depended upon. It was well that such a man had the command in Nova Scotia at this time, for the difficulties of the position were great, and not likely to be lessened so long as a passive policy was pursued.

In November 1754 Lawrence wrote to Shirley stating that he had reason to believe the French were contemplating aggressive movements at Chignecto as soon as they had repaired the fortifications of Louisbourg, and suggesting that it was high time some effort was made to drive them from the north side of the Bay of Fundy. Lieutenant-Colonel Monckton, who carried this letter to Shirley, was directed to consult with him as to the enlisting of two thousand men for an expedition against Beauséjour and the River St. John in the Spring, and the greatest secrecy was enjoined on all concerned, for it was considered almost essential to the success of the enterprise that the French should have no warning of the intended attack. Shirley had already been corresponding with Sir Thomas Robinson, the Secretary of State, with regard to the matter, and the latter had informed him that it was the desire of the Government that he and Lawrence should act in concert. Shirley scarcely needed such an order, for he was filled with zeal for the destruction of French power in America, and ready to co-operate in any enterprise to that end. He entered heartily into Lawrence's plans, and the success of the expedition was largely due to the forethought and care with which he had prepared it.

On the 23rd of May, 1755, the expedition set sail from Boston with a fair wind. It consisted of about two thousand men, under the command of Lieutenant-Colonel Monckton, with Lieutenant-Colonels Winslow and Scott under him. After calling at Annapolis, and being joined by three hundred regulars of Warburton's regiment and a small train of artillery, they got to Chignecto on the 2nd June, and on the following day all the troops were landed and camped around Fort Lawrence. Vergor, who was then in command of Beauséjour, at once sent an order for all the Acadians, capable of bearing arms, to come into the fort. The order was pretty generally obeyed, although the inhabitants demanded that, as a justification for bearing arms, he should threaten them with punishment in case of their refusal. Vergor pretended to the inhabitants that he could defend the fort successfully against the English, but, although it was well supplied with ammunition and provisions, its defences were in an incomplete state. La Loutre had kept so many of the inhabitants working on the aboteau, for which he had received a large grant in France, that the fort had been neglected. Vergor and his artillery officer Piedmont, however, endeavored to make up for lost time, and placed a large party of Acadians and soldiers at the work of completing its defences. Its armament then consisted of twenty-one cannon and a mortar, and it was manned by one hundred and sixty-five officers and soldiers of the regulars, in addition to several hundred Acadians, so that there was no lack of men.

Beauséjour could not be assailed from the front, so Monckton proceeded to take measures to enable him to attack it from the rear. On the 4th June the English troops made an attack in force on Pont a Buot, a post on the Misseguash, several miles to the eastward of Beauséjour. Here there was a block-house and a strong breastwork of timber, which the French defended for an hour, and then abandoned in a panic, setting fire to the block-house, leaving the English to lay their bridge, and cross the river unmolested. Before night they had established themselves

on the northern side of the Misseguash, half a league from
Beauséjour. As they retired, the French set fire to all the
houses between Pont a Buot and the fort, and before night
the whole of them, to the number of sixty, were burnt to
the ground. Even the church did not escape the flames.
The next day the English were busy making a bridge over
the river sufficient to transport their heavy guns, and in
cutting a road through the woods northward to the high
ground behind the fort. This work proved tedious, and it
was not until the 13th that they succeeded in getting any
of their cannon in position north of the fort. The French
in the meantime had been very busy strengthening its
defences, and had made very satisfactory progress. Two or
three slight skirmishes had taken place between small
parties, but no sortie of importance had been made. A
considerable number of Indians—both Malicites and Micmacs—had come Vergor's assistance, and they had effected
the capture of an English officer, named Hay, while going
from Fort Lawrence to the English camp at daybreak.

The English, having succeeded in getting their artillery
over the hill behind the fort, opened trenches within seven
hundred feet of it, and commenced firing small shells on
the morning of the 13th. On the 14th the firing continued,
but without much effect. That day Vergor received bad
news from Louisbourg. He had been led to hope for
assistance from that place, and in fact had given the Acadians to understand that he expected twelve hundred
soldiers from Louisbourg to relieve Beauséjour. Now
Drucourt, the Governor of Isle Royale, wrote to him that
he could send him no help, as he was himself threatened
by an English squadron. Vergor told his officers of this
depressing answer, and enjoined them to conceal it from the
Acadians, but it leaked out, nevertheless, and produced a

most demoralizing effect. That night a number of the Acadians escaped from the fort, and on the following morning those that remained asked Vergor's permission to retire, which they could easily have done, as the place was not invested. Vergor, however, refused their request. That day the English commenced firing fifteen-inch shells, two of which fell into the fort, and did a good deal of damage. On the 16th the mortar practice continued with most disastrous results to the besieged. A fifteen-inch shell rolled into one of the casemates, where the English prisoner, Mr. Hay, and a number of French officers were at breakfast. Mr. Hay and three of the French were killed, and two others wounded. This affair produced such a panic among both soldiers and Acadians, that Vergor came to the conclusion that it was impossible to hold out any longer. La Loutre and one or two others were opposed to a surrender, but Vergor sent an officer to Monckton to ask for a suspension of hostilities, with a view to a capitulation. The same afternoon the terms of surrender were agreed upon, and in the evening the English entered the fort.

The terms of capitulation granted by Monckton were—that the garrison should go out of the fort with their arms, and be sent by sea to Louisbourg, and that they were not to bear arms in America for the space of six months. The Acadians, who had been forced to take up arms, on pain of death, were to be pardoned.

All day, while the negotiations for the surrender were going on, the French officers were engaged in drinking and plundering, and great confusion prevailed in the fort. In the evening, Vergor gave a supper, at which officers of both nations were present; but there was one well known face absent from the board. The Abbè La Loutre seeing no clause in the terms of capitulation that would cover his case, had withdrawn from the fort just before the English entered it. His career, as an agitator and political incendiary, was ended. The result of all his schemes had been simply his own ruin and that of the cause for which he had labored. As in his disguise, and concealed by the shadows of evening, he wended his way towards the northern wilderness, an outcast and a fugitive, it may possibly have occurred to him that his political mission was a mistake; that he would have done better had he taken the advice of his Bishop, and attended to the proper duties of his office as a missionary priest. True, the latter position gave less scope for ambition than the role of a political agent; but it was infinitely safer, and much more likely to yield a grateful return. La Loutre had abundant opportunities, during the remaining years of his life, to meditate upon the ingratitude of man and the vanity of earthly ambition. When he got to Quebec, after a fatiguing journey through the wilderness, he met with a cold reception from the Governor, and was bitterly reproached by his Bishop for his unclerical conduct. He was glad to get away from a place where his services were so little appreciated, so in August he embarked for France, but the vessel was captured by the English, and he was kept a prisoner in Elizabeth Castle in the Island of Jersey until the end of the war. When he emerged from behind the massive walls of his prison, eight years had passed over his head, and the empire of France in North America had departed for ever.

 Monckton sent Colonel Winslow to Baie Verte with three hundred men to demand the surrender of Fort Gaspereaux, and it was given up on the same terms that had been granted to Vergor. Both garrisons were promptly forwarded to Louisbourg. About three hundred Acadians were found in Fort Beauséjour when it was surrendered, and a number of others came in afterwards and yielded up their arms. They were offered a free pardon for their past misconduct, provided they would consent to take the oath of allegiance; but they all refused to do so. They did not know then, perhaps, that the more than forty years of forbearance which the English government had exercised towards the Acadians had nearly come to an end, or they might have reached a different determination.

Monckton changed the name of Beauséjour to Fort Cumberland, in honor of the Royal Duke, who won the victory at Culloden. He placed a garrison in it, and then despatched Captain Rous, who was in command of the naval part of the expedition, to the St. John River with three twenty-gun ships and a sloop to drive the French from that place, if practicable. As soon as Rous sailed into St. John Harbor, the French burst their cannon, blew up their magazine, set the woodwork of the fort on fire, and fled up river. The commandant had already been informed of the fall of Beauséjour, and was therefore aware of the uselessness of trying to make good his defence. The Halifax Council resolved to permit this fort to remain just as the French had left it, without attempting to place a garrison there.

The Acadian expedition of 1755 was but one of four planned by the English in that year, and it was the only one that proved completely successful. The other three enterprises were an attack on Fort du Quesne by British regulars, under General Braddock, an attempt on the fort at Niagara by Colonial regulars and Indians under Governor Shirley, and an expedition against Crown Point, to be carried out by militia from the northern colonies. Braddock advanced with a large force to within a few miles of the place he was to attack, and in his arrogant self-sufficiency refused to take any of those precautions against surprise, which experience in forest warfare had shown to be necessary. The result might have been easily foreseen. His troops were attacked in the dense forest by a large body of French and Indians, thrown into confusion and defeated. Braddock was killed, and the expedition abandoned. The Niagara expedition was delayed in starting, and got no further than Oswego, where a garrison was left, but no attempt was made upon Niagara that year. The expedition against Crown Point, although it inflicted a bloody defeat on the French under Dieskau, which almost balanced Braddock's disaster, did not attain the object for which it was placed in the field. In Acadia, alone, the French had been completely defeated, for, although Boishebert, who commanded on the St. John River, still remained at the head of a few men, he was unable to hold his ground anywhere against the English, and was scarcely in a better position than the fugitive Acadians, who had escaped to him from the Peninsula.

CHAPTER XXII.

THE EXPULSION OF THE ACADIANS.

The event for which the year 1755 will be ever memorable in the history of this Continent was not the capture of Beauséjour, nor the defeat of Braddock. These were results which occurred in the ordinary course of warfare, and which grew naturally out of the struggle which England and France were waging in America. Our interest in them is merely the interest of patriotism; we feel no sympathy for the individual soldier who lays down his life for his country, for it is the business of the soldier to fight and to die, and to some a death on the field of battle, which is lighted by the sun of victory, seems the happiest death of all. The event which gives the year 1755 a sad pre-eminence over its fellows—the expulsion of the Acadians—was an occurrence of a very different character. The sufferers were men who were, or ought to have been, non-combatants, and in the common ruin which overtook them their wives and children were involved. The breaking up of their domestic hearths, their severance from their property, the privations they endured when driven among strangers, and the numberless ills which overtook them as the result of their first misfortune, have an interest for the people of every nation, for they appeal to our common humanity. It seems at the first view of the case an outrage on that humanity and a grievous wrong that such an occurrence as the expulsion of the Acadians should have taken place merely from political motives. The misfortunes and sufferings of the Acadians stand out prominently, and appeal to every eye; a great poet has sung of their sorrows; innumerable writers of books have referred to their expulsion in terms of condemnation; and so the matter has grown until it came to be almost a settled opinion that the expulsion of the Acadians was something which could not be justified, and of which its authors should have been ashamed. That is the view which one historian of Nova Scotia gives of the affair. Perhaps those who examine the whole matter impartially, in the light of all the facts, will come to the conclusion that it would have been a real cause for shame had the Acadians been permitted longer to misuse the clemency of the government, to plot against British power, and to obstruct the settlement of the Province by loyal subjects.

One statement has been very industriously circulated by French writers with a view to throw odium on the transaction. They say that the Acadians were expelled "because the greedy English colonists looked upon their fair farms with covetous eyes," and that the government was influenced by these persons. A more flagrant untruth never was told. The anxiety of the government that the Acadians should remain on their lands and become good subjects was extreme. To effect these objects the government consented to humiliations and concessions which only increased the arrogance of the Acadians. Even after the fall of Beauséjour they might have remained on their lands without molestation, if they had but consented to take an unconditional oath of allegiance to the British Crown. And as an absolute proof that no greedy English colonists were driving them out of the Province for the purpose of occupying their lands, it should be remembered that none of the lands of the Acadians were settled by the English until several years after the French were expelled, and not until most of the lands had gone back to a state of nature in consequence of the breaking of the dikes. It was not until 1759 that the lands of the Piziquid were re-settled, nor until 1761 that the marshes of the St. Croix were re-occupied. Five years elapsed after the expulsion of the Acadians before the noble diked lands of Grand Pré were occupied by English settlers, and the lands of Annapolis were not occupied by the English until nine or ten years after the French had left them.

I have said that the English Government was extremely anxious that the French should remain in Acadia. That was natural, because nearly the whole cost of maintaining the civil and military establishments in Acadia fell on the British people. From motives of economy, if for no other reason, it was considered highly desirable that the Acadians should remain on their lands, in order that they might supply the garrisons with provisions at a fair price, and so reduce the cost of maintaining them. It was also felt that the French, if they could be induced to become loyal subjects, would be a great source of strength to the colony from their knowledge of wood-craft and from their friendly relations with the Indians. It was, therefore, on no pretext that this desire to keep the Acadians in the Province—which is attested by more than forty years of forbearance—was succeeded by a determination to remove them from it. Grave and weighty reasons existed for taking so extreme a step, and on the sufficiency of these reasons its justification must depend. It must be remembered that in 1755 England was entering on a great war with France, which, although it ended disastrously for the latter power, certainly commenced with the balance of advantage in her favor. In such a death-struggle it was evident that there was no room for half-way measures, and that a weak policy would almost certainly be fatal to British power. Ever since the treaty of Utrecht, a period of more than forty years, the Acadians had lived on their lands without complying with the terms on which they were to be permitted to retain them, which was to become British subjects. Although the soil upon which they lived was British territory, they claimed to be regarded as "Neutrals," not liable to be called upon to bear arms either for or against the English. Their neutrality, however, did not prevent them from aiding the French to the utmost of their power and throwing every possible embarrassment in the way of the English. It did not prevent many of them from joining with the Indians in attacks on the garrison at Annapolis and on other English fortified posts in Acadia. It did not prevent them from carrying their cattle and grain to Louisbourg, Beauséjour and the River St. John, instead of to Halifax and Annapolis, when England and France were at war. It did not prevent them from maintaining a constant correspondence with the enemies of England, or from acting the part of spies on the English, and keeping Vergor at Beauséjour informed of the exact state of their garrisons from time to time. It did not prevent them from being on friendly terms with the savages, who beset the English so closely that an English settler could scarcely venture beyond his barn, or an English soldier beyond musket shot of his fort for fear of being killed and scalped. Yet these French Acadians had not been badly treated by the English, according to the lights of that age. At a time when the natural-born subjects of the French King were sent to the galleys because they were Protestants, French Catholics in Acadia under a Protestant Government were enjoying the fullest and freest exercise of their religion. It was not until it was discovered that some of the French priests were acting the part of political agents of the King of France, that any attempt was made to restrain them, and then all that was required of them was to take the oath of allegiance. At a time when the peasants of France were ground down to the earth by excessive taxation, and reduced to the most extreme state of misery by iniquitous and oppressive imposts, the French in Acadia, untaxed and unmolested, were growing opulent. The evils which afflicted their brethren in France they had never even heard of; the only tribute they were required to pay was the small voluntary tithe for the maintenance of their own clergy. What reason then had the Acadians for acting in such a spirit of hostility towards the English who had been so lenient in their conduct towards them? The only thing that can be said in mitigation of their conduct is that they were badly advised; they listened to the counsels of those who had other interests than theirs at heart, and so invoked the ruin which finally overwhelmed them. It was in accordance with the directions of these advisers that, in 1750, the inhabitants of Chignecto, south of the Misseguash, to the number of more than a thousand souls, emigrated in a body from their lands and abandoned their dwellings and barns, which the savages burnt as soon as they had evacuated them. This forced emigration, in which the English certainly had no hand, meets with nothing but commendation from those French writers who blame the English most severely for the forced emigration of 1755; yet it exposed the Acadians to almost the same evils which the latter brought upon them. Here is the pathetic story which a French Acadian, Augustin Doucet, writes from the Island of St. John to a friend at Quebec, after he had been forced by his own countrymen to abandon his dwelling in Acadia. He says:—

"I was settled in Acadia. I have four little children. I was living contented on my land. But this did not last long, for we have been obliged to leave all our goods and fly from under the dominion of the English. The King obliges himself to transport and maintain us until news is received from France. If Acadia does not return to the French, I hope to take my little family with me to Canada. I assure you that we are in a poor situation, for we are like Indians in the woods."

Such was the condition into which numbers of the Acadians were forced by the officers and agents of their own King. Garneau tells us that more than three thousand Acadians passed into the Island of St. John and the northern shores of the Bay of Fundy from the Acadian Peninsula at this time, and Governor Lawrence, after the fall of Beauséjour, estimated the number of Acadians north of the Misseguash at fourteen hundred men capable of bearing arms. This estimate, if correct, would raise the total number of French inhabitants, who were driven from their homes south of the Misseguash by the orders of the French Government, to nearly seven thousand souls, or more than double the number removed by the English in 1755. If it was cruel of the English to forcibly remove the inhabitants of Mines and Annapolis, because they would not take the oath of allegiance, what shall we say of the conduct of the French, who permitted their agents to entice away seven thousand Acadians from comfortable homes, to become outcasts and wanderers in the wilderness, exposed for years to all the hardships of savage life?

The presence, north of the Misseguash, of fourteen hundred Acadians, rendered desperate by their misfortunes, led by a French regular officer, and reinforced by a large band of Indians, afforded ground for the most serious alarm. The inhabitants of the settlements about Mines and Annapolis were known to be in active sympathy and correspondence with these "deserted French inhabitants," as they were termed. With consummate hypocrisy these "deserted" Frenchmen, who had claimed and professed to be neutrals, got themselves enrolled for the defence of Beausèjour, under threatening orders, which they themselves invited. With equal hypocrisy the French of Mines and Annapolis approached the English Governor with honeyed words, while they were plotting in secret with the enemies of English power. With so many concealed enemies in the heart of the Province, and so large a number of open enemies on its borders, the position of the English colonists was far from secure. And surely they deserved some consideration at the hands of their own Government, and some measure of protection against those who sought to destroy them.

During the Spring and Summer of 1755 a demand was made on the Acadians to deliver up their guns to the English commandants of the respective forts. This demand was pretty generally complied with, but the Acadians were very ill satisfied with it, and a number of the inhabitants of Mines, Piziquid and the River Canard sent in a petition early in July, asking permission to retain their guns, and demanding the removal of the restriction, which had been made some time before, forbidding the transporting of provisions from one river to the other. This petition was sent in by Captain Murray, the commanding officer at Fort Edward, who accompanied it with the statement that for some time before the presentation of the memorial the inhabitants had been more submissive than usual, but at its delivery they treated him with great insolence. This led him to think that they had some private information with reference to the movements of the French, which the Government did not possess. About that time reports were current that a French fleet was in the Bay of Fundy, and this was sufficient to account for the conduct of the people. It was always observed that any news of French successes, or any prospect of French assistance, brought out the Acadians in their true colors as the bitter enemies of English power.

The memorial was signed by twenty-five persons, and Lawrence and his Council immediately sent orders for those who had signed it to come to Halifax. Fifteen of them appeared before the Council on the 3rd July, and were severely reprimanded for subscribing and presenting so impertinent a paper; but to quote the language of the Minute of Council: "In compassion to their weakness and ignorance of the nature of our constitution, especially in matters of government, and as the memorialists had presented a subsequent one, and had shown an appearance of concern for their past behavior therein, and had presented themselves before the Council with great submission and repentance, the Council informed them they were still ready to treat them with lenity. And, in order to show them the falsity, as well as impudence of the contents of their memorial, it was ordered to be read paragraph by paragraph, and the truth of the several allegations in it minutely discussed."

Lieutenant-Governor Lawrence then read over the memorial, paragraph by paragraph, and made comments on each. As these comments contain substantially the case of the English Government in Nova Scotia against the Acadians, it is better, even at the risk of being somewhat tedious, to give it almost entire. The first paragraph of the Acadian memorial was:—

"We are affected by the proceedings of the Government towards us."

In reply to this, Lawrence observed: that they had always been treated by the Government with the greatest lenity and tenderness. They had enjoyed more privileges than English subjects, and had been indulged in the free exercise of their religion. They had at all times full liberty to consult their priests; they had been protected in their trade and fishery, and had been for many years permitted to possess their lands, which were part of the best soil of the Province, although they had not complied with the terms on which the lands were granted, by taking the oath of allegiance to the Crown. Lawrence then asked them to name a single instance in which any privilege was denied to them, or any hardship ever imposed on them by the Government. The Acadians were only able to reply by acknowledging the justice and lenity of the government towards them.

The next paragraph of the memorial was:—

"We desire that our past conduct may be considered."

This paragraph was read to the deputies, and in answer to it Lawrence said that their past conduct was considered, and that the Government were sorry to have occasion to say that their conduct had been undutiful and very ungrateful for the lenity shown to them. They had given no return of loyalty to the Crown or respect to His Majesty's Government in the Province. They had discovered a constant disposition to assist His Majesty's enemies and distress his subjects. They had not only furnished the enemy with provisions and ammunition, but had refused to supply the inhabitants or Government with provisions, and when they did supply them, they had exacted three times the price for them that the same articles were sold for in other markets. They had been indolent and idle on their lands, had neglected husbandry and the cultivation of the soil, and had been of no use to the Province either in husbandry, trade or fishery, but had been rather an obstruction to the King's intentions in the settlement. The deputies were then asked whether they could mention a single instance in which they had been of service to the Government, but were unable to make any reply.

The next paragraph was: "It seems that Your Excellency is doubtful of the sincerity of those who have promised fidelity, but we have been so far from breaking our oath, that we have kept it in spite of terrifying menaces from another power."

Lawrence told them that this paragraph argued a consciousness in them of insincerity and want of attachment to the interests of the Government. He said they had often pretended that the Indians would annoy them if they did not assist them, and now by taking away their arms the Government put it out of the power of the Indians to threaten or force them to their assistance. He told them, also, that they had assisted the King's enemies, and appeared only too ready to join with another power contrary to their allegiance to His Majesty.

The next paragraph was then read to them. It ran as follows: "We are now in the same disposition, the purest and sincerest, to prove in every circumstance fidelity to His Majesty in the same manner as we have done, provided that His Majesty will leave us the same liberties which he has granted to us."

Lawrence told them that it was to be hoped they would

thereafter give proofs of a more sincere and pure disposition of mind in the practice of fidelity to His Majesty, and that they would forbear to act in the manner they had done in obstructing the settlement of the Province by assisting the Indians and French to the distress and annoyance of many of His Majesty's subjects, and to the loss of the lives of several of the English inhabitants. He told them that it was not the language of British subjects to talk of terms with the Crown about their fidelity and allegiance, and that it was insolent to insert a proviso that they would prove their fidelity, provided that the King would give them liberties. He told them likewise that all His Majesty's subjects were protected in the enjoyment of every liberty while they continued loyal and faithful to the Crown, and that when they become false and disloyal, they forfeited that protection. That they in particular, although they had acted so insincerely on every opportunity, had been left in the full enjoyment of their religion, liberty and property, with an indulgence beyond what would have been allowed to any British subject, who could presume, as they had done, to join in the measures of another power.

In answer to the paragraph asking for the restoration of their guns in order to defend their cattle from wild animals, they were told that when they brought in their arms to Captain Murray none of them pretended that they wanted them for their defence against wild animals, and that they had another motive for presuming to demand their arms as part of their goods and their right. That they had flattered themselves they would be supported in their insolence to the Government, there being a report that some French ships of war were in the Bay of Fundy. This daring attempt plainly disclosed the falsehood of their professions of fidelity to the King, and their readiness upon every intimation of force or assistance from France to insult His Majesty's Government and to join with his enemies, contrary to their oath of fidelity.

The next paragraph was then read to the Deputies. It was in the following terms:—

"Besides, the arms we carry are a feeble surety for our fidelity. It is not the gun that an inhabitant possesses that will lead him to revolt, nor the depriving him of that gun that will make him more faithful, but his conscience alone ought to engage him to maintain his oath."

This piece of philosophy did not commend itself to Governor Lawrence as being appropriate to the occasion. He asked the deputies what excuse they could make for their presumption in treating the Government with such indignity and contempt as to expound to them the nature of fidelity, and to prescribe what would be the security proper to be relied on by the Government for their sincerity. He told them that if they were sincere in their duty to the Crown they would not be so anxious for their arms when it was the pleasure of the King's Government to demand them for His Majesty's service. Lawrence then informed them that a very fair opportunity then presented itself to them to manifest the reality of their obedience to the Government by immediately taking the oath of allegiance in the usual form before the Council.

The Acadian Deputies replied to this proposal by saying that they had not come prepared to take the oath. They were then told that during the previous six years the same proposal had been often made to them, and as often evaded under various frivolous pretences; that they had often been informed that some time or other the oath must be taken, and that no doubt they knew the sentiments of the other inhabitants upon the matter, and had fully considered and determined what course they would themselves pursue. The Deputies requested liberty to return home and consult with the other inhabitants, as they desired either to refuse or accept the oath in a body, and could not determine which to do until they had consulted the others.

Lawrence told them that he could not permit them to return home for any such purpose, but that they were expected to declare upon the spot what course they would take. They then desired permission to retire for an hour to consult among themselves, and this was granted. When the time had expired, they returned with the answer that they could not consent to take the oath of allegiance without consulting the whole body of inhabitants; but that they were ready to take a qualified oath, as they had done before. Governor Lawrence told them that no qualified oath of allegiance would be accepted, but that they must stand on the same footing in that respect as the rest of His Majesty's subjects. He then gave them until ten o'clock next day to come to a final resolution whether they would take the unqualified oath of allegiance or not.

Next day the Acadian Deputies attended before the Council and announced their determination not to take the oath. They were then informed that as they had refused to take the oath, as directed by law, and thereby sufficiently evinced the nature of their feelings towards the Government, the Council could no longer look upon them as subjects of His Britannic Majesty, but as subjects of the King of France, and as such they would thereafter be treated. They were then ordered to withdraw.

The Council then resolved that the French inhabitants should be ordered to send new Deputies to Halifax with their decision, whether they would take the oath of allegiance or not, and that none who refused to take the oath should be afterwards permitted to do so, but that "effectual measures ought to be taken to remove all such recusants out of the Province."

The Deputies were then called in again, and informed of this resolution, and, finding that matters were beginning to have a serious look, they offered to take the oath, but were informed that, as there was no reason to believe that their proposed compliance proceeded from an honest mind, and as it could only be regarded as the effect of compulsion and force, it could not be permitted. They were then ordered into confinement on George's Island.

This occurred on the 14th July; on the 14th a letter was sent by Lawrence to Vice Admiral Boscawen and Rear-Admiral Mostyn, inviting them to consult with him at a meeting of the Council, which was to be held next day. The Admirals attended the Council agreeably to this invitation, and Lawrence laid before them the recent proceedings of the Council in regard to the French inhabitants, and desired their opinion and advice. Both Admirals approved of the proceedings that had been taken, and gave it as their opinion that it was then the most proper time to oblige the French inhabitants to take the oath of allegiance, or to quit the country.

On the 25th July another meeting of Council was held, and the memorial of the French inhabitants of Annapolis River was received and read. It stated that they had nothing to reproach themselves with on the subject of the fidelity they owed His Majesty's Government, and that several of them had risked their lives to give information to the Government concerning the enemy. It stated that they had selected thirty men to proceed to Halifax with their memorial, who were charged strictly "to contract no new oath." This was signed by two hundred and seven of the inhabitants.

The Deputies sent with this memorial were then called in and asked what they had to say. They declared that they appeared on behalf of themselves and of all the other inhabitants of Annapolis River. They said that they could not take any oath different from what they had formerly taken, which was with a reserve that they should not be obliged to take up arms, and that if it was the King's intention to force them to quit their lands, they hoped that they would be allowed a convenient time for their departure.

The Council having heard their answer, questioned them in regard to the information which they pretended to have given the Government, and asked them to name a single instance in which any advantage had accrued to the Government from it. They were unable to make any reply to this request, and then Lawrence proceeded to show them that they had always omitted to give timely intelligence when they had it in their power, and when it might have saved the lives of many of His Majesty's subjects. He told them that they had always secretly aided the Indians, and that many of them had even appeared openly in arms against British authority. He further informed them that they must then resolve either to take the oath of allegiance without any reserve or else to quit their lands, for affairs were then at such a crisis in America that no delay could be admitted; that the French had obliged the English to take up arms against their encroachments, and therefore, if the Acadians were not willing to become British subjects, to all intents and purposes, they could not be permitted to remain in the country.

In reply to this the Acadian Deputies declared that they

were determined, one and all, rather to quit their lands than to take any other oath than that which they had taken before. Lawrence told them that they ought very seriously to consider the consequences of their refusal; that if they once refused the oath, they would never afterwards be permitted to take it, but would certainly lose their possessions. He said the Council were unwilling to hurry them into a determination upon an affair of so much consequence to them, and therefore that they would be allowed until the following Monday to reconsider the matter and form their resolution, and that then their final answer would be expected.

Monday the 28th July came round in due course,—a memorable day indeed for the Acadian people. The Council met at the Governor's house, and besides Lieutenant-Governor Lawrence, the members of Council present were Benjamin Green, John Collier, William Cotterell, John Rous and Jonathan Belcher. Admirals Boscawen and Mostyn were also present. The Annapolis Deputies were in attendance according to appointment, and also deputies from Piziquid, Mines and River Canard, who had arrived with memorials from the inhabitants of these districts.

The memorial of the inhabitants of Piziquid was first read, and stated that having taken the oath of fidelity to His Britannic Majesty in the time of Governor Phillips, with all the circumstances and reservations granted in the name of the King, they were "all resolved with one consent and voice to take no other oath." The inhabitants of Mines and River Canard couched their refusal in somewhat different language. They stated that they had taken the oath of fidelity to the King of Great Britain, and added, "we will never prove so fickle as to take an oath which changes ever so little the conditions and the privileges obtained for us by our Sovereigns and our fathers in the past."

The Deputies of Piziquid, Mines, River Canard and the adjacent settlements, were then called upon by the Council to take the unconditional oath of allegiance, and they most peremptorily and positively refused. The Annapolis Deputies, who had been before the Council before, were likewise called upon to take the oath, and they also refused. They had been already warned of the consequences which their refusal would entail upon them,—they were the victims of no snap-judgment. The step which they deliberately took on that memorable day in refusing the terms offered them by the Government, they must have well considered, unless indeed they supposed that the threats of the Government had no meaning. On the one side was the full enjoyment of their lands, the free exercise of their religion, and the protection of the British flag, coupled with the condition that they would become British subjects; on the other side was exile and poverty. They chose the latter, and having done so, there seems to be no reason why they or their advocates should complain of the misfortunes which were the necessary result of their deliberate choice.

But the question arises,—Had the Government a right to impose such terms upon them? Their right to do so surely is as clear as the right of a Government to defend a country against an enemy. The claims to neutrality put forward by the Acadians were wholly inconsistent with British supremacy in Acadia, even had their neutrality been real, instead of being fictitious. But when this pretended neutrality was made a cover for the most hostile acts, it became intolerable, and the Government had no other course open to them but to insist that they should either become loyal

British subjects or quit the country. No less was due to
those loyal British subjects who had come to Acadia to find
homes for themselves and families, and who were hindered
in the settlement of the country by the Acadians and their
Indian allies. Doubtless the sorrows of a famished Acadian family furnish an admirable theme for a poet who
desires to appeal to the sympathetic feelings of our nature;
but the murdered British settlers, slain in mere wantonness
by the Indians, at the instigation of the French, also had
claims upon humanity. The sad feature of the expulsion
of the Acadians is that it brought sorrow and misfortune
upon their wives and children, who certainly had not been
guilty of any political offence; but that is a feature not
peculiar to their case. Almost every man whose crimes
bring him within the grasp of justice, has innocent relations
who suffer for his fault. Yet I have never heard that
given as a reason why the guilty should go unpunished.

The determination to remove the Acadians having been
taken, it only remained to make such arrangements as
seemed necessary to carry out the object effectually. The
Council decided that, in order to prevent them from returning and again molesting the English settlers, they should be
distributed amongst the colonies from Massachusetts to
Virginia. On the 31st July, Governor Lawrence wrote to
Colonel Monckton, stating the determination of the Government with reference to the Acadians, and informing him
that as those about the Isthmus had been found in arms,
and were therefore entitled to no favor from the Government, it was determined to begin with them first. He was
informed that orders had been given to send a sufficient
number of transports up the Bay to take the Acadians of
that district on board. Monckton was orded to keep the
measure secret until he could get the men into his power,

so that he could detain them until the transports arrived. He was directed to secure their shallops, boats and canoes, and to see that none of their cattle was driven away, they being forfeited to the Crown. He was told that the inhabitants were not to be allowed to carry away anything but their ready money and household furniture. He likewise received explicit directions as to the supply of provisions for the inhabitants while on the voyage.

Lieutenant-Colonel Winslow, who was commanding the troops at Mines, received instructions relative to the removal of the Acadians in that district, dated the 11th August. He was told to collect the inhabitants together, and place them on board the transports, of which there would be a number sufficient to transport two thousand persons, five hundred of whom were to be sent to North Carolina, one thousand to Virginia, and five hundred to Maryland. After the people were shipped, he was ordered to march overland to Annapolis with a strong detachment to assist Major Handfield in removing the inhabitants of that river. Handfield's instructions were similar to those of Winslow, and he was informed that vessels sufficient to transport one thousand persons would be sent to Annapolis. Of these, three hundred were to be sent to Philadelphia, two hundred to New York, three hundred to Connecticut, and two hundred to Boston. Each master of a transport was furnished by Governor Lawrence with a circular letter to the Governor of the colony to which he was destined. This circular letter contained Governor Lawrence's justification for the extreme step which he was taking in removing a whole people from their homes, and therefore I give it entire. It was as follows:—

" The success which has attended His Majesty's arms in driving the French from the encroachments they had made in this Province, presented me with a favorable opportunity of reducing the French inhabitants of this colony to a proper obedience to His Majesty's government, or forcing them to quit the country. These inhabitants were permitted to remain in quiet possession of their lands upon condition they would take the oath of allegiance to the King within one year after the treaty of Utrecht, by which this Province was ceded to Great Britain. With this condition they have ever refused to comply, without having at the same time from the Governor an assurance in writing that they should not be called upon to bear arms in defence of the Province, and with this General Phillips did comply, of which step His Majesty disapproved; and the inhabitants pretending therefrom to be in a state of neutrality between His Majesty and his enemies, have continually furnished the French and Indians with intelligence, quarters, provisions and assistance in annoying the Government, and while one part have abetted the French encroachments by their treachery, the other have countenanced them by open rebellion, and three hundred of them were actually found in arms in the French fort at Beausèjour when it surrendered.

"Notwithstanding all their former bad behavior, as His Majesty was pleased to allow me to extend still further his royal grace to such as would return to their duty, I offered such of them as had not been openly in arms against us a continuance of the possession of their lands, if they would take the oath of allegiance unqualified with any reservation whatsoever; but this they have most audaciously as well as unanimously refused, and if they would presume to do this when there is a large fleet of ships of war in the harbor and a considerable land force in the Province, what might we not expect from them when the approaching winter deprives us of the former, and when the troops, which are only hired from New England occasionally and for a small time, have returned home?

"As by this behavior the inhabitants have forfeited all title to their lands and any further favor from the Government, I called together His Majesty's Council, at which the Hon. Vice-Admiral Boscawen and Rear-Admiral Mostyn assisted, to consider by what means we could with the greatest security and effect rid ourselves of a set of people who would forever have been an obstruction to the intention of settling this colony, and that it was now, from their refusal of the oath, absolutely incumbent on us to remove.

"As their numbers amount to near seven thousand persons, the driving them off, with leave to go whither they pleased, would have doubtless strengthened Canada with so considerable a number of inhabitants; and, as they have no cleared land to give them at present, such as are able to bear arms must have been immediately employed in annoying this and the neighboring colonies. To prevent such an inconvenience it was judged a necessary and the only practicable measure to divide them among the colonies, where they may be of some use, as most of them are healthy, strong people; and as they cannot easily collect themselves together again, it will be out of their power to do any mischief, and they may become profitable and, it is possible, in time, faithful subjects.

"As this step was indispensably necessary to the security of this colony, upon whose preservation from French encroachments the prosperity of North America is esteemed in a great measure dependent, I have not the least reason to doubt of your Excellency's concurrence, and that you will receive the inhabitants I now send, and dispose of them in such manner as may best answer our design in preventing their reunion."

The work of removing the Acadians met with no success at Chignecto, where the population was large and comparatively warlike. Boishebert, after being driven from the St. John, had betaken himself to Shediac, and from there he directed the movements of the Acadians of the Isthmus. When the English tried to collect the inhabitants for the purpose of removing them, they found that they had fled to the shelter of the woods, and when they attempted to follow them, they were met by the most determined resistance. On the 2nd September, Major Frye was sent with two hundred men from the garrison at Fort Cumberland to burn the villages of Shepody, Petitcodiac and Memramcook. At Shepody they burnt one hundred and eighty-one buildings, but found no inhabitants, except twenty-three women and children, whom they sent on board the vessel they had with them. They sailed up the Petitcodiac River on the following day and burnt the buildings on both sides of it for miles. At length the vessel was brought to anchor, and fifty men were sent on shore to burn the chapel and some other buildings near it, when suddenly they were attacked by three hundred French and Indians under Boishebert, and compelled to retreat with a loss of twenty-three men killed and wounded, including Dr. March, who was killed, and Lieutenant Billings dangerously wounded. Boishebert was found to be too strong to be attacked even with the aid of the main body of troops under Major Frye, so the party had to return to Fort Cumberland, after having destroyed in all two hundred and fifty-three buildings and a large quantity of wheat and flax.

At Mines, Lieutenant-Colonel Winslow succeeded in accomplishing his unpleasant duty without resistance. On the 2nd September he issued an order to the inhabitants of the districts of Grand Prè, Mines, River Canard and vicinity, commanding all the males from ten years upwards to attend at the church in Grand Prè on the following Friday, the 5th September, to hear what His Majesty had authorized him to communicate to them. The inhabitants attended in obedience to this summons to the number of upwards of four hundred, and were informed by Winslow that, in consequence of their disobedience, their lands and tenements, cattle, live stock and all their effects, except their money and household goods, were forfeited to the Crown, and they themselves were to be removed from the Province. He told them, however, that he would take in the vessels with them as large a portion of their household effects as could be carried, and that families would not be separated, but conveyed in the same vessel. Finally, he told them that they should remain prisoners at the church until the time came for them to embark. At Piziquid, Captain Murray collected the male inhabitants in the same way to the number of nearly two hundred, and kept them in confinement. Considering the situation in which they were placed, they manifested but little emotion, and offered no resistance worthy of the name. The task of getting so many families together, and embarking them with their household effects, proved tedious, but finally it was accomplished, and the inhabitants of Mines and Piziquid, to the number of more than nineteen hundred persons, were got on board the transports, and carried away from their homes in Acadia to lands of which they knew nothing, and where their presence was not desired.

At Annapolis many families took the alarm when the transports arrived, and fled to the woods for safety, and much difficulty was experienced in collecting them.

Hunger finally compelled most of them to surrender themselves, and upwards of eleven hundred were placed on board the vessels and sent away. One vessel with two hundred and twenty-six Acadians on board was seized by them in the Bay of Fundy, and taken into St. John, and the passengers she carried were not afterwards recaptured. The total number removed from Acadia in 1755 was somewhat in excess of three thousand souls. Some of them were taken to Massachusetts, some to Pennsylvania, some to Virginia, some to Maryland, to North and South Carolina, and some even to the British West Indies. Wherever they were taken they became for the time a public charge on the colony, and were the occasion of much correspondence between the Governments which were obliged to maintain them, and that of Nova Scotia. Many of those who went to Georgia and South Carolina hired small vessels, and set out to return to Acadia, and the Governors of these colonies were very glad to facilitate their movements northward by giving them passes to voyage along their coasts. Several hundred of those who landed in Virginia were sent by the Government of that colony to England, where they remained for seven years, finally taking the oath of allegiance, and many of them returning to Acadia. A number of these people went from Virginia to the French West Indies, where they died in large numbers. The great bulk of the Acadians, however, finally succeeded in returning to the land of their birth. Some got back in the course of a few months, others did not succeed in returning until many years had elapsed, yet they succeeded, nevertheless, and the ultimate loss of population by their enforced emigration in 1755 was much less than would be supposed.

A work of no less authority than the Census of Canada

has put forth some very inexcusable statements relative to the loss of population by the enforced emigration of the Acadians. According to it the Acadian population was reduced by 10,000 between 1755 and 1771, "without taking into account the absorption by death of a number of victims equal to the whole of the births." The Acadian population in the Peninsula is put down at 13,000 in 1749, and the total Acadian population, including Isle Royale, St. John Island and the northern portion of Acadia, is given at 16,000. In 1755, before the expulsion of the Acadians, the Acadian population is given at 18,500, of which 8,200 were in the Peninsula, 3,000 in Isle Royale, 3,500 in St. John Island, 3,500 in the district of Shediac, 500 on the shores of the Gulf, and 200 on St. John River. The absurdity of this statement lies in the fact that there could not possibly have been more than 8,000 Acadians, descendants of those who acquired rights under the Treaty of Utrecht, in the year 1755. In 1714 the two settlements of Mines and Annapolis contained but 1,773 persons; and the population of Chignecto, which had but 245 inhabitants in 1703, could not have swelled the total population of Acadia in 1714 to more than 2,500. All the authorities admit that the normal rate of increase among the Acadian population was 2·5 per annum. This would give a population of less than 8,000 souls in 1755, and that agrees pretty closely with the estimate of Governor Lawrence. The population of Isle Royale, which came direct from France, and mainly returned to France after the fall of Louisbourg, has no right to be counted as part of the population of Acadia, nor are its movements to be considered as connected with those of the Acadian people. Assuming that there were between 8,000 and 9,000 Acadians in the Province and in the Island of St. John in the beginning of 1755, at least

5,000 of these were inhabitants who had been enticed away by the French from the settlements in the Peninsula or from Chignecto, or who had originally resided north of the Misseguash. Of the remainder, about 3,000 were forcibly removed by the English, but at least two-thirds of them eventually returned to Acadia.

CHAPTER XXIII.

THE SEVEN YEARS WAR.

THE Acadians of the Peninsula no longer remained to disquiet the Government at Halifax, but those of the main land, now grown to be a numerous and powerful body, were more resolute than ever not to submit to English authority. Boishebert, who was entrusted by the Governor of Canada with the work of keeping the Acadians and Indians in a state of active hostility to the English, did his work well, and gave Governor Lawrence no end of anxiety and trouble. When the latter sent a detachment to the River St. John to attempt to recapture the transport which had been carried there by some of the Acadians, the French very deliberately burnt the vessel and fired on the party that went to recover her. The attempt of a detachment from Fort Cumberland to surprise Boishebert at Shediac was equally unfortunate, and resulted in a repulse. An armed trading schooner, with provisions for the garrion of Annapolis, which put into Passamaquoddy, was captured by the Indians there, an artillery officer of that garrison being one of her passengers. Even Annapolis was not considered secure from attack, and to make matters worse, the New England troops who had been enlisted for the capture of Beausèjour, were clamoring for their discharge, their term having expired.

The Acadians at Cape Sable and Port Latour, who had not been removed the previous year, had proved very troublesome, and Major Prebble was sent in April to capture as many of them as he could catch and take them to Boston. This measure rendered Annapolis in a manner secure; but a few days later bad news arrived at Halifax from Baie Verte. The fort there, which had been re-named Fort Monckton, was beset by the Indians, and thirty men who had gone out of it to bring in wood, were attacked and nine of them scalped. Lieutenant-Colonel Scott reinforced the garrison from Fort Cumberland, but even the latter was so closely watched, that soldiers who ventured any distance from the fort alone were almost certain to be carried off. To check this sort of warfare a company of Rangers was formed to hunt down the Indians, and a reward of thirty pounds was offered by the Government for every male Indian prisoner above the age of sixteen, or twenty-five pounds for his scalp. Twenty-five pounds was also offered for every Indian woman or child brought in alive. The killing of several private English settlers at this time by the Micmacs made it necessary for the Government to offer such high rewards for their capture or destruction.

During the summer of this year the Acadians to the number of thirty-five hundred had retired to the Miramichi, and they forwarded a memorial to Vaudreuil, the Governor of Canada, begging him to send them provisions and arms. In this document they boast greatly of their loyalty to the King of France, and attribute all their misfortunes to their attachment to that monarch. They endeavor to excuse themselves for the lack of military qualities which they displayed at Beausèjour, but announce their strong desire to avenge themselves on the English. Singularly enough they express a want of confidence in the Micmacs and in their missionary, Manach. The former they characterize as thieves and idlers, and they leave a very strong impression that they regarded the latter as a rogue. It would have been a shameful thing for the Governor of Canada to have disregarded this prayer, nor was it disregarded, for the Acadians at Miramichi and Baie Chaleur were kept supplied with provisions from Quebec until the end of the war. They became, in fact, in a large measure, a part of the combatant force with which France was striving to defend her American possessions from the English. One of them named Brossard fitted out a captured trading vessel as a privateer, and took several English vessels in the Bay of Fundy. A strong party continued to watch Fort Monckton at Baie Verte, and the losses incurred in keeping up that post became so serious that in the autumn of 1756 the English abandoned and burnt it.

Meanwhile, the war in other portions of America was going against the English. Shirley, who was Commander-in-Chief of the forces, and whose zeal, activity and knowledge would have been of the greatest service, was removed from the Governorship of Massachusetts in consequence of the partizan representations of a faction in New York, and greatly to the disgust of the people of New England, who knew his worth. He was succeeded as Commander-in-Chief in America by the Earl of Loudon, one of those titled incapables who have cost England so dear in wasted treasure, and in the blood of her sons. Loudon was described to Dr. Franklin as like St. George on the signs, "always on horseback, but never riding forward." He was wholly without decision of character, and entirely deficient in the requisites of a military leader.

While the British armies in America were under such a man, Montcalm, one of the best and bravest officers of France, had arrived in Canada; with him came Levis, Bouganville and Bourlamaque, all officers of great ability, and worthy to serve under such a leader. The French soon began to display much activity, while the English remained almost wholly inactive. Montcalm's principal achievement in 1756 was the capture of Oswego, which he attacked in August with three thousand men. It was defended by Colonel Mercer and eighteen hundred men, but, although well supplied with provisions and heavily armed, it only held out a few days. A large amount of booty fell into the hands of the French; and to conciliate the Indians, to whom they had been a great annoyance, the fortifications of Oswego were destroyed. Thus the English lost their hold on Lake Ontario, and likewise, to a large extent, their influence with the Indians, who were always ready to side with the strongest party. The consequences of the fall of Oswego were widely felt, and while the French were filled with joy and hope, the English were so much depressed that many began to despair of the ultimate success of the operations against Canada.

The military operations of 1757 were still more disastrous to the English than those of the previous year. Possibly, if Montcalm's advice had been followed, Acadia would have again passed into the hands of France, for he strongly advocated a diversion in Acadia with a squadron, a corps of French regulars, and two thousand five hundred Canadians. His plans were, however, overruled, and those of Vaudreuil for the reduction of Fort Edward and Fort William Henry adopted. In January a conference of Colonial Governors was held in New York, at the call of Lord Loudon. It was decided to stand on the defensive merely on the Candian frontier during the next campaign, but to make an effort to capture Louisbourg, with the aid of a powerful fleet, six regiments of regulars, and a contingent of Colonial troops. On the 30th June, Loudon arrived at Halifax from New York with a fleet of transports laden with troops, and a few days later Admiral Holborne came in with eleven ships of the line and six thousand soldiers. De la Mothe was at that time lying in Louisbourg with a powerful French fleet, and Loudon did not deem it prudent to attack the place, which, according to the tales of deserters, was strongly garrisoned. The whole summer was spent in useless councils of war, and the enterprise against Louisbourg was finally abandoned. Loudon returned to New York, and Holborne cruised with fifteen ships of the line in the vicinity of Louisbourg until late in September, when his fleet was scattered by a tempest, and one of his vessels driven ashore and lost on the Island of Cape Breton, most of her crew falling into the hands of the French.

While Loudon was in Halifax, Montcalm took advantage of his absence to attack Fort William Henry on Lake George with a force of eight thousand men and a powerful train of artillery. The place was defended by Colonel Munroe and twenty-five hundred men, part in the fort and part in an intrenched camp. It fell after a siege of six days,—General Webb, who had four thousand men at Fort Edward, being unable or unwilling to send any aid to the beleagured garrison. By the terms of surrender, the garrison were to return to the English colonies, not to serve again during the war. These terms were shamefully broken. The English, instead of being escorted in safety to Fort Edward, were attacked by the Indians as soon as they left the fort, and indiscriminately slaughtered, the French making no attempt to prevent the massacre. Six hundred escaped, half naked, and found their way to Fort Edward. Five hundred fled back to Fort William Henry, from which they were afterwards forwarded to Fort Edward by Montcalm. Two hundred were carried off by the Indians into captivity, and more than twelve hundred, including one hundred women, were murdered on the spot. Montcalm made a great pretence of regret at this occurrence, but it is not probable that he was sincere, for he had six thousand white troops at his command, and could easily have prevented the massacre. This deplorable event, however, hadone good effect; it stimulated the English to still greater efforts, and made them more resolute than before to compass the destruction of French power in America.

From this period the reign of incapacity in America may be said to have ceased. Notwithstanding one or two reverses, England continued steadily to gain ground from the beginning of 1758, and the French in America only sought to conduct a defensive war. The elder Pitt, the greatest war minister that ever England had, was now at the head of affairs, and by his vigor and spirit was inspiring every branch of the military and naval services with an enthusiasm equal to his own. Every soldier and every sailor was taught to feel that the honor of his country was in his keeping, and that he was expected to preserve and maintain it.

The capture of Louisbourg was the first object essayed by Pitt, and he selected men for that enterprise that he knew would not repeat the tactics of Loudon and Holborne. The command of the land forces was given to General Jeffrey Amherst, a man of singular ability, bravery and discretion, whose fame has been somewhat eclipsed by that of the hero of Quebec, but whose services to his country cannot be too highly estimated. Under him were three able Brigadiers, Wolfe, Lawrence and Whitmore, the land forces amounting to twelve thousand men. The fleet was under the command of Admiral Boscawen, an officer of distinguished courage, and consisted of twenty-three ships of the line and eighteen frigates. The fleet which, including transports, numbered one hundred and fifty-seven sail, left Halifax on the 28th May, 1758, and a part of it arrived in Gabarus Bay, near Louisbourg, on the 2nd June. The surf and fog made it impossible to effect a landing until the 8th June. The French, who had fortified the line of coast, made a stout resistance, but the heroism of Wolfe, and the courage of the soldiers whom he led, broke their line of defence and seized the key of the position, so that they were obliged to retreat.

A landing having been effected, the operations of the siege were carried on with great vigor. The French abandoned the Royal battery at the head of the harbor and the Light House battery which lay opposite Louisbourg, and General Wolfe took possession of the latter battery on the 12th with twelve hundred men. There he mounted guns from which he destroyed the shipping in the harbor and silenced the Island battery. Meanwhile, approaches were made and batteries erected against Louisbourg on the land side. The city was surrounded by a girdle of fire, and day by day the fortifications crumbled away. Of the five war vessels in the harbor, three were destroyed by the fire of the besiegers, and on the night of the 25th July a detachment from the fleet, under the command of Captains Laforey and Balfour, entered the harbor of Louisbourg, burnt one of the remaining war-ships and towed out the other. Next day articles of capitulation were signed, and on the 27th July Louisbourg was surrendered. The capitulation included the whole Island of Cape Breton and the Island of St. John.

The garrison, consisting of three thousand and thirty-one soldiers and two thousand six hundred and six sailors, were sent to England as prisoners of war. A detachment was sent to take possession of the Island of St. John, where the inhabitants, to the number of four thousand one hundred, submitted and surrendered their arms. Of the two thousand four hundred inhabitants of Cape Breton, one thousand seven hundred were sent to France at their own request. The rest remained on the Island and submitted to English rule. The Acadians soon felt the loss of their protector, Louisbourg. A squadron was sent to Miramichi and to Gaspè to destroy the settlements they had made there, and returned, after inflicting as much damage as possible upon them. Colonel Monckton was sent with a detachment of the Colonial Highlanders and Colonel Howe's light infantry to the St. John River to drive the French from the fort at its mouth. The fort, which had only two small cannon in position, was carried by assault on the land side, and a good many of the French killed. The remainder escaped up the river in boats and canoes, and the Province sloop Ulysses, which attempted to chase them, got carried into the Falls, and was wrecked. The French made their way to St. Anne's, the site of the present city of Fredericton. A strong English garrison was placed in the fort at St. John, which now received the name of Fort Frederick.

While success thus attended the enterprises of the English in Cape Breton and Acadia, the war was conducted with varied fortune on the Canadian border. Major General Abercrombie, who had succeeded the incapable Loudon as Commander-in-Chief, made an attempt on Fort Ticonderoga. He had fifteen thousand men under his command, while Montcalm, who defended it, had but four thousand; but the latter were very strongly posted behind a line of works, and the British commander made no attempt to resort to strategy. After sacrificing two thousand of his best troops in a hopeless assault, he retired to his camp on Lake George. To balance this disaster, the British could show two successes—the capture of Fort Duquesne by an army under General Forbes, and the taking of Fort Frontenac on the St. Lawrence by a force under Colonel Bradstreet. Fort Duquesne, which was burnt by the retiring French, was re-named Pittsburgh by Forbes, in honor of England's great War Minister. Fort Frontenac was also destroyed by Bradstreet, and, like Fort Duquesne, it has since become the site of a city, Kingston, once the capital of Upper Canada.

The year 1759, the most memorable in the history of Canada, opened with great preparations for the complete conquest of the French dominions in America. The financial strain was already beginning to tell on France, and while her means for the defence of her great colony were crippled, England responded freely to the demands of Pitt for men and money to carry on the war. It was resolved to make one supreme effort to plant the flag of England on the ramparts of Quebec, which had so long defied all attack, and where so many enterprises against British power had been planned. Abercromby was removed from the chief command, and replaced by General Amherst, whose conduct at the siege of Louisbourg had won him the thanks of Parliament. The plan of operations which he arranged was thought to be such as could scarcely fail of success. A fleet and army, under General Wolfe, were to ascend the St. Lawrence to Quebec, and besiege that stronghold. An army, under Amherst himself, was to force its way down Lake Champlain, and go by the Richelieu and St. Lawrence to Quebec to effect a junction with Wolfe's army. General Prideaux, with an army of regulars, Provincials and Indians, was to capture Fort Niagara, and, descending Lake Ontario and the St. Lawrence, take Montreal, and, leaving a garrison there, join Amherst and Wolfe under the walls of Quebec. A fourth corps, under Colonel Stanwix, was to clear the shores of Lake Ontario of the enemy.

These great preparations called forth corresponding efforts on the part of the French in Canada. The whole available force of the colony was embodied into militia battalions, and all the male inhabitants, capable of bearing arms, were brought into the field. The French, occupying a safe interior line of communication by the St. Lawrence, awaited with anxiety, but yet not without confidence, the approach of enemies that they had often before baffled.

General Prideaux, who had a mixed force of regulars, Provincials and Indians, the latter under Sir William Johnson, advanced to Oswego, where he left a strong detachment, and early in July reached Fort Niagara and commenced to besiege it. Prideaux was killed in the trenches a few days later, and Johnson assumed command of the army. On the 24th July he defeated a relieving force which the French had gathered from the garrisons to the westward, and next day Fort Niagara was surrendered.

Amherst, who had an army of twelve thousand men and a considerable artillery, moved with caution towards Lake Champlain. The French, unable to detect any weakness in his dispositions, and having no force capable of making a successful resistance, evacuated Ticonderoga and Crown Point, as he advanced, and retreated to Isle-Aux-Noix. Amherst spent two months in strengthening these places, and in building two vessels, to enable him to attack the armed craft which the French had on Lake Champlain, and when his preparations for a further advance were completed, the lateness of the season and the unfavorable state of the weather compelled him to put his army into winter quarters. He had gained substantial advantages, although his progress had been slow, but his inability to reach the St. Lawrence that season had placed on Wolfe the whole burthen of the campaign. Wolfe's force, which was to have been reinforced by two other armies, had to undertake the siege of Quebec alone.

The French have been trying for more than a hundred years to explain why Quebec was taken, but they have succeeded very indifferently in their self-imposed task. Although Admiral Saunders had a powerful fleet, Wolfe's land force was far too weak for the operation he had undertaken. He had but seven thousand soldiers and one thousand marines, while Montcalm had more than thirteen thousand men, regulars and Canadians, behind the intrenchments which protected the ancient capital. Fortunately, Wolfe was not the man to enter into nice calculations or comparisons between his own inadequate force and that of the enemy, and his Brigadiers Monckton, Townshend and Murray, were men of like spirit with himself. When, on the morning of the 13th September, he carried a little army of five thousand men up the precipitous heights above the St. Lawrence to the Plains of Abraham, he virtually achieved the conquest of Canada. He staked all upon the venture,—his reputation, the existence of his army, and the honor of his country; but he won, for his genius and daring carried him to victory. Montcalm, distrusting the strength of his defences, resolved to drive the English from the heights before they had time to establish themselves, and marched out against them. In the battle which followed, both leaders fell, Wolfe dying literally in the arms of victory, and Montcalm lingering but long enough to be aware of the ruin of the cause for which he fought. Five days later, Quebec surrendered, and the British flag waved over it for the first time for one hundred and twenty-seven years. The same flag waves over it still in defiance of the efforts of all England's foes, and there never was a time when it seemed less likely to be replaced by any other national banner. England's empire in Canada no longer depends on the strength of her battalions, or the might of her fleets. In all the vast region between Halifax and the shores of the Pacific there is not a single British soldier, nor a single cannon or fortress over which England claims control, yet her influence in her great colony was never so powerful before. The people of Canada, whether of French or English origin, are animated by the same sentiments of loyalty, and British interests are as secure in their keeping as in that of the people of the Metropolitan State. Such are the legitimate fruits of freedom and justice.

Quebec was surrendered to the British on the 18th September, 1759; a year later, 8th September, 1760, Montreal was also given up, and thus Canada finally passed under British rule. It forms no part of my plan to relate the details of the operations which led to this result, which, indeed, would require a volume to do them justice. The French Canadian still tells with pride of the gallant efforts of Levis to make headway against British power, after France had abandoned Canada to its fate, of his victory at Ste. Foy, and the courage with which he struggled against adverse fortune. All men delight in the recital of heroic deeds. But no courage could have saved Canada to France, for that country was at the end of her resources, and was reaping the fruits of a century's disregard of the interests of her subjects. East and west she was being stripped of her colonies. All the fruits of the courage, ability and devotion of her sons were falling into the hands of England.

CHAPTER XXIV.

THE TREATY OF PARIS.

BOISHEBERT, who had been at the head of the French and Indians in Northern Acadia for several years, was in 1758 engaged in defensive operations near Louisbourg, and in the following year assisted in the defence of Quebec. His absence did not prevent the French and Indians from continuing to annoy and harass the English settlements, and even to fit out privateers for the purpose of capturing English vessels. In 1759, they captured no less than seventeen vessels on the coast, and murdered many persons. Five soldiers were killed and scalped near Fort Cumberland, five settlers were killed near Halifax, three were killed at the St. John River, and several near Annapolis. These are but samples of many similar outrages committed at this time. A party of Acadians and Indians invested the fort at Piziquid for several days, a number of the German settlers at Lunenburg were wantonly murdered by them about the same time, and a party of committee men from New England, who went to Cape Sable to view the land, were fired on by one hundred French and Indians. The gentle-mannered Acadians had certainly no quarrel with the German settlers, however much they may have hated the English, yet they killed them all the same. The Cape Sable attack caused the Government to send a vessel there to remove the inhabitants, and they were taken, to the number of one hundred and fifty-one, and conveyed to Halifax, from which they were shipped to England.

When Quebec fell, the source of supply on which the Acadians had relied was cut off, and they began to feel the pinch of hunger. Many of the inhabitants residing near Quebec had been very prompt to take the oath of allegiance, and a large number of the French inhabitants of the upper St. John went to Quebec and took the oath. In November, about two hundred of these people and two priests came down the River St. John to Colonel Arbuthnot, who commanded at Fort Frederick, and presented a paper signed by Captain Cramahe, Deputy Judge Advocate, at Quebec, stating that they had taken the oath of allegiance, and that in consequence of their having done so Brigadier Monckton had given them liberty to return to their habitations. The Council, to whom the matter was referred, decided that, as it was evident the certificates had been granted on the supposition that the St. John was some river of that name in Canada, they should not be permitted to remain on their lands there, as that would be an acknowledgment of the French claim that the St. John was a dependency of Canada. They were ordered to be removed to Halifax, with a view to being ultimately sent to England.

In the course of the same month, Alexander Brusard, Simon Martin, Jean Bass and Joseph Brusard arrived at Fort Cumberland, under a flag of truce, as deputies for one hundred and ninety Acadians, men, women and children, residing at Petitcodiac and Memramcook, to surrender themselves to the Government. They informed Colonel Frye, the commandant, that they had not sufficient provisions to last them until Spring, and begged to be allowed some to keep them from starving. Frye agreed to keep one-third of them until Spring, and gave them permission to occupy the vacant houses in their settlements, from which the inhabitants had fled. Two days later, Peter Suretz, and John and Michael Burk arrived with a flag of truce as deputies for seven hundred inhabitants of Miramichi,

Richibucto and Buctouche. They were also short of provisions, and Frye agreed to provide for two hundred and thirty of them during the inclement season. These people had no less than twelve vessels, which were taken from the English during the summer. All these inhabitants were ordered to rendezvous at Fort Cumberland and Baie Verte in the Spring, when they were to be informed of the disposition that was to be made of them. The Council agreed to ratify what they had done, to accept the submission of these people, and to supply them with provisions. Yet these Acadians, now so submissive, had been among the most deadly enemies of the English, and had taken part in every enterprise that was calculated to annoy and distress them.

A large number of these Acadians submitted in the Spring, agreeably to their promise, and were sent to Halifax; but the majority of them still remained outside the pale of English influence. They were not without hope of the recapture of Quebec, and therefore not disposed to yield until the last chance of success had been tried. Those of them who dwelt on the shores of the Bay Chaleur were fated soon to be taught in a practical way how hopeless was the contest in which France was engaged.

In the Spring of 1760 the French Government attempted to send supplies to the relief of Levis, who was still holding Montreal. A number of store ships were despatched to Canada under the protection of a strong convoy, but when the French reached the St. Lawrence, they learned that an English fleet had already gone up that river. This induced the French Admiral to take shelter in the Baie Chaleur, and he commenced erecting batteries on its shores. Commodore Byron, who was in command of a squadron at Louisbourg, heard of the presence of the French and hastened to dispossess them. He took with him the Fame, seventy-four, his own ship, the Dorsetshire, Achilles, Scarborough, and Repulse. He captured one of the French ships, La Catherine, in Gaspè Bay, and another near Caraquet. On entering the Restigouche River, Byron discovered the rest of the fleet, consisting of Le Marchault (thirty-two), L'Esperance (thirty), Le Bienfaisant (twenty-two), and Le Marquis de Marloze (eighteen), besides twenty-two schooners, sloops and small privateers. On observing the approach of the English, the French squadron made all sail up river, and anchored under the batteries at Petit Rochelle, on the Quebec side, a little below the modern village of Campbellton. The batteries offered but a feeble resistance, and on being silenced a naval engagement took place, in which the French armed vessels were all destroyed or captured. The town of Petit Rochelle, which consisted of two hundred houses, and the two batteries near it, were reduced to ruins. Some of the French unarmed vessels which escaped during the engagement were taken by another British squadron off Port Daniel. This naval battle took place on the 8th July, 1760, just two months before the surrender of Montreal.

This year the fortifications of Louisbourg were ordered to be destroyed, and the material and munitions of war stored there were removed to Halifax. That visible sign of French power was thus obliterated and rendered incapable of ever again becoming a menace to the English. The enormous sums which it had cost the French Government, and the blood and treasure which the English had expended in its capture had yielded no better return than a heap of ruins.

Governor Lawrence, who had administered the affairs of Acadia for six years, died in October, 1760. His death was a serious loss to the Province, for his strong, resolute character was an excellent guarantee of its safety in any emergency that might arise. By his death the administration of the Government devolved upon Jonathan Belcher, the senior member of the Council. At this time the attitude of the Acadians was a great cause of concern to the Council. A large number of them had surrendered, and were living about Halifax and other settlements, working for the English inhabitants at good wages, but they were no more submissive than they had been in the days of French ascendancy, and at every rumor of French success in any part of the world their insolence became alarming. A large number of them were still at large in the Peninsula, living in places not readily accessible, and a still larger number resided on the River St. John, the Bay Chaleur, Miramichi and the other rivers flowing into the Gulf of St. Lawrence. They lived mainly by hunting and fishing. The Acadians at the Baie Chaleur fitted out privateers, and committed many depredations on English vessels in the Gulf and River St. Lawrence. Belcher, to check them, sent a detachment to the Gulf, under the command of Captain Roderick McKenzie, of Montgomery's Highlanders, in two small vessels. He surprised their settlement on the Bay Chaleur in October, 1761, and captured seven hundred and eighty-seven persons—men, women and children. He brought away three hundred and thirty-five of them to Halifax, and the remainder promised to come in when called on. Belcher soon learned that he had gained but little by the removal of those profoundly disaffected and turbulent people.

France was stricken down and well nigh destroyed; but in Europe a gleam of hope appeared. George II. was dead, and his successor, George III., a tyrant of mean capacity and worse education, had resolved on the destruction of the great war minister who had carried the country to such a height of glory. Pitt was a great man, the idol of the people, and therefore the small-minded King hated him with all the force of his petty and malignant nature. He succeeded in compelling him to resign, but England paid a fearful price in after years for the sacrifice. That price included the loss of her English Colonies in America, and a legacy of hate from what has become the most powerful branch of the Anglo-Saxon race; innumerable wars, which laid on the country the burthen of an enormous indebtedness; and, worse than all, a return to the despotic methods of ancient times, the suppression of freedom of speech, the passage of iniquitous repressive laws, and a thousand other evils which have only been wholly removed during the present century.

Pitt's resignation was forced in October, 1761. It arose out of a difference between him and Newcastle, who was supported by the King, with regard to the proposals for a peace made by France, which was using the new compact with Spain as a means of demanding better terms from England. Pitt rejected these overtures, and proposed to his colleagues to anticipate the attack of Spain by the seizure of her treasure fleet from the Indies, by the occupation of the Isthmus of Panama, and by attacking the Spanish Dominions in the New World. Unable to carry those vigorous measures in the Cabinet, Pitt resigned, and Newcastle, who had been used merely as a cat's-paw for the humiliation of Pitt, was soon afterwards driven from office. The Marquis of Bute, a Scotch adventurer, with the abilities of a gentleman usher, became Prime Minister of England.

The foresight of Pitt was vindicated by a declaration of war against England by Spain three weeks after his retirement. Fortunately for the country the impulse of conquest which England had received from Pitt's vigorous hand, was not easily stayed. War was declared against Spain, and before the year had passed, Cuba was in the hands of the English, the Philippines were seized, and Spain was humiliated and beaten.

The alliance of Spain with France gave the Acadians a fresh opportunity of displaying their desire for the humiliation of England; and the English settlers, for whom they worked, soon began to experience their insolence. They told them that they would soon regain possession of their lands, and cut the throats of all the English in the Province. In June, a French detachment seized St. John's, N. F., which was very weakly guarded, and this petty triumph filled the Acadians with so much elation and the English in Acadia with such alarm, that many of the latter left the Province altogether. The people of King's County marched the Acadians of their district into Halifax under a guard, and consigned them to the care of the Military authorities. Nothing less than a general rising of the Acadians was expected.

Under the pressure of this alarm the Council met on the 26th July, and resolved that it was absolutely necessary for the public safety to remove the Acadians in Halifax and its vicinity from the Province. Several communications on the subject of their removal had during the previous year passed between Lieutenant-Governor Belcher and General Amherst, the latter being strongly opposed to the measure, because he believed the Acadians could be made useful to the Province, and that, Canada being conquered, there was nothing more to be feared from their animosity. Now, however, the Government of Nova Scotia were resolute to get rid of them; so, in August, all the Acadians about Halifax were put on board a fleet of transports and sent to Boston. Unfortunately for the success of this plan, the authorities of Massachusetts had not been consulted with respect to it, and the Legislature of that Province passed a resolution requesting the Governor not to permit the Acadians to land. After lying for some time in Boston harbor, the transports were obliged to return to Halifax with their unwelcome freight.

In this emergency Lieutenant-Governor Belcher applied to the Lords of Trade in England for sympathy and advice, but by the time his letter reached them the war was over, and their Lordships informed him that however expedient the removal of the Acadians might have been at a time when the enterprises of the enemy threatened danger to the Province, now that hostilities had ceased, it was neither necessary nor politic to remove them. The Acadians therefore remained, receiving provisions from the Government on the military list, in proportion to their age and the number in each family. They supplied themselves with clothing by the wages they got for their work. But Governor Montague Wilmot states in a letter to Lord Halifax that they were far from being an industrious or laborious people, and that the price they demanded for their labor was so high, and their day's work so much less than that of the settlers, that few persons could afford to employ them.

The preliminaries of peace had been signed at Fontainebleau on the 3rd November, 1762, between England, France and Spain, and a definitive treaty was concluded in Paris on the 10th February, 1763. Considering the straits to which France was reduced by the war, the treaty was much less advantageous to England than it would have been had Pitt been at the head of affairs. But so far as North America was concerned, it could scarcely have been more sweeping in its terms, for there France yielded everything, except the petty Islands of St. Pierre and Miquelon. Canada, Acadia, and all their dependencies, as well as the Island of Cape Breton and all the other Islands in the Gulf and River St. Lawrence, were given up to England. Louisiana was ceded to Spain in exchange for Florida and the Bay of Pensacola, which the Spaniards ceded to Great Britain to recover Cuba and the Philippines. Of all the vast Empire which France had founded in America, nothing remained.

In the latter part of 1763, a correspondence took place between the British and French Governments relative to the Acadians. It arose out of an attempt which was said to have been made by one Rochette, a clerk to the Duke of Nivérnois, to induce the Acadians to return to France. The attempt was repudiated, and the French Government informed that of England that they did not pretend in any degree to interfere on behalf of the Acadians, but entirely acquiesced in the right of the King of England to dispose of them as he pleased. Even this did not dampen the loyalty of the Acadians. In a memorial of 12th May, 1764, which was presented to the Governor by Belonis Roy and seventy-five other heads of families, they declared that they acknowledged no other Sovereign but the King of France, and begged the Government to send them to France or to some French colony. Of course, this modest request was refused.

The Governor of St. Pierre and the Governor-General of the French Leeward Islands in the West Indies circulated papers among the Acadians for the purpose of persuading them to emigrate to these French colonies. A large number of Acadians went to St. Pierre in the Spring of 1764, built up a town, and established an important fishery, and towards the close of that year upwards of six hundred embarked for the French West Indies. The Government made no attempt to prevent them from emigrating, although at this period measures had been perfected for securing their continued residence in the Province. These measures, which were suggested by the Earl of Halifax, and which were sanctioned by the Government in October agreeably to instructions from England, seem to have been both wise and just. The Acadians, on taking the oath of allegiance, were to receive fifty acres of land for each head of a family, and ten acres more for each member of his household. Fourteen different places were selected for their settlement, the object of this arrangement being that their strength might be scattered, so that they could not again combine for any atttack on the English. The Acadians frustrated this well-meant effort to benefit them and tranquilize the Province, by peremptorily refusing to take the oath required, and soon afterwards commenced to emigrate to the West Indies, as already stated.

It was not until the year 1767 that these obstinate people commenced to yield to the force of events, and consented to take the oath of allegiance as British subjects. The Acadians of the River St. John, who were hemmed in by a powerful English colony, were the first to make their submission, and their example was speedily followed by the people of other districts. The Acadians, who had emigrated to St. Pierre and Miquelon, soon became disgusted with French rule, and during the year 1767 began to arrive by hundreds on the eastern coast of Nova Scotia, from which they spread themselves all over the Province. They were ready enough to take the oath of allegiance, which they had before refused, for the cherished illusions of their youth had been rudely dispelled, and the contrast which they drew between the easy rule of the British colony and the tyrannical system of the French Governors was very unflattering to the latter. The Acadians everywhere listened to their story, and profited by their experience. They were now as eager to take the oath as they had before been determined in refusing it, and the Governor of the Province, Michael Francklin, met them in a liberal and kindly spirit, so as to remove from their submission any appearance of humiliation. They received grants of lands as fast as they took the oath at the rate of eighty acres to each head of a family, and forty acres to each additional member of it. By the end of 1768 nearly all had submitted to the Government, and from that time they gave no reason for any complaints of their want of loyalty. Sir John Wentworth, Governor of Nova Scotia, writing in 1796, was able to state that the Acadians in feeling were "wholly British subjects, and entirely changed from their former sentiments," and that they were then "among the most faithful and happy subjects of His Majesty." They had been faithful to the King of France while any hope remained of the restoration of his rule over them; when they transferred their allegiance to the King of England, they were no less faithful to their new Sovereign, for loyalty is a characteristic of the race.

The fidelity of the Acadians to their King, great as it was, was not greater than their attachment to their native land. They struggled hard to keep Acadia a part of the dominions of France, but, having failed, most of them regarded it is a lesser evil to dwell under a foreign flag rather than to part from their beloved Acadia. Their banishment in 1755 was almost immediately followed by the return of a large number of those who had been forcibly removed from Acadia, and twenty years later Acadians were still coming back to the land of their birth. Even many of those who went to France finally returned to Acadia.

With the treaty of Paris and the submission of the French inhabitants, the History of Acadia ends. The results of the discoveries of Champlain, the labors of Poutrincourt, the struggles of Charnisay and La Tour, and the efforts of a succession of able commandants and Governors were all lost to France when the reluctant hand of De Choiseul signed the treaty of Paris. Lost, too, was the allegiance of a people who in fidelity have never been surpassed—whose devotion to a fallen cause was carried to the verge of folly. Even the name of Acadia disappeared from the maps of the world, and in the clash and clamor of greater wars, the strife of which it had been the scene passed out of memory. Acadia as a feeble English colony, although once counted a prize worthy the efforts of fleets and armies, became of small moment in the titanic struggles that were going on in both hemispheres during a half century after its final surrender to England. Yet through all these evil years a new Acadia was growing up, which, now in its vigorous youth, gives promise of greater things in the future than ever entered into the dreams of the pioneer settlers of this land. Here the descendants of the two great races who fought so long for Empire in America, toil amicably side by side for the advancement of their common country. Here new hopes and aspirations have supplanted the dreams of conquest, and the triumphs of peace are counted of more value than the trophies of war. Yet, while we rejoice in the present, we cannot afford to disregard the past, nor should we omit to pay our tribute of respect to the memory of those who here bore "the burthen and heat of the day," and braved the savage forces of nature long centuries ago.

INDEX.

A.

Acadia, probably visited by Cortereal, 7; visited by Cartier, 11; his praises of its soil, 12; visited by De Monts, 64–5, *et seq.*; trading companies in, 109; given up to France, 123; seized by English, 198; restored to France, 209; surrendered to England, 280; limits of, 375; final surrender to England, 428.

Acadians, attack Annapolis, 279; origin of, 282; method of diking, 283; numbers, 284–5; names of, 285–6, 289, 290; preponderance of males, 291–2; marriage with Indians, 293–6; Cadillac's account of them, 297; Abbe Raynal, 298; under priestly rule, 299; accusations against, 301; litigious disposition, disregard of civil authority, 303; Costabelle's account of them, 304; good character of the modern Acadians, 305–6; their numbers, 307; their status, 309; refuse to take the oath of allegiance, 310–11; under French influence, 312; their deputies, 313; take the oath from Governor Phillips, 323; unfriendly to English, 344; become numerous, 355, again refuse the oaths, 357, 358; menaced by La Loutre, 362; abandon Beaubassin, 363; aid in defence of Beauséjoir, 377; their faithlessness, 386; ordered to deliver up arms, 389; refuse oath of allegiance, 397–99; removal from the Province, 405–6; their number, 408; hostility of, 410, 411; many of them surrender, 422–25; at Halifax, 427; remove to St. Pierre, 429; take the oath of allegiance and receive grants of land, 430; their loyalty, 431.

Alexander, Sir William, receives a grant of Acadia, 111; project for its settlement, 112; meets Claude La Tour, 117; his grant to the La Tours, 118; colony at Port Royal, 120, 123, 126.

Amherst, General, captures Louisbourg, 414–15; at Isle-aux-Nois, 418.

Andros, Governor of New England, 225; seizes Penobscot, 226.

Annapolis, attacked by Acadians, 279; Phillips, Governor at, 311; invested by Indians, 316, 332; besieged by DuVivier, 335; by Marin, 337; by Ramezay, 348; seat of government removed from, 356.

Argal, Samuel, destroys St. Saveur colony, 101; destroys Port Royal, 102; conference with Biencourt, 103.

Armouchoquois, Indian tribe at Saco, 43; war with Micmacs, 87.

Armstrong, Lieutenant - Governor, 322–23; his suicide, 327.

Aubrey, lost in the woods, 66; discovered by Champdore, 73.

Aukpaque, Indian village on the St. John, 255.

B.

Baronets of Nova Scotia, 112.
Beaubassin, son of La Vallière, his piratical conduct, 220.

INDEX.

Beauséjour, erected, 370; shelters 'deserted inhabitants,' 372; measures taken to reduce it, 376; captured by English, 379; named Fort Cumberland, 381.
Belcher, Lieut.-Governor, 425.
Belleisle (see Le Borgne), his seigniorial claims, 325; his son attacks Annapolis, 332.
Bergier, establishes shore fishing company, 217; complaints of La Vallière, 218; appointed Lieutenant for the King under Perrot, 219; robbed by La Vallière, 220.
Berwick, attacked by Hertel, 230.
Biard, Pierre, Jesuit father, 91: quarrels with Biencourt, 94, 96; goes to St. Saveur, 100; at Port Royal with Argal, 102.
Biencourt, son of Poutrincourt, 91, 92; in command of Port Royal, 93; quarrels with the Jesuits, 94, 96; visits Chignecto, 97; his colony destroyed by Argal, 102; remains in Acadia, 104; death, 114.
Bigot, Jesuit missionary, 242.
Boishebert, at St. John River, 359; at Chignecto, 404; at Quebec, 420.
Bonaventure, naval commander, 237, 240, 245; commandant in Acadia, 264; charges against him, 266.
Breedon, Capt., Governor of Acadia, 203.
Bruillon, Governor of Acadia, his character, 260–61; goes to France, 264; dies at sea, 264.
Byron, Commodore, defeats French in Restigouche, 424.

C.

Cabot, John, 3; discovers North America, 4; knighted, 5.
Cabot, Sebastian, 3; first voyage to America, 4; second voyage, 5, 6.
Campbell, Mrs. Agatha, seigniorial claims, 324–25.
Canada, origin of its name, 15; Cartier's voyage to, 20; Roberval's colony, 23.
Canso, captured by Du Vivier, 331.
Cape of Good Hope, discovered by Diaz, 6.
Cartier, Jacques, first voyage to America, 10; visits Acadia, 11; at Gaspè, 13; second voyage, 15; at Quebec, 16; at Montreal, 18; winters at Quebec, 19; returns to France, 20; third voyage, 22; deserts Roberval, 23.
Caulfield, Lieut.-Governor, tenders oath of allegiance to Acadians, 311.
Central America, ruined cities of, 31.
Chaleur Bay, visited by Cartier, 12.
Chedabucto, fishing establishment at, 217, 233.
Chignecto, visited by Biencourt, 97; settlement founded, 213; La Vallière's farm there, 219; ravaged by Church, 254, 264; a principal settlement of Acadia, 307; inhabitants abandon villages south of Misseguash, 363; English fort at, 368; inhabitants resist removal, 404.
Chubb, Capt., commander at Pemaquid, his treachery, 250; surrenders Pemaquid, 253.
Church, Benjamin, 228, 238, 254; his expedition against Port Royal, 263; destroys Chignecto, 264.
Columbus, discovery of America, 1.
Company of New France, 113, 125, 127, 137; dissolved by Louis XIV, 205.
Copan, ruins of, 33.
Cope, an Indian, murders How, 371.
Cornwallis, Hon. Edward, Governor of Nova Scotia, 356; founds Halifax, 356: the Acadians, 357, 358, 359, 362, 363; his speech to the Acadians, 365–66.
Chambly, commandant in Acadia, 213; attacked by Dutch, 214; leaves Acadia, 216.
Champdore, in Acadia, 69; discovers Aubrey, 73.

INDEX. 435

Champlain, Samuel de, first voyage to the St. Lawrence, 61; accompanies De Monts to Acadia, 63; winters at St. Croix Island, 75; at Port Royal, 84; founds Quebec, 110.
Charles I. of England, confirms Sir W. Alexander's grant, 112; restores Acadia to France, 123.
Charles II. of England, 25; orders Temple to surrender Acadia, 207, 208.
Charnisay, D'Aulnay, 126; at Penobscot, 132, 140; quarrels with La Tour, 141, 145, 148, 151; attacks fort Latour, 155; beaten off, 160; his hatred of Lady La Tour, 162; treaty with Massachusetts, 167; his anger, 168; defeated by Lady La Tour, 170; massacres garrison of Fort Latour, 172; in France, 180; treaty at Boston, 184; favored by King, 186; attacks Denys, 187; drowned, 187; his bad reputation, 188.
Charnisay, Madame, married to La Tour, 191.
Chauvin, voyage to Tadoussac, 60.
Cortereal, Gaspar de, voyages to America, 7.
Couriers de bois, 220; prohibited 223.
Cumberland, Fort (see Bausèjour), 381.
Crowne, John, dramatist, born in Acadia, 201.
Crowne, William, grantee of Acadia, 200-1.

D.

D'Amours, the, their grants in Acadia, 220; at Fort Nashwaak, 255.
Daniel, Capt., 116, 117.
D'Anville, Duc de, fate of his fleet, 346–47.
De Chaste, 60.
De La Roche, his colony on Sable Island, 26.
De Monts, 61; voyage to Acadia, 64; winters at St. Croix Island,

75; second voyage to Acadia, 81; at Quebec, 110.
D'Entremont, Procureur du Roi, removed, 224.
Denys, Nicholas, 126, 128, 187, 193.
Des Goutins, Judge of Port Royal, 224; quarrels with Menneval, 228; consults with Villebon, 235; quarrels with Villebon, 258; hatred of Brouillan, 264, 266.
De Villiers, his expedition to Grand Pré, 349; attacks English detachment, 350; captures them, 351.
Diaz, Bartholomew, 6.
D'Iberville, 230, 240; captures Pemaquid, 252.
Donnacona, Indian King, 16; taken to France, 20.
Du Bourg Morillon, comes to Acadia, 207; at Boston, 208.
Du Breuil, Procureur du Roi, 224.
Dudley, Governor of Massachusetts, his attempt on Port Royal, 267.
Du Thet, Gilbert, Jesuit father, 95; killed at St. Saveur, 101.
Du Vivier, great grandson of La Tour, 328; captures Canso, 331; attempt on Annapolis, 335.

E.

Endicot, John, 159; Governor of Massachusetts, 163.
English colonization, 100, 106, 107, 110.

F.

Fishing Company of Acadia, 217, 221, 244, 246.
Flesche, Jossé, missionary in Acadia, 90.
Francis I. of France, patron of Verazzano, 8; schemes of colonization, 8; sends Cartier to America, 10.
Franquet, M., engineer officer, 362; visits Acadia, 372.
Frontenac, Governor of New France 218, 229.
Frye, Major, defeated by Boishe-

436   INDEX.

bert, 404; Acadians submit to, 422.
Fundy, Bay of, visited by De Monts, 66.

G.

Gaspè, Cartier erects a cross at, 13.
Gaspereaux Fort, at Baie Verte, 369; taken, 380; re-named Fort Monckton, 410.
Gibbons, Edward, 157-58, 175.
Gilbert, Sir Humphrey, voyage to America, 24; lost at sea, 25.
Gorges, Sir Fernando, 106, 108, 109.
Gorges, Thomas, 158.
Grand-fontaine, Chevalier, in command in Acadia, 209; takes census of Province, 210; recalled to France, 213.
Grand Prè, English attacked at, 340.
Guercheville, Madame de, 92; her religious zeal, 94; establishes a colony at Mount Desert, 100.
Gyles, John, his account of the Indians, 47; taken at Pemaquid, 227.

H.

Halifax, founded, 356.
Hanfield, Capt., occupies Mines, 360.
Hawkins, Thomas, 157, 160-61.
Hawthorne, Colonel, supersedes Church, 254; attacks Fort Nashwaak, 256.
Henry IV. of France, patron of De la Roche, 26; grants patents to Pontgravè, 60; patent to De Monts, 62; interest in Acadia, 88; assassinated, 91.
Henry VII. of England, 2; sends the Cabots to America, 3, 4, 5.
Henry VIII. of England, patron of Thorne, 10.
Hochelaga, site of Montreal, visited by Cartier, 18.
Hopson, Governor of Nova Scotia, 373.

Hore, voyage to the St. Lawrence, 20.
How, Edward, Capt., taken prisoner at Mines, 351, murdered by Indians, 371.

I.

Indians of Acadia (See Micmacs and Malicites), described by Cartier, 13; number of, 43; mode of living, 45; habitations and food, 46; feasts, 48; as warriors, 49; weapons, 51; torture of prisoners, 53; religion, 54; funerals, 55; superstitions, 56; diseases, 57; converted to Christianity, 90; at war with the English, 226, destroy Dover, 227; attack Falmouth, 230; at Wells, 237; at Pemaquid, 240; attack Dover, 243; stricken by plague, 244; capture Pemaquid, 252; end of the war, 257; renew the war, 262; assist in attack on Annapolis, 279; new war with English, 315; attack Annapolis, 332-34; their hostility, 360; controlled by La Loutre, 362; attack Dartmouth, 371; at Beausèjoir, 378; beset fort Monckton, 410.
James I. of England grants Acadia to Sir Wm. Alexander, 111.
Jemseg, fort at, erected by Temple, 203; surrendered to Grand-fontaine, 209; destroyed by Dutch, 214; occupied by Villebon, 237; abandoned, 240.
Jesuits, sail for Acadia with Briencourt, 92; quarrels with Briencourt, 94, 96; colony at St. Saveur, 100; colony destroyed, 101.
Jonquiere, Governor of Canada, 347; his fleet defeated, 352.

K.

Kirk, Sir David, 115; takes Quebec, 116; Govern'r of Newfoundland, 177.

L.

Labrador, discovered, 7.
La Corne, sent from Quebec to hold Chignecto, 359; erects Beausèjoir, 369.
La Have, settled by De Razilly, 127; French colonists at, 128; removal of colonists to Port Royal, 141; burnt by Le Borgne, 194; taken by English, 202, 233.
La Loutre, Abbè, missionary, 332; collects the Indians, 337; his character, 361; influences the Indians, 362, 370, 371, 374, 375; opposed to surrender Beusèjour, 379; escapes to Quebec, 380.
La Saussaye, establishes St. Saveur colony, 100.
La Tour, Charles de La, 104, 114; his fort near Cape Sable, 115, 117; grant from Alexander, 118; defends his fort against English, 119; at Machias, 131; grant of St. John, 137; his fort at St. John, 142; differences with Charnisay, 144, 146; ordered to France, 147; commission revoked, 148; sends for aid to Rochelle, 149; goes to Boston, 156; obtains aid in New England, 157; defeats Charnisay, 160; in Boston, 163; his fort taken, 172; goes to Newfoundland, 177; at Quebec, 178; restored to his governorship, 179; returns to Acadia, 190; marries Madame Charnisay, 191; Le Borgne's designs against him, 195; fort taken by the English, 197; receives grant of Acadia from Cromwell, 200; death, 206.
La Tour, Claude de La, 114–15, 117; grant from Alexander, 118; attacks his son's fort, 119; at Port Royal, 120; at Cape Sable, 122; at Penobscoot, 130.
La Tour, Lady de La, 114, 143; goes to France, 162; escapes to England, 163; in Boston, 165; defends her fort against Charnisay, 170-71; her heroism, 172; death, 173.

Latour, Fort, 123, 138, 142, 155, 170, 171,; taken by Charnisay, 172; mortgaged, 175; taken by the English, 197; restored to the French, 209; a ruin, 210; rebuilt by Villebon, 257; re-occupied, 258; abandoned and demolished, 260.
La Valliére, commandant in Acadia, 216; permits English to fish and trade, 217; appointment cancelled, 218; attacks Bergier, 220.
La Verdure, 193; surrenders Port Royal, 198.
Lawrence, Col., sent to Chignecto, 363; establishes fort there, 368; Lieut.-Governor, 375; and the Acadians, 390–92; removes the Acadians, 400, 406; death, 424.
Lawrence, Fort, established at Chignecto, 368.
Le Borgne, Alexander, Sieur de Belleisle, comes to Acadia, 207; at Port Royal, 208; lawless conduct, 212; Seignior of Mines, 222.
Le Borgne, Emmanuel, creditor of Charnisay, 152; arrives in Acadia, 193; beaten at Port Royal, 197.
Le Borgne, Emmanuel, Jr., captured at La Have, 203.
Lescarbot, 70; visits Acadia, 81; his diligence, 83.
Leverett, Capt. John, commander of Port Royal, 198.
Lous XIII., 91; aids Company of New France, 113, 145; Letter to La Tour, 145, 147; death, 156.
Louis XIV. King of France, 185; commission to La Tour, 189; interest in Acadian affairs, 224.
Louisbourg, 307; its great strength, 337; captured by New Englanders, 342; restored to France, 354; taken by the English, 415; demolished, 424.

M.

Machias, English driven from, 131.
Malicites, of Acadia, 43 (see Indians).

438   INDEX.

Marie, M., commissioner of Charnisay, 166–67, 182.
Marin, his attack on Annapolis, 337; recalled to Louisbourg, 344; joins Ramezay, 345; heads party of Indians, 353.
Marot, Capt., 121–22.
Martin, Abraham, Heights of Abraham named after him, 147.
Mascerene, Paul, Lieut.-Governor, 327–28; defends Annapolis, 332, 334–36, 348; his advice to the Acadians, 353.
Masse, Enemond, Jesuit father, 91; at the St. John, 93; quarrels with Biencourt, 94, 96; leaves Port Royal, 99.
Matakando, Chief of Penobscot Indians, 215; at Falmouth, 230; at Quebec, 240; made Chief of St. John River, 247.
Mazarin, Cardinal, treaty with England, 199.
Membertou, Micmac Chief, 85; quarrel about his place of burial, 94.
Menneval, M. De, appointed Governor of Acadia, 222; directions from the King, 223; quarrels with des Gautens, 228; surrenders Port Royal, 233.
Meulles, M. De, Intendant of Canada, visits Acadia, 222.
Mexicans, traditions of origin, 39.
Mexico, its ancient civilization, 36.
Micmacs of Acadia, 43; at Port Royal, 79; friendship of, 85; (see Indians.)
Mines, settlement established, 213; population in 1686, 222.
Miramichi, visited by Cartier, 11; Acadians at, 410.
Miscou, mission at, 109; re-established, 138.
Monckton, Col., takes Beauséjour, 377; occupies St. John, 416.
Musquodoboit, 211.

N.

Nashwaak, fort erected by Villebon,
240; attacked by the English, 256; abandoned, 257; demolished, 260.
Nelson, John, nephew of Sir T. Temple, 225; prisoner at Quebec, 240.
Newfoundland, discovered by Cabot, 4; Basque and Breton fishermen at, 8; visited by Cartier, 11; Roberval at, 22; visited by Gilbert, 25.
North West Passage, attempted by Cabot, 5.

O.

Ouygoudy, Indian name of St. John, 69.

P.

Palenque, ruins of, 33.
Pemaquid, English at, 149, 225; fort taken by Indians, 227; Fort William Henry built, 239; D'Iberville at, 240; captured and demolished, 253.
Pennoniac, Micmac Chief, 55.
Penobscot, or Pentagoet, La Tour's fort there, 114; English trading house plundered, 129; seized by Charnisay, 132; Charnisay at, 140; Temple at, 202; Grandfontaine occupies fort, 210; taken by Dutch, 214–15; settled by St. Castin, 215; seized by Andros, 226; ravaged by Church, 263.
Pepperell, Gen'l, 339; commands expedition against Louisbourg, 340.
Perrot, M., Governor of Acadia, 218; his character, 219; jealousy of St. Castin, 221; imprisons him, 222; ordered to return to France, 222; robbed, 233, at Port Royal, 235; captured by pirates, 235.
Peruvians, traditions of their origin, 38.
Phillips, General, Governor of Nova Scotia, 311–13; tries to conciliate the Indians, 314; returns

www.ingramcontent.com/pod-product-compliance
Lightning Source LLC
Chambersburg PA
CBHW022145300426
44115CB00006B/347